METHODISTS AND THEIR MISSIONARY SOCIETIES 1760–1900

Ashgate Methodist Studies Series

Methodism remains one of the largest denominations in the USA and is growing in
South America, Africa and Asia (especially in Korea and China). This series spans
Methodist history and theology, exploring its success as a movement historically
and in its global expansion. Books in the series will look particularly at features
within Methodism which attract wide interest, including: the unique position
of the Wesleys; the prominent role of women and minorities in Methodism; the
interaction between Methodism and politics; the 'Methodist conscience' and its
motivation for temperance and pacifist movements; the wide range of Pentecostal,
holiness and evangelical movements, and the interaction of Methodism with
different cultures.

Methodists and their Missionary Societies 1760–1900

JOHN PRITCHARD

ASHGATE

Published by
Ashgate Publishing Limited
Wey Court East
Union Road
Farnham
Surrey, GU9 7PT
England

Ashgate Publishing Company
110 Cherry Street
Suite 3-1
Burlington, VT 05401-3818
USA

www.ashgate.com

British Library Cataloguing in Publication Data
Pritchard, John.
   Methodists and their Missionary Societies 1760–1900. –
   (Ashgate Methodist Studies Series)
   1. Methodist Church – Missions – History – 18th century. 2. Methodist Church –
   Missions – History – 19th century. I. Title II. Series
   266.7'1–dc23

The Library of Congress has cataloged the printed edition as follows:
Pritchard, John, 1941–
   Methodists and their Missionary Societies 1760–1900 / by John Pritchard.
      pages   cm
   Includes bibliographical references and index.
   1. Missions – Societies, etc. 2. Wesleyan Methodist Church – Missions – History –
   18th century. 3. Wesleyan Methodist Church – Missions – History – 19th century.
   4. Methodist Church in Ireland – Missions – History – 18th century.
   5. Methodist Church in Ireland – Missions – History – 19th century. I. Title.
   BV2550.P75 2013
   266'.75–dc23   2012051545

ISBN   9781409470496 (hbk)
ISBN   9781409470502 (ebk-PDF)
ISBN   9781409470519 (ebk-ePUB)

Printed in the United Kingdom by Henry Ling Limited, at the Dorset Press, Dorchester, DT1 1HD

Contents

List of Illustrations

Notes

*   © Trustees for Methodist Church Purposes, used by permission.

**   Paintings: property of TMCP, used by permission. Images by the Public Catalogue Foundation, used by permission of Oxford Brookes University (Oxford Centre for Methodism and Church History).

List of Maps

Note: All maps © R.A. and M.J.T. Lewis

Abbreviations

AME(C)	African Methodist Episcopal (Church)
AMEZ	African Methodist Episcopal Church Zion
BC	Bible Christian
BFBS	British and Foreign Bible Society
BMS	Baptist Missionary Society
CIM	China Inland Mission
CMS	Church Missionary Society
DMBI	Dictionary of Methodism in Britain and Ireland
FRCS	Fellow of the Royal College of Surgeons
HMG	Her Majesty's Government
JMA	Juvenile/Junior Missionary Association
JRUL	John Rylands University Library, University of Manchester
LMA	Ladies' Missionary Association (MNC)
LMS	London Missionary Society
MARC	Methodist Archives and Research Centre (JRUL)
MCCA	Methodist Church of the Caribbean and the Americas
MCOD	Methodist Church Overseas Division
MD	Doctor of Medicine
MEC	Methodist Episcopal Church
MMS	Methodist Missionary Society
MNC	Methodist New Connexion
PM(AMS)	Primitive Methodist (African Missionary Society)
SOAS	School of Oriental and African Studies, University of London
SPCK	Society for Promoting Christian Knowledge
SPG	Society for the Propagation of the Gospel
UMC	United Methodist Church (1907–1932)
UMFC	United Methodist Free Churches
WA	Wesleyan Association / Women's Auxiliary (WM)
WHS	Wesley Historical Society
WMF	Women's Missionary Federation (PM)
WM(MS)	Wesleyan Methodist (Missionary Society)
WW	Women's Work

Brief Glossary of Methodist Terms

Chairman of the District: The minister appointed by the Conference to oversee a District and chair the Synod. Overseas, the title 'Chairman of the District and General Superintendent' was often used to make clear that the Chairman did not merely chair Synod meetings. This book normally abbreviates to 'Chairman'.

Circuit: A group of Methodist societies in a given area.

Class: The basic unit in Wesleyan Methodism: all members were expected to meet regularly in a group with a designated Class Leader for prayer, testimony and mutual exhortation.

Class ticket: Issued quarterly to all members as proof of their good standing, of use especially when away from home. It served as a ticket of entry to meetings; in many places to Holy Communion; and was often placed in a member's coffin as a ticket of entry to heaven...

Committee: Here used, unless otherwise defined by the context, to denote the General or managing Committee of the Society in question.

Conference: The central governing body of the denomination, meeting annually.

Connexion: The network of local churches, circuits and districts governed by the Conference.

District: A sub-unit of the Conference, normally comprising a number of circuits, governed by a Synod.

Preacher: Until the early nineteenth century, an itinerant stationed by the Conference, later to be styled 'minister'; in this book given a capital P, to distinguish from unremunerated local preachers.

President of the Conference: In Britain, an annual appointment.

Quarterly Meeting: The ministers and lay representatives of all the societies in a Circuit, meeting four times per annum to conduct the affairs of the Circuit, with the superintendent minister in the chair.

Secretary: With a capital S, a Secretary of the Missionary Society in question (the Wesleyan Secretaries were styled 'General Secretary' from 1843).

Society (1): Used in this book with a lower case s, the original and enduring term for a local Methodist congregation – Methodists at first avoided using the term 'church' in order to make it clear they were not competing with the local parish (Anglican) church.

Society (2): With a capital S, the particular Missionary Society in question (most often the WMMS).

Stations: A list, published annually, of the Circuits and other appointments to which ministers had been assigned by the Conference.

Steward: A lay leader: the term was used for a variety of roles, the chief being Society Steward (in current usage Church Steward) and Circuit Steward.

Place-Names

Since, in accordance with common usage, Deutschland is in these pages invariably referred to as Germany and Xianggang as Hong Kong, the same principle has been applied to most other names, however they are rendered locally. Thus, for example, Mumbai, Chennai and Kolkata are referred to as Bombay, Madras and Calcutta.

Chinese names present their own problem. In 1958 a new system of romanizing Chinese characters, known as *Pinyin*, was officially endorsed, replacing the Wade–Giles spelling previously used. To enable readers to locate places on modern maps, the new spelling is used, even though the old spelling is used in the Societies' records. Peking, for example, is thus Beijing and Canton is either Guangzhou, for the city or Guangdong, for the province. To use Hong Kong's familiar name may be considered an anomaly; the alternative would be bizarre. Personal names, on the other hand, retain the spelling found in the records.

New Zealand and Aotearoa have been used interchangeably. The people of the Gold Coast are Ghanaians.

Preface

In October 1813 the first meeting of a Wesleyan Methodist Missionary Society (WMMS) took place. It was held in Leeds and its remit was limited to the Leeds District; the nationwide Society was formed only in 1818. The appearance of this history thus coincides – more by accident than design – with the bicentenary of that Leeds meeting. It was conceived at a gathering of a small group of Methodist historians on Wesley Day, 24 May 1994 and has, therefore, had a longer gestation period than Findlay and Holdsworth's massive *History of the Wesleyan Methodist Missionary Society*, which George Findlay was commissioned to write for the centenary celebrations of 1913.[1] It was completed by William Holdsworth after Findlay's death in 1919 and the five volumes appeared between 1921 and 1924. This much more concise and less comprehensive history covers the same ground from a more distant vantage point; it also describes the foreign missions of the other Churches – Primitive Methodist and United Methodist, the latter incorporating several streams – which were merged as the Methodist Missionary Society at Methodist Union in 1932. A companion to this volume reviews twentieth century developments.

Harold Wood began to compile his four volume *Overseas Missions of the Australian Methodist Church* (1975) as that Church was about to unite with others, 'before its identity ceases'.[2] He said in his Preface, 'To write such a complete history is an audacious venture, and an ageing minister must have misgivings about the attempt.'[3] The present work, together with the companion volume, is much wider in scope, in terms of both time and place, than his and commensurately less detailed in its account. But the author's audacity and his misgivings are of the same order.

The eighteenth and nineteenth centuries have been treated in much greater detail by previous historians. William Moister's *Conversations on the Rise, Progress, and Present State of Wesleyan Missions in Various Parts of the World* (1869) is a remarkable work.[4] It takes the form of a series of conversations between an experienced missionary – Moister had worked in West Africa, the West Indies and South Africa – and George, an inquisitive and intelligent teenager. Brief quotations give the flavour of its style. George asks:

---

[1] G.G. Findlay and W.W. Holdsworth, *The History of the Wesleyan Methodist Missionary Society,* (5 vols, London, Epworth Press, 1921–24).

[2] A.H. Wood, *Overseas Missions of the Australian Methodist Church,* (4 vols, Melbourne, Aldersgate Press, 1975–80).

[3] Wood, vol. 1, p. iii.

[4] W. Moister, *Conversations on the Rise, Progress and Present State of Wesleyan Missions in Various Parts of the World*, (London, Hamilton Adams & Co, 1869).

I shall be glad if you will kindly inform me by whom, and under what circumstances, the work was commenced, as I know of nothing more interesting than a narrative of facts connected with the introduction of the Gospel into a new country, whether it be inhabited by heathens, properly so-called, or by our own countrymen, without the means of religious instruction.

I shall feel obliged if you will now have the goodness to favour me with some account of the Missionary enterprise in ...[5]

Moister's favourite words for most of the people among whom missionaries went to work were 'degraded', 'depraved', 'disgusting' and 'savage'. He had a fondness for calling Africans 'the sable sons of Ham'. Dying – the all too common lot of missionaries in his period – is too simple a word; he preferred 'removed to their eternal rest', 'expired', 'finished his course', 'breathed her last', 'cut down by fever', 'fell a sacrifice to the climate' or 'called to his reward'. He described Islam as 'the religious dogmas of the False Prophet'.[6] Already in *Makers of our Missions*, published in 1895, another Methodist historian, John Telford, wrote: 'His books are too antique in phrase and style to win anything like enduring popularity, but they form a mine of information.'[7] The information was geographical as well as historical and he recycled pertinent statistics from the WMMS annual reports at the end of each chapter.

In 1905 Telford wrote *A Short History of Wesleyan Methodist Foreign Missions*,[8] and in 1912 George Findlay and his daughter Mary wrote *Wesley's World Parish*.[9] This was variously described in the Minutes of the WMMS Centenary Committee as a shorter, smaller or popular history: a sketch of the larger work Findlay never completed. The five volumes which Holdsworth saw through the press contained a wealth of detail – not always entirely accurate – sourced from the Society's annual reports and from the *Missionary Notices,* by and large without citing references. The inaccuracies probably arose from Holdsworth's inability to comprehend fully the working papers he inherited after Findlay's death.

The overseas missions of the Methodist New Connexion (MNC), United Methodist Free Churches (UMFC) and Bible Christians (BC) are the subject of chapters in the MNC Centenary volume edited by George Packer and others (1897), Oliver Beckerlegge's *The United Methodist Free Churches* (1957) and Frederick

---

[5]   Moister, pp. 46, 43.

[6]   Moister, pp. 103, 116, 136 for example.

[7]   J. Telford, *Makers of our Missions*, (London, Charles H. Kelly, 1895), p. 183.

[8]   J. Telford, *A Short History of Wesleyan Methodist Foreign Missions*, (London, Charles H. Kelly, 1905).

[9]   G.G. and M.G. Findlay, *Wesley's World Parish*, (London, Hodder & Stoughton, 1912).

Bourne's *The Bible Christians: Their Origin and History* (1905) respectively.[10] A resolution of the 1892 Primitive Methodist (PM) Conference read 'That as it will be the Jubilee of the formation of our Missionary Society next year, we deem it desirable that a history of our missionary work be written, and we request the Revs John Atkinson and James Travis to undertake the work.' This potentially valuable resource never materialized, but there are brief accounts in Aquila Barber's *A Methodist Pageant* (1932)[11] and Geoffrey Milburn's *Primitive Methodism* (2002).[12] While drawing on all of these secondary sources, I have not attempted to replicate them. I have described these as 'Parallel Missions'; to call them 'non-Wesleyan' is both unnecessarily negative and a denial of their Wesleyan roots and ethos. But these parallels, in defiance of geometry, were destined to meet in 1932.

Barber contributed a masterly article on the *Methodist Foreign Missionary Enterprise, The Work of the British Societies* to volume two of *A New History of Methodism* (1909).[13] Barber's was a straightforward chronological account packing an immense amount of information into under eighty pages. There is nothing comparable for the later period. However, papers produced for a series of annual *MMS History* conferences, organized by Andrew Walls from 2001, explored a wide and eclectic range of subjects from 'The Social Impact of John Wesley's Mission to Georgia' to 'Women's Perspectives on Contextual Missiology'.

There is a wealth of primary sources – minutes and correspondence – in the Methodist Missionary collection at the University of London School of Oriental and African Studies (SOAS), much of it as yet un-mined. The collection also includes a library of some 7,000 volumes, almost all out of print, as well as annual reports and magazines. Many of the books listed in the bibliography, although long out of print, can be accessed at SOAS.

Earlier histories made a distinction, apparent in the first quotation from Moister's friend George, between 'colonial missions' and 'missions to the heathen'. This book is largely about the latter. It does not deal with American Methodism after the foundation of the Methodist Episcopal Church. It sketches the early history of Wesleyan Methodism in Canada, Australia and Aotearoa but does not take their story beyond the mid-1850s, when autonomous Wesleyan Conferences took over responsibility from the British Conference and WMMS. The Pacific island Districts belonged to the Australasian Conference from its inception, though when

---

[10] T.D. Crothers, W. Longbottom, W.J. Townsend, T. Rider, G. Packer (eds), *The centenary of the Methodist New Connexion 1797–1897*, (London , Geo. Burroughs, 1897); O.A. Beckerlegge, *The United Methodist Free Churches*, (London, Epworth Press, 1957); F.W. Bourne, *The Bible Christians: Their Origin and History*, (London, Bible Christian Book Room, 1905).

[11] B.A. Barber, *A Methodist Pageant*, (London, Holborn, 1932), pp. 167–96.

[12] G. Milburn, *Primitive Methodism*, (London, Epworth Press, 2002), pp. 34–7.

[13] G. Eayrs, W.J. Townsend, H.B. Workman, (eds), *A New History of Methodism*, (2 vols, London, Hodder & Stoughton, 1909).

eventually they assumed their own autonomy they once again welcomed mission partners from Britain.

The period treated here saw the expansion of British influence and interests overseas and the emergence of the British Empire. The extent to which missionaries were complicit in the colonial enterprise, sympathetic to either imperial or nationalist aspirations or marginal to the geopolitical scene is keenly debated. The evidence of Methodist records suggests, unsurprisingly, that some were and some were not. The theme is explored notably by Jean and John Comaroff in *Of Revelation and Revolution: Christianity, Colonialism and Consciousness in South Africa* (1991, 1997), by Andrew Porter's *Religion versus empire?* (2004) and in *Missions and Empire*, edited by Norman Etherington (2005).[14]

A concise history must necessarily be selective. Dates matter, for without them the record would be even more confused, but not every significant date is included in the narrative. Still less is every missionary mentioned. Time and again we have to remind ourselves that those officially designated as missionaries or mission partners played a relatively small part in the spread of Christianity, compared with the indigenous believers, most of whose names are recorded in heaven but in no earthly text, who shared their faith with their compatriots.

The historian E.P. Thompson, the Marxist son of Wesleyan missionary parents, wrote in the Preface to *The Making of the English Working Class*:

> I am seeking to rescue the poor stockinger, the Luddite cropper, the 'obsolete' handloom weaver, the 'utopian' artisan, and even the deluded follower of Joanna Southcott, from the enormous condescension of posterity.[15]

The Indian biblewoman, the Chinese evangelist, the African catechist and the Caribbean class-leader are in the same way easily overlooked; I have tried to give them their due. But such a history as this inevitably pays more attention to the heroes, the saintly characters, the achievers whose lives and accomplishments are well-documented. So it is important to recognize that 'interpreting missionary records requires constant attention to the multiple levels of exclusion in the narratives'.[16] There is a hidden history which is undocumented. The missionaries whose service left them frustrated and disillusioned tend to leave little trace; few of them trumpeted their complaints and official correspondence and minutes were inclined to gloss over the tensions. Regrettably few first-hand accounts from

---

[14]   J.L. and J. Comaroff, *Of Revelation and Revolution: Christianity, Colonialism and Consciousness in South Africa*, (2 vols, Chicago, University of Chicago Press, 1991, 1997); A. Porter, *Religion versus empire?*, (Manchester, Manchester University Press, 2004); N. Etherington (ed.), *Missions and Empire*, (Oxford, Oxford University Press, 2005).

[15]   E.P. Thompson, *The Making of the English Working Class*, (London, Gollancz, 1963; reprinted Penguin, 1980), p. 12.

[16]   J. Cox, *Imperial fault lines: Christianity and colonial power in India, 1818–1940*, (Stanford, California, Stanford University Press, 2002), p. 5.

indigenous Christians exist. This is partly because so many converts were illiterate, or barely literate, to the end of their days. And even the literate were, by and large, far too preoccupied to put pen to paper. The sheer business of survival – earning a living and supporting a family – together with their involvement in church life and Christian witness, took all their time and energy. The few with the ability and resources to write tended to regard Biblical studies and theology as more urgent than writing history or autobiography. Seldom, moreover, do indigenous believers get due recognition in the publications of their day. The Mende Hut Tax war in Sierra Leone claimed the lives of numerous African Christians in 1898, including five Krio Methodist workers from Freetown. The UMFC *Missionary Echo*, preoccupied with the narrow escape of the English missionary Charles Goodman, completely ignored the loss of his African colleagues. On the other hand, the PM *Advance* in 1923 included this tribute to *The Native Preacher*:

> When the missionary journeys in his district here and there,
> Giving counsel to the churches, sharing all the people's care,
> Holding forth the Gospel message to the heathen as he can,
> He is sure to be attended by a native preacher-man.
>
> And it's tramp, tramp, tramp as he trudges through the dust,
> While his eyes are nearly blinded by the rushing, whirling gust;
> And it's splash, splash, slump as he struggles through the mud,
> While the rain that falls in torrents sends a chill into his blood,
>
> For he is working for the Master, and not for Mission pay,
> With his apostolic labours, and his thirty pence a day.
> He's a map and a directory, a walking gazetteer;
> He's a Daniel come to judgement; he's a constant source of cheer.
> No fatigue and no discomforts are too great for him to bear;
> Call him late or call him early, when you call you'll find him there…
>
> We have travelled through the jungles, he and I, these many years,
> And I hope to keep him with me till he leaves this vale of tears;
> Then when God sums up the records that are written down on high,
> I shall not begrudge it if he wears a brighter crown than I.[17]

For much of the nineteenth century the woman's voice is muted too. Not only are there few indigenous women of whom much is known, the same is true of many British and Irish women whom the Societies sent abroad. In some cases it has been impossible to discover the forenames of women. A painstaking search of marriage

---

[17]   David Gilmour, published in the PM monthly missionary magazine *Advance*, June 1923, p. 115.

registers would doubtless fill the gaps, but it is likely that they were hardly ever addressed or spoken of except as 'Mrs'.

It is difficult, within this compass, to avoid some generalization. Max Warren, General Secretary of the Church Missionary Society (1942–62), faced the same problem and in the introduction to his *Social History and Christian Mission* (1967) quoted wise words of the historian Kitson Clark who wrote that

> ... most historical generalizations are necessarily founded on guesses, guesses informed by much general reading and relevant knowledge, guesses shaped by much brooding on the matter in hand, but on guesses none the less. This is, however, not a matter of which there is any reason to be ashamed ... If it were not for guesses the historical imagination could never build up a complete picture of any period ... and all of the most attractive work of the historian would remain undone.[18]

Yet, given such a diverse collection of individuals, working in so many different situations, one must be wary of generalizing. I have not attempted to impose any overarching thesis on a very disparate set of circumstances, experiences and theological stances.

I have refrained from inserting 'sic' after every mention of 'man', 'brotherhood' and terms such as 'kaffirs' and 'coolies' where they appear in quotations; it must be taken as read. Spellings such as 'Fejee' or 'Fegee', 'Hankow' and 'Canton' are likewise unaltered in quotations but become Fiji, Hankou and Guangzhou when I have referred to them – see the note on place-names.

I am greatly indebted to Lance Martin, the archivist at the School of Oriental and African Studies in London with a prodigious knowledge of the MMS archive, for his encouragement and advice; to Albert Mosley, former General Secretary of the Methodist Church Overseas Division (MCOD), who in retirement has compiled a massive and informative database of almost every Methodist missionary that ever was, which I have consulted ceaselessly; to Norman Taggart, another former officer of MCOD and past President of the Methodist Church in Ireland, for his advice on the Irish contribution; to John Vickers, who has compiled the index; to Alison and Michael Lewis, who have produced the maps; and to Edward Royle, for reading the typescript and saving me from sundry errors of fact and interpretation. Andrew Walls has arranged and Kirsty Murray has administered a series of Methodist Missionary History conferences and an associated website.[19] Others whose help I gratefully acknowledge include Scott Anderson, Brian Beck, John Clapham, Kenneth Cracknell, Deborah Gaitskell, Bill Gibson, Dorothy Graham, Elizabeth Harris, Peter Howson, John Lenton, John Neal, Peter Nockles, Donald Phillipps, Jennifer Potter, Israel Selvanayagam, Geoffrey Senior, Rosemary Seton,

[18]   M.A.C. Warren, *Social History and Christian Mission*, (London, SCM Press, 1967), p. 13.
[19]   http://www2.div.ed.ac.uk/other/mms [accessed 1 November 2012].

Betty Venner, Kevin Watson, Ian Welch, Martin Wellings and John Young. My debt to Pat, my wife, is incalculable; since I was prevailed upon to undertake this history, retirement has turned out rather differently from what we anticipated and without her support it would not yet be completed.

JOHN PRITCHARD
1 November 2012

Chapter 1
Beginning with Wesley

The first Methodist missionaries were the Wesley brothers.[1] The narrative dear to later Methodists tells how the 'great flame'[2] of Methodism was kindled in Epworth, nurtured at Oxford, all but dowsed in Georgia, but rekindled by the grace of God and the Moravian influence they first encountered at sea. From May 1738 it began to blaze as they shared their intense personal experience of God's love. The possibility and promise of God's love for all – *all* is one of the key words in Charles Wesley's hymnody – was the motivation that drove them for the next half-century and drove hundreds of thousands inspired by them in the ensuing two centuries of Methodist participation in world mission.

Antecedents and Influences

The first decade of the eighteenth century saw not only the birth of John and Charles Wesley but the beginning of the Protestant missionary era. Catholic missions to peoples beyond Europe began to be established earlier, as Spain and Portugal in particular embarked on the colonial enterprise. Indeed, it was the Jesuits of the sixteenth century who began to use the word *missio* to denote bringing the unbaptized to faith. The predominantly Protestant countries, on the other hand, had very little contact with non-Christian peoples until the end of the seventeenth century, nor did the theology of the early Reformers inspire them to extend their activity beyond their borders. *Cuius regio eius religio* (the 'follow-my-leader' principle that the ruler's religion is the people's religion) was the rule of the times – religion followed the flag. But then the flag of Denmark was hoisted over Tranquebar in South India and in 1705 King Frederick IV recruited two Lutheran missionaries to work in Tranquebar.

Bartholomew Ziegenbald and Henry Plutshau came from Halle in Germany. They were products of the pietist movement, the first flowering of religious renewal which proved the forerunner of the evangelical revival of the eighteenth century. It 'reacted against the official stress on formal theological correctness and

---

[1]   *pace* J.A. Vickers, *Myths of Methodism,* (Oxford, Wesley Historical Society, 2008), p. 34, who regards such statements as among the myths and rightly points out 'that the Methodist movement, as part of the much wider "Evangelical Revival", had already begun before the Wesley brothers had their hearts "strangely warmed"'.

[2]   C. Wesley's hymn 'See how great a flame aspires' (*Hymns and Sacred Poems*, 1749) was a favourite at missionary meetings.

merely conventional churchgoing … to create a more personalized and inward type of piety and stressed the importance of good works'.[3] Reaching India in 1706, Ziegenbald, a gifted linguist, applied himself to learning the Tamil language and then to translating the Bible. The New Testament in Tamil was published within a decade, in 1714. It was printed on a press which had been supplied by the recently founded Society for Promoting Christian Knowledge (SPCK) in England, where the Royal Danish Mission and Ziegenbald's prolific letters home had attracted much interest. Susanna Wesley was one who was enthused by the letters and she set about imparting to her children her enthusiasm for missions to the heathen.[4]

When the German missionaries began to extend their activity beyond the confines of Tranquebar and King Frederick insisted that the resources he supplied were not to be employed outside Danish territory, the SPCK again took an interest and funded their work in British territory. The SPCK had been founded in 1699 to promote Christian knowledge both in England and in the Church of England's colonial parishes, mainly by providing books, libraries and schools. It was swiftly followed by another voluntary society: the Society for the Propagation of the Gospel in Foreign Parts (SPG) was founded in 1701 by royal charter, with a seal that bore the text 'Come over and help us'.[5] The charter referred to the lack of provision for the Church of England's ministry in 'the Plantations, Colonies and Factories [that is, trading stations] beyond the Seas'. The SPG's objective was to send personnel, especially to the American colonies; Thomas Bray, the instigator of both these High Church societies, had seen for himself the situation in Maryland. The colonies were regarded as parts of the home country established overseas, subject to English law and the care of English souls was the prime concern. Although the SPG charter's reference to 'such other Provision … as may be necessary for the Propagation of the Gospel in those Parts' was intended to promote the conversion of indigenous peoples, it was a concern that took a distant second place behind establishing a less erratic and inadequate supply of ministers to the colonists.[6]

1738, Before and After

It was under the auspices of the SPG that John and Charles Wesley, the former in his early thirties and the latter in his late twenties, worked briefly in Georgia. Their motives were mixed. Two months before he sailed, John (whose heart had not yet been 'strangely warmed') wrote: 'My chief motive, to which all the rest are subordinate, is the hope of saving my own soul.' He went on: 'I hope to learn

---

    [3]   H.D. Rack, *Reasonable Enthusiast* (London, Epworth Press, 1989), p. 162.
    [4]   S. Neill, *A History of Christian Missions* (London, Penguin Books, 1964), pp. 228–31.
    [5]   Acts 16:9.
    [6]   H.P. Thompson, *Into All Lands*, (London, SPCK, 1951), p. 17.

the true sense of the gospel of Christ by preaching it to the heathen. They have no comments to construe away the text; no vain philosophy to corrupt it; no luxurious, sensual, covetous expounders to soften its unpleasing truths ...'. And then: 'it is commonly objected that there are heathens enough in practice, if not in theory, at home; why, then, should you go to America? Why? For a very plain reason: because these heathens at home have Moses and the Prophets, and those have not; because those who *have* the gospel trample upon it, and those who have it not earnestly call for it'.[7] His intention, plainly, was to work among the native peoples. That was not how it worked out. In the words of the SPG historian, 'His dearest hope, to convert the Indians, proved unattainable: the authorities discouraged it, his time was over-full, and his illusions as to their simple and noble qualities did not stand the light of experience.'[8] The colonial community was just as big a disappointment. In his eyes they lived up to all the prejudice with which he set out, having the gospel but trampling on it. John Wesley the pioneer missionary was a disaster, while Charles Wesley's stay in Georgia was even more short-lived.

The story of the Georgia experience and its aftermath, their intensely personal experience of God's grace and their whole-hearted, warmed-hearted immersion in the burgeoning evangelical revival, has been told and retold. In a reversal of his letter to Dr Burton, John Wesley chose to preach to the heathen in Britain. Many years were to pass before new ventures abroad were contemplated, let alone begun.

Allen Birtwhistle, in his contribution to *A History of the Methodist Church in Great Britain*, discussed some of the Wesley hymns which have inspired generations of Methodists.[9] Yet they were not the launch-pad for missionary activity among 'the fullness of the Gentiles'. In a hymn published as early as 1742 John Wesley wrote

> Let all earth's sons thy mercy prove,
> > Let all thy saving grace adore...
> Abroad thy healing influence shower,
> > O'er all the nations let it flow...[10]

But he took a lot of persuading that the time was ripe for matching action to his prayer. Charles Wesley is renowned for such lines as

> The world he suffered to redeem
> > For all he has the atonement paid...

---

[7]   Letter to Dr John Burton, 10 October 1735, in J. Telford (ed.), *The Letters of John Wesley*, (8 vols, London, Epworth Press, 1931), vol. 1, pp. 188–91.

[8]   Thompson, *Into All Lands*, pp. 53–4.

[9]   N.A. Birtwhistle, 'Methodist Missions' in R.E. Davies, A.R. George, G. Rupp (eds), *A History of the Methodist Church in Great Britain, vol. 3*, (London, Epworth Press 1983), pp. 38–9.

[10]   From 'Son of thy Sire's eternal Love' (headed 'The Lord's Prayer paraphrased') in *Hymns and Sacred Poems* (Bristol, Felix Farley, 1742).

> And all shall own thou dieds't for all

and

> For all my Lord was crucified,
> For all, for all my Saviour died.[11]

Less familiar, because the hymn was not included in the 1779 hymn-book, are the lines

> Master, be thou my might, my mouth,
> And send me forth to North or South,
> To farthest East or West...[12]

Charles Wesley's verses expound the scriptures in which he was steeped, but he was not issuing a call to world evangelization. The emphasis on 'all' was in deliberate contrast to that Calvinism which limited the possibility of salvation to the elect: a theological rather than a geographical point.

Nor did John Wesley's oft-quoted statement 'I look upon all the world as my parish' indicate any enthusiasm to get involved in foreign missions. It must be understood in the light of the rest of the sentence he wrote to James Hervey in 1739: 'thus far I mean, that, in whatever part of it I am, I judge it meet, right, and my bounden duty to declare unto all that are willing to hear the glad tidings of salvation'.[13] It was then over a year since John Wesley had found peace with God; eighteen months since his brief spell of service in Georgia had come to an abrupt end. The energy and enthusiasm with which he had sailed for America and which had subsequently fallen victim to his failures and doubts, were again evident. For the last few months he had been based in Bristol where he had, at first with severe misgivings, begun to preach in the open air. John Wesley would not accept the normal limits placed on the activity of an Anglican priest. Parish boundaries could not confine him. But his travels over the next half-century were confined to Britain and Ireland, apart from a couple of visits late in life to Holland. His youthful ambition to preach the gospel to the American Indians was of the past.

It took a long time for John Wesley to shed his reluctance to contemplate any venture in mission 'among the heathen'. He was a cautious conservative and shunned such a rash enterprise. His reputation as a radical innovator is only part of the record, for in other respects too his hesitations are notorious. Open air preaching was initially repugnant to him and it was only after casting lots that he joined George Whitefield in Bristol and 'submitted to be more vile'.[14] One account

---

[11]   From 'Father, whose everlasting love' in *Hymns on God's Everlasting Love* (London, W. Strahan, 1741).

[12]   C. Wesley, *Hymns for the Use of Families*, (Bristol, William Pike, 1767), no. 151; quoted by Birtwhistle, p. 49.

[13]   Letter to James Hervey, 20 March 1739, in Telford (ed.), *Letters*, vol. 1, pp. 284–7.

[14]   J. Wesley, *Journal*, 2 April 1739, in N. Curnock (ed.), *The Journal of the Revd John Wesley*, (8 vols, London, Epworth Press, 1911), vol. 2, p. 172.

says that he could not abide the thought of unordained preachers until, compelled by his mother to listen to Thomas Maxfield, he was obliged to admit 'It is the Lord; let Him do what seemeth good.'[15] And his attitude to separation from the Church of England was ambivalent to the end. 'In the Church I will live and die, unless I am thrust out' he wrote in 1788, despite courting separation by his ordinations.[16] So his attitude to foreign missions was typical of the man. They happened, at first, by accident.

First Societies Abroad

Those who gathered together in response to the preaching of John Wesley and his colleagues were formed into local groups known as societies. As societies grew in numbers, they were divided into smaller groups for fellowship and mutual encouragement, known as classes (a term not yet strongly associated with education, but denoting classification, as used in the emerging biological sciences). This was the pattern naturally adopted when Methodism began to take root beyond Britain and Ireland.

The first Methodist class meeting and preaching place outside the British Isles were established in the colony of Antigua by the planter and lawyer Nathaniel Gilbert, who was a member of the island's House of Assembly and was to be its Speaker between 1763 and 1769. Gilbert's brother, Francis, in England, had fallen under John Wesley's influence and become a travelling preacher. Nathaniel visited Britain in 1757 with the express intention of hearing John Wesley preach, after reading during a period of illness his *Earnest Appeal to Men of Reason and Religion* which Francis had sent him some time earlier. He was accompanied by three of his black servants, two of whom received baptism at John Wesley's hands in November 1758, prompting Wesley to write of the first African Christian he had known. On returning home in 1759, Gilbert, a changed man, began a house church. He wrote to John Wesley:

> I signified to one or two persons that as there was no service at the church in the afternoon, any person disposed to join my family was welcome. I had on the first Sunday six besides my own family, on the second nine, and on the third about eighteen; and it is now not only spread through the town that I have preached, but I believe through this island.[17]

---

[15]   T. Coke and H. Moore, *The Life of John Wesley*, (London, Paramore, 1792), pp. 219–20; doubts about the authenticity of this account are summarized in J.H. Lenton, *John Wesley's Preachers*, (Milton Keynes, Paternoster, 2009), pp. 32–3.

[16]   Letter to Henry Moore, 6 May 1788, in Telford (ed.), *Letters*, vol. 8, p. 58.

[17]   10 May 1760, reproduced in the *Arminian Magazine*, 3 (1780): pp. 387–9.

Gilbert's initial audience was made up primarily of white people, but he wanted to share his faith with his slaves too. His domestic servants could be accommodated at the house meetings, but to his 300 plantation workers he preached from the steps of the house. As happened in many another place subsequently, it was a private initiative, not a conscious act of the Methodist Conference, which founded the first Methodist society overseas.

Francis Gilbert went back to Antigua in 1763 and the two brothers shared an energetic ministry for over a year, but then he returned to England for health reasons. In 1769 Nathaniel relinquished his office as Speaker of the House of Assembly and immediately fitted up a large room above the place where his plantation stores were kept. He furnished it with a pulpit and benches for his black congregation. Francis was once more in Antigua when Nathaniel died in 1774 and preached at the funeral service. For a while he carried on the work, but then ill health compelled his return to England once more. Leadership of the society was assumed by the black and mulatto members, including Sophia Campbell, Mary Alley and possibly – the oral tradition, though much repeated, is undocumented – by one of Gilbert's domestic slaves, known only as Bessie, who may have been one of those baptized by John Wesley. They were joined in 1781 by Francis's widow: ethnic diversity was evident from the outset. Yet when John Baxter, a government shipwright and local preacher, was posted to Antigua in 1778, it was said, with more than a hint of chauvinism, that he 'found the Methodist flock unshepherded'.[18]

It was in spontaneous unplanned fashion that Methodism also reached New York. The first Methodists there came from Ireland, but their migrations had begun in Germany. Around the time of John Wesley's birth a small group of Protestant refugees from the Palatinate settled in Limerick, where in 1749 some responded to Methodist preaching. Among them was Philip Embury, a carpenter, who became a local preacher himself. Successive parties of 'Palatines' moved on to America in the early 1760s, but for some years their religious zeal cooled, until in 1766 Embury's cousin, Barbara Heck, urged him to resume preaching. The result was a little congregation which soon outgrew Embury's cottage and took a room near the barracks. Here they were joined by English soldiers, most notably Captain Thomas Webb, another Wesleyan preacher. Within a short space of time these and other premises again proved too small and at the instigation of Barbara Heck a chapel was built in 1768. Captain Webb headed the subscription list.

Other local, lay initiatives followed elsewhere in the colonies. Before long the New York society appealed to John Wesley for an able and experienced minister, who must be 'a man of wisdom, of sound faith, and a good disciplinarian'.[19] Wesley recognized both the need and the opportunity and the Leeds Conference of 1769 appointed Richard Boardman and Joseph Pilmoor, the first to New York and

---

[18]   Findlay and Findlay, p. 49.
[19]   Letter to J. Wesley from Thomas Taylor, 11 April 1768, quoted in A. Stevens, *A Compendious History of American Methodism*, (New York, Phillips & Hunt, 1868), p. 43.

the other to Philadelphia. The two Yorkshiremen, who had walked over fifty miles from Ryedale to Leeds, were the first preachers the Conference sent overseas. Two years later, a further appeal produced two more, including Francis Asbury who was to spend the next forty-five years establishing, consolidating and expanding American Methodism.[20]

New Initiatives

Another volunteer for America was the young Irish preacher, John Prickard, who had a different object in view and was twice discouraged. 'John Prickard wants to go to missions work to America [among the] American Indians' wrote one of John Wesley's associates, Walter Churchey, to another, Joseph Benson, in 1774. 'He's needed here. Indians! Why go to America to look for them! Their black souls are visible at home.'[21] The time for a mission to the heathen had not yet come.

Haphazard and hesitant beginnings were however to take a more deliberate shape after Dr Thomas Coke joined the Methodist movement. Coke, a Welshman from Brecon and a schoolmate of Churchey, was the only son of an affluent and respected family. Coke was a bright Oxford graduate, elected mayor of Brecon while in his twenties, then ordained in the Church of England and later awarded a doctorate in civil law by his alma mater. At the age of 30 he came under Methodist influence and experienced a profound spiritual change; he was dismissed from his curacy at South Petherton in Somerset on account of his Methodist tendencies and became one of John Wesley's preachers. Contemporary accounts suggest that when, shortly afterwards, he met Wesley, he sought advice as to what he should do next and Wesley is supposed to have said 'Brother, go out, go out, and preach the Gospel to all the world.'[22] Whatever John Wesley meant by these words, there is no doubt what Coke made of them. He was to take the principal role in developing Methodism's foreign mission. At the 1778 Conference, probably the second which Coke attended, a request was considered from two African princes who had fallen under Methodist influence in Bristol. They had been freed from slavery by virtue of Lord Chief Justice Mansfield's ruling in 1772 that slavery was illegal in England and that any slave who set foot in England automatically became free.[23] They had returned to Calabar and asked for missionaries to be sent to them. Two German

---

[20] See J. Wigger, *American Saint, Francis Asbury and the Methodists*, (New York, Oxford University Press, 2009).

[21] Methodist Archives and Research Centre, (MARC), Manchester, MAW PLP 24.1.1, Walter Churchey to Joseph Benson, 18 May 1774.

[22] *Wesleyan Methodist Magazine* 1824, p. 568; but see J.A. Vickers, *Thomas Coke, Apostle of Methodism*, (London, Epworth Press, 1969), p. 33.

[23] No definitive text was printed of Mansfield's 600-word speech in the Court of King's Bench; it was reported in a letter to the London *General Evening Post* of 21–23 June 1772.

brothers from Bristol went, only to die on reaching Calabar, and this renewed appeal followed.

Two men had expressed an interest in going to Africa: Prickard again and Duncan M'Allum to whom John Wesley wrote on the eve of Conference, 'You have nothing to do at present in Afric [sic]. Convert the heathen in Scotland.'[24] (This M'Allum proceeded to do, travelling in all for fifty-one years.) For his part, Prickard later reported:

> I received a circular letter respecting an African Mission. As soon as I read it, I felt a strong desire to offer myself to go; yet my nature shuddered at the thought of leaving father and mother, brothers and sisters, friends and country, but especially my dear brethren in Christ. I also dreaded the intense heat of the sun by day, and the damps of the night; which I had heard were in general fatal to an European constitution. In this deep distress I prayed to the Lord that he would give me direction and strength. The next morning I went to church, when one of the Psalms for the day was the one hundred and twenty-first. In reading it, I viewed it as an answer to my prayer. But when we came to the fifth verse, my soul was so overwhelmed with Divine love, that I could no longer doubt the will of God concerning me. As we read on, I resolved to offer myself to go, on which all my fear and dread vanished away …[25]

> Having received this clear answer to my prayer, I hesitated no longer; but offered myself freely and fully, if approved of by my brethren in Conference. But they did not approve of the Mission itself, on account of the war: so the matter was for that time laid aside.

> I have often thought since, that they were too cautious … I have always been of opinion that we ought to have gone; and if the Lord ever restored me to tolerable health, and it is judged right to send out a Mission into those dark regions, I hope I shall be as ready to go as ever.[26]

Prickard suggested that the American War of Independence was the obstacle to the execution of this plan, though Joseph Benson, a preacher who was at the Conference that year, simply recorded: 'after the matter was seriously considered, it was concluded that the time had not arrived for sending missionaries to Africa'.[27]

---

[24]   Letter 14 July 1778, in Telford (ed.), *Letters*, vol. 6, p. 316.

[25]   Psalm 121, verses 5–6: The Lord himself watches over you; the Lord is your shade at your right hand. So that the sun shall not strike you by day, nor the moon by night.

[26]   T. Jackson, *The Lives of Early Methodist Preachers*, (6 vols, London, Wesleyan Book Room, 1865), vol. 4, pp. 184–6.

[27]   Benson's report was quoted by Vickers, *Coke,* p. 132 from J. Macdonald, *Memoirs of Joseph Benson*, (London, T. Blanshard, 1822), p. 75.

So the request was turned down – after more prolonged deliberation than might have been expected, given that John Wesley's mind was so clearly made up. But Coke, still a newcomer, was deeply impressed by the challenge. A few years passed and then, towards the end of 1783, he and Thomas Parker, a barrister and local preacher from York, discussed and issued a *Plan of the Society for the Establishment of Missions among the Heathens*. It was addressed 'To all the real lovers of mankind' and stated:

The candid of every denomination (even those who are entirely unconnected with the Methodists, and are determined to be so) will acknowledge the amazing change which our preaching has wrought upon the ignorant and uncivilised at least, throughout these nations; and they will admit, that the spirit of a missionary must be of the most zealous, most devoted, and self-denying kind; nor is anything more required to constitute a missionary for the heathen nations than good sense, integrity, great piety, and amazing zeal. Men, possessing all these qualifications in a high degree, we have among us; and we doubt not but some of these will accept of the arduous undertaking, not counting their lives dear, if they may but promote the kingdom of Christ, and the present and eternal welfare of their fellow creatures; and we trust nothing shall be wanting, as far as time, strength, and abilities will admit, to give the fullest and highest satisfaction to the promoters of the plan.[28]

The *Plan* proposed that everyone subscribing at least two guineas annually should be a member of the society; it announced that the first annual general meeting was fixed for Tuesday, 27 January 1784; and that a committee of seven was to be appointed. A list of subscriptions already received, amounting to £66, 3s, was printed with the *Plan*.

Nothing was to come of this first scheme. Coke's biographer John Vickers related: 'What final sum was received, and how it was disbursed, remains a mystery ... The first general meeting was presumably held as planned, at No 11 West Street, Seven Dials, though from his Diary it would appear that Wesley did not attend.'[29] But on 14 February John Wesley recorded in his Journal:

I desired all our preachers to meet and consider thoroughly the proposal of sending missionaries to the East Indies. After the matter had been fully considered, we were unanimous in our judgment that we have no call thither yet, no invitation, no providential opening of any kind.[30]

---

[28]   Quoted by Vickers, *Coke*, pp. 133–4.
[29]   Vickers, *Coke*, p. 134.
[30]   Curnock (ed.), *Journal*, vol. 6, p. 476

John Wesley's Diary for that day includes the laconic entry '11 Dr Coke, etc',[31] so Coke was presumably party, however reluctantly, to the judgment.

But in 1786 Coke, undeterred, launched another appeal. It was headed 'An Address to the Pious and Benevolent, Proposing an Annual Subscription for the Support of Missionaries in the Highlands and Adjacent Islands of Scotland, the Isles of Jersey, Guernsey and Newfoundland, the West Indies, and the Provinces of Nova Scotia and Quebec'.[32] Again it was addressed to a broader audience than Methodists, but on this occasion it did receive John Wesley's backing. Prevarication and procrastination were over. For circumstances had changed irrevocably after he notoriously 'set apart' Coke to be 'superintendent' of the Methodist Church in America.[33] Coke's star was in the ascendant. John Wesley wrote:

> Dear Sir,
>
>   I greatly approve of your proposal for raising a subscription in order to send missionaries to the Highlands of Scotland, the Islands of Jersey and Guernsey, the Leeward Islands, Quebec, Nova Scotia, and Newfoundland. It is not easy to conceive the extreme want there is, in all these places, of men that will not count their lives dear unto themselves, so that they may testify the gospel of the grace of God.[34]

'Missions to the Heathen' would become known, successively, as Foreign Missions, Overseas Missions and World Mission. Though the Antigua class meeting of 1759 and the stationing of Boardman and Pilmoor in 1769 were each significant beginnings, there is much to be said for the view that 1786 'marks the birth of the Methodist Missionary Society some thirty years before it was formally constituted'.[35]

---

[31] Ibid.
[32] London, un-named publisher, 1786 – a copy is held at MARC.
[33] See p. 14.
[34] Quoted by Vickers, *Coke,* p. 136, from Telford (ed.), *Letters,* vol. 7, p. 322.
[35] Vickers, *Coke,* p. 138.

Chapter 2
Coke's World Parish

The end of the eighteenth century was an era of revolutions. The settlers in America revolted against British rule and won their independence. The French Revolution followed, violently ending the old order with a series of coups under the banner Liberty, Equality, Fraternity, which struck fear into some and caught the imagination of others. Most significant of all was the industrial revolution. Its defining feature was speed: speed of manufacture made possible when machinery replaced hand production, together with accelerating speed of travel and international communication. There was also a consumer revolution. Tea, coffee, sugar and tobacco became popular in England and the volume of sea traffic increased dramatically in the course of the century to satisfy demand. This made possible Thomas Coke's eighteen transatlantic voyages before he embarked on his last journey to Asia. Commercial shipping not only brought the goods home to British ports, but transported the means of production, in the form of slave labour, from Africa to the plantations of the Caribbean and the Americas.

Exploration, Enlightenment, Enthusiasm

Trade had long been the driving influence behind exploration. But by the eighteenth century it was also driven by a thirst to learn what lay beyond the horizons of the known world. Captain James Cook's voyages, which were well chronicled, encouraged others to venture inquisitively around the globe. In the early 1790s George Vancouver charted America's north-western coast. The Association for Promoting the Discovery of the Inland Districts of Africa (generally known as the African Association) was founded in 1788 by Sir Joseph Banks, who had sailed with Cook, and others. European settlers in Asia and Africa had hitherto scarcely ventured beyond the coastal enclaves they established as trading centres. Local people brought their produce – or brought captives destined for slavery – to these settlements to barter. The new spirit of enquiry now led adventurers into the interior. The Scot, Mungo Park, for example, made two expeditions into West Africa in 1795 and 1805. Banks described him as 'my missionary in Africa' – an interesting secular use of the term. After reading Park's diary, published as *Travels in the Interior of Africa* in 1799, Banks wrote:

> I have little doubt that in a very few years a trading Company might be established under the immediate control of the Government, who ... would govern the Negroes far more mildly, and make them far more happy than they now are under

the Tyranny of their arbitrary Princes ... by converting them to the Christian
Religion ... and by effecting the greatest practicable diminution of the Slavery of
mankind, upon the Principles of natural Justice and commercial Benefit.

This 'grand civilizing mission', he said, should include 'the more intelligible
doctrines of the Scriptures and the more useful branches of European mechanics'.[1]

The geographical horizon was extending: the enlightenment was also making
its mark. While Roman Catholicism resisted enlightenment thought and treated
faith and reason as opposites, the Protestant tradition was profoundly influenced
by it. The philosopher John Locke (1632–1704) had written a treatise entitled *The
Reasonableness of Christianity*. The view that Christian principles can be deduced
by reasonable people anywhere lay behind Banks's expectation that religion could
and should be taught and it spurred and steered the missionary movement. William
Wilberforce, the Anglican evangelical, argued that if missionaries combined
general education with religious instruction, 'the combination of reason and truth,
enlightenment and Christian mission, would be irresistible'.[2]

Enlightenment thought was not incompatible with the emotion and enthusiasm
that fuelled the evangelical revival.[3] John Wesley himself has rightly been called
a 'Reasonable Enthusiast'. Features of this enthusiasm included the believers'
peace, joy and relief at knowing themselves to be saved, in a right relationship with
God, delivered from the everlasting hell which was the destiny of the unbeliever;
the desire to share their experience and excitement so that unbelievers might be
saved; and the expectation, fuelled by such cataclysmic events as the Lisbon
earthquake in 1755, that the Last Days were at hand. An appendix to Thomas
Coke's *Commentary on the Bible*, published in 1807, was entitled *The Recent
Occurrences of Europe Considered in relation to such prophecies as are either
fulfilling or unfulfilled*. Coke wrote: 'of this we may rest ourselves assured, that the
great period of the consummation is at hand, – that it is even at the door.'[4]

Put these factors together and the time was ripe for a change of gear in the
missionary enterprise. Two zealous and intrepid Christians were there to recognize
the new opportunities and seize them. One of these was the Baptist, William Carey.
In his influential pamphlet of 1792, *An Enquiry into the Obligations of Christians to
Use Means for the Conversion of the Heathens*, Carey wrote about 'The Lord's Still-
binding Commission'. He challenged the view, widely held in his day, that Jesus'
words, 'Go and make disciples of all nations' (Matthew 28:19), were addressed
solely to the apostles and that the charge had been fulfilled by them. It had, according
to this view, no relevance to eighteenth-century Christians. Carey thought differently.

---

[1]   See R. Holmes, *The Age of Wonder: How the Romantic Generation Discovered the
Beauty and Terror of Science*, (London, Harper Press, 2008), p. 222.

[2]   Porter, p. 101.

[3]   D. Hempton, *Methodism: Empire of the Spirit*, (New Haven, Yale University Press,
2005), pp. 32–54.

[4]   Quoted by Porter, p. 34.

He was an impoverished pastor, part-time shoemaker, of little consequence in the eyes of theologians, and the pamphlet did not sell well. Yet such was its impact that within months the Baptist Missionary Society (BMS) was formed, to be followed in quick succession by the London Missionary Society (LMS), the Church Missionary Society (CMS), the British and Foreign Bible Society (BFBS) and others, while Carey himself left for an outstanding forty years of service in Bengal.

Thomas Coke was the other pioneer. He made the first of his many overseas journeys some years earlier, in 1784, at John Wesley's behest.

1784

The year 1784 was of great significance for Coke and for Methodism. As one of the few ordained clergymen among the Methodist preachers and because of his exceptional gifts, Coke had already become John Wesley's lieutenant. Until 1782 Wesley had tried to visit every major Methodist society each year. But, as he approached the age of 80, he decided to visit only every other year and asked Coke to take his place in alternate years, even presiding in Wesley's stead over the Irish Conference. As the year 1784 began John Wesley had a lot on his mind. That fruitless meeting convened by Coke which was intended to launch a missionary society came to nothing due to Wesley's lack of support. Then in the months before the Conference met, Coke, with his doctorate in Civil Law, was busy advising Wesley in a legal capacity. John Wesley had come to accept that the 'Society of People called Methodists' would continue after his death and that its government by an annual Conference needed to be set on a sound legal footing. The 'Deed of Declaration' adopted at the Leeds Conference in August owed much to Coke's legal acumen. It effectively turned the Methodist movement into the Methodist Church (though it was only in 1891 that the Wesleyan Conference approved the change of nomenclature from 'Society' to 'Church').

A few weeks after the Conference, in an even more momentous step, Coke joined Wesley in Bristol. Wesley wanted him to go and report on the situation of Methodism in America, where the war of independence had finally ended the previous year. Boardman, Pilmoor and their colleagues had been hounded out. Even Asbury, who supported the colonists' stance, had been forced into hiding. Most of the Anglican clergy had fled and there was no-one to celebrate the sacraments. The Bishop of London, under whose jurisdiction overseas parishes fell, resolutely refused to consider ministering to the 'rebels' and turned down John Wesley's request that he should ordain Methodist preachers to supply the need. Through the preceding months, alongside their legal consultations, Wesley and Coke had been in theological discussion about what other course could be taken. Wesley had concluded that he must himself take on the mantle of a bishop and ordain preachers. When Conference met he shared the idea with a select handful of associates, who were strongly opposed to it. The only exception was

Figure 2.1   Thomas Coke, 1747–1814, Oil painting by David Grice, 1976

Coke. He not only went along with the proposal; he reasoned that if John Wesley had the right to ordain then so, as an ordained presbyter himself, did he.

Two of the preachers had volunteered to go to America and they, without suspecting what lay in store, were summoned to Bristol. On 2 September 1784 Coke and James Creighton, another Anglican priest, assisted John Wesley in ordaining Richard Whatcoat and Thomas Vasey to the ministry of word and sacraments. Next Coke himself received the imposition of Wesley's hands as 'superintendent' of the Methodist Church in America – effectively, its bishop. There was no intention that he should remain long in America and he was instructed to ordain Asbury as 'joint superintendent'. This would ensure the continuity of American Methodism; it also meant that the Methodist Church in America would become an episcopal body.[5]

Whatcoat, Vasey and Coke sailed on 18 September 1784. In their baggage they carried a certificate of Coke's ordination. Wesley also sent a letter to the American

---

[5]   The 1787 American Conference minuted, 'We have constituted ourselves into an Episcopal Church under the direction of bishops, elders, deacons, and preachers, according to the form of ordination annexed in our prayer-book, and the regulations laid down in this form of discipline.'

brethren explaining his ordinations, another letter indicating his choice of Coke and Asbury to be joint superintendents, a hymn-book and a prayer-book that included Wesley's modifications of the Church of England's doctrinal guidelines. The voyage took six and a half weeks. They landed at New York and set out to track down the nomadic Asbury, eventually catching up with him in Delaware. The two agreed to convene a Conference of all the preachers in Baltimore at Christmas and between them drew up the constitution of the American church. Sixty of the preachers managed to gather and with their agreement the constitution was adopted and Asbury was duly ordained and set apart as superintendent. A few other preachers were ordained as well. The Conference appointed one of them, Jeremiah Lambert, to the West Indies, but after a few months in Antigua he fell ill, returned to America and died.[6] However, just before embarking for home, Coke met the shipwright John Baxter, who had come from Antigua to Baltimore expressly for ordination. Baxter told of his work among the slaves. In the weeks before and after the Christmas Conference, Coke had ridden far and wide to visit the scattered societies and what he had seen of the way slaves were treated had left him aghast. He was impressed by what Baxter had to say and had no hesitation in ordaining him also.

Antigua Again

Full of his experiences in America, Coke returned to Britain even more determined to spread the gospel both at home and abroad. In the next few months his journeys took him from the Gaelic-speaking regions of Scotland to the Channel Islands and the *Address to the Pious and Benevolent* was launched.

John Wesley's and the Conference's willingness to respond to the *Appeal* came with one major reservation: how much would it all cost and where would the money be found? Coke would not be deterred. He had inherited a considerable amount. He had paid from his own pocket the expenses not only of his own voyage to America, but Whatcoat's and Vasey's as well. He would do the same again. Indeed, his entire fortune and that of his wives, when at length he married, were to be devoted to the missionary cause for the next twenty-seven years.

So the Conference endorsed the proposal. William Warrener was designated to join Baxter in Antigua. John Clarke and William Hammett were appointed to Newfoundland. Coke would sail with them and make a second visit to the American church as its co-superintendent. This time the voyage was a nightmare. From the English Channel right across the Atlantic they were beset by storms and

---

6   Vickers, *Coke,* p. 99, wrote 'he died of consumption before he could take up the work there' but two letters in the MMS archives refer to his preaching in Antigua. William Warrener told the Leeds Missionary Meeting of 1813 how 'Mr Jeremiah Lambert was then sent to him (Baxter) from America, whither he was soon obliged to return, on account of his being consumptive.'

driven off course. After all of three months at sea they finally made landfall, not in Nova Scotia as intended but in Antigua, on Christmas Day 1786. John Baxter, about to conduct Christmas services, could not believe his eyes; nor could Coke when he faced an almost entirely black congregation of two thousand, for the most part slaves, gathered to worship.

He went on to tour some of the Leeward and Windward Islands with Baxter for two months and the American mainland with Asbury for another two. On his return to England he had exciting news for the Conference. There were 25,000 Methodist members in the United States and 3,000 in the West Indies. Moreover, he had taken it upon himself to alter the stations of his companions. Newfoundland would have to wait. Warrener remained in Antigua; he left Clarke in St Vincent and Hammett in St Kitts.

Coke the Itinerant

John Wesley's preachers were continually on the move. They were appointed to circuits round which they circulated on a methodical basis, returning to visit each society every few weeks. After a year or two Conference usually moved them on to a different part of the country. 'Home' was an ever-changing location. Coke was a different sort of itinerant. His home from 1778 onwards was in London. Until 1784 he was stationed at the prestigious new chapel on City Road and even so he was away from home much of the time. Thereafter he was constantly on the move, even after he married at the age of 57. In the first six weeks of married life he and Penelope covered 400 miles. A few years later he wrote that they were 'continually on the wing'. 'I annually visit and preach at more places than I did for many years before my marriage.'[7]

Between 1784 and 1803 he made nine visits to America. On the fourth outward voyage his ship was captured by a French privateer, but he and his companions were allowed to board a brig and proceed. Between 1786 and 1792 he made four visits to the West Indies. He was abroad less often after Wesley's death in 1791, when he was immediately elected Secretary of the Conference, a post he held in all 14 times. He was President in 1797 and 1805. He instigated Methodist outreach among Welsh-speakers and Irish-speakers and tried, unsuccessfully, to establish Gaelic-speaking work in the Highlands of Scotland. He continued to preside regularly at the Irish Conference and travelled as extensively there as in Britain. But his chief preoccupation remained the work overseas. He took three main duties upon himself. One was to keep the Methodist people informed and enthused. Another was to recruit volunteers for the growing number of overseas stations. He found them, full of zeal and enthusiasm, if not always with sufficient ability and stamina, and personally ordained them. Financing them was the problem. From 1786 onward the Conference showed itself willing to support his plans as long as it could devolve on

---

[7]   Vickers, *Coke,* p. 252.

him responsibility for funding them. So the third consuming task was fund-raising. In 1793, two years after John Wesley's death, the Conference did agree to an annual collection in all the chapels for missionary funds. But Coke's own generosity and his indefatigable quest for subscribers were the mainstay of the enterprise.

New challenges attracted him. He attempted to plant work in France – he started polishing his French in 1786 and was not deterred by the revolutionary turmoil which soon arose. In 1791 it seemed to him that the time was ripe; he imagined that the French Revolution, in breaking the hold of Roman Catholicism, had opened the door to the gospel. He travelled via Jersey to Normandy and on to Paris, where he bought a disused church for £120. But the venture failed. Parisians were in no mood to go and listen to foreign evangelists. The tumbrel and the guillotine were more popular attractions. His preaching was met at first with apathy and then with threats that he would be strung up from a lamp-post if he did not depart. He did however leave two of the Channel Islands preachers in Normandy, with more fruitful prospects.

In his imagination and in his prayers Coke constantly travelled even further afield than horses, carriages and ships could take him. Africa commanded his attention. His favourite text was 'Ethiopia shall stretch out her hands to God' (Psalm 68:31). Returning from his first visit to the Caribbean, he had written in his Journal, 'Since my visit to the islands, I have found a peculiar gift for speaking to the blacks. It seems to be almost irresistible. Who knows but the Lord is preparing me for a visit in some future time to the coast of Africa?'[8] That visit he never made, but when the Sierra Leone Company was formed in 1791 to organize a settlement for refugees from the American colonies, he took a keen interest. 'We are going to send Missionaries to Sierra Leone', he wrote in a letter. 'The Company has chosen two Chaplains. One of them is a zealous Methodist Preacher of my recommendation.'[9] The chaplains were in fact the son and nephew of Nathaniel Gilbert, the Antiguan pioneer. Nathaniel Gilbert, the son and Melville Horne, the nephew, were both Anglican clergymen. Horne preached to the settlers four or five times a week. He hoped to be a missionary to the native Temne people as well, but the opportunity was not there. He only managed to 'preach one single sermon by means of an interpreter' and left in disappointment after fourteen months. Nonetheless for several years from 1792 the statistics record 223 members in Sierra Leone, but it seems they were not a shining example of disciplined Christianity.

Coke was then closely involved, albeit in a personal rather than any representative capacity, with a 'Plan for establishing Missions in the Foulah Country of West Africa', the brainchild of the governor of Sierra Leone, Zachary Macaulay. Coke planned to be part of the team of missionaries that sailed, after much delay, in 1796, but went to America instead. The whole venture was a disaster and Coke's part in it inept. Mortified, he reported its failure to the next Conference, which decided 'that trial should be made in that part of Africa on

---

8   Ibid., p. 288.
9   Ibid.

the proper missionary plan'. It was another fifteen years, however, before, in response to repeated calls from the Sierra Leone Methodists, a preacher and three schoolmasters were appointed. In his old age the impetuous Coke had perhaps learned a little of John Wesley's natural caution.

Bishop and Superintendent

From its inception the American church had chosen to be known as the Methodist Episcopal Church (MEC). In 1788 its Conference decided that its two leaders should have the title Bishop Coke and Bishop Asbury. Wesley's displeasure was unbounded, but the MEC was master in its own house. In 1789 George Washington was elected the first President of the United States and the Conference resolved to send him a declaration of loyalty to the new constitution and government. Asbury and Coke drafted it and both signed it. Eyebrows were raised in America that one from the old colonial power should play such a part; and at the next British Conference, when the question 'Is there any objection to any preacher?' was asked, Coke was instantly cited and given a very hard time. But he was back in America in 1791 and was there when he heard of Wesley's death. There were grounds for expecting he would take over as President of the Conference. When he was passed over, many in America hoped he could be persuaded to take up his episcopal role there permanently.

But there was much to retain Coke in Britain. After 1792 his visits to the MEC became less frequent. The 1792 visit itself lasted only a few weeks and nearly ended in disaster. After chairing the Conference because Asbury was ill, he was preparing to sail for the West Indies when he had an accident which might have killed him. He slipped and fell between the ship and the quayside. Fortunately a spar wedged to prevent the ship from grinding against the quay saved him from the water and he was rescued.

He did not return to America until the 1796 Conference. There was growing concern at the burden an exhausted Asbury was shouldering alone and on an impulse Coke suddenly offered to abandon his other responsibilities and devote himself wholly to America: 'all I am and have, with my talents and labours in every respect, without any mental reservation whatsoever'.[10] There were some who wanted to insist on the condition that he first become an American citizen, but the case was not pressed. He sailed for England with a letter requesting the British Conference to release him. The response of the Conference was to elect him President at last and the moment passed.

Coke had been made Superintendent for America and there was nothing episcopal about Methodism in Britain. But the time came when the Conference accorded him the title 'Superintendent of the Missions'. It reflected the reality. The origin and the development of missionary activity abroad were down to him and

---

[10]   Minute book of the Baltimore Conference, quoted by Vickers, *Coke*, p. 233.

the enterprise has been justly described as a 'One-man Band'.[11] While Asbury had to carry the leadership of the American church without his co-bishop, Coke single-handedly managed the growing missions both overseas and at home. Although the 1790 Conference appointed a committee 'for the management of our affairs in the West Indies' it never met and a 'Committee of Finance', set up in 1798, seems to have met only once.

But administration was not his forte. Given 'Coke's own impulsiveness, his chaotic personal control swelling debts and a complete lack of any financial or administrative system',[12] it is remarkable that he did not completely forfeit the confidence of his fellow Methodist leaders. Nor did he have much confidence in them. During his final, nine-month-long visit to America in 1803–04, the arrangements he made for his absence fell into disarray and a new committee was formed. It demanded to see the accounts of the missions on a regular basis and a young minister, Jabez Bunting, was asked to draw them up. It instructed every missionary to keep a journal and submit it twice a year with a view to publication. These eminently reasonable steps provoked Coke's resentment on his return. An explosive situation was defused at Conference by replacing this committee with yet another, which Coke accepted as long as it was true to its name, a Committee of Finance and Advice and not, he made clear, a 'Committee of control and superintendency'. But the friction did not abate. The committee was critical of his selection of candidates, which was not always judicious. Fewer volunteers for overseas were forthcoming from among the itinerant preachers and those he recruited without that previous experience were not always suitable.[13]

Coke's prime concern as Superintendent was for the welfare of those he chose and sent out. In the opinion of his biographer, he was not called the 'Father of the Methodist Missions' for nothing – he displayed a paternal concern for them.[14] Unlike most members of the successive committees he had to work with, he knew from personal experience the sort of conditions that confronted them. He once wrote: 'Umbrellas may be esteemed as luxurious in this country, but are highly necessary for Europeans under the torrid zone. We should not study the health of the Missionaries, if we did not allow each of them an umbrella.'[15] His chief fear was that they should find themselves penniless far from home. Bills of exchange must at all costs be honoured; he guaranteed to meet them out of his own dwindling fortune if there was not enough in the fund. It was a time of financial hardship in the country, exacerbated for Methodists by the schism which formed the Methodist New Connexion in 1797, and the annual collections authorized by the Conference were not especially productive. To make up the deficit he was

---

[11]   See J. Vickers, 'One-man Band: Thomas Coke and the origins of Methodist Missions', in *Methodist History*, 34/3 (April 1996): pp. 135–47.

[12]   Porter, p. 32.

[13]   Vickers, 'One-Man Band': pp. 7–11.

[14]   Vickers, *Coke*, p. 271.

[15]   Ibid., p. 272.

ceaselessly writing begging letters and even begging from house to house. It must have afforded him some relief to retreat to Lincolnshire and work on his massive Bible commentary and his three-volume History of the West Indies.

Missionary Mindset

Coke and the many who shared his commitment and ambition had one overriding aim: to bring men and women to a saving faith in the love of God made known in Jesus Christ. The objective was the same among people who had never heard the name of Jesus as it was among those who may well have done so but did not live according to the light of the gospel.

> O that *the world* might taste and see
> The riches of his grace!
> The arms of love that compass me
> Would *all mankind* embrace! [16]

No lesser motivation than 'the apprehension of the wholesale perdition of the heathen'[17] drove Coke, his envoys and his subscribers. His mishandling of the accounts caused frustration because every passing day consigned more men and women to eternal damnation and 'discontent at the thought that through carelessness the Lord's coming might be delayed'.[18]

However they shared the attitudes and prejudices of the times. The notion of a 'great chain of being' ranked the 'White', 'Red', 'Yellow' and 'Negro' races in that descending order of humanity. A similar hierarchy applied to the world's religions, as can be seen from an article on Religion in the 1797 edition of the *Encyclopedia Britannica*:

> When the different systems of religion that have prevailed in the world are comparatively viewed with respect to their influence on the welfare of society, we find reason to prefer the polytheism of the Greeks and the Romans to the ruder, wilder religious ideas and ceremonies that have prevailed among savages; Mahometanism, perhaps, in some respects to the polytheism of the Greeks and Romans; Judaism however to Mahometanism; and Christianity to all of them.[19]

In like vein William Carey in 1792 divided the world's religions into 'Christian, Jewish, Mahometan, Pagan' and subdivided the final category into 'civilized

---

[16]　　C. Wesley, from the hymn 'Jesu, accept the grateful song', in *Hymns and Sacred Poems*, (Bristol, Felix Farley, 1749 edition).

[17]　　Findlay and Holdsworth, vol. 1, p. 193.

[18]　　Porter, p. 10.

[19]　　*Encyclopaedia Britannica* (1797), vol. 16, p. 77.

Pagans' – Indians and Chinese, who possessed their own literature – and 'savage and barbarous pagans' – preliterate societies notably in Africa, described as 'without literature, arts, sciences, government, Laws ... as destitute of civilization as they are of true religion'.[20]

Coke's thoughts returned again and again to India, where Carey had been working since 1792. 'Civilized pagans' they might be; but their eternal destiny was no different from that of barbarous savages. Back in 1784 Coke had corresponded with a director of the East India Company, Charles Grant, in Calcutta. Grant noted in his journal: 'Read two days ago a letter from Dr Coke, in connexion with Mr Wesley, with a scheme for a Mission in this country, and queries for information and assistance. A great project! May it be well influenced.'[21] Grant replied with sound advice, but in his next letter Coke had to say that the plan was in abeyance until 'the present extraordinary calls from America are answered'. When the opportunity at last arrived, a now elderly and twice-widowed Coke determined that he would lead a missionary party in person. He was familiar with Europeans and Africans; he longed to make Christ known to Asians too. It would be his final voyage:

> Happy if with my latest breath
> I might but gasp his name,
> Preach him to *all* ...[22]

---

[20]   W. Carey, *An Enquiry into the Obligations of Christians to Use Means for the Conversion of the Heathens*, (Leicester, Ann Ireland, 1792; Kindle edition, 2004).

[21]   F.D. Walker, *William Carey: Missionary Pioneer and Statesman*, (London, Cargate Press, 1926). p. 137.

[22]   C. Wesley, from 'Jesu, accept the grateful song'.

Chapter 3
1813

The Methodist leaders of the mid-nineteenth century decided that the Jubilee of the WMMS should be marked in 1863. Their choice was bizarre. For 1813 was not the year the first Methodist society outside the British Isles was formed; that was in Antigua in 1759.[1] It was not the year that Boardman and Pilmoor were stationed in America, though the *Methodist Magazine* seventy years later described them as 'the first Methodist missionaries'; nor when Warrener, Hammett and Clarke, who have a rival claim to that distinction, were stationed in the West Indies.[2] It was not the year the first autonomous Conference overseas was constituted; the Methodist Episcopal Church in America dates from 1784. Nor was it the year when Conference adopted the *Laws and Regulations of the General Wesleyan Methodist Missionary Society*; there was no such Society until 1818. But 1813 had its own significance.

In Parliament

The charter of the East India Company, which exercised control over British merchants and other British subjects in India, had to be renewed by Parliament every twenty years. The Company was founded in 1600. It let nothing stand in the way of its commercial interests, though it provided chaplains to minister to its employees. From time to time it issued directives requiring the chaplains to learn a local tongue in order to bring Indians under the civilizing influence of Christianity, but these directives invariably remained a dead letter. By 1770 the Company was resolutely committed to non-interference with local custom. Religious propaganda, it feared, might easily stir up trouble and harm trade prospects. One of its directors, Charles Grant, after an intermittent correspondence with Thomas Coke, produced *A proposal for establishing a Protestant Mission in Bengal and Behar* (1787) but it was given short shrift. The Company's permission was technically required before any British subject could reside in India. So when William Carey and his party arrived in 1792 they were in effect illegal immigrants. They eventually settled in Serampore,

---

[1]   Although the Methodist Church of the Caribbean and the Americas (MCCA) marked the 250th anniversary of Wesleyan Methodism in the western hemisphere in 2010, the celebration was a year late; the dates were discussed by J. Neal in *WHS Proceedings*, 58 (May 2012): pp. 226–35.

[2]   See N.W. Taggart, 'Methodist Foreign Missions. The First Half Century', in *WHS Proceedings*, 45 (October 1986): pp. 157–82.

a Danish enclave near Calcutta. There, free from harassment, they studied Indian languages and made Bible translations at a prodigious rate; the translations may not have stood the test of time but they laid the foundation for others.

When the Company charter came up for renewal in 1793, Grant and Wilberforce pressed for the inclusion of a 'pious clause' which would oblige the Company to make provision for the religious instruction of Indians. The directors were adamantly opposed, rallied support and ensured the proposal was roundly defeated. In 1801, in a memorial to Parliament, they declared 'The sending of Christian Missionaries into our Eastern possessions is the wildest, maddest, most expensive, and most unwarranted plan that was ever proposed by a lunatic enthusiast.'[3] Yet there was a different result at the 1813 renewal. Wilberforce and his allies lobbied hard. The parliamentary debates continued from March to July. The 'pious clause' which was eventually enacted did not achieve much – missionaries were not specifically mentioned – but the virulent opposition was at an end. The Company undertook to support an Anglican bishop of Calcutta and three archdeaconries, while Nonconformists welcomed a clear statement that promoting 'the Interests and Happiness of the Native Inhabitants' involved 'religious and moral improvement' and an undertaking to provide 'sufficient facilities … to persons desirous of going to and remaining in India, for the purpose of accomplishing these benevolent designs'.[4]

In fact this was only a partial victory for the missionary cause. Carey wrote that 'our going into the interior depends as much upon the rule of Government as before'.[5] It was not so much the outcome as the publicity given to the debate which brought new heart to such as Coke and encouraged them to put a foot in the door which was now at least ajar. At the next renewal of the charter in 1833 all restrictions on missionary activity were lifted; in 1858, following the war sparked by the sepoy mutiny, the powers of the Company passed to the government.

In Leeds

The BMS and LMS had been energetic participants in the campaign to lift the East India Company's restrictions and they were keen to take swift advantage of the opportunity. The LMS was a non-denominational society and, though it was chiefly supported by Congregationalists and Presbyterians, it had no reservations about soliciting funds in Methodist circles. Wesleyans realized that it was none too soon to overhaul their fund-raising methods. For years they had relied on Coke's exertions and personal generosity and mostly turned a blind eye to his chaotic book-

---

[3]   Quoted by the Bishop of Tasmania in an address on 'The Church and Foreign Missions' delivered in London in 1897 and printed in *The Churchman*, July 1898, p. 506, where the resolution is wrongly dated 1793.

[4]   See Porter, pp. 74–5.

[5]   Ibid.

keeping. Not only was Coke now aged 66; he was preparing to sail for the East. His imminent departure prompted much heart-searching. By this time there were forty-two serving missionaries to be supported, in the Caribbean, North America and Bermuda, in France, Gibraltar and now, at last, in Sierra Leone. There was too a pressing call from Cape Town. The 1805 directive that every society should hold once a year a collection for foreign missions did not produce the £7,000 to which the budget had already risen, quite apart from any South African or Asian venture. The Conference was now committed to a costly missionary enterprise without any active or effective home organization.

Two Wesleyan leaders took a bold initiative. The LMS was pressing its cause in Yorkshire and George Morley, the Leeds Circuit Superintendent and Jabez Bunting, the Leeds District Chairman, were spurred to action. Bunting had some familiarity with the funds, which he had taken in hand during Coke's long absence in 1804–05. They resolved to set up a missionary society of their own.

It may be thought surprising that no such Methodist Society as yet existed. The Baptists had theirs from 1792, the LMS was founded in 1795 and within the established Church the SPG was joined by the Society for Missions to Africa and the East, later known as the Church Missionary Society, in 1799. One reason why Methodism had not followed suit is doubtless that as long as the indefatigable Coke was around – and officially appointed the Conference's 'Agent' for the foreign missions from 1798 – there was no need for more organization. Indeed collaborative ministry was not his style and that in itself was perhaps the major obstacle. But there is a more fundamental reason: the Methodist movement itself was a missionary society.

The titles of the earliest published missionary reports are instructive. The first, in 1804, was entitled 'An Account of the Rise, Progress and Present State of the Methodist Missions by the Rev Dr Coke, General Superintendent of these Missions'. It began 'To the Subscribers for the Support of the Missions among the Negroes in the West Indies, the Roman-Catholics in Ireland, and the Welch in North-Wales.' The next appeared in 1809: 'The Annual Report of the State of the Missions which are carried on Both At Home and Abroad by The Society Late in Connexion with the Rev John Wesley'. Then came the 1812–13 and 1813–14 reports, each entitled 'The Annual Report of the State of the Missions, Foreign and Domestic, conducted by the Conference and supported by the members and friends of the United Societies late in Connexion with the Rev John Wesley'. These last were employing terminology which went back to the union of two societies in Bristol in 1739. The term 'United Society' came to be used, by extension, of all the societies in Wesley's orbit. The Methodist movement was thus itself a network (or connexion) of local societies with a missionary purpose: societies, or even a Society (as in the 1809 report) within the established Church.

When a Wesleyan Missionary Society eventually came into being, it was a quite different body from the BMS, LMS or CMS. It never had responsibility for the selection, stationing and control of missionaries. Its constitution left the Conference firmly in charge of these matters. Its task was to raise the funds. That was the urgent need that led the Irish Conference of July 1813 – the last attended by Coke – to call for auxiliary societies to be established throughout Ireland to raise annual subscriptions for 'our missions throughout the globe' and which prompted Bunting and Morley to call a meeting in Leeds that October with the same end in view. Above a thousand people came to hear numerous speakers, among whom was William Warrener, the 1786 Antigua missionary, in person. Morley, in his address, explained:

> When at the last Conference the subject of Missions was brought forward and proposals were made for extending them to the East, though all joined in the common wish for extending Christianity to those countries, many were discouraged, and some absolutely terrified, from making the attempt at this time, on account of the exhausted state of the funds. But it was at last agreed to diminish the number of Preachers at home, in order that we might be enabled by our frugal savings to maintain a greater number of Missionaries in foreign countries ... It was then that I resolved on returning to my circuit to propose some extraordinary effort for the continuance of the present scale of our important Missions, and for their yet farther extension.[6]

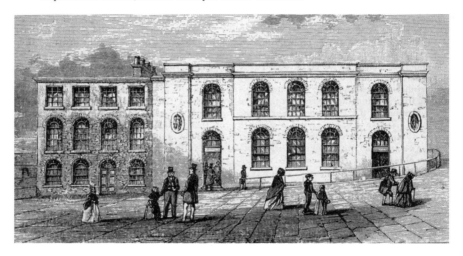

Figure 3.1   The Boggard House, Leeds, where the Methodist Missionary Society for the Leeds District was formed on 6 October 1813

---

[6]   *Report of the Principal Speeches delivered at the Formation of the Methodist Missionary Society for the Leeds District,* (London, James Nichols, 1813) quoted in R.E. Davies, A.R. George, G. Rupp (eds), *A History of the Methodist Church in Great Britain,* vol. 4, (London, Epworth Press, 1988), pp. 344–5.

When Bunting's turn came, he observed that 'Preceding speakers have brought forward almost every topic on which I might otherwise have presumed to dwell.' But there was 'one point which they have left untouched':

> Permit me, sir, to offer to the Meeting my congratulations on the public and avowed accession to the Missionary cause of those valuable *Female* Auxiliaries who crowd the galleries this day … They deliver no speeches in *public*; but they will both speak and act in *private* life. They do not *make* or *second Motions* in assemblies like this; but they will do what is better, they will *make subscriptions* for our Fund in their several domestic and social circles, and thus show themselves ready to *second all our efforts* for the honour of God, and the evangelization of the world.[7]

Numerous resolutions were passed. The first approved the foreign missions 'as established by Conference', the third set up 'The Wesleyan Methodist Missionary Society for the Leeds District'; the second described its purpose as 'augmenting the Fund by which these benevolent undertakings are supported'. Another determined that membership of the Society should be by subscription and 'all donors of ten guineas and upwards, and annual subscribers of not less than one guinea' were invited to Committee Meetings. This Society and others which soon followed the Leeds District's example in Halifax, Hull, Sheffield, York, Newcastle, Cornwall and Dublin, were voluntary associations of missionary-minded Methodists. They were not part of the connexional organization and (apart from the Dublin Society, which in 1817 became the 'Hibernian Auxiliary') had no authorization from the Conference. However when Conference met at Bristol in 1814 it congratulated them all and 'strongly recommends the immediate establishment of a Methodist Missionary Society in every District'. Thus, in the space of a few years culminating in 1818, 'Wesleyan Methodism did not so much *found the Missionary Society*; it realized that it was a Missionary Society by its calling of God.'[8]

Coke's Last Voyage

India had long figured in Coke's dreams and ambitions. In 1800 the Conference authorized him to send a missionary to Madras where Sergeant Armour had formed a society.[9] Nothing came of it. In 1805 he was discussing how to circumvent the restrictions of the East India Company. One possible way forward was to take up a suggestion of working in Malabar, on the opposite side of the subcontinent from the Company's headquarters in Calcutta. Nothing came of that either. In 1813 he came up with a bold but utterly implausible idea. He had lost two wives in the space of

---

[7] Ibid.
[8] Findlay and Holdsworth, vol. 1, p. 183.
[9] See p. 44.

twenty-four months and there was nothing to prevent him from journeying to the East in person. He wrote to the Prime Minister Lord Liverpool offering to be the first Bishop of Calcutta, if the scheme being debated in parliament was adopted. He was, after all, in Anglican orders and observed

> that I should, in case of my appointment to the Episcopacy of India, return most fully and faithfully into the bosom of the established church, and do everything in my power to promote its interests, and would submit to all such restrictions in the fulfillment of my office, as the government and the bench of bishops at home should think necessary – that my prime motive was to be useful to the Europeans in India; and that my second (though not the least) was to introduce the Christian religion among the Hindoos by the preaching of the Gospel, and perhaps also, by the establishment of schools.[10]

Needless to say – for the estrangement of Methodism from the established Church was now unequivocal – this ambitious initiative was yet another non-starter.

In any case Coke now had a different destination in view: the island of Ceylon. Ceylon was a Dutch colony when the French invaded the Netherlands in 1795 and turned the country into a satellite republic. Britain's swift riposte was to occupy the Dutch colonies. Ceylon became for a time part of the East India Company's fief, but was made a crown colony after the Treaty of Amiens in 1802 and the Company's restrictions no longer prevailed. Sir Alexander Johnston, the Chief Justice of the island, returning to England in 1809, spoke to Wilberforce of the need for Christian missionaries and Wilberforce advised him to approach the Methodists. This he did and in 1811 Conference decided to take action – or rather, as it had throughout the two decades since Wesley's death, asked Coke to take action. By 1813 he already had several volunteers, one of whom was none other than Jabez Bunting. Coke however discouraged him, even as he encouraged him to proceed with his plans for the public meeting in Leeds. The Irish Conference produced another three names and ultimately a team of seven was chosen.

The Conference resolution of 1813 read:

> The Conference authorizes and appoints Dr Coke, to undertake a Mission to Ceylon and Java, and allows him to take with him six Preachers for that purpose, exclusively of one for the Cape of Good Hope.[11]

Like Ceylon, Java and the Cape were former Dutch possessions taken over by Britain. Java was returned to Holland by the Treaty of Vienna in 1815 and was dropped from the enterprise. The Cape was far too valuable for Britain to concede – setting the stage for bitter struggles to come.

---

[10]   Recounted in a letter to Wilberforce, 14 April 1813; see Vickers, *Coke,* pp. 341–3.
[11]   *Minutes of the Conference*, 1813, p. 389.

Before the party left, there was one last disagreement with the missionary committee over expenses. They considered Coke had overspent his outfit budget – not that any budget had been made, agreed or requested. He, once again, defended his purchases and said he would personally pay for whatever they found superfluous. Then he gathered his team in London and proceeded to ordain them: William Ault, Benjamin Clough, George Erskine, William Harvard, James Lynch, John McKenny and Thomas Squance. (It had for some time been his practice to ordain men who went overseas, even though Methodist preachers were not as yet generally ordained for ministry in Britain.) They had scant preparation: they found no-one to introduce them to Sinhala or Tamil, nor apparently were they given any grounding in Buddhist, Hindu or Muslim beliefs and practice.

On 31 December, Coke and six of the group, together with Mrs Ault and Mrs Harvard, embarked at Portsmouth. The seventh, McKenny, would sail early in the new year to answer the call from Cape Town; but, after a few futile months there, he too continued to Ceylon.

The voyage to Asia was slow, storm-tossed and sad. Sarah Ault died before they crossed the Equator. On 13 April Coke wrote to Bunting and colleagues from 'the South Pacific Ocean, not a great way from the island of Madagascar', his head still full of projects:

> I have earnestly requested the Conference to send me two missionaries licensed for the Continent (with a license for myself) to meet me in Calcutta in May or June in the next year, 1815 ... I will certainly be at Calcutta God willing in time to meet them.[12]

But seventeen days later, 3 May 1814, he was found dead in his cabin and was buried at sea that afternoon.

A memorial tablet was placed in the City Road Chapel where Coke had begun his Methodist ministry. Its language is of its day. After referring to his labours in America and the Caribbean, it says of his last missionary journey:

> He died on the voyage ... his days were past; but his purposes were not broken off: the work which he had planned has been made to prosper; and through the preaching of the Gospel, the circulation of the Scriptures in the native tongues, and the establishment of Christian Schools, many once-deluded Cingalese[13] have exchanged the wretchedness of an Atheistic Creed, and the worship of idols and devils, for the light and comfort of the true religion.

The language of 1822, when the tablet was erected, is unpalatable today. Although Buddhism, which is not named, can be held to be an atheistic creed, the derogatory

---

12 WHS *Proceedings,* 2 (1900), pp. 91–2; original letter at MARC.
13 i.e. Sinhalese.

tones are deplorable. They are expressed even more strongly and less acceptably in a hymn composed in 1819 by Reginald Heber, who went on to be Bishop of Calcutta:

> What though the spicy breezes
> Blow soft o'er Ceylon's isle;
> Though every prospect pleases,
> And only man is vile;
> In vain with lavish kindness
> The gifts of God are strown;
> The heathen in his blindness
> Bows down to wood and stone.[14]

Heber's hymn, 'From Greenland's icy mountains', manifested all the confidence of the enlightenment: 'They call us to deliver Their land from error's chain'; 'Can we, whose souls are lighted With wisdom from on high, Can we to men benighted The lamp of life deny?' It was sung by generations of Methodists, oblivious alike to the insult to Ceylon's ancient culture and religious tradition[15] and to the arrogant comparison between those 'whose souls are lighted' and 'the men benighted'. But this was the spirit in which the missionaries – Coke foremost – forsook all comfort and security and sacrificed their lives.

It was in 1814, the year of Coke's death, that Jane Austen wrote *Mansfield Park* and had Miss Crawford saying to Edmund Bertram the zealous young clergyman, 'When I hear of you next, it may be as a celebrated preacher in some great society of Methodists, or as a missionary in foreign parts.' Dr Coke had made his point.

---

[14]   First published in the *Evangelical Magazine*, 1822; original ms. in JRUL.

[15]   The verse concerning Ceylon (unaccountably altered by Heber's widow to 'Java's isle') was included in Methodist hymnals until 1933.

Chapter 4
Colonies and Dominions

North America was the new world of choice for refugees and fortune-hunters turning their backs on Europe. Several generations of colonials had taken possession of the eastern seaboard by the time the first Methodists arrived. The colonization of remote Australia came later; few chose to settle there at first, but convoys of convicts were given no choice. In South Africa, Dutch settlers were followed by an influx of British migrants from 1820.

The Methodist Episcopal Church

About the time that Philip Embury began preaching in New York, Robert Strawbridge settled in Maryland. Like Embury, Strawbridge had been a preacher in Ireland. His farming took second place to preaching and he was soon touring Maryland, establishing societies, erecting log chapels and, controversially, celebrating the sacraments. Unlike the New York Methodists, he sought no aid from Britain and, although his name appeared sporadically on the American stations, he did not welcome oversight. He was one of the reasons John Wesley sent an experienced preacher, Thomas Rankin, to superintend the American work and enforce discipline.[1] Shortly after he arrived in 1773 Rankin called the first American Conference. Its *Minutes* stressed that the preachers were in connexion with John Wesley and subject to his authority. They were not to administer the sacraments; Anglican clergy were to do that. An exception was however made, in a spirit of conciliation, for Strawbridge.

In spite of the war, which began well before the Declaration of Independence on 4 July 1776, Methodist Conferences continued to be held each year, but as time went by all but one of the British missionaries departed, in the wake of the Anglican clergy. The exception was Francis Asbury, who spent much of the war in hiding in Delaware. Methodists were suspect and liable to ill-treatment as royalists, especially after John Wesley published his *Calm Address to our American Colonies* in 1775 and Captain Webb was convicted of passing information about Washington's troop movements to the British. But that did not discourage twenty-eight new American preachers from joining the itinerant ranks between 1777 and 1779.[2] At the end of the war Wesley sent Coke to ordain Asbury and draw up a

---

[1] An extract from Rankin's journal of his American experience is in T. Jackson, vol. 5, pp. 185–212.

[2] Lenton, p. 245.

Figure 4.1   Francis Asbury, 1745–1816, Oil painting, early nineteenth century

constitution for the American connexion. Henceforth there would be a quadrennial General Conference and regional Annual Conferences, a pattern which survives. After the Christmas Conference of 1784 the Methodist Episcopal Church was no longer subject to the British Conference and had its own history.

For some years that history continued to revolve around Coke and Asbury, as one sailed back and forth from Europe and the other rode ceaselessly round the vast territory of the MEC. Asbury's 'model of episcopal leadership was not to reside in a dignified palace issuing pastoral addresses, but to accept the hardships of an evangelizing itinerancy with even greater alacrity than most of his charges'.[3] The Methodist community grew from 500 to 218,000 during his forty-five years in America; by the centenary of independence in 1876 there were two million members and 14,000 ministers. But it was a largely white church: the slavery issue split it as it split the nation and in 1844 the anti-abolition Methodist Episcopal Church South took nearly half the connexion. Black Methodists had long taken their own course: the African Methodist Episcopal Church Zion (AMEZ), though not fully organized until 1821, traces its origin to a charter in 1801, while the

---

[3]   Hempton, p.101.

African Methodist Episcopal Church (AMEC) broke away from the MEC in 1816, the year that Asbury was lifted down from his horse for the last time.

Maritime Northern America

The Church born in Baltimore that Christmas went on to become the world's largest Church in the Wesleyan tradition, notwithstanding the early breakaway of the black congregations and a tumultuous history of separation and reunion. The missionary spirit it inherited from its founders not only ensured its expansion westwards as the frontier of the United States advanced towards the Pacific, but led to the creation of associated Methodist Churches in Africa, Asia and back in Europe and throughout Latin America. But its first, intermittent outreach beyond the new republic's borders lay to the north. William Black arrived at the founding Conference from Nova Scotia to ask for help.[4]

Black, then 24, had left Yorkshire with his family ten years earlier and was converted and called to preach at the age of 19. He was untrained, but became the *de facto* leader of Nova Scotia Methodists. He wrote to Wesley for advice and Wesley's replies, together with books he sent, constituted Black's correspondence course. As the War of Independence drew to its end, some 30,000 'United Empire Loyalists' fled to Nova Scotia, together with a number of black refugees. He needed help. Wesley told him of Coke's mission and he set out for Baltimore. There he pleaded his cause successfully and the Conference sent Freeborn Garrettson, one of Asbury's protégés, and James Cromwell. These, the MEC's first foreign missionaries, stayed only until 1787. Coke and Asbury wanted to appoint Garrettson as Superintendent of the Missions in British North America and the West Indies, but instead he was called back to the States. Democracy (of sorts) now reigned there and the bishops did not always get their own way.

John Wesley was dissatisfied at this turn of events, coming on top of the redeployment of Clarke and Hammett from their designated station in Newfoundland. He sent James Wray, one of the Legal Hundred, out to Nova Scotia as superintendent; but Wray did not get on with Black and his fellow-preachers. Black, who with two others was ordained in Philadelphia in 1789, was then appointed by Coke as 'Presiding Elder' in Wray's place. The nomenclature presumes that Nova Scotia was under MEC's jurisdiction, yet it was listed in the British stations. In time the confusion was resolved; it was made one of the British Conference's overseas Districts. Most of the black members sailed for Africa in 1791 when the Sierra Leone Company was formed and became the nucleus of the Methodist Church there. Thereafter Methodist ministry and outreach in Nova Scotia was almost wholly among those of European extraction.

The Methodist presence in Newfoundland began with an Irishman, Laurence Coughlan. He could speak Erse, which commended him to the sizable Irish

---

[4] See Lenton, pp. 280–82.

community around Conception Bay on the south-eastern coast of the island. He had been one of John Wesley's itinerant preachers, until with five others he received ordination at the hands of Bishop Erasmus (allegedly a bishop of the Greek Orthodox Church), for which they were dismissed. The following year he emigrated, in a lay capacity, though still fired with the passion of a preacher. His ministry was so greatly appreciated that his hearers petitioned the SPG, which had long been working in Newfoundland, to have it recognized. He travelled to England in 1767 and was 'properly' ordained by the Bishop of London, with John Wesley's blessing and recommendation. He remained true to his Methodist ways and when, eventually, there was a surge in the number who met in class with him, he encountered a storm of protest. His health gave way under the strain and he had to return to London. The classes, much diminished in size by reason of intimidation, struggled on for eighteen years. The settlements were scattered, the terrain rocky, roads and bridges scarce, the climate harsh. Neither the handful of lay leaders nor the missionary sent to join them (fully twelve years after Coughlan left) made progress. They were in despair, until in 1791 William Black, now Presiding Elder for all the Maritime Provinces, came on a brief visit, rekindled their enthusiasm by his preaching and organized the societies on a sustainable basis. Thereafter Newfoundland figured annually on the overseas stations. In 1818, at the creation of the WMMS, Newfoundland was the first overseas contributor, sending £30. Nova Scotia set up the first overseas Auxiliary of the Society and collected over £300.

Newfoundland's economy revolved around fishing, a precarious and hazardous occupation. In the 1830s the fisheries failed, the potato crop was blighted and for a while a state of famine prevailed, with its customary toll of disease and death. Under these conditions people turned to God. Between 1830 and 1833 Methodist membership doubled from 1,000 to 2,000. A devastating hurricane in 1847 provoked another Godward movement.

Besides witnessing in their own locality, efforts were made from time to time to reach out further afield. There was a short-lived mission to the Inuit of Labrador, but no missionary capable of sustaining it. In 1841 began a serious attempt to extend the work beyond the better-populated Conception Bay area to the scattered fishing communities further along the coast. 'Visiting missionaries' were appointed. Because of the rigours of the climate they could only make their visits in the summer months.

Newfoundland remained separate from Canada, with its own Dominion status from 1907, until 1949. Methodism took a different line. Ministers moved from District to District. In 1855 the Maritime Districts of Nova Scotia (including Prince Edward Island) and New Brunswick came together to constitute the Conference of Eastern British America; after some hesitation Newfoundland was persuaded to be part of it. It was time to relieve the WMMS of its responsibility for their welfare and form a self-governing Affiliated Conference, such as had recently been created in France and Australia.

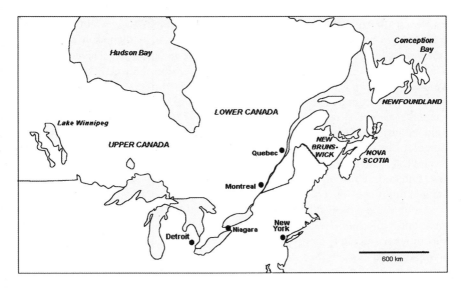

Map 1   British North America

Mainland Canada

The Canadian mainland was first colonized by the French and came under British rule after Wolfe's capture of Québec in 1759. The size of the indigenous population at that time is unquantifiable; most of the 70,000 settlers were French Catholics. They were joined by an influx of migrants from the new republic, who mostly settled in Ontario, then known as Upper Canada, leaving Lower Canada – Québec – to the French. Methodism began in the same way in both Upper and Lower Canada. A British officer named Tuffey preached in Québec while posted there from 1780 to 1784. Another, Major Neal, was allocated land near Niagara when he was discharged at the end of the war and won hearers there. Barbara Heck and a group of Palatines, the German–Irish families who planted the seeds of Methodism in New York, continued their migrations when the war began and eventually settled on the banks of the St Lawrence. Another pioneer was James Lyons on the shores of Lake Ontario. He was a schoolteacher from the republic. Yet another, James M'Carty, was arrested for unlicensed preaching and on his release was kidnapped, abandoned on a desolate island at the mouth of the Lake and left to an uncertain fate.[5]

These disparate sources of evangelical influence lacked cohesion. It was the MEC that took them in hand. Freeborn Garrettson was, in the 1790s, in charge of

---

[5]   T. Webster, *History of the Methodist Episcopal Church in Canada*, (Hamilton, Canada Christian Advocate Office, 1870), pp. 37–9.

the New York Annual Conference and seconded William Losee, who had relatives in Canada, to 'range at large' there. Others followed and by the turn of the century the Upper Canada District had its first thousand members. The subsequent history is a complicated mélange of co-operation and tension, between the British and American Conferences, British/Irish and American missionaries, pro-American and pro-British Canadians, loyalists and republicans; forms of church government – whether or not to follow the episcopal route – and the provision of personnel were in question. The key individuals in the saga are too many to mention; besides the colourful characters there were, in Canada as elsewhere, numerous ministers and layfolk with their strengths and weaknesses, their prejudices and convictions, their faith and faithfulness, who contributed in prominent and unsung ways to the life and mission of the church.

Among the colourful characters was William Case. American-born, he served the church in Canada for half a century. He arrived in 1805, along with an impetuous Irishman, Henry Ryan. Both were MEC ministers and they lost no time in importing a fresh style of ministry: the Camp Meeting. Lorenzo Dow, who two years later held the first Camp Meeting in England at Mow Cop, claimed that 'for a considerable time in America, as much good has been done and as many souls brought to God at Camp Meetings as at all the other meetings put together'.[6] It was an innovation well suited to the Canadian backwoods. One of Case's early stations was Detroit, which was in the USA after 1796 but gave good access to the country gradually being settled on both sides of the border. It was a 240 mile ride round his circuit.

Asbury, now an old man, paid his one episcopal visit to Canada in the summer of 1811, reinforcing the co-operation between independent Americans and colonial Canadians. But when the next year another war broke out between Britain and the USA, he recalled Case, who engaged in a valuable ministry caring for Canadian and British prisoners-of-war, among whom were a lot of Methodists. Most of the American ministers also went home. Canadians got by without them, thanks to the vigilance of Henry Ryan who remained at his post as Presiding Elder in Upper Canada. Case took over from him on his return in 1815, while Ryan transferred to Lower Canada to preside there. They exercised strong leadership for several years, exchanging roles more than once.

Ryan took exception to the wartime arrival of British missionaries. The Montreal society had already made a direct request for aid from England and the Conference, perhaps assuming the Americans' departure was permanent, began to send missionaries before the war came to an end. Ryan was not consulted by either party. The calming influence of Case was needed to restore relationships and from 1820 Lower Canada became a District of the British Conference, but not without the loss of the Montreal society which ceased to be Episcopal and called a Presbyterian pastor.

---

6   B.A. Barber, p. 17.

In 1828 Case found himself with two fresh challenges. As Presiding Elder he had been encouraging outreach to indigenous groups; now he was set apart as Superintendent of Indian Missions, a responsibility he held for five years. Little by little converts were made among the 'redskins', though they were retreating westwards as the colonists encroached incessantly on their homelands. For the same period Case served as 'President' (not Bishop) of the Methodist Episcopal Church of Canada. In 1824 Upper Canada had become an Annual Conference of the MEC, no longer under the tutelage of an American Annual Conference, and four years later it declared its independence. Case's appointment was described as interim and temporary, but he accepted re-election year on year, until in 1833, after much debate, a new decision was taken. It was a radical one: to unite with the British connexion. A minority seceded, preferring to retain the Episcopal label, and remained separate until 1884.

The 1833 amalgamation was not the end of the saga. It ruptured in 1840. The issue this time was whether or not the colonial government should subsidize religious bodies. In Britain the view was that the church should take whatever was offered, especially if it served to support the Indian missions. Canadian Methodists were opposed to anything that smacked of ecclesiastical privilege, especially as Anglicans and Presbyterians were likely to benefit more than Wesleyans. Case chaired the special Conference at which matters came to a head and Upper Canada unilaterally separated from the British connexion once again. Then, to general surprise, he along with ten others took the British side and made his departure with sorrowful dignity. He had given himself unreservedly to the Indian cause, which the WMMS was supporting liberally, and in that service he continued.

Case lived to see the end of the rupture, followed by unification with Lower Canada which had throughout the period remained a British District and finally the creation, this time by mutual agreement, of a self-governing Affiliated Conference. Autonomy was effected in 1854, a year before the Eastern British America Conference was established. Case preached the Conference sermon to mark the occasion; it also marked the Jubilee of his own ministry. Not long afterwards, at the age of 75, he fell from his horse and died within weeks.

Peter Jones was another significant character. He was the son of a Welsh surveyor and an Ojibway mother. All three of their children became active Methodists. Jones responded to the gospel invitation at a camp meeting led by Case in 1823. Speaking their mother's language, he and his brother John preached to Ojibways and Mohawks with some success. Case encouraged Peter to full-time Christian service, first as a schoolteacher and evangelist, eventually as an itinerant. He was influential in bringing to faith another Ojibway, Shawundais, who was baptized John and ordained John Sunday. Sunday was almost illiterate when converted at the age of 30 and was said to know only three words of English: pint, quart and whisky. He had a gift for story-telling and had a long and popular ministry, both in Ojibwa and in broken English.

Jones visited England twice, in 1831 and 1844, to solicit funds for the Indian missions. He spoke powerfully, with the *hwyl* inherited from his father and the challenging story of his Indian kin to tell. He addressed missionary meetings up and down the country and excited both the Methodist public and the WMMS leadership. But they made it clear at the outset that he was not to make his appeal specifically for Canada. All collections, they explained, were always for the general funds of the Society. They offered a grant of £300, on condition that he should be at the Society's disposal during his stay in England. He had no choice but to accept. As a result of this visit the Society assumed responsibility for the Indian missions and, along with finance, more direct control. It was the Society's application for government funds for the Indian work that precipitated the 1840 rupture. Like Case, Peter Jones lived to see the new beginnings of 1854 and died shortly after his mentor.

New opportunities for evangelization opened as the frontier advanced to the Pacific, though they were not seized until later. They opened to the north too, well beyond the area controlled by the colonial administration, where the Hudson Bay Company had its scattered trading outposts. Back in 1837, during the first period under the British Conference, the Company invited the WMMS to undertake missionary work. Here the pioneer was James Evans, who established a base at the head of Lake Winnipeg in 1840.[7] He had ten years' experience of service among the Indian communities of Upper Canada and was a talented linguist. He survived for only another six years, but in that time he learned the Cree language and his great achievement was to devise a way of committing it to writing. The syllabic characters he had been working on for some years were easy to learn and corresponded so well with Indian vocalization that he found they were as applicable to Cree as to the dialects he had previously encountered – usable indeed with all the North American indigenous languages. The Evans Syllabary made it possible to produce translations of the Bible, hymns and other literature. But to make good use of it there were enormous problems to be surmounted. With no equipment Evans improvised a printing press for the portions of scripture he translated, using birch bark for paper, mixing soot and sturgeon-oil for ink and moulding his type from lead foil he collected from the traders' tea boxes. His genius, resourcefulness and persistence were the foundation on which literacy, education and the Christian message were brought to some of the loneliest places of North America.

Australia

After the War of Independence, Britain could no longer send convicted criminals to the American colonies and settled on New South Wales (so named a few years

---

[7]   See A. Lewis, 'Bicentenary of Rev James Evans' in *WHS Proceedings*, 53 (May 2001): pp. 38–41 and J. Maclean, *James Evans, inventor of the syllabic system of the Cree language*, (Toronto, Methodist Mission Rooms, 1890).

earlier by the explorer Captain James Cook) for the purpose. A 'First Fleet' sailed in 1787; its avowed intention was:

> 1st, to rid the mother country of the yearly-increasing number of prisoners, who were accumulating in the prisons; 2d, to afford a proper place for the safe custody and punishment of the criminals as well as for their progressive and ultimate reformation; and 3d, to form a free colony out of the materials which the reformed prisoners would supply, in addition to free emigrants, who might settle in the country from time to time. [8]

The first boatloads numbered over a thousand, of whom 757 were convicts: some of them ruffians, others sentenced for trivial offences. They landed at Botany Bay, where Sydney now stands, and raised the Union Jack. Groups of indigenous Australians approached them in curiosity and were immediately repulsed with bullets, setting in motion a history of ill treatment for which the government finally apologized in 2008.

Wilberforce pressed for a chaplain to be found for the colony and in 1800 Samuel Marsden, an Anglican priest with Methodist connections, was appointed. He appealed for schoolmasters and two of those who responded were Methodists, Thomas Bowden, a class leader, and John Hosking, whose son became the first mayor of Sydney. Over the seventy years of transportation, some 160,000 convicts were landed in Australia, but they were far outnumbered by free immigrants; it was among these that a class began meeting in Bowden's home in 1812. Soon there were several classes. The teachers wrote home in vivid terms:

> The lower orders are indeed the filth and offscouring of the earth, in point of wickedness. Long accustomed to idleness and iniquity of every kind, here they indulge their vicious inclinations without a blush. Drunkenness, adultery, Sabbath-breaking, and blasphemy, are no longer considered as indecencies … we call upon you in our own behalf: leave us not forsaken in this benighted land.[9]

Samuel Leigh, a young man from Staffordshire who had found his way back to Methodism after studying at the Congregational academy in Gosport, was the answer they were sent. His tombstone in Reading churchyard bears the inscription 'The first Methodist missionary to the South Seas'. Landing in 1815, he rapidly developed a Circuit with fifteen preaching-places, which he rode around in three weeks. On his first journey into the interior he came across an isolated farm where the farmer, John Lees, was a retired soldier who turned out to be a fervent Christian. He built the first Methodist chapel in Australia and presented it to Leigh in 1817.

---

[8]   R. Young, *The Southern World: Journal of a Deputation from the Wesleyan Conference to Australia and Tasmania*, (London, John Mason, 1858), pp. 71–2.

[9]   Quoted in J.G. Turner, *The Pioneer Missionary: Life of the Rev Nathaniel Turner*, (Melbourne, George Robertson, 1872), pp. 19–20.

Another chapel was opened in Sydney thanks to the generosity of Sergeant James Scott, who had been converted when his regiment was on duty in the West Indies. Samuel Marsden was still in the colony, working at Parramatta; Leigh and he struck up a friendship which was subsequently renewed in New Zealand.

Tasmania – then still known as Van Diemen's Land – was the site of a penal station for incorrigible convicts. Here another soldier, Corporal George Waddy, gathered a class meeting. Benjamin Carvosso preached there when his ship called briefly at Hobart on his way to join Leigh. Later he worked for five years on the island. It is noteworthy that in 1833 there were more members in Tasmania than on the Australian mainland – but the numbers were pitifully small, 157 and 111 respectively. It was some time before Methodism spread south to Victoria and north to Queensland, with the first regular stations opened in 1841 in Melbourne and 1850 in Brisbane.

Neither Methodists nor other missionaries had any great success with the indigenous Australians. The most sustained Methodist venture was made by Francis Tuckfield between 1836 and 1848. He worked on what was becoming the classic pattern: acquire land, preferably on a prominent, often hilltop, site; build a house, chapel and schoolroom; welcome the first-fruits of the local population to settle in the grounds. The station, eighty miles west of Melbourne, was christened Buntingdale. Some children came sporadically to school, some adults intermittently to worship; but they were a nomadic people and could not be persuaded to settle. Tuckfield had zeal, energy and stamina, but he was not a James Evans and made little progress in their language. Buntingdale was not far enough removed from the adverse influence of unprincipled settlers and Tuckfield realized that the station needed to be relocated. After searching over an area of 200 miles he identified a suitable site, only to learn that the Missionary Committee in London had decided to abandon the experiment.

In Western Australia John Smithies, who had previously worked in Newfoundland, had a different approach. For twelve years from 1840 he combined his colonial pastorate with his determination to serve the native Australians. He had no colleagues; his District Chairman was 2,000 miles away in Sydney; his nearest brother minister was a 1,500-mile voyage away in Adelaide. Yet he not only kept the work going, he established a school for aborigine children which he and his wife ran single-handedly. The Anglican Bishop of Adelaide, on a visit, declared that 'more had been well done there than in any of the colonies eastward'. But that initiative too came to an end when Smithies moved on and no successor could be recruited.

In 1846 the redoubtable William Boyce arrived in Sydney.[10] He had already served with distinction for thirteen years in South Africa and would later spend eighteen years as a WMMS Secretary in London. He came as the General Superintendent of Wesleyan Missions in Australia and Van Diemen's Land. He

---

[10]   See P.M. Gunnar, *Here am I, Lord, Send Me: the life of missionary leader William Binnington Boyce*, (Sydney, The Federation Press, 2003).

brought outstanding leadership at a time of significant church growth as well as social disruption.

The population of Victoria mushroomed after gold-fields were discovered in 1852. Methodism rose to the challenge of the gold rush. Many of the prospectors came from South Australia, leaving the churches there half-emptied. Daniel Draper, the missionary assigned by Boyce to Adelaide as Superintendent, promptly asked his colleague John Symons[11] to follow them, ensure the Methodists met together and collect funds for the straitened churches they had left. Symons, with no regard for clerical conventions, camped among the gold-diggers and made himself their friend, exhorting them to set their hearts on the treasure laid up in heaven. With each story of a new strike, miners rushed off in search of their pot of gold and promising contacts would disappear overnight, but he persevered, remaining in Victoria for sixteen years. In another initiative a Wesleyan Emigrants' Friendly Society was started and an Emigrants' Home opened in Melbourne to cater for the shiploads of fortune-hunters who were arriving daily and found themselves friendless and penniless. A third result was the Chinese Mission.[12] Between 1854 and 1856 large numbers of Chinese fortune-seekers made their way to Victoria. A short-lived interdenominational Victoria Chinese Mission was then replaced by denominational missions, including the fledgling Australian Auxiliary of the WMMS. Though Chinese emigrants were at first rarely willing to accept Christianity, there were more conversions pro rata in Australia than anywhere else in the Chinese diaspora in the nineteenth century. This was due in part to the friendship offered by the little Methodist community, as one testified:

> I thought there must be something in this religion to induce these persons, who were strangers to me, to be so kind to me, who could neither speak nor understand English.[13]

But it was largely due to Chinese Christians such as Leong On Tong. How, when and where he became a believer is unclear, but he was instrumental in leading some of his compatriots to faith. He was eventually ordained and worked in Victoria for over thirty years before retiring to Hong Kong.

Draper in Adelaide and William Butters in Melbourne were invaluable colleagues for Boyce. He recognized that, with men of such calibre in place, the Australian church was ready to take control of its own destiny. He had been directed at the time of his appointment to keep in view 'the duty and privileges of self-support'. The Secretaries and Committee in London felt that they must focus

---

[11] See J.C. Symons, *Life of the Rev. Daniel James Draper*, (Melbourne, Wesleyan Book Depot, 1870).

[12] I. Welch, 'The Wesleyan Methodist Church and the Evangelization of the Chinese on the Victorian Goldfields in the 19th Century', unpublished paper delivered at an MMS History Conference, 2003.

[13] *The Wesleyan Chronicle*, Melbourne, 20 December 1865, p. 184.

their resources on 'our Missions in purely heathen countries' and reduce their expenditure on the colonial constituencies. This was the period when the fly-sheets controversy caused a haemorrhage of Wesleyan members and a fall in missionary income – in other circumstances the establishment of the Affiliated Conferences might not have come about so soon. In 1852 the Conference despatched Robert Young, a highly respected minister, on a two-year visit to the Australian Districts, New Zealand and the South Sea islands, charged with negotiating the establishment of an Australasian Conference. The Australian Districts, prepared by Boyce, welcomed the proposal and the Pacific Districts concurred. Annual grants-in-aid from WMMS were to be continued, a pattern which was followed when in the twentieth century most overseas Districts became autonomous. As in the case of the two North American Affiliated Conferences, the scheme reserved two powers to the British Conference: that of choosing one of its own number, whenever it judged desirable, as President and a veto on any regulations held to infringe the doctrinal or disciplinary principles of Methodism. The second of these powers never had to be enforced. The other took immediate effect and William Boyce was made the first President, to general acclaim. The founding Conference was held in 1855. Boyce was re-elected in 1856. Then he returned to England for twenty years, before making his retirement back in Sydney.

Australia became a self-governing nation in 1900. Australian Methodism was nearly half a century ahead and thereafter its history and that of the Missionary Society divide. Australia had its own missionaries, not only in the Pacific but in India, where they worked in harmony with British colleagues. In 1977 the Uniting Church of Australia brought together Methodists, the Congregational Union and two-thirds of the Presbyterian Church.

Chapter 5

Pioneers

Christian evangelism has generally been most effective when people have told of their faith within their own culture, speaking of God in their own language and in terms and thought-forms they have grown up with. But the spread of the gospel was from the start only possible because of pioneers who crossed linguistic and cultural frontiers or who, like the apostle Paul, were at home in more than one cultural environment. Not all of these pioneers, however fervent their religion, had evangelism as their primary motivation. Usually, if not invariably, the arrival of Christianity in a particular region predated the appearance of any specifically appointed agent of a missionary society. The Australian experience was untypical, in that no Christian activity is recorded before Marsden arrived. Generally, 'the first missionary was not the first'.[1] Often, it was an indigenous person, a native of the region, returning home after travels (captured, enslaved, trading or adventuring) in the course of which he or she had been led to Christian belief. It might have been a soldier or sailor on a military expedition. It might have been a European merchant or settler. Consequently many a missionary found a company of believers waiting. In Antigua, Gilbert preceded Baxter; both acted on their own initiative and Baxter's appointment as an elder (in American Methodist usage) at the 1784 Baltimore Conference came about because he went to Baltimore on his own initiative and at his own expense. In North America the Palatine emigrants preceded Conference appointees on both sides of the Canadian border.

There is nothing surprising in this. Islam has, since the era of its military expansion came to an end, spread in much the same way. In Coke's day foreign travel, while still slow and hazardous, was no longer a rarity. Horatio Nelson and his crews were scurrying across the Atlantic and around the Mediterranean. James Cook had charted the southern seas. Hard on the heels of explorers followed armies, settlers, traders, planters, convicts. There were Methodists among them all, even the last – for example among the Tolpuddle martyrs from Dorset who were transported to Australia. The story of Methodist mission (and in this the Methodist story is not unusual) is one of partnership: between ordained or officially commissioned missionaries and layfolk 'gossiping the gospel', between men and women, between expatriates and indigenous Christians.

---

[1]   The thesis of the Swedish missiologist Bengt Sundkler, in private conversation, January 1987.

Military Methodists

The British Army took men to many lands and regularly played a role in planting the gospel. In 1769, while Captain Thomas Webb, the Albany barrack master, was preaching to the troops around New York, Sergeant Henry Ince was posted to Gibraltar.[2] He would become famous for his work on the Rock's defences during the Great Siege of 1779–83. But already in 1769 he was writing to John Wesley describing how he and a few friends had started the first Methodist society in Gibraltar. Then from 1792 Andrew Armour led a meeting for worship and fellowship in Gibraltar. On one of the occasions when Methodists were threatened with being prohibited, he was instrumental in securing the Governor's approval for them to continue their activities as long as they did not neglect their military duties. Constant regimental movements interrupted the life of the society but around 1797 a chapel was built (which cost £120).

In 1798 Armour was transferred to Madras. It can be assumed that there again he shared in and maybe organized such fellowship meetings and that these continued after his departure. James Lynch, one of the missionaries who sailed with Coke to Ceylon, reported from Jaffna in 1815:

> I have received a letter lately from Madras signed by five serious persons, who appear to experience the power of religion. They have received much light into the doctrines of the Gospel by reading Messrs Wesley's and Fletcher's works, and most earnestly request one of us to visit them.[3]

The link between this group and Andrew Armour seventeen years previously is speculative but very likely. What is known is that Armour was a gifted linguist. In Madras he learned Tamil and became so proficient that he was moved to Colombo to serve as interpreter in the Supreme Court. He later obtained his discharge from the army and remained in Ceylon as a teacher. In 1812 he was licensed to preach in Portuguese and Sinhalese. He was there to welcome the Methodist missionaries to the island, helped them to acquire a house in Colombo and was listed in the Minutes of Conference for 1816 and 1817 as an 'Assistant Missionary'. A few years before his death in 1828 he was ordained to the Anglican ministry.

The Methodist Church of Southern Africa owed its origin to the capture of Cape Town by British forces in 1806.[4] George Middlemiss of the 72nd Regiment of Foot was a preacher who gathered a society of forty persons. He told in a letter

---

[2]   See S.I. Jackson, *In the Shadow of a Mighty Rock*, (Oxford, Wesley Historical Society, 2009).

[3]   7 October 1815, published in *Methodist Magazine,* 39 (1816): p. 398.

[4]   During an earlier British occupation of the Cape a handful of soldiers 'met together and were called Methodists' – L.A. Hewson, *An Introduction to South African Methodists*, (Cape Town, Standard Press, 1950), p. 1, quoting *The Christian Magazine or Evangelical Repository,* 1802.

dated 16 September 1807 how, in 1806, he and a few other Christians tried to trace the Methodists or any that were 'striving to work out their own salvation' among the regiments at the Cape. About forty-two Christians were traced – a few of these were 'sincere Methodists'.[5] These early meetings and services were held in adapted buildings: a hayloft above a stable and a disused wine store. When Middlemiss was posted to another garrison, Sergeant Kendrick of the 21st Yorkshire Light Dragoons took over and the numbers grew to 120 soldiers plus a number of Africans.[6] Kendrick recognized that he could not give them adequate spiritual guidance. Besides, as a military man he could not be sure how long he would remain stationed in Cape Town. He wrote to a friend in England:

> Dear Sir, – In the name of the Methodist Society at the Cape of Good Hope I request that my letter may be laid before Dr Coke … that a Preacher may be sent to be stationed at the Cape, if he conceives that it is practicable, and that it will tend to the glory of God. You know, sir, that our stay at the Cape may be short, and that therefore there is more need for a prop for those who may be left behind. We are very weak and illiterate, and stand in need of every advice which we may receive from you, our brethren. I hope that the Society will take fresh courage from knowing that there are those in their Native country whose study it is to promote holiness in the hearts and lives of their fellow creatures in a remote land, who are not privileged as our brethren at home.

> The whole Society express their warmest thanks to you, hoping that we shall all, by continuing to the end, meet together in heaven.[7]

Although Kendrick died before he could receive a reply, the outcome was that when the 1813 Conference authorized Coke's mission to Ceylon it further specified that an additional missionary should be appointed to Cape Town. John McKenny duly went, but he stayed only a few months. The Governor of the colony refused him permission to hold services, on the grounds that there was already an Anglican military chaplain in Cape Town. But a successor, Barnabas Shaw, was sent in 1816 and Methodist mission in South Africa has been unbroken ever since.

Methodism in Trinidad originated with a discharged soldier, Thomas Talboys, who in 1809 found a few scattered Methodists. By 1812 they numbered 138, only two of whom were white. In 1815 Talboys moved to Guyana in order to organize the Methodists there.[8]

In 1815 Sergeant James Scott in Australia prepared the way for the arrival of Samuel Leigh. He renovated a property for Leigh's manse and at his own expense

---

[5]   16 September 1807, published in *Methodist Magazine*, 31 (1808): p. 188.

[6]   See W.G. Mears, *Sergeant John Kendrick*, (Cape Town, Methodist Publishing House, 1963).

[7]   30 December 1812, published in *Methodist Magazine*, 36 (1813): p. 475.

[8]   See p. 167.

built the first Wesleyan church in Sydney. Corporal George Waddy began the first class meeting in Tasmania.

In 1843 Rowland Rees of the Royal Engineers was posted to the newly-formed colony of Hong Kong. Before sailing his minister gave him a 'class book' to use in his new home and he soon started a Methodist class meeting, consisting mostly of soldiers but also a few Cantonese. Rees's letter to the WMMS calling for missionaries, with which he enclosed a contribution raised locally to reinforce his request, met with rejection at the 1846 Conference. When he returned to England, the class was taken over by a devout Highlander, Sergeant Ross and at Ross's death in 1851 by Sergeant Dewar. It was Dewar who welcomed the Yorkshire farmer George Piercy – another pioneer who proceeded on his own initiative before being formally appointed.[9]

Local Forerunners

On his historic first tour of the Caribbean in 1787, Coke spent two weeks on the Dutch island of St Eustatius. Here, as in Antigua, he found a congregation already gathered. The pioneer was a slave known as 'Black Harry', who had been converted in America before he was sold on. He had the gift of eloquence and when he began preaching even the Governor of the island went to hear him. When other slaves were deeply affected, however, their owners took fright and persuaded the Governor to prohibit him. Coke arrived the day after the order was issued and even he was not allowed to preach. But he organized the Christians in class meetings and appointed Harry class leader. Harry however could not be silenced. He was threatened with a flogging and retorted 'Christ was flogged, and why should not I?' So he was whipped, then imprisoned and in the end was sold back to America. He was eventually freed and Coke later met him, still testifying to his faith. It was a long time before the Christians of St Eustatius were able to meet undisturbed, but they owed their beginnings to 'Black Harry'.

Buried under volcanic ash on the island of Montserrat is a memorial tablet in the church at Plymouth to another pioneer:

IN MEMORY OF
KITTY DORSET
A BLACK CHRISTIAN SLAVE
WHOSE ARRIVAL IN 1810 HISTORICALLY
INTRODUCED METHODISM UNTO MONTSERRAT
FOR NOTWITH STANDING ACRIMONIUS PERSECTION
HER ABIDING AND UNWAVERING FAITH IN GOD
AND IN METHODISM SUSTAINED AND ENABLED HER
TO WORSHIP REGULARLY WITH ANOTHER MEMBER WHO HAD

---

[9]   See p. 120.

COME FROM ST. KITTS UNTIL THE ARRIVAL IN 1820
OF THE REV JOHN MADDOCK
AFTER WHICH SHE SERVED AS A DEDICATED
FAITHFUL AND UNREMITTING CLASS LEADER
TO GOD BE THE GLORY[10]

Nor were missionaries the first Methodists in West Africa. The earliest Methodists in Sierra Leone were liberated African slaves. Freetown got its name when a settlement was established there after Lord Mansfield's judgment in 1772 left free black folk homeless and destitute in London. A handful of these were joined by a group of 1,200 from Nova Scotia, an inhospitable home they had been found after taking the British side in the American war. Most of the Scotians were already Baptists, Methodists or members of the Countess of Huntingdon's Connexion. They arrived with their own preachers and maintained their denominational divisions. Moses Wilkinson was the Methodist leader. He was neither well-tutored nor well-disciplined, but he outstayed the first preachers Coke sent out[11] and his return of 223 members was recorded in the Minutes of Conference for 1792 and several years thereafter. In 1800 five hundred Jamaican Maroons (whose African slave ancestors had escaped their Spanish masters a century earlier and who had been living, free and troublesome, in the Jamaican interior) were deported to Freetown and in due course built their own church. In 1807 a preacher named Joseph Brown wrote – in vain – appealing for

> a pious person, who could assist in preaching to the people, and taking charge of our small flock ... as I am old. My assistant, Mr Gordon, is likewise advanced in years, and there is not any suitable person being raised up here.[12]

So when at length the Conference stationed George Warren to Freetown in 1811, he found a Krio-speaking society that had been established for twenty years and Gordon, a white local preacher who had come from Nova Scotia in 1792 was there to greet him. Warren came with three schoolmasters. He died after only eight months, West Africa's first casualty in Methodist annals, but two of the teachers, John Healey and Thomas Hirst from Dewsbury, were still at their posts when Warren's successor William Davies arrived in 1815, working faithfully with a small African congregation.[13]

In Ghana Joseph Dunwell is regarded by Methodists as 'the first', yet here too there were antecedents. There had been a school in the castle at Cape Coast ever since the 1690s which had been staffed sporadically by Anglican clergy. The most

---

[10]   Kitty Dorset's obituary was printed in the *Wesleyan Methodist Magazine,* 50 (1827): pp. 328–9.

[11]   See p. 17.

[12]   *Methodist Magazine,* 30 (1807): pp. 203–4.

[13]   The third, Jonathan Raynor, had become a minister and gone to Antigua.

notable of these was Philip Quaque, an African who had been educated in London at the expense of the SPG and returned to give fifty years' service as the castle's chaplain-schoolmaster between 1766 and 1816. After Quaque's death the work was again staffed only fitfully, but Charles Macarthy, during his brief tenure as Governor of the Cape Coast colony between 1822 and his death in 1824, was keen to improve educational standards and open other schools along the coast.

> Accordingly he placed an order, the size of which had never been known before, for suitable books. Between April 1822 and April 1824 the SPCK sent out two shipments of books, valued at £71 and £294 ... Twenty dozen Psalters, twenty dozen prayer-books, ten dozen Bibles and ten dozen New Testaments to mention only a few of the items in Macarthy's order, reached the people, and with them the name of the publishers ... The Bible Band of Cape Coast which supplied the first members of the Methodist Church ten years later, did not have to look far for a suitable name or for material to study.[14]

This Bible Band, which held its first official meeting on 1 October 1831, consisted of a handful of Africans who had been educated at the castle school and used to attend the 11a.m. service there on Sundays. In the absence of a chaplain at the castle the Prayer Book service would simply be read by one or other of the British officers. They wanted much more and resolved to study the scriptures assiduously. The African head of the castle school, Joseph Smith, thought this a dangerous development and reported them to Governor Mclean, who had two of them, William de Graft and John Sam, imprisoned until a heavy fine was paid. Nothing daunted, they resumed meeting and wanted more Bibles. They approached Captain Potter of the Bristol vessel *Congo* who met them in Cape Coast. As a devout Wesleyan, he was so impressed that, once back home, he approached the Missionary Committee and said that if they would appoint a missionary he would take him on his next voyage.

The Committee acted with remarkable speed. Potter had arrived home in August 1834; in mid-October he sailed again with Joseph Dunwell on board. Dunwell was welcomed politely by the Governor and the resident European merchants, enthusiastically by the Bible Band. Within a week he had formed them into a Methodist class-meeting. Joseph Smith, no longer hostile, became his principal interpreter and a good friend of de Graft. By March, the class had grown so much that it had to be divided and he issued the first 'class tickets' to fifty of them. But after less than six months in Africa, Dunwell died. A few hours before, he sent for Joseph Smith and asked him to 'watch over the flock, and strengthen them in the Lord'. It would be fifteen months before another missionary arrived and the local lay leadership did not fail. Joseph Smith's journal for 26 June reads:

---

[14]   F.L. Bartels, *The Roots of Ghana Methodism*, (Cambridge, Cambridge University Press, 1965), pp.7–8.

Figure 5.1   Thomas Birch Freeman, 1809–1890, Oil painting by David Grice, 1975

> Friday evening – I met the class on purpose to know whether they would continue in the profession they had recently entered into, or desire to return to their former ways, in consequence of the death of the missionary. They said they would remain in the profession; for though the missionary was dead, God lives. [15]

A stream of missionaries eventually followed in Dunwell's wake, almost all of them succumbing to the unaccustomed climate within a brief period. The exceptions were Thomas Birch Freeman[16] and Henry Wharton, who each had African blood in his veins. Freeman's father was an ex-slave who married an Englishwoman. He worked vigorously from his arrival in 1838 until his death in 1890. He established societies along the Gold Coast and was swift to realize the strategic importance of Accra, which was not yet the capital.

> His one dominant passion (was) to preach the acceptable year of the Lord but he did not let it obscure his clear insight into the needs of the situation. He believed in giving people something to do, and often that meant building their own church. He had the Cape Coast chapel completed within six months of landing…

---

[15]   Bartels, p. 19.

[16]   http://www.dacb.org/stories/ghana/freeman_t.html [accessed 31 October 2012].

It was this sound practical instinct that made him a great pioneer and carried him to Kumasi, Abeokuta, and the heart of Dahomey, at a time when the death-throes of the slave trade and the superstitions of the people made his journeys really dangerous.[17]

Wherever Freeman went he was careful to observe the custom that a stranger's first call must be on the chief. He described in his journal his arrival in Kumasi at the court of the Asantahene, the Ashanti king.[18] He was amazed at the opulence of the court, but appalled at the human sacrifices which were part of royal funerals. He was received courteously but cautiously. He exercised patience and persistence. Eventually, on a second long visit in 1841, he obtained a site for a mission house and permission to hold services. Ossu Ansah,[19] the Asantahene's nephew, went back to Cape Coast with him, trained as a catechist and from 1850 worked in Kumasi alone. Relations between Britain and Ashanti had soured and the missionaries were obliged to withdraw. Later Anglo–Ashanti wars brought Methodist work in Kumasi to a complete halt until the twentieth century.

Freeman had limitations. He never learned an African language and always relied on an interpreter. He was hopeless at keeping accounts and constantly overspent his budget. When he realized he had incurred a debt of £7,000 he offered his resignation from the ministry. From 1857 to 1873 he became initially the civil commandant of the Accra district and after that a farmer, before returning at the age of 64 to another thirteen years of circuit work.

Freeman's Travels

It was in 1842 that Freeman first took ship for Nigeria. It came about because some of the Christian ex-slaves in Freetown spoke Yoruba. In 1838 a few of them bought a small ex-slave vessel, renamed it the *Wilberforce* and began trading along the coast. To their surprise and delight, they arrived at a place they recognized, where Yoruba was spoken. Great was the excitement when they got back to Freetown and over the next three years about 500 Yorubas left Freetown for their homeland. Soon Thomas Dove, the Wesleyan missionary in Freetown, began to be bombarded with letters calling for missionaries for Nigeria and, at the request of WMMS Secretary John Beecham, Freeman went to investigate. With him went de Graft and his wife. Disembarking at Badagri, they almost immediately set about building a house where the de Grafts would live and a little bamboo chapel. At the same time he was in touch with Shodeke, who ruled the Yorubas of Abeokuta and had offered a

---

[17]   N.A. Birtwhistle, *Thomas Birch Freeman*, (London, Cargate Press, 1950), p. 9.

[18]   T.B. Freeman, *Journal of Various Visits to the Kingdoms of Ashanti, Aku, and Dahomi*, (London, John Mason, 1844; third edn, London, Frank Cass, 1968).

[19]   http://www.dacb.org/stories/ghana/owusu-ansa_prince.html [accessed 31 October 2012].

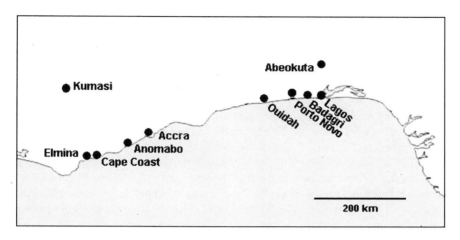

Map 2   West Africa, showing places visited by Thomas Birch Freeman

welcome to the compatriots from Freetown, and with Gezo, the King of Dahomey. Before he returned to Ghana he was able to visit them both, although Gezo kept him waiting for nine weeks at Ouidah, a port where Portuguese slave-traders were still defying the ban on their activities. These were tenuous beginnings, but the Methodist Churches of Nigeria, Dahomey (confusingly renamed a little after independence as Bénin) and Togo each trace their origin to Freeman. His role is known because he kept a journal, but Yoruba Christians were the first pioneers.

South Africa: Africans, Settlers, Missionaries

European settlers abroad were pioneers in many senses. With unremitting determination and unbelievable endurance they established their farms and their cities. Their achievements were as formidable as their disregard for the local inhabitants was culpable. But there were some, from the Pilgrim Fathers onwards, who took their faith with them and became pioneers of the gospel. In far-flung, isolated places in North America and Australia, Methodist preachers found shelter and support. In South Africa, in contrast, Methodists encountered a different situation; they were suspected and rebuffed by fellow-Europeans.

Africa was and remains a continent in migration, from those prehistoric times when our earliest ancestors began to people the earth, to the twenty-first century as refugees from famine and warfare trek to and fro across borders determined by Europeans. Treks in search of more fertile land or to escape invaders were commonplace in the south of the continent until long after the Dutch began to settle there. The settlers brought their own *dominees* with them; but these men were chaplains to the Dutch rather than missionaries to the Africans. In the course of the French wars the British navy took Cape Town in 1795; it was returned to Dutch rule by the Treaty of Amiens which briefly interrupted the war in 1802, but was recaptured in 1806. The British administration opted in the early years to maintain Dutch law, protect the settlers and respect the role of their pastors. Thus it was that Barnabas Shaw was at first rebuffed as McKenny had been two years earlier.

But Shaw was a determined man. He reported: 'Having been refused the sanction of the Governor, I was resolved what to do, and commenced without it on the following Sabbath. If his excellency was afraid of giving offence either to the Dutch missionaries or the English [military] chaplains, I had no occasion to fear either the one or the other.'[20] Initially he ministered to the society that Middlemiss and Kendrick had formed, but his ambition and prayer were to take the gospel to the Africans. Within a few months the opportunity arose. The LMS missionary Johann Hinrich Schmelen came down from the Orange River and moved the Shaws with his account of the Nama people – ethnic Khoi, at the time known to Europeans as Hottentots. He invited the Shaws to go north with him; while Barnabas hesitated out of concern for his wife's health and comfort, she declared, 'We will go with you, the Lord is opening our way.' By this time the Governor had begun to recognize Shaw's worth and was even prepared to offer him a Dutch pastorate to keep him in Cape Town, but Shaw roundly told him that if he had wanted to preach only to Christians he would have stayed in England.

On the journey north the party encountered a group of Africans who were actually on their way to the coast to seek a Christian teacher and the Shaws at once decided to settle among them. Parting from the Schmelens,[21] they made their home at a place they called Leliefontein (fated to be the scene of a massacre in the course of the Boer War, in 1902). The Nama people were nomadic hunter-gatherers. Shaw decided that to become a wanderer like them would take the concept of itinerancy too far. Instead he made a plough, built a smithy and successfully demonstrated the possibilities of agriculture. His letters home, published in the *Missionary Notices*, told how he built his house, made soap, planted his garden, celebrated the first baptisms and the first communion service and how Leliefontein became a prosperous settlement with herds and flocks and church and a little Christian fellowship. His appeal for colleagues produced prompt action from the Missionary Committee, now becoming efficiently organized at its London base. When in 1826 Shaw was recalled to Cape Town, it was to be Chairman of a much expanded District. Several of his Nama friends had been made 'Assistant Missionaries' – this was the label given to locally recruited workers. Two, indeed, had lost their lives the previous year: Jacob Links[22] and Johannes Jager accompanied William

---

[20]   B. Shaw, *Memorials of Southern Africa*, (London, John Mason, 1841; reprinted by C. Struik, Cape Town, 1970), p. 60.

[21]   U. Trüper, *The Invisible Woman*, (Basel, Basler Afrika Bibliographien, 2006), recounts how Zara, Schmelen's Nama wife, translated the New Testament into Nama.

[22]   See J.A. Millard, *Malihambe: Let the Word Spread*, (Pretoria, Unisa Press, 1999), pp. 28–30.

Figure 5.2   A missionary convoy crossing the Orange River, 1821

Threlfall[23] beyond the Orange River, into what is now Namibia, intending to plant work among the San people. (The San, or Bushmen, were regarded as a primitive people by the Khoi – in the Nama language San means 'outsider' while Khoikhoi denotes 'first people'.) The murder of these pioneers put a temporary end to the venture, but it resumed eight years later when Peter Links, Jacob's brother, helped the missionary Edward Cook to found a station at Warmbad, which they named Nisbett Bath after the benefactor who contributed £300 to make their mission possible. From this centre the outreach soon extended over several hundred miles into the German colony of South-West Africa and the Cape Town District stretched for over a thousand miles. But it was not realistic to administer such a huge area and later – between 1850 and 1867 – the churches in German territory were ceded to the Rhenish Mission.

Wesleyan activity developed eastwards more quickly and more intensively than to the north. In 1820 another wave of settlers arrived. The economic downturn in Britain in the aftermath of the Napoleonic Wars led to poverty and distress for many and, when Parliament voted £50,000 to encourage emigration to the Cape Colony, some 90,000 applications flooded in of whom 4,000 were selected and taken to the eastern border area, christened Albany. Only on arrival did they realize that the scheme was designed not only to relieve distress at home but to guard the frontier against the 'Kaffirs', the Xhosa raiders and cattle-thieves. From the Xhosa perspective, of course, the colonists were encroaching on their land

---

[23]   See p. 255–7.

and appropriating their cattle. The so-called 'Kaffir Wars', or Cape Frontier Wars, were for Africans the 'wars of dispossession'. War continued intermittently for over half a century, fuelling a resentment on all sides that would blight the region for generations.

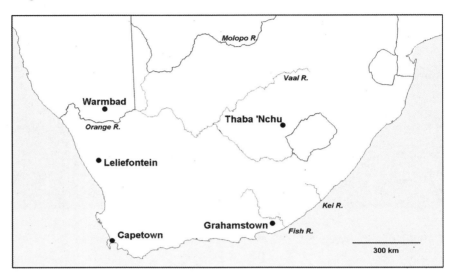

Map 3   South Africa: the early Wesleyan stations

With the 1820 settlers sailed William Shaw – no relation to Barnabas – an energetic young preacher who at 21 already had a wife and two children. His prime responsibility was to serve as chaplain to the settlers, but like Barnabas he aspired to evangelize the Africans. His circuit comprised 1,300 square miles with no roads or bridges; his vision encompassed the whole continent. There was hardly a Christian to be found, he said, between his home and the Red Sea, with the exception of one LMS mission station and in Ethiopia. He proposed to establish a chain of mission stations from Albany to Natal.

Gradually the settlers settled down, the farmers on their farms, the artisans soon moving on from their allotted lands to the growing towns of Port Elizabeth and Grahamstown where Shaw later made his base. He enlisted some zealous settlers to help in his ministry and in 1823 obtained permission to prospect beyond the Great Fish River. In order to keep the Xhosa at bay, the authorities had at first prohibited any communication with them, but with the veto removed he set out on a hazardous journey, visiting a succession of kraals and eventually arranging with a group of chiefs to plant the first of his chain of missions among them. The opposition and dire warnings of his Albany friends made him waver, but his wife

Ann settled the matter: 'We shall be under the Divine protection. Let us go, in the name of the Lord!'

Within seven years six stations were opened and named Wesleyville, Mount Coke, Butterworth, Morley, Clarkebury and Buntingville. Joseph Butterworth, the WMMS Treasurer, died in 1826; Morley, Adam Clarke and Bunting were very much alive when these names were awarded. Later on Newtondale was founded; but Richard Watson, the WMMS Secretary who approved the scheme and deployed the missionaries, was not similarly remembered. Among the men Watson sent to reinforce Shaw were William Shrewsbury,[24] who had needed to flee Barbados for his life on account of his opposition to slavery, and William Boyce, later to be President of the Australasian Conference.[25]

Boyce swiftly made a name for himself. In his first appointment he compiled and published a Xhosa grammar. He replaced the experienced LMS missionary, John Philip, as a confidential advisor to the controversial governor, Sir Benjamin D'Urban. D'Urban wanted to extend the frontier to the Kei River,[26] a move which Philip and others opposed. 'I do not object', wrote Philip to the LMS in 1835, '... provided the lands are secured to the Caffres as has been the case in all our conquests in India'; but he knew that the outcome would be a further European land-grab. Boyce took issue with Philip and while Philip was in London successfully lobbying Lord Glenelg, the Colonial Secretary,[27] for the removal of D'Urban and the reversal of his policy, the Wesleyans were presenting the governor with a congratulatory address.[28]

During D'Urban's brief governorship a new Cape Frontier war broke out, provoked by a fresh dispute over cattle and military reprisals. These wars were as disastrous for the missions as for race relations. Wesleyville was demolished three times. The third time it was not rebuilt because the local population, depleted by warfare, had moved on and British settlers had moved in. In 1835, while Boyce was advising D'Urban, Shrewsbury provoked an outcry by the advice he gave to Colonel Smith on how to conduct the Frontier War:

> The Chiefs who have invaded the Colony to forfeit their chieftainship, & their people to forfeit their Country, their Arms and their Property ... The actual

---

[24]   See p. 64.

[25]   See p. 40.

[26]   In the apartheid era two Bantustans, Ciskei and Transkei, lay on either side of this river.

[27]   Glenelg, whose full title was Secretary of State for War and the Colonies, was the eldest son of Charles Grant of the East India Company (see p. xxx).

[28]   Boyce's *Notes on South African Affairs*, (London, John Mason, 1839) and William Shaw's *A Defence of the Wesleyan Missionaries in southern Africa*, (London, John Mason, 1839) were sharply and unfairly critical of Philip; Findlay and Holdsworth, vol. 4, p. 272, uncritically repeat their view that D'Urban was 'one of the best and wisest Governors ever sent to South Africa'. See Porter, pp. 113–15.

murderers of British subjects, to be everywhere demanded; & when obtained, executed on the spot…[29]

Shrewsbury's blunt and brutal tone contrasted surprisingly with his report of the Covenant Service he had conducted in January with the white congregation in Grahamstown, where

> most of the congregation – including many who had lost loved ones and all their possessions – took a pledge to 'renounce all anger and malice and bitterness and revenge against the Kafir tribes'.[30]

He had a low view of black South Africans, whom he compared unfavourably with the slaves he had known in Barbados. These had, in their adversity, 'embraced the Gospel as the only source of their consolation' whereas in South Africa 'we have to do with a proudly independent people … too apt to consider themselves alike independent of God and Man'. His stance was not acceptable to the WMMS Committee with its unswerving humanitarian instincts; when they met early in 1836 they recorded their 'most entire and unqualified disapprobation' and he was dismissed. Glenelg was told at once of the Committee's action.[31]

The Frontier War of 1850 was even more disastrous. The cost of mission was apparent in Francis Gladwin's account of the loss of Butterworth, when the station was abandoned on the orders of the Governor as his troops closed in on the marauding Kaffirs:

> Imagine five thousand human beings of all ages … men, women and children and cattle, drinking up every little puddle of water they met with; old people and children fainting from the heat of the sun; the Kafirs attacking, killing one and wounding another. Thus we moved on amidst the lowing of cattle, the firing of musketry, and crying of children, enveloped in a cloud of dust … In this state we reached the river, and here our circumstances were not improved, for we found scores of the carcasses of dead cattle in a putrid state … To our great annoyance the river was not fordable, and in the midst of this putrid flesh we had to spend the night…[32]

These were far from the only instances of destruction and dispersion. Yet throughout every vicissitude William Shaw kept his head and his influence. He was careful to keep the Missionary Committee informed and commanded their trust. After thirty-six

---

[29]   Shrewsbury's report of the advice he had proffered, sent to the Committee on 24 December 1835, quoted in D. Cragg, *A Spark of Grace: The Wesleyan Methodist Mission in South Africa 1816–1883*, (Cape Town, Methodist Publishing House, 2011), p. 73.

[30]   Shrewsbury's letter to the Committee, 16 January 1835, quoted in Cragg, p. 47.

[31]   Porter, pp. 136–9.

[32]   *Missionary Notices*, October 1852, p. 155.

years, following his wife's death, he returned to Britain. By then the Grahamstown District had become the Albany, Kaffraria and Bechuana District and extended to the borders of Natal to the east and northwards beyond the Orange River towards the Vaal. Shaw's work was not yet done. He served for ten years in English circuits and was President of the 1865 Conference.

Another migration, which came to be known as the Great Trek, had begun in the 1830s. The Dutch farmers, or Boers, had grown increasingly restless. A number of factors provoked their discontent. Not only had the arrival of the English settlers taken much of the fertile land available to them. Dutch law had now been replaced by British law. They took exception to an 1828 Ordinance guaranteeing equal legal rights to all free persons of whatever colour and prohibiting inhumane treatment of workers. When slavery in the Cape was abolished on 31 December 1834, 30,000 slaves were emancipated and their Dutch owners, who claimed £3 million in compensation, were aggrieved to be awarded only £1¼ million. Their grievance was compounded by the reversal of D'Urban's annexation policy. And they were weary of the relentless border wars. The Cape, they concluded, was no place for them; between 1836 and 1840 some 12,000 Boers, mostly from the east of the colony, harnessed their ox-wagons and left. They went in various directions, but chiefly to the veldt beyond the Orange River where Sotho and Tswana peoples were settled.

The Rolong were a Tswana[33] people who had been constantly on the move before they established themselves at Thaba 'Nchu (Black Mountain). Their migrations were part of the domino-effect resulting from Ndebele and Zulu expansion, which was violent and bloody. From the 1820s on, when Barnabas Shaw sent a succession of colleagues to work amongst them, the Rolong were accompanied and indeed guided by Wesleyans. Foremost among these was James Archbell, who arrived in the Cape at the age of 20. With Thomas Hodgson he identified a suitable place where the Rolong settled and the years between 1826 and 1832 saw peace and progress. But then more internecine warfare brought thousands of their Rolong cousins from their ancestral lands on the Molopo River to settle with them. It soon became evident that the land could not sustain so many people. Both pasture and water were in short supply. Drought and hunger threatened. Again Archbell took matters in hand. He negotiated with King Moshoeshoe of the Basotho to occupy Thaba 'Nchu and 12,000 Rolong embarked on a 200 mile trek which was likened to Israel's journey to the Promised Land; hymns were written which made the parallel explicit. The missionaries and their families lived in their ox-wagons for months on end as they slowly crossed the veldt. Thaba 'Nchu then became a major centre, with schools, a printing press and a busy church life. Archbell published a Setswana grammar and New Testament. Some Tswana converts became Local Preachers, including Molema who was the son of the Molopo Rolong chief.

---

[33] The terms *Batswana* for the people and *Setswana* for the language only came into use at the independence of Botswana in 1966. Before that it was *Bechuana* for the people and for their land (which was not identical with present-day Botswana) and *Sechuana* for the language. For consistency the modern terms are used throughout this history.

But then it was rumoured that their ancestral lands were being looked on with covetous eyes by Dutch *voortrekkers*. Yet again the Molopo group moved on, resolved to re-occupy their homeland. Between 1841 and 1847 successive parties made the 300 mile journey. Molema and other Local Preachers maintained worship and teaching on the trek and established schools when they got there. Sadly they found life on the Molopo still as precarious as it had been two decades earlier and were soon forced to flee again, this time across the river into the land which eventually became Botswana. No missionary accompanied them once they left Thaba 'Nchu and their appeals were unanswered. Thaba 'Nchu was still a thriving centre of ministry to other Batswana, local Basotho and *voortrekkers*, but there was no-one to spare for the Rolong until from 1851 Johann Ludorf made annual visits for some years. Ludorf had medical qualifications and later left the ministry to set up a practice in Potchefstroom. He continued to be an intermediary between the Rolong and the Boers until his death in 1871, but it was Molema who sustained the Methodists of Botswana until he died in 1882.[34]

Many other African Christians played a similar part spearheading the numerical and spiritual growth of the church. Kama[35] was a Xhosa chief who showed himself friendly to William Shaw on his first reconnaissance beyond the Great Fish River and returned with him to Grahamstown where he admired the Christian community he found there. In 1825 he was baptized and he became as effective a leader in the church as of his people. He refused to take a second wife though it cost him a political alliance. For much of his life he was isolated by the Frontier Wars from missionary support, but he showed himself wise, reliable and compassionate. There was a bizarre and tragic event in 1856, which did long-term harm to the Xhosa people, when a soothsayer declared that the spirits of departed chiefs had promised to return and expel the foreigners, inaugurating a time of peace and affluence for the Xhosa with abundant cattle and overflowing granaries. This would come about on condition that the people prove their faith by destroying their herds and burning their stores. Unbelievably the Xhosa in their thousands took the soothsayer at her word. It is estimated that 200,000 cattle were slaughtered and the granaries emptied. When the prophecy proved a figment of a deranged imagination, mass hunger was the inevitable outcome; 25,000 people died of starvation. Kama, whose people had not been taken in, did everything he could to assuage the distress and shared such meagre resources as he could muster with the survivors of the calamity.

Kama died in 1875, acknowledged as 'a noble man, a just governor, a faithful Christian'. It was a rare accolade, yet he and Molema were by no means rarities, either in the pioneer years or later, as the church expanded into Natal and Transvaal.

---

[34]   J.M. Potter, 'Methodist Missionaries and State Formation in Nineteenth Century Southern Africa', paper delivered at MMS History Conference, November 2007.

[35]   See Millard, pp. 25–7.

Chapter 6
Gospel and Justice

Sydney Smith (1771–1845), a canon of St Paul's, had no time for either Methodists or missionaries. He wrote of 'the nasty and numerous vermin of Methodism'. And in one of his diatribes on the subject of foreign missions, he thundered: 'If we wish to teach the natives a better religion, we must take care to do it in a manner which will not inspire them with a passion for political change.'[1] Yet the story of world mission is bound up with social and political change of all kinds. The struggle for justice is a dimension of mission which does not normally divide Christians along denominational lines, so that the Methodist involvement is only part of the total picture. Wherever Christians found practices that they could not reconcile with their understanding of God's will, they made efforts to remove them. Some of these practices were murderous: human sacrifice, the strangling or burning of widows at their husbands' funerals, the killing of twins. Others were degrading and dehumanizing when they were not deadly: the caste system in India, the opium trade, slavery. What to do about the practice of polygamy was a constant source of debate. Recognition of the horrors of female circumcision came much later.

The condemnation of practices like cannibalism was more forthright and universal than the attack on slavery or, later, on apartheid. Evils perpetrated by Europeans, the missionaries' own kith and kin, who generally claimed to be Christians themselves, were not so easy to tackle; forceful if specious arguments, advanced from positions of power, had to be confronted. But the social witness of missionaries abroad and of their colleagues at home was instrumental in effecting their abolition. The question whether this social witness was incidental or integral to their mission was debated from an early stage. In 1816 the Committee forbade James Lynch to start a project for the relief of the poor in Jaffna, declaring:

> There are strong temptations in the East for trade and commerce but all our brethren must keep themselves totally disentangled from the world. As men of God and Ambassadors for Christ you must have nothing to do with trade in any way whatever. Let the whole of your time and strength be given to the salvation of your own souls and of the souls of those among whom you labour.[2]

By 1830, however, Richard Watson, one of the authors of that letter, told the annual WMMS Anniversary Meeting:

---

[1]   *Edinburgh Review*, April 1808, p. 118.

[2]   Marsden and Watson to Lynch, 29 October 1816, quoted in N.W. Taggart, *The Irish in World Methodism 1760–1960*, (London, Epworth Press, 1986), p. 117.

All our Missionary enterprises, all our attempts to spread Christianity abroad …
tend to increase our sympathies with the external circumstances of the oppressed
and miserable of all lands. It is impossible for men to care for the souls of others
without caring for their bodies also.[3]

The matter appeared to be settled until at the end of the nineteenth century the
'social gospel' began to be disparaged, vehemently by some, as a version of
Christianity that was disloyal to its biblical roots.

In his famous sermon on 'The Use of Money' John Wesley qualified
his exhortation to gain, save and give all you can by listing ways in which it
was wrong to make money. Besides illegal activities, gambling and the liquor
business, he wrote: 'We cannot study to ruin our neighbour's trade in order to
advance our own.'[4] It took over two centuries before a Fair Trade movement
translated his stricture into action: two centuries of unfair commerce, enriching
the West, incidentally facilitating the efforts of missionaries and their Societies
and exploiting those among whom they went to work by buying cheap and selling
dear. Other causes were taken up more promptly.

Slavery

John Wesley's stance on slavery was unequivocal: in pamphlet, sermon and letter
to the press, he denounced 'that execrable sum of all villainies'. 'Never,' he wrote,
'was anything such a reproach to England, since it was a nation, as having a hand
in this infernal traffic.'[5] His last letter, dated 24 February 1791, was addressed to
William Wilberforce. He had been reading *The Interesting Life of Olaudah Equiano*
(also known as Gustavus Vasa) who was born in Africa in 1745, kidnapped as a
boy, sold as a slave in Barbados and sent to England in 1757. His statement that
no black man's testimony was admitted in the West Indies against any white man
whatsoever made a great impression on John Wesley, who wrote to Wilberforce:

> … if God be for you, who can be against you? O be not weary of well doing! Go
> on, in the name of God and in the power of His might, till even American slavery
> (the vilest that ever saw the sun) shall vanish away before it.

> Reading this morning a tract wrote by a poor African, I was particularly struck by
> that circumstance, that a man who has a black skin, being wronged or outraged
> by a white man, can have no redress; it being a *law* in all our Colonies that the
> *oath* of a black against a white goes for nothing. What villainy is this!

---

[3]   *Missionary Notices*, June 1830, p. 283.
[4]   J. Wesley, *Sermons on several Occasions*, vol. 4, (Bristol, J. Grabham & W. Pine,
1760), Sermon XLIV, (4th edn, London, Epworth Press, 1944), p. 580.
[5]   J. Wesley, *Thoughts upon Slavery*, (London, R. Hawes, 1784).

That He who has guided you from youth up may continue to strengthen you in this and all things is the prayer of, dear sir,

Your affectionate servant

In April 1791 the Commons rejected Wilberforce's motion for the abolition of the slave trade. At the time Methodism had, throughout the islands of the Caribbean, 6,500 members; only 120 of them were white. Coke, who had personally visited thirteen islands[6] in the course of his four visits, had seen the way in which slaves were treated. Befriending them was risky. Some missionaries were violently treated.[7] As early as 1793 an act of the St Vincent House of Assembly prohibited preaching to black congregations. Although preachers licensed by the government were exempt from this order, no one might be licensed before completing twelve months' residence in the island. The legislation was specifically aimed at Methodism and Matthew Lumb fell foul of it. To accept the veto was to obey human law rather than God's, so he preached on the Sunday after its promulgation as he had before. By Thursday he was in a dank prison where he was kept for several months.

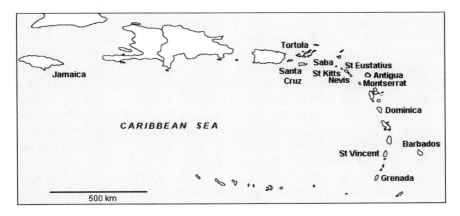

Map 4   The islands visited by Thomas Coke

---

6   Antigua, Barbados, Dominica, Grenada, Jamaica, Montserrat, Nevis, Saba, Santa Cruz, St Eustatius, St Kitt's, St Vincent, Tortola.

7   According to Findlay and Findlay, p. 52, Robert Gamble in St Vincent 'was waylaid by a band of white ruffians and so cruelly beaten that in a few days he expired (1791) – the first on Methodism's roll of missionary martyrs.' This account is not however borne out by the 1791 *Minutes* (which says he was seized with a putrid fever in February 1791 and after sixteen days died) or any other contemporary evidence.

The Irishman John Stephenson took a similarly principled stand in Bermuda, where he arrived in 1799. Because he preached in the house of a person of mixed race, gathered black people for worship and shook hands with them and criticized the clergy of the Established Church, an Act was passed in the local Assembly which allowed no-one to preach unless licensed by the Church of England or the Church of Scotland. The penalty for offenders was a fine of £50 and six months' imprisonment. In the belief that the Act was both un-constitutional and un-Christian, Stephenson decided to defy it. After preaching in two private houses in June, he was arrested. His case was heard on 6 December 1800 and, despite presenting a well-argued defence, he was found guilty, fined and imprisoned for the full six months. Colourful accounts were handed down of his time in prison, exhorting the 'listening and often weeping blacks' through the grating of his prison window. He left the island in 1802 and returned to Ireland but was never well enough to resume normal circuit ministry.[8]

In Jamaica in 1802, 'The conversion of some females of colour who used to be the easy prey of licentious men exasperated the enemies of religion, many of whom were armed with wealth, place and power. The rabble, under such patronage, began to interrupt the meetings and disturb the public peace.'[9] An attempt was made to close the preaching-houses as 'public nuisances' but it failed in the courts. Then an Act was passed in the Jamaica House of Assembly prohibiting any person not duly qualified and authorized according to 'the laws of this island and of Great Britain' from preaching. At the time it was the practice for Methodist missionaries to be provided with a license signed by the Lord Mayor of London as well as their ordination certificates, but any Jamaican magistrate might now treat these as inadequate and some did. The Acts were eventually overturned by the Privy Council.

In 1807 Wilberforce's twenty-years-long campaign to abolish the slave trade was successful; another quarter of a century elapsed before the Act emancipating all slaves in British territories was passed. In 1807 also the Conference, prompted by Thomas Coke, declared that no Methodist minister might own a slave.[10] From the beginning many of the planters in the Caribbean had viewed the Methodist mission with suspicion because black people were being welcomed into its fellowship. Coke in *A History of the West Indies*[11] said 'poor slaves' were 'the primary objects' of the Methodist mission and missionaries were in places derided as 'Negro Parsons'. However not all the white families in the islands were implacably opposed to Methodist preachers and over the years some of the missionaries married into local families. They came to appreciate the planters'

---

[8]   N.W. Taggart, 'The Irish Factor in World Methodism in the Eighteenth and Nineteenth Centuries', (PhD thesis, Queen's University, Belfast, 1981): pp. 75–8.

[9]   Samuel, p. 34.

[10]   For Coke's own brief and salutary experience as a slave-holder, see Vickers, *Coke*, p. 171.

[11]   T. Coke, *A History of the West Indies*, (3 vols, Liverpool, Nuttall, Fisher, & Dixon, 1808, 1810, 1811).

perspective on slavery and saw how, under humane owners, slaves were well-treated and apparently contented. Such owners had the well-being of the slaves at heart and preached to them of the love of God; but to set them free, as the 1807 Conference resolution required, was another matter. The slaves – in their judgement – would not have the wit and perseverance to fend for themselves, or the opportunity for work; their last state would be worse than the first. This point of view led the Antigua Synod of 1808 to declare 'the publication of the Minute in question to be impolitic, its execution impracticable, and its effect injurious'. The Chairman of the District, Edward Turner, wrote to Coke: 'I do not think that the Methodist Preachers are the persons to effect a revolution; it is their business to make all people good without interfering with their civil condition, and I am deeply convinced that the opposite of bad is not always good. Allowing Slavery to be bad, yet general and immediate emancipation would be worse.' He said that the mistake, 'if mistake it be', of marrying wives who own slaves could not be rectified at a stroke. And, since there had never been any question of excluding slave-owners from the church, he wanted to know on what grounds ministers could be banned from holding slaves while it was permissible for members.

In 1823 Wilberforce issued a powerful *Appeal to the Religion, Justice and Humanity of the Inhabitants of the British Empire*[12] and the Anti-Slavery Society was formed. Its first Secretary was Richard Matthews, a Methodist barrister who later served on the WMMS Committee for twenty-two years and on other committees of the Conference too. He published an attack on slavery in 1824 which went so far as to argue, in terms that would be used in the twentieth century by the freedom movements of southern Africa, that:

> If the slave is denied by the law the protection it ought to give him, he has a right
> to rebel and no moral guilt can be attached to a resort to violence.[13]

The demands of his legal work caused him to resign as Secretary in 1825, but he remained on the committee of the Anti-Slavery Society until it was wound up in 1839.

In 1823 also, the House of Commons made its first clear commitment to the principle of abolition, in the vain hope that the various colonial legislative bodies would put it into effect. The Colonial Office immediately wrote to all colonial Governors, reporting the vote:

> That this House is anxious for the accomplishment of this purpose at the earliest
> possible period compatible with the well-being of the slaves themselves, with

---

[12]   W. Wilberforce, *Appeal to the Religion, Justice and Humanity of the Inhabitants of the British Empire*, (London, J. Hatchard and Son, 1823).

[13]   R. Matthews, pamphlet under the pseudonym 'Anthropos', entitled *The Rights of Man (not the Paines) but the Rights of Man in the West Indies*, 1824, quoted by B.E. Beck in *Epworth Review*, July 2008, p. 57.

the safety of the colonies, and with a fair and equitable consideration of the interests of private property.[14]

Orders in Council were issued limiting the daily hours of labour to nine and prohibiting all field whipping and in no case the flogging of female slaves. Slaves were to be given religious instruction and issued with passes to attend religious services. In the South American colony of Demerara the Governor and the Court of Policy, still controlled by Dutch planters under Dutch civil law, decided to withhold this dispatch, but the news filtered out and a large number of slaves rioted.[15] This brief Demerara uprising was brutally put down; insurgents were shot, hanged, flogged; and the LMS missionary John Smith, accused of inciting it, died in prison. The incident made slave-owners throughout the Caribbean all the more harsh and spurred them to fight their losing battle all the more fiercely.

In the West Indies as a whole there were seven times as many black people as white, but in Barbados whites outnumbered blacks. On his second voyage to the islands in 1788 Coke and his party were met by sympathizers and heard with enthusiasm. Two years later he found hostility. Benjamin Pearce, the missionary he had left there, was friend to black and white alike. That was enough to awaken suspicion that he was an agent of the anti-slavery movement bent on encouraging a slave rebellion. Though the mob made his life a misery, he persevered, building a chapel in the centre of Bridgetown. But for years the services were subject to interruption and disturbance. The itinerant system moved ministers frequently. For thirty years membership never exceeded the fifty-one recorded when the chapel opened in 1793. William Shrewsbury was transferred from Grenada to Bridgetown in 1820. In 1823 he married Hilaria King from a wealthy slave-owning family, with whom they remained on good terms although they renounced any share in the family estate. But Shrewsbury made enemies. Prior to his arrival Methodism was habitually treated with scorn. Shrewsbury's forthright denunciations of vice, compounded by news of the Demerara uprising, aroused resentment, anger and violence. Within a few months of his marriage, the chapel was attacked and wrecked by a party of almost 200 white men and he and his wife were run off the island.

Other instances both of opposition and of compliance are recorded from all over the Caribbean. Jamaica offers contrasting examples. In 1823 a petition was presented to the Jamaica legislature, by free blacks and people of mixed race, calling for an extension of civil rights. The House of Assembly, suspecting missionaries to be behind this, authorized the Governor to expel any suspected persons from the island. In consternation four of the Methodist missionaries met in Kingston and drafted a series of resolutions, intended to allay suspicion, which amounted to an apology for slavery: 'Christianity does not interfere with the civil condition of slaves, as slavery is established and regulated by the laws of the British West

---

[14]   *Hansard,* 16 March 1824.
[15]   See E.V. da Costa, *Crowns of glory, tears of blood: the Demerara Slave Rebellion of 1823,* (Oxford, Oxford University Press, 1994).

Indies'.[16] The document bluntly repudiated the designs of 'Emancipationists and Abolitionists'. Although these 'Jamaica Resolutions' of 1824 had no formal status, they were leaked to the press and caused an uproar when published in England. The unequivocal response of the Missionary Committee in London echoed the resolution of Parliament:

> They hold it to be the duty of every Christian Government to bring the practice of slavery to an end as soon as can be done prudently, safely, and with a just consideration of the interests of all parties concerned; and that the degradation of men merely on account of their colour, and the holding of human beings in interminable bondage, are wholly inconsistent with Christianity.[17]

The attempts of some to ingratiate themselves with planter society were in any event unavailing. Most Methodist members were from the black community and Methodists and other Dissenters remained under suspicion of complicity with every manifestation of anti-slavery feeling. The slave insurrection of 1831–32 saw the imprisonment under martial law of missionaries falsely accused of provoking acts of sedition and Henry Bleby, who arrived in Jamaica only in 1832 (to begin forty-six years of service in the West Indies), was within days tarred, feathered and all but burned alive. Among the factors which provoked the Jamaica rebellion was the legislation enacted by the Jamaica Assembly in February 1831 reducing the annual number of free days allowed to slaves from three to two, to take effect immediately after the following Christmas. The instigator, Sam Sharpe, who had considerable influence in the slave community of western Jamaica, organized a meeting where they declared that after Christmas they would no longer work except for wages. Their owners did not agree. The slaves rebelled; after several months the uprising was suppressed. Bleby interviewed Sharpe as he awaited execution and reported:

> I had much conversation with him whilst he was in confinement; and found him certainly the most intelligent and remarkable slave I have ever met with … Sharpe acknowledged to me that he had as an individual, no reason to find fault with the treatment he had received as a slave. His master, Samuel Sharpe Esq. and the family, were always very kind to him, and he had never been flogged beyond the occasional and slight correction which he had received when a boy. But he thought that he learnt from his Bible that the whites had no more right to

---

[16]   Quoted in WMMS General Committee Minutes, 5 January 1825: SOAS, MMS/ Home/General Minutes/FBN1.

[17]   General Committee Minutes, 5 January 1825, quoted in WMMS *Report* 1824, p. 107.

hold black people in slavery, than the black people had to make the white people slaves and, for his own part, he would rather die than live in slavery.[18]

In Britain the Conference of 1832 again condemned the Jamaica Resolutions of 1824, which were still being quoted by defenders of slavery. The Resolutions expressed 'sentiments opposed to those which the Conference has at all times held on the subject of negro slavery, and not less so to the views and convictions of the great majority of its Missionaries who have been, and now are, employed in the West Indies'. Another resolution addressed the question 'Shall any further means be adopted by the Conference to promote the early and entire abolition of slavery in the British dominions?'

> The Conference feels that it is rendered imperative ... year by year, until some effectual step shall be taken by the Government to terminate it, to call upon the members of the Wesleyan Societies throughout Great Britain and Ireland to promote that important event by their prayers, by their influence, by diffusing all such publications as convey correct information upon this subject, by supporting those institutions which are actively engaged in obtaining for our enslaved fellow men and fellow subjects the rights and privileges of civil freedom, and by ... giving their votes at the election of Members of Parliament only to those candidates [in whom on] this most important question they have entire confidence.[19]

The members heeded the call. They joined in a general petitioning campaign and by May 1833, when they were presented to parliament, petitions promoted by Wesleyans had obtained 229,426 signatures. That figure amounted to 95 per cent of the membership, though not all who signed the Wesleyan petitions were necessarily members.[20] By then half of the 380 circuits in Britain had had at least one returned West Indies missionary on its staff for at least one year and through their first-hand testimony – 'not from the chapel pulpit but by the cottage fireside – an immense number of grass-roots Methodists developed a conviction that here was a wrong in need of righting'.[21]

The Emancipation Act was passed that August. It did not wholly satisfy the most ardent abolitionists, since it required the slaves to remain 'apprenticed' to their former owners for a transitional six years. It also provided £20 million compensation to the slave-holders, which inevitably provoked the criticism that they were being rewarded for their past evils. But Wilberforce, who died just

---

[18]   H. Bleby, *Death Struggles of Slavery*, (London, Hamilton, Adams, & Co., 1853), pp. 115–16.

[19]   *Minutes of Conference* 1832, p. 175.

[20]   C. Midgley, *Women Against Slavery: The British Campaigns 1780–1870*, (London, Routledge, 1992), p. 65.

[21]   P. Howard, 'A case of returned empties – former missionaries in 'home' circuits in the early years', unpublished paper read to MMS History Conference, November 2005.

before the bill completed its passage through parliament, commented 'Thank God, that I should have lived to witness a day in which England is willing to give twenty millions sterling for the Abolition of Slavery'.[22]

The Act could not miraculously transform the lives of a million slaves overnight; exploitation and discrimination were to be their fate and their children's for generations. But from 1 August 1834 slavery was, according to the Act, 'utterly and for ever abolished throughout the British colonies, plantations, and possessions abroad'. The date was awaited with apprehension by white and black alike. But fears of rioting and threats of martial law were not realized. 'The self-restraint with which the mass of the Negroes awaited the hour of release, the devout and sober joy with which its advent was hailed, were due, by admission of all candid observers, to the influence the Ministers of the Gospel had acquired over them and the leaven of Christian principle infused into their nature. It cost the Missionaries in some instances their utmost exertions to secure this peaceable issue. To them largely fell the duty of expounding the Emancipation Act and explaining the intentions of the Government.'[23]

The reports filed by the missionaries describe the remarkable way in which throughout the region the slaves celebrated their freedom. Even in Nevis, where passions were fired and rumours rife as the day approached, it passed off peacefully and joyfully. Henry Britten reported that there was 'no drunkenness, no fiddling or dancing, no carousing'. He rode round the island to preach at four services at which the congregations far surpassed the capacity of the chapels and 'poured out their heartfelt praises in songs of holy triumph'. The *Missionary Notices* for October 1834 carried a similar report from Matthew Banks in Antigua:

> I am happy to inform you that our most sanguine hopes have been more than realised. I have not heard of the slightest disturbance of the public peace in any part of the island ... On Thursday evening, July 31ˢᵗ, we held watchnight services in all our chapels ... When the clock struck twelve, I announced that the first of August had arrived, and exclaimed, 'You are all free!' The voice of their weeping was more distinctly heard, and it became general, and mingled with 'Glory to God!' 'Praise the Lord!' &c. We then sang 'Praise God from whom all blessings flow'...[24]

The fight against slavery was by no means over. Not all the islands were under British rule and there were Methodist societies on Danish, Dutch, French and Swedish islands, where emancipation came years later. Sweden freed the slaves on St Bart's in 1847, Denmark and France followed suit in 1848, while in the

---

[22]   Quoted by most biographers and by E.F. Hurwitz, *Politics and the Public Conscience: Slave Emancipation and the Abolitionist Movement in Britain*, (London, Allen & Unwin, 1973), p. 154.

[23]   Findlay and Holdsworth, vol. 2, p. 310.

[24]   *Missionary Notices,* October 1834, p. 553.

Netherlands Antilles they were liberated only in 1863. Decades were to pass before slavery was officially abolished throughout North and South America and even longer before it was ended in East Africa where missionaries again played an important role. Nor did emancipation put an end to the miseries of the black people. They continued for generations to battle on their own against economic and political marginalization.

Freedom of worship was one of the new liberties. Between 1833 and 1840 Methodist membership in the West Indies increased by 50 per cent – from 32,000 to 48,000. Black members predominated; they could no longer be forbidden from attending services or punished for holding prayer meetings. To mark emancipation the WMMS raised a Special Fund of over £9,000 'for the general furtherance and enlargement of our West Indian Missions and negro schools'. As a result, the number of missionary staff increased in the same period from fifty-four to eighty-five and a programme of school building was executed. For a short time the government made a grant-in-aid to the Society, as to other Societies, to support their educational work; but the schools were inevitably a substantial charge on the Society's budget.

Meanwhile, back in West Africa, domestic slavery was still a social reality. The Fanti élite of the Gold Coast held both slaves and debt-pawns, whose situation, given the size of most such debts, was akin to slavery. The Wesleyan baptismal register at Cape Coast identified 20–25 per cent of all those baptized between 1838 and 1878 as slaves or pawns. In 1840 the Colonial Office sent a Commissioner of Enquiry to investigate reports that British officials owned and traded in slaves themselves and supplied ships still engaged in the transatlantic slave trade. The commissioner, Richard Madden, was shocked by the way they turned a blind eye to slavery and pawning. The result was that all the British settlements came under Crown control in 1843. Although the WMMS ethos was strongly abolitionist, the Gold Coast missionaries were not renowned for outspoken opposition. Secretary John Beecham issued clear instructions: no church members were to own either slaves or pawns. But the missionaries had to tread warily. There were slave-owning coastal merchants who, if not actually members, were patrons of the mission; they provided meeting places and accommodation and, vitally, honoured the Society's bills of exchange. Furthermore it was from them that Freeman and his colleagues hired workers to build and maintain their chapels and schools, a workforce consisting entirely of slaves and pawns. William de Graft and Joseph Smith, from the outset foremost among Ghanaian Methodists,[25] were fierce critics of the governor's proposal to ban slave-holding among educated Africans in 1851. On the other hand the missionaries acquired a reputation for benevolence, intervening on occasion in cases of maltreatment and sometimes finding small sums of money to redeem pawns from bondage.[26]

---

[25]   See p. 48.

[26]   I am indebted to S. Anderson's MMS History Conference paper, 'Masters, Slaves and Missionaries on the Gold Coast, 1838–1851', November 2005, for this paragraph.

Cannibal Feasts

In the twentieth century the South Pacific was the theatre of a vicious war which was not of the island peoples' making and the site of nuclear weapons testing well into the 1990s. Christian comment on the subject of these barbarities was much less vocal than it was when the early missionaries found the local customs of tribal warfare and cannibalism in the region. The Maoris of Aotearoa (New Zealand) were known to celebrate their victories by feasts on human flesh. In other islands religious ceremonies occasionally included such orgies. But in certain of the Fijian islands the cannibal appetite had developed to the extent that if a chief used the expression 'I'll eat you' to someone who crossed him this was no idle threat. Some indeed kept a tally of the victims they had devoured and one, known to the first missionaries, claimed a score of 900. The practice was on the whole confined to the chiefs and their retainers and women did not normally participate. On the other hand the victims were generally commoners, of either sex. A banquet to honour a visiting chief could well include people waylaid and slaughtered expressly for the purpose of providing meat for the table.

The extent of cannibalism was overplayed in missionary propaganda, for nothing could be more sure to raise horror – and money – in Europe. Unlike slavery, it was alien to the European experience and the missionaries' endeavours won unqualified support. An appeal from James Watkin, a missionary in Tonga, was published by the WMMS in its *Missionary Notices* for February 1838. It was accompanied by an apology for its content, described as 'almost too horrible for publicity'. Readers were informed that the editors 'have omitted several disgusting particulars included in the original communication ... neither the whole nor the worst is even here told in detail. But as such abominations do exist, we think it would be a criminal delicacy that would withhold the substance of these recitals from the public view ... They may shock our feelings; but no matter for that, if they do but teach us our duty and stimulate us to a due performance of it.' Watkin wrote:

> Let all the horrors of a cannibal feast be present to your minds, while you read; and if you love your species (and we know you do), 'put on bowels of mercies' and hasten to send more Missionaries to Fegee, that its inhabitants may be prevented from any longer literally 'biting and devouring one another'. You must not, for the love of God and for the love of souls, dare to reject our petition ... We feel persuaded that you will not![27]

After referring to other appeals on behalf of 'the burning widows from the East' and 'the manacled slave from the West', he went on: 'Pity poor Africa' has often been heard by you, and not heard unheeded ... and now we cry ... 'Pity, oh, pity cannibal Fegee!'.

---

[27] *Missionary Notices,* February 1838, p. 25.

The Fijian islands were among the last in the Pacific to be visited by missionaries. They were reached, in the end, via New Zealand and Tonga. The Anglican Samuel Marsden was the pioneer in New Zealand as in Australia and he encouraged his Wesleyan colleague Samuel Leigh to explore the opportunities there. In 1818 Walter Lawry arrived from England to support Leigh in Australia and Leigh was able to make a brief visit to the North Island where the CMS already had a station. [28] Not long afterwards Leigh went on furlough, convinced there was work to be done among the Maori people and volunteering his services. Unfortunately he found the Committee preoccupied by a debt of £10,000. He was however permitted to appeal, not for money for a Maori mission, but for gifts in kind. He made such an impression as he toured the country that the response could be measured in tons: ploughs, spades, fish hooks, clothes and cloth, pots and pans and, from one generous donor, a hundred wedding rings. The Committee took due note of the widespread interest and the mission to New Zealand was agreed. For twenty years both Methodist and CMS activity were confined to the far north. Auckland was unknown to Europeans until shortly before it became the colonial capital in 1841. Methodist stations were not established on the South Island until the 1850s.

When Leigh returned to New Zealand in 1822, he found a brutal internecine war in progress. After one battle, hundreds of the vanquished were roasted and eaten on the spot. To Leigh's dismay, the victorious chief was someone he had been depending on to facilitate the mission. Hongi had been brought to England on a short visit by the CMS in order to publicize their Maori work and Leigh had met him, hosted him and set his hopes on him. But Hongi was more interested in muskets than missionaries. Now the most Leigh could hope for was that Hongi would let him work unmolested. He established a station which he named Wesleydale, where he was joined by reinforcements. But his health suffered and he had to return to Australia. After his departure Hongi's warriors attacked. The missionary families escaped, but Wesleydale was destroyed. However Hongi fell in battle the following year and a sea-change ensued. The 'musket wars' came to an end and cannibalism effectively ceased. Before long a chain of mission stations was in place and in 1831, at last, a Maori class meeting began. By 1842, when the Bible Society presented the missions with Maori New Testaments, 10,000 were inadequate for Methodist needs.

Hard on the heels of the missionaries, increasing numbers of *pakeha* (as Maoris call white people) began settling in New Zealand. The New Zealand Association, set up in London in 1837 to promote the colonization of the islands, displayed little concern for the character of the recruits enlisted in England and still less for the Maoris they would dispossess. Bribery, brutality and fraud were used by the company's agents to obtain Maori tribal land. In 1840 a group of chiefs in the north signed the Treaty of Waitangi by which Aotearoa was ceded to

[28]   R.F. Snowden, *The Ladies of Wesleydale*, (London, Epworth Press, 1957) is a concise account of Leigh's brief ministry in New Zealand with particular reference to the experience of his wife Catherine and of his colleague Nathaniel Turner's wife Anne.

the crown. They could not represent their compatriots throughout the islands, but the British assumed they did. There followed bitter disputes over land ownership, with the Maori often outwitted by unscrupulous *pakeha*. Robert Young, on his visit[29] in 1853, interviewed Epiha Putini (a chief whose baptismal name was Jabez Bunting), who told him: 'If Missionaries had not come to the land, great would have been our darkness and death. You came and told us the name of God, – that stopped our fighting.' Young then asked about the land question. Epiha replied: 'I gave the Governor a *pukapuka*, (a book or letter) with all my lands written in it; and told him, when anybody came from my district to sell land, to look into the *pukapuka*. But some of those lands have been sold. This is the crooked place about our land.' Young remarked that the Queen was very anxious that there should be no crooked place, but that justice should be done to all her Maori subjects. 'That is good,' said Epiha. 'When your children are under your eye, you control them: you make them do right. But when they get out of your sight, they sometimes fall into mischief. And when the Queen has her children in England around her, she can keep them right; but when they get as far away as New Zealand, what can she do to keep them right? Like children out of their parents' sight, they sometimes get into mischief.'[30] Epiha was not a mighty warrior like Hongi, but a wise and discerning Christian. Thirty years of mission were bearing fruit.

At the same time as Leigh began work in New Zealand, his colleague Lawry attempted a similar venture in Tonga, in the Friendly Islands. He sailed from Sydney in 1822 at his own expense with a carpenter and a blacksmith and received such an encouraging welcome that he wrote to London asking for more missionaries (a term which at the time was applied only to ordained preachers) and a surgeon, a printer and teachers. But the atmosphere soured and the venture was aborted. Tindall the blacksmith remained in Tonga however and a few years later, in 1826, greeted another blacksmith, John Thomas[31] from Dudley and John Hutchinson from Tasmania, who were both newly ordained and sent in response to Lawry's first report. Thomas and his young wife Sarah were to spend twenty-three unbroken years in Tonga and then another three from 1856. But at first they were disheartened. They found that the people were more interested in the missionaries' property than in the *lotu* (their name for Christian teaching). Repeatedly raided and robbed, the couple were on the point of withdrawing when reinforcements arrived. They were joined by Nathaniel Turner and his wife after their escape from Wesleydale and by William Cross, intended by the Committee in London for New Zealand but diverted to Tonga by Turner's unilateral decision.

The Friendly Islands, so named – misnamed, at the time – by Captain Cook, comprise three groups of islands: Tongatapu in the south, Vavau in the north and

---

[29]   See p. 42.
[30]   A.K. Davidson and P.J. Lineham (eds), *Transplanted Christianity*, (Palmerston North, NZ, Dunmore Press, 1989), document 1.34.
[31]   See J.L. Luckcock, *Thomas of Tonga, 1797–1881: The Unlikely Pioneer*, (Peterborough, Methodist Publishing House, 1992).

Ha'apai in between. The missionaries were initially based in Tongatapu, where King Tupou was the first Tongan chief to adopt *lotu* and receive baptism. He had been influenced by Christian teachers from Tahiti and then sought instruction from Turner and Cross. But Ha'apai was the scene of the first big breakthrough. Taufaahau was a vassal of Tupou and frequently visited his suzerain, with whom he was on good terms. He was intrigued by Tupou's experience and asked for a missionary. There was no-one to spare, but Turner sent a Tongan teacher, Pita Vi, across to Ha'apai. The chief's initial reaction was scornful; why should Ha'apai people listen to a Tongan? But soon he was persuaded and publicly declared his faith in Jesus, dramatically destroying the images and shrines of his former practice. Within a few weeks, fifteen of the eighteen islands under his rule had followed his example. After this it became imperative to transfer John Thomas to Ha'apai. But Thomas scrupulously waited for permission from London. Amazingly, the ship on which the answer was brought sank without trace, apart from one package washed ashore which contained the authorization. Not long afterwards Taufaahau fell dangerously ill. Poison was suspected. Thomas administered what little medication he could; Pita Vi recorded that 'all the Christian chiefs, and ourselves, met to pray for him. No Christian slept that night.' The ruler recovered and shortly afterwards was baptized. He took a suitably regal name, George. His wife was baptized Charlotte (in Tongan, Salote). Some years later, in 1853, George accompanied Robert Young to Sydney on the *John Wesley*. When he preached there, he displayed his little fingers, mutilated in boyhood in a traditional rite. He then proceeded to Hobart, where he was made his first pair of shoes.

At the time of George's baptism in 1831 Finau, who ruled in Vavau, was visiting Ha'apai. He had already expressed some interest in *lotu*. On a return state visit to Vavau George was accompanied by Christians who, with all the passion of new converts, proved effective evangelists long before foreign missionaries appeared. When they did come, they found that although there was a general turning to Christianity it was at a shallow and superficial level. These pioneers, Peter Turner – no relation of Nathaniel – and David Cargill, with his wife Margaret, prayed for a Baptism of the Holy Spirit and the 'Tongan Pentecost' of 1834, with poignant emotional outpourings, answered their prayer. It began in Vavau but spread to Ha'apai and, in lesser degree, to Tongatapu.

George himself was caught up in the awakening and went on to become a local preacher with a gift for oratory. That gift served him well in politics too. He was wily and ambitious. When Finau died, the people of Vavau elected him as their sovereign and eventually he united all the Friendly Islands under his authority. As King George Tupou I he founded a long-lasting dynasty. He realized that the widespread adoption of Christianity was a unifying factor that would cement his position. He encouraged the practice of daily public worship which gave his subjects something other than rebellion to occupy them – his realm was so fertile and fish so abundant that daily toil alone was not time-consuming enough to keep them out of mischief. Much later in his long reign, in 1875, he declared Tonga a constitutional monarchy, at which time he emancipated the 'serfs', enshrined a code of law, regulated land tenure, guaranteed press freedom and limited the power of the subordinate chiefs.

There was regular traffic by canoe between the Friendly Islands, the Society Islands (Tahiti) where LMS missionaries were at work and the islands which Tongans called Fiji – their pronunciation of *Viti*.[32] Tongans, of light-skinned Polynesian stock and Fijians, darker-skinned Melanesians, had sometimes fought in times past but were generally more interested in trading. For Tongans, cannibalism was by the start of the eighteenth century an occasional practice; for Fijians, it was customary. He who had eaten the greatest number was at the top of the social order. It is impossible to say for how long this was the case before contact with Europeans. While the subject is prone to lurid and sensational reportage the accounts are well authenticated.

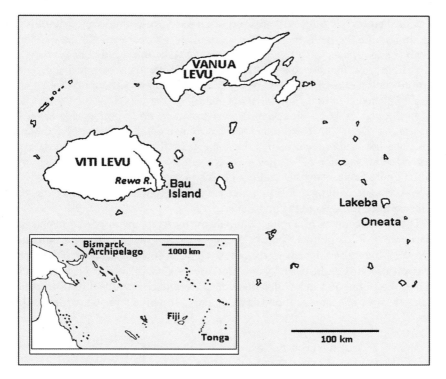

Map 5   Fiji, and its far-flung neighbours

[32]   Viti Levu is the principal island of the archipelago.

Tongans were skilful boat-builders and experienced seafarers. Some of their double canoes carried as many as 150 people. The outlying island of Lakeba[33] was their usual destination in the Fijian archipelago. Even before the Tongan Pentecost, Tongan sailors were telling of the *lotu* in Lakeba's harbour and some Fijians had been baptized in Tonga. After 1834 Tongan Christians spread the word with renewed zeal and the synod of the South Seas District, chaired by John Thomas from its inception in 1832 until 1848, decided to send two of its missionaries to Fiji. William Cross, who had tragically lost his wife at sea when they struck a reef between Tongatapu and Vavau, was ready to make a fresh start. David Cargill, with his Aberdeen MA, was the WMMS's first graduate missionary. The two had already immersed themselves in the Tongan language. Now they began to learn Fijian and sailed to Lakeba in 1836. They were not the first missionaries to the archipelago; three Tahitian teachers, Tahaara, Hatai and Arue[34] had preceded them in 1830. The LMS's John Williams promised to return within twelve months but did not and the Tahitians were left to work alone for six years. Obliged to leave Lakeba under threats in 1832, they settled on Oneata, thirty miles away; they lost their Bibles and hymn-books in a shipwreck but did their best to hand on the portions they had memorized. Cross was not impressed with them, though later Cargill reached a more favourable judgement.[35]

At the end of 1837 Cross sailed west to Rewa, an important centre on the coast of Viti Levu.[36] In 1838, a team of six Tongan couples, including the King's brother-in-law, Julius Naulivou, joined the Cargills on Lakeba. David Cargill treated them as senior colleagues, asking them where they would like to serve. With dignified simplicity they deferred to his judgement, 'We are entirely at your disposal, and are willing to labour wherever you appoint us.' ... In due course they were scattered throughout the mission.[37]

The disappearance of Fijian cannibalism, the conversion of the people and the course of Fiji's political history during the 1840s and 1850s were intimately related.[38] Although Christians were not actively persecuted on account of their faith, the stress of living amidst cruelty and brutality took its toll on the missionaries. As a handful of foreigners in a violent land, they lived in constant fear of ill-treatment and anxiety for one another. Food scarcity and destructive typhoons added to their

---

[33]   The Fijian *b* is pronounced *mb*.

[34]   Also known as Jacero, Fuatai and Faaruea.

[35]   See A. Thornley, 'The Legacy of Siloam: Tahitian Missionaries in Fiji', in D. Munro and A. Thornley (eds), *The Covenant Makers: Islander Missionaries in the Pacific*, (Suva, Institute of Pacific Studies, 1996), pp. 91–110.

[36]   Rewa, with the nearby offshore island of Bau, Cakaudrove on the island of Vanua Levu and Lakeba were the principal seats of power at this period.

[37]   M. Dickson, *The Inseparable Grief; Margaret Cargill of Fiji*, (London, Epworth Press, 1976), pp. 117–18.

[38]   For a fuller account see J. Darch, *Missionary Imperialists?*, (Milton Keynes, Paternoster, 2009), pp.78–89.

trials and several of the early British missionaries died young. Maggie Cargill, after nursing her husband through a dangerous illness, succumbed in 1840. He took their four children back to Britain and remarried. But he went through much mental suffering and soon after his return to the Pacific, depressed and ill, he died of an overdose in Vavau. In 1842 Cross died from exhaustion and dysentery. He was 45; the Cargills both in their early 30s.

John Hunt[39] was one of four British missionaries sent to reinforce the team, arriving a few months after the Tongan party at the end of 1838. Hunt, a Lincolnshire farmhand, illiterate until the age of 16, had exceptional physical and intellectual energy. The missionary learned Fijian as quickly as the teenager had learned to read. Bible translation and theological writing filled what was left of the day after preaching, training Fijian teachers, extending the District to more of the islands and constantly seeking the conversion of the influential and aggressive chiefs. Foremost among these was Cakobau (pronounced Thakombau).[40] An intelligent but a ferocious and vengeful warrior, Cakobau enjoyed the company of the missionaries and loved discussing with them, but was unconvinced.

Hunt died after ten years in Fiji, aged only 37. Two others who arrived with him were spared to give long service and see some favourable answers to their prayers. James Calvert was his fellow student at Hoxton.[41] He had as a teenager been apprenticed to a printer and after revising and completing Hunt's translation of the Bible he published it himself. Richard Lyth was both minister and qualified doctor and served for a short while in Tonga before he came to Fiji. First Lyth, later Calvert, followed Hunt as Chairman of the Fiji District.[42] The determination of the missionaries to stand against cannibalism at whatever personal risk is evident again and again in the record. On one occasion while the ministers were away at a Synod, their wives, Mary Calvert[43] and Mary Ann Lyth, heard that fourteen women had been seized to supply a special banquet for some guests. They at once set out by boat to plead for their lives, but discovered on landing that the killing had already begun. Undeterred, they made their way to the chief's house. Entrance was strictly forbidden to women; but the guards fell back as they marched boldly through to offer, with suitable presents, their protests and their petition. The chief was sufficiently impressed to answer: 'Those who are dead are dead; but those who are still alive shall live.' Another time, when three women were strangled at the death of a warrior, Calvert arrived to find the tragedy finished. He sought an audience with Cakobau himself to remonstrate and Cakobau said afterwards: 'Aye! how the Missionaries labour to save life! They take any trouble and go

---

[39]   See N.A. Birtwhistle, *In his Armour: The Life of John Hunt*, (London, Cargate Press, 1954).

[40]   The Fijian *c* is pronounced *th*.

[41]   See C.M. Hall, *Calvert of Cannibal Fiji*, (London, WMMS, 1918).

[42]   The South Sea Islands District was divided into the Tonga and Fiji Districts in 1838.

[43]   P.M. Webb, *Women of our Company*, (London, Cargate Press, 1958), pp. 13–23.

anywhere for our salvation; and we are always trying to kill one another! What a pity he was too late! Had he been in time I would have spared her.'[44]

The conversion of a powerful young warrior, Verani of Viwa,[45] in 1845 was a critical factor in bringing such practices to an end. Verani was the local pronunciation of the word 'French'. He was given the name after sharing in the capture of a French ship, whose crew were eaten. On becoming a Christian, he took the name of Elijah. Cakobau of Bau, his overlord, who had threatened that on the day Verani was baptized he should be killed and eaten, admitted: 'He is a man of one heart. When he was with us he was fully with us; now he is a Christian he is decided and not to be moved'. This led to a considerable movement to the *lotu*. But it was not for another nine years, after Verani's murder and at the urging of King George of Tonga who visited him with Robert Young in 1853, that Cakobau himself accepted *lotu* and the death-drum which only ten days previously had announced a cannibal feast was used to summon a great assembly for worship. A short while later his great enemy Nggara of Rewa, pressed to accept Christianity in his turn, refused with the pertinent observation: 'If we all *lotu*, we must give up fighting; it will not do to pray to the same God and fight with each other.'[46] Nggara however fell ill and died; the coalition opposed to Cakobau fell apart. Little by little peace spread from island to island, while the church grew. Tongan missionaries continued to play their part – there were fifteen at work in Fiji in 1853.

Both Lyth and Calvert remained in Fiji until 1855 and witnessed Cakobau's change of heart. That was also the year in which the WMMS ceded responsibility for its Pacific missions to the new Australasian Conference. Calvert went back to England where he continued to revise the Fijian Bible, before returning to Fiji as Chairman at the invitation of the new Conference. 'Were you not afraid of being killed?' he was once asked and replied, 'No: we died before we went.' Lyth went initially to New Zealand and then to England. Both had further overseas postings, Calvert in South Africa and Lyth in Gibraltar.

Another name to conjure with during this period was Waterhouse. John Waterhouse had been a minister in England for twenty-nine years before he was appointed 'General Superintendent of the Wesleyan Missions in Australia and Polynesia', based in Hobart, in 1838. He was a greatly valued support to his far-flung team and travelled extensively over the area for four years but could not sustain the pace and died in 1842. Eight years later his son Joseph was stationed in Fiji and played a part in wresting Cakobau from his old ways. He took the helm of the District when it came under Australian tutelage. He died in a shipwreck off New Zealand in 1881.

The conversion of chiefs was an important target and a major achievement, but there was far more to the mission in Fiji, just as there was more in the Caribbean

---

44   J. Calvert, *Fiji and the Fijians*, (London, Alexander Heylin, 1858), p. 302.

45   Viwa and Bau are small islands off the east coast of Viti Levu, while Rewa is nearby, at the mouth of the river Rewa on the main island.

46   Calvert, p. 186.

than the anti-slavery cause. Fijians themselves, most unremembered, played as important a role as those whose names are recorded. The missionary ship *John Wesley,* bought by the Society to supply the Pacific outposts because of the irregularity and unreliability of merchant shipping, carried Lyth and others to more remote locations to begin the work of evangelization anew; Captain Buck and his crew made an often perilous contribution to the advance of the faith. In another few decades the Methodist Church was able to claim the allegiance of the majority of Fijians. The annexation of Fiji by Britain in 1874[47] and the arrival of indentured labourers from India in 1879 belong to a later chapter in Fiji's history.

So under Christian influence Caribbean-style slavery and Pacific-style cannibalism disappeared. Caste discrimination in India was another matter altogether. Not all missionaries were aghast at its pernicious influence; in any case their own influence was powerless to change a system so deeply embedded in Indian culture.

---

[47]　See Darch, pp. 91–111.

Chapter 7

The WMMS: The First Fifty Years

Until William Carey's *Enquiry* was published in 1792 the propagation of the gospel had not been thought of in terms of the Great Commission (Matthew 28:19–20); thereafter, 'Go into all the world and make disciples' was the watchword of the Missionary Societies. Another New Testament text was cited by some who went to serve abroad: 'The love of Christ leaves us no choice,' an argument which led the apostle Paul to conclude, 'Therefore we are ambassadors for Christ'.[1] Many missionaries saw themselves in that light – it was Francis Asbury's text for a mid-Atlantic sermon on 13 October 1771, sailing to America. The Methodist sub-conscience, however, was strongly influenced by what they sang and Charles Wesley's 'Jesus, the Conqueror, reigns'[2] and lines like 'till all his foes submit' left their mark: mission was often spoken of – not only by Methodists – in terms of conquest and military metaphors abounded. The distinction between an ambassador and a conquistador is plain but it was lost on most of the men and women who poured their energies and resources into the missionary enterprise. Their hymn-book began, as did all Wesleyan hymnals for over two centuries,

O for a thousand tongues to sing
My great Redeemer's praise…
…Assist me to proclaim,
To spread through all the earth abroad
The honours of thy name.

The Society Established

The Leeds District Missionary Society of 1813 was swiftly joined by other District-based Societies, dedicated to enthusing supporters and raising funds. Wesleyan missions remained, however, the business of the Conference, which had first appointed a committee of oversight in 1789. Jabez Bunting, the instigator of the Leeds Society, was a prominent Conference figure, elected its Secretary in 1814 and elected at the same time to the Legal Hundred, the first person to be chosen

---

[1]   2 Corinthians 5:14, 20.
[2]   First published in *Hymns and Sacred Poems,* 1749.

otherwise than by seniority.[3] He was as passionate about foreign missions as Coke and used every effort to give them pride of place in the Conference agenda.

In 1816 *The Report of the Executive Committee for the Management of the Missions First Commenced by the Revd John Wesley, the Revd Dr Coke and Others, and now carried on under the direction of the Methodist Conference* listed work underway in Gibraltar, Brussels, France, Ceylon, Sierra Leone, the Cape, the West Indies and the North American colonies, while no news had as yet come from New South Wales of the arrival of 'brother Leigh, appointed more than eighteen months ago'. The Missionary Fund, said the report, was devoted 'solely to foreign missions, with the exception of a sum voted by the Committee towards the expenses of the mission in the Irish language'. Richard Watson,[4] a rising connexional leader who had returned to the Wesleyan fold in 1811 after eight years in the Methodist New Connexion, was appointed General Missionary Secretary. He was a gifted preacher, whose sermon in Leeds on the morning of the founding meeting in 1813 made his reputation. He combined the post with circuit ministry until 1821 when he was 'separated' and moved to London. He wrote the Society's annual report for many years. Self-educated, Watson was a prodigious systematic theologian. His four-volume *Theological Institutes* (1823–29)[5] was a standard text for Methodist scholars on both sides of the Atlantic for fifty years.

The District Societies and connexional Committee were brought together in 1818 as the Wesleyan Methodist Missionary Society. The *Laws and Regulations*, drafted by Bunting and Watson, declared that:

> The object of this Society is to excite and combine ... the exertions of ... Methodists (and of others, who are friends to the conversion of the Heathen World, and to the preaching of the Gospel, generally, in Foreign Lands) in the support and enlargement of the Foreign Missions, which were first established by the Rev John Wesley, AM, the Rev Thomas Coke, LLD and others ...[6]

They prescribed that every person subscribing a guinea per annum and every benefactor donating at least £10, would be a member of the Society, though the provisions about branch societies in circuits and local societies meant that in practice the distinction between church membership and Missionary Society membership was soon blurred. Monthly Missionary Prayer Meetings should be held in every chapel in the connexion. Ladies' Branch Associations and Juvenile Branch Associations were commended. There were to be three Secretaries, one

---

[3]   J.H. Rigg, *Jabez Bunting, a great Methodist leader*, (London, Charles H. Kelly, 1905).

[4]   E.J. Brailsford, *Richard Watson, theologian and missionary advocate*, (London, Charles H. Kelly, 1906); T.A. Langford, *Methodist Theology*, (London, Epworth Press, 1998), pp. 20–24.

[5]   R. Watson, *Theological Institutes*, (London, John Mason, 1823, 1829).

[6]   First Report of the General Wesleyan Methodist Missionary Society, 1818, p. viii.

resident at the 'Mission House' who would devote his weekdays exclusively to the service of the Society. Joseph Taylor and, in 1821, Bunting therefore joined Watson as Secretaries of the Society. Dedicated management of the missions had become imperative as the number of missionaries grew. In 1813 there had been forty-two. Ten years later there were 111 and the numbers were growing fast.

There were several thrusts to this missionary work: care for the emigrants from home; the evangelization of the heathen; a mission to Islam; and the conversion of Roman Catholics. Colonial Methodism prospered and autonomous Conferences in North America and Australasia came into being within fifty years. These Churches consisted in the main of people of British stock and British culture and could be trusted to govern themselves in a seemly manner. They were encouraged to be self-supporting. In a letter to John McKenny, as he moved from his long spell in Ceylon to leadership in New South Wales in 1835, John Beecham, one of the Secretaries, wrote:

> The funds of the Socty. are especially designed for the support of Missions among the Heathen, & missionaries cannot be multiplied in an English colony where the labours among the Settlers are unconnected with any efforts on behalf of the Aboriginal Inhabitants, excepting on the principle of their support being chiefly raised by those among whom they exercise their ministry.[7]

The heathen – a term that was applied essentially to dark-skinned people, living in places scarcely explored – received the greatest attention, the largest number of missionaries, the bulk of the funds.

The evangelization of peoples under Muslim rule was a project particularly dear to Richard Watson. The disintegration of the Ottoman Empire encouraged the belief that the time was ripe and Charles Cook, who had recently embarked on a lifetime's ministry in France, was despatched on a reconnaissance mission. His report was favourable; several young Preachers began to study Arabic; from 1823 to 1831 Palestine was listed on the Stations, but always with mentions such as 'two [or three] to be sent' or 'vacant for the present'. From 1830 to 1835 James Bartholomew was stationed in Alexandria, but his successor returned after a year and the Middle East never became a theatre of Methodist activity. The 'conquest' of Islam was a mirage.

Elsewhere in the Mediterranean there was a succession of ministers in Malta from 1824 to 1843, with the aim of exploiting the island's strategic position between Catholic Europe and Muslim North Africa. From 1827 to 1834 Walter Croggan worked on the Greek island of Zakynthos (then known as Zante) in the Ionian Sea, looking in vain for an opening in Greece. Tentative missions in Europe were equally

---

[7]   9 October 1835, quoted in N.W. Taggart, 'Methodist Foreign Missions, The First Half Century' in *WHS Proceedings*, 45 (October 1986): p. 160.

short-lived: in Sweden from 1826 to 1843, with never more than a dozen members, and in Spain where outreach from Gibraltar was thwarted again and again.[8]

Communication Difficulties

Evidently the Committee in its enthusiasm was over-stretching itself. Their plan was to scatter seed in all directions, not knowing in advance which ground would prove rocky or prickly and which would produce a harvest. As a result their resources were too thinly dispersed. Beyond Europe their ambitions were complicated by immense distances, the slow speed of travel and unpredictable communications. For example they wanted to extend the South African operation to Madagascar and at one point in 1824 Barnabas Shaw, under obedience, had his boxes packed awaiting a passage from Cape Town. His colleagues were not so ready to co-operate in a plan that had been formulated in ignorance of local realities. They wrote to the Committee pointing out the consequences of uprooting them: a language on which they had expended much effort no longer of use and a new language to be learned, outposts they had established and nurtured left without oversight. After consulting among themselves the group decided to ignore the Committee's instructions and stationed themselves on the basis of known needs and prospects. Appointments listed in the *Minutes of Conference* did not always correspond with the facts on the ground.

Communication with the Pacific was even slower. Christianity reached Samoa (the Navigators' Islands) through seafarers from Tonga, just as it did Fiji. In Samoa indeed, the faith was known as the '*lotu* Tonga'. In 1832 the Committee directed the infant South Seas District to extend its care to Samoa, but it was three years before Peter and Mrs Turner were sent.[9] They found 2,000 Wesleyans waiting for them. They knew that elsewhere in the Islands there were Tahitian teachers, left there by the LMS missionary to Polynesia, John Williams. Williams, the 'hero of a hundred islands' was the first European missionary to set foot in Samoa.[10] Turner was under instruction to complement, not compete with the LMS's work. Within twenty months the 2,000 Methodists had become 13,000. What Turner did not know was that the Secretaries in London were in discussion with the LMS and that early in 1836 they had agreed that Samoa should be left to the LMS and the WMMS would concentrate on Tonga and Fiji. Turner first learned of this from an LMS party later in the year. They regarded him as an interloper and asked him to hand over the Wesleyan congregations to their care. His pleas to the Committee were in vain; the deal had been done. The correspondence had taken months in

---

8   James Scott, President of the South African Conference in 1892 and 1897, was born in Stockholm in 1835 during the ministry of his father George Scott.

9   Née Smallwood; Mrs Turner's forename is not recorded.

10   See J. Williams, *A Narrative of Missionary Enterprises in the South Sea Islands*, (London, J Snow, 1837).

each direction. In 1839 Williams returned to oversee the transfer and the Turners left on his schooner. The Wesleyans, however, declined to join 'the other *lotu*' – and shortly after the Australasian Conference became autonomous, the new Australian WMMS decided it was not bound by the compact with its parent Society and took them under its wing.

The unreliability of Pacific shipping led the Society to invest in its own vessel. In 1839 Bunting was instrumental in raising a Centenary Fund – marking the centenary not of the Wesley brothers' heart-warming but of the first Methodist society, in Bristol – and in determining its allocation. The previous year the LMS had acquired, primarily for the use of John Williams, its own missionary ship, the *Camden*, and put Captain Robert Clark Morgan, an experienced mariner who was a Wesleyan, in command.[11] The WMMS followed suit and with a grant from the Centenary Fund bought the *Triton,* for the purpose of

> conveying Missionaries and stores between the Colonies of New South Wales and Van-Diemen's Land and the Friendly Islands, New-Zealand, the Fejees and other groups and islands of the Great South Pacific Ocean … It is expected that advantage will be taken of this opportunity to send a reinforcement of Missionaries to the several Stations in that part of the world, as well as a large supply of goods of all kinds for the use of the Missions; but especially for such as have no circulating medium, and where the necessaries of life can only be obtained by barter.

This announcement was coupled with an appeal:

> … merchants, manufacturers, and others, who are friendly to the operations of the Wesleyan Missionary Society, have now an opportunity of testifying their good-will, by contributions of goods, which though, in some cases, they may be almost unsaleable in this country, in consequence of changes and improvements, or from being broken sets or remnants, will be of great value in those parts of the world to which they will be carried by the Missionary ship.[12]

There followed a long list of articles which 'would prove most acceptable presents to the Society'; the *Triton*'s manifest would be a revealing snippet of social history.

The *Triton* plied between the islands until 1846 when it was replaced by the *John Wesley.* This ship gave valuable service until 1865 when it struck a Tongan reef. Amazingly, just as the ship's back was breaking, an earthquake occurred and the ensuing surge of water lifted the ship off the reef and swept it into a shallow lagoon. All the passengers and crew and most of the cargo were saved. The *John*

---

[11]   Morgan had commanded the whaling vessel which took the first emigrants to South Australia in 1836.

[12]   *Missionary Notices*, April 1839, p. 61.

Wesley II was built in Aberdeen. It was eventually sold in 1881, made redundant by a more regular shipping service.

Secretaries and Missionaries

The organization and management of the missionary enterprise was a huge task for the Secretaries. But they could not spend all their time on administrative and pastoral duties. The work had to be resourced and so they were constantly on the platform at missionary meetings, inspiring the swelling numbers of Wesleyans in Britain and winning both large collections and offers of service. Watson and Robert Newton (both of them Bunting's neighbours in Yorkshire when the Society was taking shape) were especially powerful and popular speakers. Then there was the selection, training and stationing of missionaries. This was a delicate responsibility and every time the news arrived that one had died brought more heartbreak and heart-searching. Nor was the Society's business conducted in isolation from the social and political issues of the day. Bunting was a founder member of the Anti-Slavery Society set up by Thomas Clarkson and William Wilberforce in 1823 and, being Bunting, no back-pew member. And after slavery was officially ended in British territories, there was the Frontier controversy in South Africa, which can be seen as a portent of twentieth century struggles.[13]

What sort of men were Methodist missionaries? 'My brothers,' wrote the apostle Paul to Corinth, 'think what sort of people you are, whom God has called. Few of you are men of wisdom, by any human standard; few are powerful, or highly born.'[14] The same was the case in the eighteenth century; yet some, nonetheless, showed themselves of outstanding ability. John Hunt the Lincolnshire farmhand was illiterate at 16 but when he died a mere twenty years later he had translated the New Testament into Fijian and written a book which became a standard text for ministerial students.[15] William Boyce, after service in South Africa, went on to be the first President of the Australasian Conference and then for eighteen years (1858–76) an influential Secretary of the WMMS, before retiring in Sydney where he wrote *The Higher Criticism and the Bible* (1881)[16] and was elected a member of the Sydney University Senate. His Irish colleague at the Mission House, William Arthur, was another influential writer.[17] There were doubtless others of great potential who did not live to fulfil it. In fifty years no fewer than sixty-

---

[13]   See pp. 54–6.

[14]   1 Corinthians 1:26.

[15]   J. Hunt, *Letters on Entire Sanctification*, edited by his colleague J. Calvert, (London, Wesleyan Conference Office, 1853).

[16]   W.B. Boyce, *The Higher Criticism and the Bible*, (London, Wesleyan Conference Office, 1881).

[17]   See N.W. Taggart, *William Arthur, First among Methodists*, (London, Epworth Press, 1993).

three Wesleyan missionaries or missionary wives died in West Africa or at sea en route. So fearful was the climate that at one meeting in 1832 the first five men accepted for missionary service all indicated their willingness to go anywhere, 'Sierra Leone excepted'. A few months later it was noted that Isaac Clarke, a lace-weaver, was 'willing to go to any part of the world,' with a marginal note to the effect that he was 'willing to go to Sierra Leone.'[18] To Sierra Leone he went and was dead within a year.

For Wesleyans, the label 'Missionary' – spelt with a capital M – was, with rare exceptions, reserved for the ordained. Although the style 'Reverend' was being used in the connexion by 1818, those who itinerated in Britain were deemed to have been 'virtually ordained' by the vote of the Conference admitting them to 'full connexion'. Those proceeding abroad, however, received the imposition of hands (which only became the general Wesleyan practice in 1836) but were not admitted to full connexion until they had satisfactorily completed four years of probation. There continued to be exceptions. Epistolary (rather than Episcopal) ordination was the experience of George Piercy, the first Methodist missionary to China.[19] He was ordained, received into full connexion and appointed superintendent of the work in China at one and the same time by a letter which was brought by the colleagues appointed to join him. The ordained missionaries were sometimes accompanied by laymen who were missionaries by nature but not designated Missionaries in name. When George Warren went to Freetown in 1811 he sailed with three schoolmasters from Dewsbury, who outlived him. Dr Porter Smith, appointed to China in 1864 and the first 'medical missionary', was the first to be given the title Missionary without ordination, whereas Richard Lyth FRCS went to the Pacific in 1838 with ministerial status as well as surgical qualification.

Headquarters

In the days of Thomas Coke, the Book Room at City Road served as the base for connexional business, though from time to time Coke made use of the office of Mr Bruce, a prominent Methodist, at 4 City Road. The occasional meetings of a Missionary Committee were held in the vestry of Wesley's Chapel. In 1816 two rooms on Mr Bruce's first floor were rented for £24 per annum, but already the volume of activity had increased and they were unsuitable from the outset. Not only were there letters to be written and accounts to be kept, there were visitors to be received, baggage to be stored, supplies to be kept in stock. In 1817 the Conference directed

> that suitable premises for a Mission House and office shall be immediately
> secured in some central situation in London, affording sufficient accommodation

---

18   SOAS: MMS/Special Series/Candidate Papers/FBN 43.
19   See p. 121.

for the transaction of all our missionary business, and for a depot of proper articles which are wanted for the outfit of Missionaries ...

This empowered the Secretaries to rent and later buy a large house in Hatton Garden, just north of London's Holborn Circus, which served as the Mission House for twenty-three years. It had ample room for the Secretaries and the growing number of clerical staff, as well as a Committee Room; upstairs lived the resident Secretary; a warehouse was built in the garden. By 1830 the business of the Society had so expanded that the upstairs rooms were taken over and a house nearby was rented for the Secretary. It served too as a hostel for candidates coming to be interviewed and missionaries awaiting their passage. The only training most of them received was such instruction as the Secretaries could give in those few weeks before departure.

Bunting was determined to make better provision, both for the headquarters and for the training. One of the purposes of the 1839 Centenary Fund, which raised £222,589, was to acquire a 'Centenary Hall' for the WMMS. The 'City of London Tavern', containing one of the largest lecture halls in London, does not sound like an ideal set of premises, but it was on the market and £15,000 for one of Sir Christopher Wren's buildings, with 'two thousand dozen of the finest Port, sherry, Madeira and other wines' thrown in, was a bargain. It was adapted – in part entirely rebuilt – for a similar amount and was opened in 1841. The Mission House occupied the site in Bishopsgate for almost a hundred years. Until Westminster Central Hall was opened in the next century, connexional committees of all kinds made use of its rooms. It had space for the occasional Sale of Work, one of which, in June 1851, attracted crowds to buy articles sent as a thank-offering by Tongan and Fijian converts: 'temple cloths and mats, spears and clubs, shells and bowls, elephants' and whales' teeth, costumes, idols and musical instruments'. But it was 'a dark, dingy and highly inconvenient agglomeration of halls, passages, staircases and rooms, beset with missionary baggage and other impedimenta.'[20]

For training, the vision of a Theological Institute was realized earlier. The premises of the LMS's Hoxton Academy, where men such as John Philip and the pioneer China missionary Robert Morrison had been prepared, became available when the Academy moved to Highgate in 1828. They were rented in 1834 and here those preparing for ministry both at home and overseas were trained. The two-year course focused on the Bible, theology and the liberal arts. Specific training for missionary service was informal; cross-cultural encounter did not figure on the syllabus and anthropology was as yet an infant science. It was *in situ* that experiential learning reshaped attitudes and assumptions.[21]

---

[20]   E.W. Thompson, *The Methodist Mission House: its history and its treasures*, (London, WMMS, 1933?), pp. 8–9.

[21]   See for example p. 234.

Finance and Policy

The income of the Society climbed at a steady and rapid pace until 1841, but fell significantly after 1846 – unsurprisingly, for the connexion was in turmoil. Bunting had always been a controversial figure; there were those who regarded him as an impudent upstart when he launched the Leeds District Society over thirty years earlier. He wielded immense power: Secretary of Conference 1814–19 and 1824–27, Connexional Editor 1821–24 (then the only full-time separated office apart from the Missionary Society), President of Conference at regular eight-year intervals from 1820 to 1844. In 1833 he began a second term as WMMS Secretary and soon combined that role with the Presidency of the new Theological Institution. He knew his own mind and did not suffer fools gladly. His intransigence led to the secession of the Protestant Methodists in 1828 and the Wesleyan Association in 1834. The crisis that erupted over the publication of five anonymous 'fly-sheets' between 1844 and 1849 had even more serious consequences. These papers were severely critical of Bunting in sundry respects, including what was claimed to be Mission House extravagance. Eventually a third of all Wesleyan members seceded, mostly to the Wesley Reform body which united with the two previous break-aways in 1857 to form the United Methodist Free Churches. It may well be that devotion to the missionary cause restrained many who might otherwise have seceded; nonetheless loss of members meant loss of income and loss of income necessitated a review of WMMS policies.[22]

No new initiative had been undertaken since 1836. The Mediterranean and Middle East ventures had come to nothing. In 1843 the Committee met with a Captain Gardiner R.N., who was so enthusiastic about a mission to Patagonia that he offered £100 per annum to support it and was ready to accompany the appointed missionary and introduce him to the people. After ten days' consideration the offer was respectfully declined.[23] In Europe a little German church depended on one man, Gerhard Muller, who had become a class-leader while trading in London. Returning to his birthplace he worked as an Agent of the Society, at trifling cost, from 1831 and built up a Society in Wurttemberg which peaked at 1,100 members in 1854 and then dwindled as his health declined. French Methodism did a little better, due to the itinerant ministry of Charles Cook, who was appointed to Normandy in 1818 and in the course of forty years formed a network of little congregations as far afield as Switzerland and Sardinia as well as in the Midi and remote Huguenot villages of the Cevennes.

By the 1850s the Committee, stimulated by John Beecham and Elijah Hoole – two far-sighted and long-serving Secretaries to whom Bunting's baton was handed on – resolved to encourage the most mature of the overseas Churches to become self-governing. That France should be the first was remarkable, given that the

---

[22] Findlay and Holdsworth, vol. 1, p. 190.
[23] General Committee Minutes, 5 May and 15 May 1843: SOAS, MMS/Home/ General Minutes/ FBN2.

District comprised only 821 members and would need the continued support of the Society right up to its union with the French Reformed Church in 1939. But the financial pressures were not the primary motives for this policy, contributing factor though they were. Beecham went over to North America to persuade both Canada and Eastern British America to assume autonomy, while Robert Young undertook an arduous tour of the Pacific for the same purpose. In all cases the overseas Churches concurred with the Society's proposals and became Affiliated Conferences.[24] The *Minutes* of the British Conference continued to print the names and stations of the ministers – many of whom had begun their ministry in Britain or Ireland – until 1873 in the case of Canada, 1875 for Australasia and for France until 1939.[25]

In 1852, the year of French autonomy, the WMMS at last felt able to embark on a new venture. Since the Treaty of Nanjing ten years earlier many western missions had entered China. The Society had held back, but, with income beginning to rise again after the fly-sheets slump, held back no longer.

Over the fifty years to 1863 the 17,000 Methodists overseas became almost 200,000 – two-thirds of them in the care of the Affiliated Conferences. The number of missionaries grew from forty-nine to 1,120, if the ministers of the Affiliated Conferences are included. By the year of the Jubilee the four-fold thrust of the missionary endeavour discernible in the early years had given way to an agenda dominated by the evangelization of the heathen. But a distinction was now being made between the 'barbarian heathenism' of the black and Pacific peoples and the 'civilized heathenism' of Asia. Asia was proving stony ground for the gospel seed. After fifty years the number of converts was small, Ceylon and India between them numbering only 2,095 members. After ten years in China there were eighty-five and that included missionary wives. In the coming years these would be the areas that absorbed the highest number of missionaries and the largest input of funds.

---

[24]   See pp. 34, 37 and 42.

[25]   The stations of the South African Conference were printed from its inception in 1883 until 1927 and the West Indian stations throughout the lifetime of the West Indian Conference, 1884–1903.

Chapter 8

Into India

The India of the nineteenth century was vast enough to be called 'the sub-continent', encompassing what later became India, Pakistan, Bangladesh and, from 1886 to 1937, Burma. It was a region divided in many ways. The Moghul Empire, which at its height around 1700 had ruled most of the sub-continent, was already in decline when European armies began fighting for control of the coastal trading areas. Outside those areas, Indians were subject to the nawabs, nizams and maharajahs whose kingdoms ranged from huge to minuscule. Even when an 'Act for the Better Government of India' transferred the functions of the British East India Company to the crown in 1858 and when Queen Victoria was crowned Empress of India in 1877, suzerainty in much of the territory was exercised through these Princely States. It was a land of many languages: four major Dravidian languages spoken in the south, Hindi and a dozen other Indo–Aryan tongues in the north, many more mutually unintelligible languages spoken by smaller groups in the north-east. It was also divided religiously. The majority of Indians were Hindus. Sikhs and Jains, Parsis (Zoroastrians) and Buddhists, as well as the ancient Christian churches, were all relatively small minorities, whereas Muslims formed a significant proportion of the population, with considerable power and influence. The Hindu community in turn was divided by the age-old caste system with its impenetrable social barriers and cruel discrimination.

Long before the nineteenth century a rigid caste system was in place, comprising *brahmans* (priests), *kshatriyas* (warriors), *vaishyas* (at first cultivators but in time prosperous landowners and traders) and *sudras,* peasants tied to the land and heavily taxed on their produce. Outside these castes altogether, the aboriginal people of India were made to do the most menial work, to live on the margins of society and to avoid all contact with caste people. They too developed their own miserable hierarchy of clans and sub-tribes. One, the *paraiyurs,* gave the name pariah to them all. The terms 'untouchable', 'harijan' (Gandhi's word) and 'dalit', were all coined in the twentieth century; in the nineteenth the word was '*panchamas*', while the British government called them the 'depressed classes'.

This was the Indian social context in which Christian missionaries lived and worked.[1] They faced not only the indifference of Indians whose religious traditions were highly developed and deeply ingrained, but also the hostility of those Europeans who, long after the 1813 Act had set aside the East India Company's

---

[1]   For a social rather than an institutional history of Christian India, see the volumes published by the Church History Association of India: various authors, *History of Christianity in India*, (Bangalore, CHAI, 1982 and ongoing vols).

objections, continued to deplore any interference with local custom, which, they argued, undermined their commercial interests.

Ceylon

The Wesleyan Mission in Asia began in Ceylon, the largest island of the Indian Ocean. In 1972, by then an independent nation, it was renamed Sri Lanka, from the Sanskrit for 'resplendent isle'. By the western European explorers and merchants it was called Ceylon, from the same Sanskrit root as *Sinhala*. The majority of the island's population was Sinhalese and Buddhist, but the northern region of Jaffna had been Tamil and Hindu since at least the second century BCE. The same divisions as in India – territorial, linguistic, religious – prevailed, together with caste discrimination in the north. Sinhala society had a less strict caste system.

Although the East India Company established control of much of the island in 1796, it was declared a crown colony in 1802 and never became part of British India. The Wesleyans arrived in 1814, a year before the central kingdom of Kandy fell and the island was gradually unified under British rule. The little missionary party, deprived of Coke's leadership, wasted no time in taking stock of the situation. Ten days after landing they held a 'little Conference' to decide how they would proceed. They recognized that, because of the different vernaculars and faiths and the considerable distances, they would have to split up. It was the Governor and his staff who suggested where they should establish themselves and offered to pay them as schoolteachers until regular financial support from London was assured. There were already 85,000 children in school when the British ousted the Dutch and maintaining educational standards was a priority. So Lynch and Squance went north to Jaffna, Ault north-east to Batticaloa and the others south to the old Dutch port of Galle. William Ault, whose wife Sarah had died at sea, survived only a few months. Harvard had remained for a while in Bombay; when he arrived he was based in Colombo and with the help of Andrew Armour[2] soon built the first Methodist chapel in Asia at the Pettah. The little society, barely a class, was composed of English, Portuguese, Dutch and Sinhala speakers and Armour, who was employed as interpreter to the Supreme Court, interpreted for them all. Harvard also took control of the printing press which had come in Coke's baggage.

The missionaries at once looked for local collaborators. Armour himself left his government post for a year to be an 'assistant missionary'.[3] Other recruits disappointed and had to be discharged, but two proved their worth over many years. William Lalmon, a Burgher – the name proudly borne by the Eurasians of Ceylon with Dutch or Portuguese ancestry – served the mission from 1817 to

---

[2]   See p. 44.

[3]   This terminology was adopted by the Conference of 1833 to designate locally recruited ministers throughout the foreign missions. Some found it demeaning however and they were later styled 'native ministers'.

The first Methodist Church in Asia in Dam Street, Colombo, founded 1814.

Figure 8.1   The first Methodist Church in Asia: The Pettah, Colombo

1863. Cornelius Wijesingha, a Sinhalese, served from 1819 to 1864. John Philips Sanmogam, a Tamil converted under Squance's influence at the age of 15, also went on into the ministry and showed himself a diligent pastor, greatly loved. The first reinforcements from England joined the team in 1816 and in 1818 Daniel Gogerly[4] was sent to relieve the missionaries of the printing work – not being ordained, he was not classed as a missionary himself. But Gogerly was more than a printer. He sorted out the chaotic finances he found, he was a competent linguist and before long he was called to the pastoral ministry. Accepted in 1823, he served in Ceylon to his death in 1862, not once returning to Europe. He made a close study of Buddhism, mastered Pali, the ancient language of Theravada Buddhism and acquired such a thorough grasp of the subject that Buddhist teachers came to respect his learning and fear his influence.[5] His studies led him to conclude, as he wrote to Elijah Hoole, one of the Secretaries, in 1858, that 'The institutions of Brahminism and Buddhism may be regarded as the citadels of Satan's kingdom.' Robert Spence Hardy, who worked in Ceylon from 1825 to 1848 and 1862 to 1865, was inspired by Gogerly and he too became an expert on Buddhism, although he preferred to work with Buddhist texts in Sinhala rather than the Pali Canon.[6]

---

[4]   W.J.T. Small (ed.), *A History of the Methodist Church in Ceylon,* (Colombo, Wesley Press, 1964), pp. 116–23.

[5]   His writings were eventually collected, edited by A.S. Bishop and published as D.J. Gogerly, *Ceylon Buddhism*, (Colombo, Wesleyan Methodist Book Room, 1908).

[6]   E.J. Harris, 'Wesleyan Witness in an Interreligious Context', in P.R. Meadows (ed.), *Windows on Wesley*, (Oxford, Applied Theology Press, 1997), pp. 66–8.

Relationships with the Secretaries and Committee in London were uneasy from the start. The first letter received in Ceylon contained no word of sympathy at Coke's death, but a complaint that the news had reached them by way of private letters. Formal notification had been sent from Bombay and the missionaries should not have been blamed for the unreliability of mailboats, but they were. In 1816 Lynch, appalled by the poverty and distress he found in Ceylon, suggested setting up a workshop in which people would be employed in carding and spinning cloth. Local Europeans would help to defray initial costs of acquiring cotton, spinning wheels and looms until profits from the manufacture and sale of calico and muslin made the establishment self-supporting. He was told in no uncertain terms that the missionaries must

> have nothing to do with manufactories or worldly traffic of any description
> whatever; … give yourselves entirely to prayer and the ministry of the word, not
> entangling yourselves with the affairs of this world that the word of the Lord be
> not hindered.[7]

Later came another complaint, this time about Gogerly's press. Clough, who joined Harvard in Colombo, had wasted no time in producing a Sinhala translation of the New Testament with the help of two converts. He also produced a Sinhala–English dictionary, which the Committee's report for 1819 described as 'a work which will be of incalculable importance to missionaries and to civilians in acquiring this difficult but comprehensive language'. Yet in 1821 the Secretaries wrote a stinging letter of reproof calling it 'a literary speculation' on which neither Clough nor the press should have spent time and energy. Another issue, which arose in all overseas Districts, was the Committee's insistence on its right to station missionaries in the name of the Conference, despite the time it took to send recommendations in one direction and decisions in the other. Circumstances could easily change in such a long interval and inevitably those on the spot assumed discretionary powers. It was only after years of recrimination that these were formally recognized, by which time, ironically, communication was becoming more regular, reliable and rapid.

Two Districts, as envisaged from the first, were officially recognized in 1819, with Lynch in charge in the north and Buckley Fox, a newcomer, in the south. Clough, though he hated administration and, after the rebukes he received, wanted nothing more to do with bills of exchange, was nonetheless persuaded to take over from Fox on his return from furlough in 1825. He persevered amid trials and tribulations until he retired in 1838. In 1825 another important site was purchased in Kollupitiya, then a village on the outskirts of Colombo but eventually in the heart of the city, and the next year an Institute for training native agents was begun. This was a short-lived experiment, revived only in 1851 at Richmond Hill, a large property two miles from Galle. In the intervening years each missionary

---

[7]   Buckley to Lynch, 23 August 1816, quoted in N.W. Taggart, *The Irish in World Methodism 1760–1960*, (London, Epworth Press, 1986), p. 117.

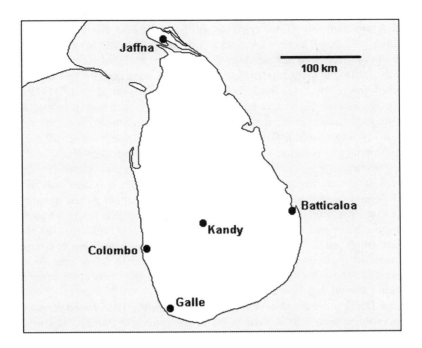

Map 6   Ceylon

was expected to have one or two promising young men living with him, to receive instruction and shadow him. In this way the number of indigenous ministers and of lay catechists increased steadily. But although Lalmon, the first Ceylonese candidate, had been accepted in 1816, not until 1887 were 'native ministers' entitled to be members of the Synod as of right.

The central region surrounding Kandy, the last area of the island to come under British rule, was predominantly Buddhist. Early dreams of getting to work there came to nothing. As in so many places, it was when converts from elsewhere settled there that a church was formed. They asked for a minister and the post was opened in 1866. Ten years later, the congregation was in a position to build a chapel and mission house, to support a Ceylonese minister and to contribute £150 per annum towards the costs of the missionary.

The place and style of education in mission was hotly debated throughout the century, especially in relation to caste questions. Among the Sinhalese it was a less divisive issue than in India. The first Methodist missionaries, after their brief spell of employment in government schools, lost no time in opening their own. There were already fourteen in Colombo when, in 1818, two men were sent out specifically for educational work. But they were provided with no budget and were diverted into circuit ministry. Schools however continued to open; Wesleyans championed education in the vernacular. In 1841 the non-denominational 'Ladies' Society for

Female Education in the East' opened two 'Superior Schools for Girls' in Galle and Jaffna and Mary Twiddy,[8] a Wesleyan minister's daughter from England, took charge of the latter until her marriage. There was a period of retrenchment at the end of the 1840s due to the financial difficulties created in England by the secession of the Reformers but it was not long before the work resumed. In 1866 Catherine Scott, sister of John Scott who had just succeeded Spence Hardy in the District Chair, started a Girls' School at Kollupitiya. One large room was divided into three sections – two for the Sinhala and English classes and the third for Miss Scott's private Sinhala lessons. She stayed for seventeen years and saw the school grow into a grant-aided English High School, later to flourish as Methodist College Colombo. Its counterpart, Wesley College Colombo, opened at the Pettah in 1874. Daniel Pereira, a second generation minister and polymath paved the way and was its first Vice-Principal, under successive missionary Principals. The school's scholastic achievements belied the shabby state of its first buildings, which were eventually replaced as the twentieth century began. Meanwhile a major complex of educational institutions grew at Richmond Hill near Galle. Ministerial formation and teacher-training – with a practising school next door – were complemented by boys' and girls' High Schools in 1876.

In the Tamil areas, the first Methodist missionaries in 1814 found support from a remarkable woman, a schoolteacher who spoke Dutch, Portuguese and Tamil. At the age of 56 Mrs Schrader, a Dutch Presbyterian, learned English; she taught in the Wesleyan school in Jaffna for many years as well as leading a society class and translating some Wesley hymns and sermons into Portuguese. Other centres of work were established in Batticaloa and Trincomalee and before long across the straits in Tamil Nadu. Lynch chaired the northern District even when he removed to Madras, until a separate Madras District was created in 1824. Among his successors, Peter Percival and Ralph Stott are noteworthy. Percival was a scholar and translated the whole Bible and the Book of Offices into Tamil. He was posted for three years to Calcutta but otherwise served the District from 1824 to 1851. He was a great believer in education and opened a number of schools around Jaffna. He had many disputes with Stott, who with equal fervour argued for the priority of vernacular preaching in the villages, which was his focus in Batticaloa. Stott feared that the energy spent on running schools was a distraction from evangelism. The two approaches were complementary, but that is not how they saw it at the time. Until around 1840 the congregations in the north consisted almost entirely of Europeans and Burghers. Stott went into the jungles to seek out nomadic or cave-dwelling hunter-gatherers. Nobody built on his work once he left. Richard Watson Vyramuttu, a young man born and nurtured in Hindu temple precincts, lived with Stott for some years and eventually entered the ministry. His baptismal name, presumably chosen by Stott, was apt, for like the English Watson he became an eloquent preacher.

[8]   See p. 247–8.

In 1847 John Kilner joined the District staff. He was then transferred to India as part of the cost-cutting exercise of 1849. He returned in 1853 and was the District Chairman from 1859 to 1875. He was a strategist and based his policy on the principles first enunciated in 1854 by Henry Venn of the CMS for native autonomy. Thus, as soon as possible, the Tamil Christians should take over responsibility for their government, their finances and their evangelistic outreach. This meant, he argued, that stipends and allowances should be fixed at rates which would not surpass the capacity of the local people. His major concern and his greatest achievement was the development of Tamil leadership. In the first fifty years North Ceylon had produced just two Tamil ministers; by 1875 there were eleven and there were twenty-one catechists where there were none in 1860. The number of schools in the District rose under his administration from twenty-two to ninety-five. In 1875 Kilner returned to England to be a WMMS Secretary until his death in 1888.

The creation of the Women's Auxiliary and later of the Wesley Deaconess Order brought new missionaries to both Districts. They undertook teaching in the schools and opened much-needed dispensaries. They did evangelistic work among village women. With their help the number of schools for girls grew and 'industrial' schools were opened to equip girls from the poorest families with the skills to earn a livelihood.

As the century progressed, increasing numbers of Tamils moved south, both to Colombo as the economic pole and political capital of the island and to the plantations of the central hills. Coffee planting was developed in the 1820s but after 1869, when coffee rust began to blight the crop, tea cultivation took over. Migrant workers thronged in, not only from Jaffna but from India. The Tamil mission in Colombo was begun in 1873, when John Wesley Philips was dispatched from Jaffna; he was the son of Squance's protégé Sanmogam. By the end of the century Tamil members in the capital outnumbered the Sinhalese.

The Sinhalese were proving resistant to the gospel and towards the end of the century a Buddhist revival brought more open hostility to Christianity. This was in part a reaction to the scholarship of Gogerly and Spence Hardy, which the leading Buddhist teachers respected but saw as a threat. They sensed that missionaries were contemptuous of Buddhism. Buddhist monks had shown remarkable hospitality to the missionaries at first, giving them manuscripts and teaching them some Pali; now they felt betrayed. The revival was also a reaction to the huge expansion of Christian schools such as Kingswood School in Kandy, a private school taken over by the Wesleyans; it was encouraged by the theosophical movement in the west which took inspiration from Buddhism. Furthermore political nationalism was beginning to surface and was hostile to an alien religion.

At the close of the century the Ceylon Districts reported 4,443 members in 64 chapels and 227 other preaching places and 27,140 scholars in 358 schools with 891 teachers. Forty-five Ceylonese ministers (the term 'native minister' had ceased to be used) worked alongside twenty missionaries and one Joyful News agent.[9]

South India

By 1900 Wesleyan missionaries were working in Tamil, Kannada and Telugu-speaking areas, though most of their educational work was done in English. In each area – Madras, Mysore and Hyderabad – the first approaches came from British soldiers. There were Wesleyan soldiers in Madras by the end of the eighteenth century and James Lynch visited them from Jaffna, sailing in a small open boat, in 1817. He returned on a permanent basis the next year and at first ministered principally to the English and Eurasians, needing an interpreter for Tamil. This was a common pattern in the early days. Strangers in a foreign land, the missionaries naturally gravitated towards their compatriots in the military cantonments. Lynch lodged initially with a well-to-do resident, Bradford Dunford. Hospitable and generous, Dunford facilitated the purchase of a property in the Royapetta district of the city, where a chapel and manse were built – and which 130 years later became the headquarters of the Church of South India.

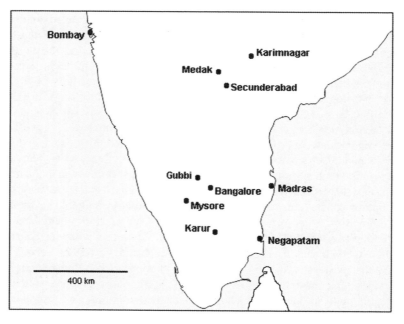

Map 7   South India

---

[9]   See pp. 202–4.

Lynch shuttled between Madras and Jaffna for some years, but in 1824 the Tamil District was split. The Madras District consisted of 198 members, most of whom were soldiers. There were a few other Europeans and just fifteen Tamil Christians. By then two other centres had been opened in India. Negapatam, formerly a Dutch trading post, was half-way from Jaffna to Madras and Lynch had been warmly welcomed as he passed through. The other was far away in Bangalore, on the Mysore plateau. The people of Mysore are the Kanarese and their tongue Kannada, but evangelism was carried on in English and largely among the English and to some extent among the migrant Tamil community. Here in 1821 arrived a youthful Elijah Hoole, having survived shipwreck on the voyage out. Within a matter of months he was transferred to Madras and soon made himself competent in Tamil. He translated Wesley's Order of Morning Prayer, the Rules of the Society, a selection of hymns and a catechism, before ill health forced him to return home after only seven years. But his experience prepared him for his marathon service as a WMMS Secretary from 1834 to 1872.

Wesley's preachers were itinerants by calling if not always by temperament. At home the practice was to tour large circuits every few weeks and they assumed that what worked in England would work in India. Hoole had the twin advantages of speaking Tamil and being a bachelor and spent weeks at a time on trek. But in India the strategy was misplaced. The missionaries were stationed too far apart, their circuits too scattered. Most worked in isolation and replacements were not readily available should one fall ill or be posted elsewhere. Then whatever property they had built could quickly become derelict. It was a costly policy in terms of money and of stress. When Titus Close, the first missionary to join Lynch in Madras, was transferred to Negapatam, he found a completely empty mission house; and Lynch, calling in on his return journey from Synod in Jaffna, informed him that Synod had determined to spend no money on houses for the ensuing year. The Committee in London, itself overstretched, had not yet come to appreciate the expense entailed in opening new stations. Perhaps they assumed that conversions would come fast enough to make the work self-supporting. As a result the missionaries were thrown back even more on the support of the British and Anglo–Indians, which distracted them from the study of Indian tongues, culture and religion. No wonder they met with so little success. When, in cases of dire need, those on the spot incurred unauthorized expenditure, they brought severe criticism down upon their heads. Fearful of further censure, they became paralysed, unwilling to risk any initiative. The letters they received from London not only failed to give any clear guidance, but lacked words of sympathy for their privations, bereavements and frustrations.

This sorry state of affairs took a turn for the better with the appointment of Hoole and of John Beecham as WMMS Secretaries and when, in 1832, Thomas Hodson was posted to Bangalore. Hodson, with Peter Percival, had spent three years in Calcutta learning Bengali when they were withdrawn on the grounds that 'results had not come up to expectations'. Before moving to Bangalore Hodson wrote a long letter to the Committee. He pointed out that, after working hard at Bengali which he would no longer use, he had now to start on Kannada. He sought an assurance that he would not be wasting his efforts again. He went on to propose a complete change of method, an intensive approach with missionaries stationed only a few miles apart and with schools at each station. Each missionary should engage in teaching as well as preaching. Beecham was sympathetic. His letters were couched in the sympathetic tones so markedly absent from earlier communications and his words were coupled with action. Several able missionaries were sent, specifically to work among Hindus. Hodson did supervise the Tamil work in Bangalore, but limited his direct involvement. Then, after prospecting the region, he made his base at Gubbi, a market town where there was no European population to divert his attention from the Kanarese. While a thatched cottage was being built in Gubbi he lived in a tent, just as Charles Wesley had when he arrived in Georgia a century earlier.

Among the new staff were Peter Batchelor and William Arthur. Batchelor, who had come to India as a layman to run the CMS Press in Madras, had joined the Wesleyan ministry and was appointed to the Tamil congregation in Bangalore. Arthur, an Irishman, went to Gubbi. Neither stayed long. Batchelor was transferred to Negapatam; in 1842 he married Mary Twiddy, who had been his young son's governess. Together they ran a school in Negapatam and two of the pupils went on to become the first Indian ministers. William Arthur's eyes could not cope with the strain of poring over his Kannada homework. He had to return to England, where he had a distinguished ministry including seventeen years as a WMMS Secretary.[10] Hodson too was obliged to leave for health reasons and spent ten years in England before returning to India. Around the same time a succession of discontented missionaries and assistant missionaries transferred their allegiance to the SPG. Hard won advances were thwarted again and again, though in 1848 work among the Kanarese was deemed sufficiently developed to warrant the separation of a Mysore District from Madras.

At last however a turning point came. In any history of India in the colonial era, the most significant nineteenth century date is 1857–58, when sepoys – Indian soldiers in the British army – mutinied.[11] Among many causes of rancour among both Hindus and Muslims was the mistaken view that the East India Company was masterminding mass conversion to Christianity. Nothing could be further from the truth – Company bosses were as resentful as the Indians of anything that smacked of privilege for missionaries. Nevertheless social reforms such as the abolition of *suti* in 1829 were regarded as interference with local tradition.[12] The final spark to the mutiny was the equally mistaken belief that the cartridges of the new Enfield rifle, which the infantrymen had to bite open, were greased with either lard (pork fat), anathema to Muslims, or tallow (beef fat), unthinkable to Hindus. Some

---

[10]   See Taggart, *Arthur* and W. Arthur, *A Mission to the Mysore*, (London, Partridge & Oakey, 1847).

[11]   See S. David, *The Indian Mutiny*, (London, Penguin Books, 2002).

[12]   See Warren, pp. 72–4.

civilian groups joined in the uprising, which has been labelled the first Indian war of independence. There was heavy loss of life on both sides and savage reprisals as the British troops relieved beleaguered garrisons and gained the upper hand. Missionaries and members of their families were not specifically targeted, though almost forty died. The insurrection, which lasted thirteen months, did not spread to the south and Methodists were not directly affected. But there was henceforth a much greater awareness of India in the minds of the British public. The WMMS sent funds to assist post-war relief and at last missionaries began to be sent in greater numbers.

The India to which they came had changed. The East India Company had been shorn of its power. The Raj had come into being. Signing the Act into law, the Queen proclaimed:

> Firmly relying ourselves on the truth of Christianity, and acknowledging with gratitude the solace of religion [these opening words being her own composition], We disclaim alike the right and the desire to impose Our convictions on any of Our subjects. We declare it to be Our royal will and pleasure that none be in anywise favoured, none molested or disquieted by reason of their religious faith or observance, but that all alike shall enjoy the equal and impartial protection of the law.[13]

Among the influential Methodist missionaries in South India in the latter part of the century were Henry Little (1862–92), William Burgess (1867–96), Henry Haigh (1874–1901) and William Holdsworth (1884–1900). Little came to Madras in 1862 and served in a succession of circuits before moving to Karur in 1874. He remained there until 1892 and turned an unpromising station into a hive of activity. The great famine of 1876–78, which killed some six million people in south India, left countless children orphaned. Henry Little did whatever he could to assist famine relief operations and in the aftermath he opened an orphanage where youngsters from a wide area were accommodated. He set up a vocational training programme which grew into a notable industrial school where young men and women acquired skills that would give them a livelihood; some of them became Christians. The reputation of the school was such that at one point five different Missionary Societies were sending people for training and regular government grants were obtained. Little's ministry entailed long journeys by bullock-cart, such as his 1889 tour to map out potential centres for the mission in Konga Nadu, an area south of Karur dominated by huge and wealthy Hindu temples, a striking contrast to the tiny thatched prayer sheds of the Christians. Alongside all this he was the Chairman of the Madras District from 1881 and of the Negapatam and Trichinopoly District when it separated from Madras in 1885.

---

[13] Quoted by Neill, p. 323.

Figure 8.2   Karur Industrial School, cane department, circa 1890

In 1878 Little and Burgess visited Secunderabad, the British cantonment on the north side of Hyderabad in Andhra Pradesh, in response to a letter from a Sergeant Goodwin. The prospect of a mission in the Telugu-speaking area had been considered earlier; this time it was begun. Burgess, previously in charge of ministerial training in Madras, returned there for a little while, ministering to migrant Telugu-speakers and learning their language. He was joined by a young evangelist, Benjamin Wesley. Then in 1880 they removed to Secunderabad, a move made possible because the Madras District agreed to divert £500 of its District grant. From there the Telugu mission spread to Medak, sixty miles north and Karimnagar, further north again. Converts came much more quickly than elsewhere; Burgess and his team avoided the mistakes of their forerunners. His colleagues were men already acclimatized, both physically and culturally, and proficient in Telugu. He refused to divide his time between the local people and the British soldiers – there were 150 Wesleyans among the troops in Secunderabad – and insisted on a designated military chaplain from home. He saw that Indian colleagues like Benjamin Wesley were vital to success. When success came, he was faced with the usual financial difficulties. There were chapels to be built, workers to be housed, schools established and yet, as it turned out, the church was made up almost exclusively of the most impoverished people in the area. Burgess had no qualms about appealing directly to congregations at home and the response far exceeded the Committee's grants. When he spent six months in Australia, supposedly convalescing, he spent his time on advocacy and returned with over £1,700. Direct appeals of this sort were never welcomed by those who had to raise the general funds of a missionary society but in Hyderabad it was an effective measure. Frederick Lamb, a later Chairman of the Hyderabad District, defended the policy vigorously:

> God's work must be carried on, and when ordinary resources fail others must be opened up. Those who protest should remember that red-hot appeals from the field touch hundreds who would never give to the same extent through the ordinary channels.[14]

In support of these appeals Burgess had an impressive story to relate. He told how they had opened five girls' schools in the first year – there were plenty of boys' schools in Secunderabad already. His wife Lilian and her sister Miss Hay worked energetically in the schools and would make home visits to the *zenana* quarters where women were closeted. He told how he had managed to win over (though not convert) the Muslim Nizam of Hyderabad, who was reckoned at one time to be the richest man in the world. The Nizam at first refused permission to open a mission in Karimnagar. Yet within two years he was persuaded to give his authorization and in that area the church began to take root. In 1885 came the first baptisms and by the end of the century there were fifty-four congregations in the area and 2,000 Christians in the circuit. It could hardly be described as a mass movement but the growth was at a more rapid pace than it had been anywhere in India hitherto.

Burgess spoke too of the dispute over open air preaching. Some of the Nizam's officials objected and banned it; after some sensitive negotiation he secured the right but, as a gesture of good will, never again exercised it. To establish such a rapport with a Muslim ruler was an achievement in itself. But then tragedy struck. Lilian Burgess and one of the children, returning from a visit to England to see her parents, were drowned. Like so many other bereaved missionaries he remained at his post and saw the beginnings of a mass movement to Christianity in Medak, when Karon Rajamnah, the headman of over 1,100 Mala villages, was baptized. Burgess left in 1896, the year that the redoubtable Charles Posnett arrived. Posnett recruited his sister Emilie and her friend Sarah Harris for medical work and the three of them worked in Medak for over forty years. Their first four years, the last of the century, were years of famine and cholera. The trio, at great risk to their own lives, sheltered and aided the most destitute of their neighbours who were 'untouchable' Mala people. Posnett made a schoolboy's coffin with his own hands because no carpenter would venture near his corpse. By the time the worst was over several hundred, astonished at such unaccustomed kindness, had turned to the faith from which it sprang. Even the Muslim nobility were impressed. Whereas in 1888 they had petitioned the Nizam 'to refuse the infidel dogs a foothold among the company of the faithful in Medak', ten years later they were asking him to 'give freely to the Padri Sahib and his pious sisters all the land they ask'. Although unqualified, Emilie Posnett and Sarah Harris had some basic medical training and the healing ministry formed the substance of their work. After the cholera

---

[14]   F. Lamb, *The Gospel and the Mala*, (Mysore, Wesleyan Mission Press, 1913), p. 58.

Figure 8.3   Emilie Posnett (1866–1966) and Sarah Harris (1867–1955) on tour

epidemic they ran a mobile clinic in the shape of a bullock-cart in which they toured the rural area. The people of the region then took the initiative themselves and found the land in Medak for a hospital which opened in 1902.

Henry Haigh worked in Mysore from 1874 to 1901, then became a WMMS Secretary and in 1911 President of the Conference, after which he went to serve in Ceylon and died in China. He was far-sighted, his enthusiasm was unbounded and his energy inexhaustible. Alongside circuit ministry he was for a time the editor of *The Harvest Field,* a journal on mission issues started by Thomas Hodson, which became renowned throughout India and appeared monthly until 1919. Haigh himself founded a weekly in Kannada, *Vrittanta Patrike,* which was not a church paper but was intended to provide the general public with a Christian viewpoint on current affairs. Its circulation grew to 5,000 and in remoter villages a single copy might be read aloud to large groups. For thirty years until 1870 the Mysore District's press in Bangalore had produced a stream of vernacular and English literature but it was then closed due to competition from more modern presses. Haigh, on his appointment to Mysore City in 1889, re-established a quality press there on which *Vrittanta Patrike* and many other publications were printed. In due course its reputation for quality became such that for years the Oxford University Press found it economical to have books printed in Mysore. As Chairman of the District, Haigh welcomed colleagues from the Women's Auxiliary (WA) and *Joyful*

News Evangelists. He implemented his vision of a hostel where WA workers could live together in their early years of orientation and language study.

Haigh's colleague in Mysore City was William Holdsworth. Several of their schemes were effected through the generosity of Australian women who financed Hardwicke College, named after their own high school in Adelaide. Holdsworth secured more donations while on furlough, which enabled the College complex to develop. The campus housed the press and the women workers' residence, alongside the boarding school for boys where Holdsworth was head teacher, a hostel for Christian young men working in the city, a commercial school and a small theological institution. In 1898 an outbreak of Bubonic Plague spread to Mysore and raged virulently in the slum quarters where untouchables lived in insanitary squalor. Holdsworth found a plot of land where some could be rehoused in cleaner conditions and it became known as Karunapura, 'City of Mercy'. At this time he saw how inadequate, or non-existent, were medical facilities in Mysore and determined to build a hospital. He had returned to England by the time it was completed and his wife Mary had died shortly after their return: when it was opened by the Maharaja of Mysore in 1905 it was named after her. This was the same William Holdsworth who twenty years later was called on to finish Findlay's monumental *History of the WMMS*.

North India

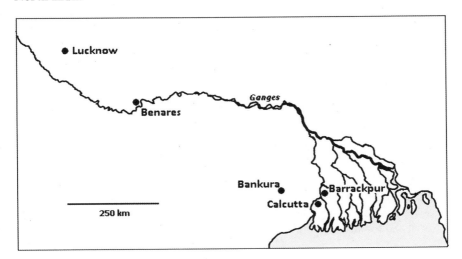

Map 8   North India

Short-lived and unproductive ministries in Bombay and Calcutta were the extent of the Society's activity in the north in the first half of the nineteenth century. Each was terminated by a Committee short of funds and impatient for quick results.

Among the European community, however, Methodism was known and appealed to some. Fanny Parks, the wife of a civil servant, recorded in her journal for 1830:

> Methodism is gaining ground very fast in Cawnpore; young ladies sometimes profess to believe it highly incorrect to go to balls, plays, races, or to any party where it is possible there may be a quadrille. A number of the officers also profess these opinions, and set themselves up as New Lights.[15]

It was only after the rebellion, with the British public now far more aware of India and its army of occupation, that Methodism returned to the north, with appointments made 'for the spiritual benefit of the Methodist soldiers' in Karachi (later taken over by American Methodists) and Barrackpur, the garrison ten miles from Calcutta. There was still no focused work among Indians and though mission stations were opened in Calcutta and Lucknow in the 1860s this second venture met with no more success than in 1830. George Baugh, appointed Chairman of the District in 1876 after 16 years in Ceylon, wrote a forthright letter to the Secretaries about 'the fatal error of spreading ourselves over more ground than we can cover':

> ... one or two Missionaries doing mixed work, frequently exchanged and never mastering a knowledge of the language or of the manners of the people, is really no more than playing at mission work, very little more than mere waste of time and money.[16]

His words are reminiscent of the Cape Colony missionaries' stance in 1824[17] and were equally unheeded. Eventually, however, J. Milton Brown, who also had sixteen years' experience in Ceylon, came to Calcutta. Between 1883 and 1900 he revitalized the work. Schools were opened. Bengali ministers were trained. Energetic young missionaries made extensive tours of rural areas. Camp meetings were held. There were signs that the Santal people – a tribal group occupying a large area north-west of Calcutta where mining was replacing agriculture – might be responsive to the gospel, although there was as yet nothing approaching a mass movement among them. The CMS withdrew from this region and shortly after the Methodists took over baptisms began to be recorded. The town of Bankura became, half a century after Hodson and Percival had to abandon their plan to establish an outpost there, a significant Methodist centre. Among the missionaries who worked there was Ambery Smith who took note of the ravages of leprosy in the area and founded asylums both in nearby Raniganj and in Bankura itself. The

---

[15]   Journal 7 October 1830, in F. Parks, *Wanderings of a pilgrim in search of the picturesque*, (2 vols, London, Pelham Richardson, 1850; reprinted Karachi, Oxford University Press, 1975), vol. 1, p. 161.

[16]   Baugh to 'Brother Kilner', 23 April 1877: SOAS, MMS/India/Correspondence/Calcutta/FBN1 – one of several such strongly worded letters.

[17]   See p. 82.

Ambery Smiths served in Bengal from 1886 to 1911. One who made life difficult for them early in their ministry was a Brahmin, Kulada Prasad Pande, of whom his son said:

> He was very hostile to the Christian missionaries. He couldn't stand them going about preaching the Gospel ... Then once, when there was an epidemic of cholera in the city, and hundreds of our poor, sweeper-class community were dying, he was greatly struck by the service which the two church missionaries [the Ambery Smiths] ... rendered to these untouchable sweepers. My father used to persecute them ... But he was struck by their service, and that has drawn him in, and at last made him the servant of Christ.[18]

Pande announced his conversion at Christmas 1890 and a communal riot ensued. The Pandes's son was baptized 'Christa Charan' meaning 'at the feet of Christ'.[19] C.C. Pande was the long-serving Chairman who led the Bengal District into the Church of North India in 1970.

The Lucknow and Benares District was separated in 1879, for administrative reasons and not because the work had grown – the District had just sixty-one members at its inception. In Lucknow they came from the troops. In Benares, that great centre of Hindu pilgrimage, the tiny Methodist presence had no more impact than had the other Societies working there. A new attempt to promote the cause in Bombay began in 1887, but the missionaries' activity was confined to Europeans while an evangelist, Samuel Rahator, worked unaided in Marathi. A Hindu converted through the witness of William Burgess, Rahator was ordained in 1894 and built up a little congregation which was still numbered in single figures at the century's end.

The last years of the 1890s were marked throughout India by famine, plague (which almost took Rahator's life), earthquake and cyclone. These calamities prompted generous gifts from England and enabled the church to engage with the needs, particularly providing Homes for orphans and widows. Once the glare of publicity faded, however, the funds dried up – a story repeated again and again in many places. The Mission struggled to maintain its institutions and had no resources to respond to other opportunities.

Caste and Conversion

Missionary activity took place against the background of the caste system. The churches founded by the early Protestant missionaries were accustomed 'to sit at church in two separate divisions, and had communicated separately at the Lord's

18   C. Mayhew, *Men Seeking God*, (London, Allen & Unwin, 1955), p. 81.
19   J. Clapham, 'Bengal Methodism: First Hundred Years', in N.B. Mitra (ed.), *Methodist in Bengal*, (Kolkata, Diamond Art Press, 2007), p. 28.

table, drinking out of the same cup, but high-caste converts drinking first'.[20] The second Anglican bishop, Reginald Heber, concluded that caste distinction was a worldly matter irrelevant to Christian mission:

> It is an intelligible and appreciable Christian principle that all men in the sight of God are equal. But it is equally certain that all are not equal in the sight of Man; and it is a fair presumption that God never intended them to be equal. Social distinctions exist everywhere ... why should we endanger the success of our efforts by endeavouring to enforce a law of equality, which is maintained among no other classes of men?[21]

But on closer acquaintance the pernicious element in the system could not be denied. Back in 1814, Andrew Armour had written from Colombo about the lingering influence of caste among converts, commenting that 'heart conversion' was required as well as 'head conversion'.[22] By 1833 Bishop Daniel Wilson was ready to write a pastoral letter denouncing caste 'eating as doth a cancer into the vitals of our infant Churches' and declaring that 'the distinction of caste must be abandoned, decidedly, immediately, and finally'. Methodists were of the same view and Wilson's long letter was printed in full in the WMMS *Missionary Notices*.[23] In 1847 two able Tamil Christians who had been recognized as 'Assistant Missionaries' and were due to be ordained were dismissed because they refused to renounce caste privileges and rules. This incident prompted a categorical declaration:

1. No person holding caste in any respect shall be employed as a paid agent in the Church.
2. No person holding caste in any respect shall be admitted as a member of our Society.
3. No candidate for admission into the Church shall be baptised until he has given satisfactory proof of having entirely renounced caste.[24]

The result was a decline in membership. The majority had until then been Sudras but before long the proportion of Sudra and outcaste members was reversed. Other denominations had similar experiences, though in Negapatam the Lutherans took a more relaxed view and all but a few Wesleyans transferred their allegiance to a church which tolerated their prejudices.

---

20   J.W. Kaye, *Christianity in India: An Historical Narrative*, (London, Smith, Elder & Co., 1859), p. 352.

21   Kaye, pp. 355–6.

22   Letter to the Committee, 29 July 1814, quoted in Taggart, 'Methodist Foreign Missions, The First Half Century', in *WHS Proceedings*, vol. 45, October 1986, p. 167.

23   *Missionary Notices*, July 1834, pp. 493–6.

24   Findlay and Holdsworth, vol. 5, p. 139.

Plenty of unequivocal statements were made down the years. A Conference of Protestant missionaries in Bangalore in 1879 pronounced:

> … it is diametrically opposed to the Christian doctrine of the unity of mankind and of the brotherhood of all true Christians. It is therefore the duty of all Missionaries and Societies to demand an absolute renunciation of caste and all its outward manifestations from those who desire to be received into the Church of Christ.[25]

Similar declarations were made by successive Conferences, but in 1906 the Anglican J.A. Sharrock was driven to say 'We speak against it, we write against it and in fact we do everything but act against it.' A socio–cultural structure that had been 3,500 years in the making proved impervious to such resolutions. In so far as it was a cultural or socio–economic phenomenon, caste was challenged, just like slavery and apartheid, by Paul's resounding 'There is no difference between Jews and Gentiles, slave and free, men and women; you are all one in union with Christ Jesus' (Galatians 3:28) and by Jesus' mission statement at Nazareth, 'to set free the oppressed' (Luke 4:18). But it had also to be challenged at the level of the Hindu belief system sustaining it. It was bound up with the doctrine of *karma*, according to which people are reborn according to their deeds. The supreme reward of good deeds is to be born a Brahman; the penalty for evil is to be born into a lower form of animal life. To be an untouchable is scarcely better than the latter. That much was easy to grasp, but few westerners were equipped to engage at a deeper level with Hinduism. Missionary reports fed the home constituency with a simplistic vocabulary composed of words like *deluded, benighted* and *idolatrous heathen*. Though men like T.E. Slater, the LMS missionary who went to India in 1866 and has been called 'the earliest missiologist of the modern kind',[26] were far more respectful, it would be many years before his approach – 'We shall never gain the non-Christian world until we treat its religions with justice, courtesy and love' – was taken seriously.[27] James Cooling, Chairman of the Madras District from 1888 until his death in 1915, took up what was very much a minority position when he claimed that while caste was not to be tolerated in the church it was not necessarily a bad thing in Hindu society. Nobly attempting to see the world as a Hindu sees it, he made the extraordinary claim that the caste system was 'practically the only bulwark Hinduism has against immorality'.[28]

---

[25] Findlay and Holdsworth, vol. 5, p. 140.
[26] K.R. Cracknell, *Justice, Courtesy and Love*, (London, Epworth Press, 1995), p. 108.
[27] Ibid., p. 119.
[28] G.A. Oddie, *Social Protest in India: British Protestant Missionaries and Social Reforms 1850–1900*, (New Delhi, Manohar, 1979), p. 57.

Wesleyans on the whole engaged with Hinduism at a practical rather than philosophical level. Converts were shunned by their families and excluded from community life. In law the male convert forfeited the right to inherit family property, the right to hold any public office and the right to remarry if deserted by his wife. The abolition of these 'disabilities' – the first two by 1830, the third in 1866 – affected the convert's legal status but not his social position. There was an incident in Madras in 1858 when a schoolboy made a confession of faith and sought baptism. When his parents failed to deter him, the manse where he was staying was stormed by a mob and both he and the missionaries had to clamber over the compound wall to escape. The house was wrecked. New Christians, in general younger people, had not only to be nurtured in the faith but sheltered and equipped to make a living without the support of their caste. Some found employment in missionaries' homes or, if better educated, in mission schools, but that could provide for only a few. Industrial schools, as at Karur, were another part of the answer.

Writing in 1891, William Goudie vividly described the situation he found in the Paraiyur communities around Madras:

> It is often the case that in a Pareiyah village there is not a family that has not been plundered and ruined through having to put their 'sign' to what they could not read, and yet these very people will say, 'Why should our children read and write? Will that fill their bellies?' They are so poor and oppressed that every child of four and upwards has to help in seeking food. They are scarcely old enough to come to school when they are sent to the fields to pick up cow dung for fuel or manure, to tend sheep and cattle, or to seek crabs in the streams for food ... It is often pitiful to see a poor little girl of scarcely five years striving to keep awake at the night school after a long day of toddling in the scorching heat after the sheep and goats. Our work is almost entirely among the Pareiyahs or non-caste people. It would be more correct to say that we work among all, but our fruit is chiefly among them, and that has made us feel committed to them as a class. Their condition is one of great destitution, and they have been for twenty centuries the victims of cruel oppression, oppression which has not yet ceased.[29]

In 1893 a convert in Mysore saw his wife and children removed by his relatives the moment he was baptized and a lawsuit for the recovery of the children was thrown out on the grounds that in becoming a Christian he had forfeited his civil rights, his children and his property. Even under the Raj, the disabilities persisted in the Princely States. The WMMS Secretaries joined with those of the LMS and CMS in petitioning for a change in the law. But the Viceroy, more concerned to avoid unrest than to uphold justice, would have none of it. He took the view that such legislation, 'while it would be unpopular and might become a source of trouble, would fail to benefit those in whose interests it was designed'. In

---

[29]   J. Lewis, *William Goudie*, (London, WMMS, 1923), pp. 50–51.

corroboration the Prime Minister of Travancore State, a Brahman, advised him that in his jurisdiction there would be no point, since converts came from classes owning little or no property.

The last statement was undoubtedly true. For most of the century the number of conversions had been small. By the final decade there were many more, drawn chiefly from the outcaste communities.[30] Yet so ingrained was the discriminatory system, even among the 'untouchable' *panchamas*, that those who found freedom in Christ could not shake themselves free of it. In 1887, as the gospel began to change lives in Karimnagar, both low-caste Sudras and outcaste Malas were baptized but the Sudra converts could not accept that they were now 'one body' with people they despised and drifted away. The Mala themselves had no dealings with the leather-worker Madigas and, while willing to worship with converted Madigas, would not eat with them; so the Medak seminary (reported Edgar Thompson in 1919) had two kitchens. Mala–Madiga disputes persisted into the twenty-first century, but within the Christian community sensitive handling of the issue by church leaders defused them. In 1921, when the first Madiga children were admitted to Siddapett circuit boarding school,

> Only three Mala boys ran away … The Mala and Madiga children became quite friendly in a surprisingly short time, walking arm in arm and playing with each other as if they had always been the best of friends.[31]

Education

There was not the scholastic tradition in India that the missionaries found in Ceylon. The education of Indians was no more encouraged by the East India Company than was the propagation of Christianity. The foundation of Carey's 'College for the instruction of Asiatic, Christian and other youth, in Eastern Literature and European Science', opened at Serampore in 1819, was a significant step, though it began with only thirty-seven students. Wesleyan schools had more humble titles and more modest aims, but were deemed an indispensible ancillary of church-planting. It was axiomatic that a pioneer missionary would start a school, built of mud and thatch, usually on the same plot as chapel and manse. Not only the scholars but the teacher had to be recruited, for in the early days few missionaries had sufficient command of the vernacular to teach and they were, in any case, often away from home. The first teachers were hardly ever Christians themselves. When it came to Christian instruction, they interpreted for the missionary and were perhaps more likely than the pupils to be enlightened.

---

[30]   See J.R. Pritchard, *Methodists and their Missionary Societies 1900–1996* (Aldershot, Ashgate Publishing, 2014), chapter 6.

[31]   WMMS *Report*, 1922, p. 40.

There were three major debates about educational policy in the course of the century. One, as in Ceylon, was about the relative value of schooling and preaching. Another was about concentrating resources on English-medium or on vernacular schools. The third concerned whether or not to accept government grants after policy changed in the 1850s.

Thomas Cryer (Madras District, 1829–52), like Stott in Ceylon at the same period, argued for the priority of itinerant evangelism. Ideally it would be best for each station to have two missionaries, one of whom would be touring the villages and the other engaged in schoolwork, alternating every few weeks as Hodson had proposed. But it was a pipe-dream: there was no prospect of getting enough staff to make that work. Furthermore schools were costly and funds were as deficient as personnel. Others supported Hodson's line and pressed for intensification rather than dispersion, even if it meant contacting fewer villages. To visit many places at infrequent intervals, they said, was a waste of effort. Concentrated teaching was far more likely to win disciples. It did indeed win some and very gradually Indian Christians with a measure of education did begin to emerge as village teachers or catechists, often combining both roles. Yet numbers were depressingly small.

The case for English language teaching in India is associated with the name of Alexander Duff. He was a Church of Scotland missionary sent to Calcutta in 1830 with a remit to set up vernacular teacher-training. But he was soon persuaded by the views of Thomas Macaulay, the MP and historian, who held that the way forward was to give the brightest and best Indians a solid grounding in western languages and sciences. He expected them in turn to hand their learning on, for the ultimate benefit of all India. For Duff this meant that even in elementary schools English should be used. There was a desire for it and there were Indians ready to pay school fees for it. Of course those who could afford it were members of the higher castes and the debate was also about élitist or popular education. If big investments were to be made, said opponents of Duff's policy, it should not be for the benefit of high-caste families. Brahmins were arguably the people least likely to be influenced by the gospel, but most likely to accrue more social, economic and political power and it would be wrong to reinforce their privileges to the detriment of the poorest Indians. Yet Duff's policy was akin to that of missionaries elsewhere who encouraged kings and chiefs to put their sons in school: convert the chief and the people will follow. His goal was unequivocally evangelistic and his methods were widely adopted.

The Wesleyan solution was to establish 'Anglo-vernacular' schools, with teaching in the local tongue and English as a foreign language at upper grades. Hostels for boarders were common, accommodating scholars from outlying villages. What became of most pupils is not recorded, but small numbers became Christians and some went on to ministerial training and ordination. Noteworthy efforts were made to get girls into school, for as one missionary pertinently remarked, 'What is needed for the conversion of India is a new race of grandmothers.'[32] Many missionaries' wives were able to devote themselves to this work; it was easier to be a working mother where there was an *ayah* to care for the children. Mary Batchelor started a girls' school in Negapatam immediately after she married in 1842 and, after much itineration round the District, was still running it in 1858. With as many as sixty scholars, half of them boarders, she needed help. Eventually two women were sent from England to assist her. One was her own daughter and the other did not arrive as she promptly married a missionary. It was however Mary Batchelor's persistence that led to the appointment of more women missionaries, for teaching, medical and evangelistic work.[33] Another notable figure was Mrs Joseph Roberts. Her husband, Chairman of the Madras District, died in 1849. She stayed on for another ten years and saw the orphanage she had begun grow into the Madras Wesley Girls' High School, becoming its first headmistress.

The two conflicting pressures remained. There was still a demand for vernacular schools, but the cry for English language High Schools grew more strident. When Edward Hardey went on furlough in 1853 he took a petition in nine languages, signed by prominent figures of Mysore City, asking the WMMS to provide an English school. The Committee could offer no help, but it opened anyway, funded briefly by the donations of well-wishers and within a short while by charging fees.

The availability of government grants eventually set mission schools on a sounder footing. Even before the transfer of power the East India Company's Board of Control in London was working on a scheme to extend educational provision. But if its hostility to missions had waned, wariness remained. To be eligible for a grant-in-aid, officials insisted, there could be no Bible teaching at the new school in Mysore during school hours. After the war a more detailed and less inflexible scheme was produced and implemented. Any agency running schools or colleges could claim grants provided they followed government syllabuses and agreed to government inspections. Religious instruction would be allowed provided other subjects were taught satisfactorily.

The missions decided to co-operate with this plan. Some warned they would soon find themselves compromised, but there was no strong resistance. Before long two-thirds of the cost of education was being borne by the government and the missions were able to expand both their schools and their other activities. The number of institutions multiplied. Fed by a network of elementary schools, the Methodist High Schools in Madras, Negapatam, Bangalore and Mysore all expanded during the 1860s and 1870s and were able to offer better qualifications to the most successful students. The Madras Christian College, run jointly by the Church of Scotland, CMS and Wesleyan Mission from 1878, had exceptionally high standards.

There was, however, a price to pay. One of the great evils of the day was the opium trade. Opium 'is small in bulk, light, not quickly perishable, and very expensive. The revenue derived from the export duties was an essential item in the

---

[32]   Webb, p. 30.
[33]   See p. pp. 247–8.

Indian government's budget.'[34] A long war was waged against the trade, with as much fervour and as little success as the campaigns against the slave trade in the eighteenth century and the arms trade in more recent times. Ashley, the future Lord Shaftesbury, moved a resolution in parliament in 1843, after the first Opium War,

> That it is the opinion of this House that the continuance of the trade in opium, and the monopoly of its growth in the territories of British India, are destructive of all relations of amity between England and China, injurious to the manufacturing interests of the country by the very serious diminution of legitimate commerce, and utterly inconsistent with the honour and duties of a Christian kingdom.[35]

But to no effect: the trade 'continued for three generations to enrich individuals, to disgrace governments, and to perplex the Christian conscience of the world'.[36] When Company rule ended in 1858, revenue from the opium trade amounted to one seventh of its total income.[37] The missionary conscience was especially perplexed and lamentably divided. The most vociferous missionary apologists for the traffic were found among those working in education, who feared the loss of opium revenue would mean cuts in government grants. In 1893, after a Missionary Conference in Bombay failed to condemn the trade, the *Bombay Guardian*, a Christian weekly, thundered:

> When men who have been deputed to come to India by the Churches of Great Britain to work for the salvation of souls confess that they are silent on an official crime that is dragging millions down to perdition, through fear of having their grants diminished, it is time the home Churches should consider their relationship between the work of God and mammon.[38]

and Hugh Price Hughes, speaking at a meeting of the Anti-Opium League at Exeter Hall in London, said that never in his life had he

> witnessed anything more deplorable than this exhibition of sane men, professing to represent the missionary societies in India, standing up to resist the protest that comes to us from the bleeding hearts of missionaries in China.

It was, he said, 'the most appalling proof of the demoralising effect of associating with Indian officialdom'.[39]

---

34   Neill, p. 131–2.
35   Lord Ashley's speech was reported in *The Times,* 5 April 1843.
36   Neill, p. 135.
37   Oddie, p. 222.
38   *Bombay Guardian*, 7 January 1893.
39   15 February 1893.

Not until 1916 did the 'Anglo–Oriental Society for the Suppression of the Opium Trade' achieve its ends. The matter was never at the forefront of WMMS concerns, whereas educational policy was subject to constant review. Repeated reports recognized that the schools served a tiny fraction of India's people and that out of that fraction only a very few actually became Christians. Whatever the quality of the education, it needed to be complemented by a more direct proclamation of the faith in terms that would engage lively young minds. However encouraging the response of lowly villagers to the gospel, it was vital to invest in the evangelization of the educated.

The Missionary Controversy

That focus on the cultured, high-caste élite was vigorously challenged by four articles which appeared in the *Methodist Times* in April 1889. They were written by Henry Lunn (later Sir Henry), a minister and doctor who had just returned from India. The Society had sent him to establish a hospital at Tiruvalur, near Negapatam, but illness had forced him to return within a year and he was then stationed at the West London Mission with Hugh Price Hughes, the editor of the paper. The first article was endorsed by Hughes's leader headed *The Fatal Mistake of Dr Duff*. Lunn observed that after seventy years of Wesleyan mission in India the number of Christians was pitifully small. The expense on English-medium schools was unproductive and the diversion of resources from vernacular evangelization was a disaster. He detected a feeling in some circles that, if the depressed class groups really did become Christian *en masse*, it would undermine the decades of painstaking work among the higher castes, by confirming their suspicion that Christianity is after all only for the poor and ignorant.

A second criticism concerned the life-style of missionaries. In Africa the pioneers built their own homes, fetched their own water, grew and hunted their own food and all too often died on the job. In India, with a well developed economy, an approximation to western modes of living was possible, life was less hard and death less frequent. The prerequisite to being an effective missionary is to survive, which meant being 'properly fed and housed, and ... so provided for that [they are] able to work without distraction'.[40] Some tried to live Indian-style, on an Indian diet and with the rudimentary facilities of Indian village homes. All too often the result was that they fell ill and had to be repatriated or needed a long period of recuperation. Others erred in the opposite direction. Lunn and Hughes charged the whole missionary corps with an unnecessarily lavish lifestyle, akin to that enjoyed by the upper échelons of the European community, and with failing to socialize with their Indian colleagues. In sum, they were accused of preoccupation with the élite and aloofness from the masses. They had abandoned their proper sphere of work and entailed the Society in needless expense.

---

[40]   G. John, *A Voice from China*, (London, James Clarke & Co, 1907), p. 215.

These articles echoed the findings of an eminent Baptist MP, W.S. Caine, after a visit to India the previous year. They brought immediate denials. The controversy dominated the Methodist papers for months. Thomas Champness entered the fray, supporting the criticisms in his halfpenny-a-week, *Joyful News*. He had just begun to send lay evangelists to India under his own independent low-budget arrangement and, on the basis of very limited experience, had concluded that European agents could be maintained a deal more cheaply than the missionaries were. The Missionary Committee resisted the charges. They were debated in the 1889 Conference before there had been time for anything more than an initial, appalled reaction from India. On the education question, Conference followed the Committee's line: 'It is necessary to maintain our existing educational enterprises' but 'the main energy of our Missions in India is devoted to directly evangelistic efforts'. On the lifestyle question, Conference was firm: 'The Conference is convinced that there is no ground for believing that our Missionaries live, or wish to live, in habits of self-indulgence; but that, on the contrary, they are an earnest and self-denying class of men.'

That was by no means the end of the matter. Hughes accepted the resolution but declared he could not retract the statements in his paper that had caused offence. Then protests from India began to arrive and a Conference of Wesleyan Missionaries representing all the Indian Districts met in Bangalore. It issued a sweeping repudiation of the allegations and called for a commission of enquiry. In London a sub-committee was appointed in due course, chaired by the President. Two missionaries (George Patterson of the Madras Christian College and William Findlay from Negapatam) were sent home from India specially to testify before it. Hughes, Lunn and Champness were heard, the household accounts of missionaries' wives were subjected to scrutiny, many hours were spent in cross-examination of witnesses and compiling a report. It found

> that our Indian Missionaries have not the means to live, and do not desire to live, in luxury, as our English middle classes understand the word

and

> that the assertion that the manner or place of living of the Indian Missionaries tends to alienate them from the Native population, or hinders the success of their Native work, is not sustained. In the cases in which the attempt has been made to live in Native quarters and in the manner of the Native population, the sacrifice of life and health has been great, and it appears to have been attended by no compensating advantage as regards the success of the labour so carried on. The Sub-Committee also is of the opinion that the relations between the Missionaries and the Native Ministers are cordial and fraternal.[41]

----

[41]   WMMS (corporately compiled), *The missionary controversy: discussion, evidence and report*, (London, WMMS, 1890), pp. 241–2. Longer extracts from this report are in

The 1890 Conference endorsed these findings and exonerated the missionaries and Lunn soon resigned from the ministry. But damage had been done. Wesleyans in Britain were deeply troubled and the Society's income fell to the lowest level it had reached in 40 years.[42]

Burma

The British occupation of Burma began in 1824 and in 1886 it was made part of the Raj. Only then did the Society contemplate extending its work in that direction. A challenge to 'attempt something fresh' had come from Hugh Price Hughes the

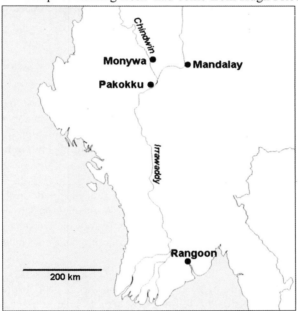

Map 9   Burma

previous year. Critical as he was of some things, he was an enthusiast for foreign missions. He pointed out with typical candour that in twenty-five years 'only one fresh mission in heathen lands' had been launched. So when the experienced Ripley Winston told the Committee that he felt called to go to Burma, where, he wrote, 'the population of several million has been suddenly released from ... tyranny and misrule and thrown open to the Gospel', they took up his offer. Winston had worked in Ceylon and was then in south India. After a preliminary

Davies, George and Rupp, vol. 4, pp. 575–84.
[42]   Findlay and Holdsworth, vol. 1, pp. 137–60.

Figure 8.4   Mandalay, Burma Girls' Boarding and Training School, 1894

visit to explore the terrain, he settled in Mandalay; other Missions were already engaged in Rangoon and Lower Burma. He was joined by two evangelists from Ceylon, familiar with the Theravada Buddhism dominant in both countries. He was soon reporting with excitement and optimism. But his high hopes were not to be fulfilled.

> Successive generations of missionaries ... struggled with heat, disease, political nationalism, systematic opposition from Buddhist leaders and a sense of frustration ... A mere trickle of converts [was] won over to Christianity from Buddhism. 'Successes' were measured in ones and twos rather than in thousands.[43]

Following the usual pattern, an English school was opened in Pakokku, some seventy miles from Mandalay, followed by a girls' boarding school. The news that a Burmese princess had become a Christian was joyfully regaled in England. 'No girl,' said Winston roundly but wrongly, 'can pass through the school without being converted.' An 'Asylum for Lepers' was opened in Monywa, with financial support from the Leprosy Mission and the moral but categorically *not* financial support of the WMMS. At first the victims of leprosy could not believe anybody cared about them and suspected they were being lured there to be poisoned. Once these suspicions were disproved, the Asylum developed rapidly and by 1898 there were three brick-built wards, another five built of wood, a dispensary, a children's home and a chapel. Winston could look at these achievements with satisfaction when he left Burma in 1898, disappointed as he must have been that there were

---

[43]   E.A. Bishop, 'Leaving Burma for Good', (privately circulated, 2006): p. iii.

fewer than two hundred Christians under his care. The extension of the mission to the hill people of the north-west came later.

Harbingers of Things to Come

There was no thought of separating the Indian Districts from the British Conference, as happened in Australasia and Canada in the 1850s and South Africa in 1883. A measure of devolution took place when in 1893 three Provincial Synods were established, for Ceylon, for South India and for North India including Burma. They met annually, the members being appointed by the District Synods. Indian ministers and even a handful of laypeople were representatives, but the dominant voice was still that of the missionary.

Wesleyans did not work in isolation from other missionaries. Nor did they take their holidays in isolation. In May every year Europeans and Americans would leave the sweltering plains for a vacation in one of the hill stations, where they would meet and exchange their stories and hopes. In 1852 a gathering of missionaries was organized at Ootacamund, the summer seat of the Madras government. Similar assemblies took place in Kodaikanal, the favoured retreat of most missionaries in the south, and in other parts of India. Decennial Missionary Conferences in Calcutta began in 1862. There was a General Missionary Conference in Allahabad in 1872, followed by a South India Conference in Madras in 1879. In between such events, the degree of co-operation varied from place to place. Comity – agreements not to duplicate others' efforts but to concentrate on discrete areas – had limited effect. The concept of organic union still lay in the future. But the hill resort meetings became more formalized; a South India Missionary Association was formed in 1897 and set up a Conference in Madras in 1900 which brought together about 150 missionaries, not self-selected but appointed by their churches or organizations. Forty-five bodies were represented, forming a Christian community of 350,000, of whom 150,000 were Anglicans and 12,000 Wesleyans.

Out of the 150 participants, only twenty-four were Indians. Indian nationalism was still in its infancy – the Indian National Congress was formed in 1885, the Moslem League not until 1906. Self-government, in church as in state, was still on the distant horizon.

Chapter 9
The Challenge of China

By the nineteenth century the Qing dynasty, which had ruled China since 1644, was struggling to retain its authority. The Emperor and his court were Manchus from the north-east. Most Han Chinese lived in the south, subject to and resentful of their overlords. Lord Macartney, Britain's first envoy to China, described in 1795 'the tyranny of a handful of Tartars over more than three hundred million Chinese'. The next 120 years were a time of economic stagnation, social unrest and western penetration, culminating in the downfall of the Qing and the advent of a republic in 1912.

Macartney's mission failed to establish diplomatic relations or negotiate a trade treaty. China, which gave the world paper, gunpowder, the compass and the printing press and vaunted its self-sufficiency, was unaware of, uninterested in and eventually undone by the European industrial revolution. Macartney was told that China had no use for manufactured products and would only accept payment for its exports in silver. For the East India Company, banking on a continued supply of tea, silk and porcelain, this had by the 1830s become problematic. Europe's stocks of precious metals were seriously depleted. However, the Company found a lucrative alternative in opium and deliberately stimulated its production in India.

In 1839 the Emperor sent a special commissioner to Guangzhou (known to Europeans as Canton), where all international trade was carried on. Foreign merchants were banned from the rest of China; one of Macartney's aims and failures had been to get the restrictions lifted. The commissioner's instructions were to stamp out the opium business. He had all the stock in the warehouses destroyed and refused any compensation. Tension escalated. The British were formally excluded from Guangzhou and the Opium War broke out. China's forces were routed. Their wooden junks and ill-equipped troops were out-manoeuvred and out-gunned. A humiliated emperor was compelled by the Treaty of Nanjing in 1842 to cede Hong Kong and open up five 'Treaty Ports' to international trade. In each of these cities there were to be 'concessions' where British subjects were immune to Chinese law.

It was a sordid episode. William Gladstone's judgement was that 'a war more unjust in its origin, a war more calculated in its progress to cover this country with permanent disgrace, I do not know, and have not read of'.[1] It fuelled Chinese resentment not only of the emperor who was responsible for their humiliation, but even more of the 'long-noses' – or, less politely, 'foreign devils'. It also paved the way for Missionary Societies. On the one hand they could see that the trade, the

---

[1]   *Hansard*, 8 April 1840.

war and the 'Unequal Treaties' were deplorable; yet on the other, they concluded that God had wrought good out of evil by opening China to the gospel.

Map 10   China: Wesleyan stations

South China[2]

The first Protestant missionary to work in China was Robert Morrison of the LMS, in 1807; over the next 30 years barely fifty followed in his wake. By 1842 seven societies had arrived on the scene; twenty more appeared in a dozen years after the Treaty was signed. Wesleyans did not immediately join the influx. The Society was in debt and Bunting and Beecham urged the Conference of 1846 not to embark on another costly venture when there were insufficient funds to consolidate the work being pioneered in other places. However, donations earmarked for China were received, including one from a Royal Engineer stationed in Hong Kong. Rowland Rees, who was leading a class-meeting there, accompanied his gift with a letter urging that a missionary be sent to each of the five Treaty Ports. But these contributions could only be held in a special account to await a more opportune moment. When in 1850 George Piercy, a Yorkshire farmer's son and local preacher, declared he had a call to go to China, the Society was unable to

---

[2]   J.R. Rose, *A Church Born to Suffer*, (London, Cargate Press, 1951) recounts the 100-year-long history of the South China District.

support him. Piercy, however, was a determined young man. He persuaded his father to pay for a one-way passage and extracted from the WMMS Secretaries a letter of introduction.

In January 1851 he arrived in Hong Kong. The letter was to Sergeant Ross, who had taken over Rees's class. But Ross died a week before Piercy landed. The class had shrivelled to one. Undeterred, Piercy gathered another group of soldiers, rented a house where he led worship and applied himself to studying Chinese and acquiring a rudimentary knowledge of medicine. For him Hong Kong was only a staging post. As soon as he felt able, he took a junk up the Pearl River to Guangzhou. In both places it was due to the support and encouragement of LMS missionaries that he managed to survive and establish himself.

From Guangzhou in 1852 he again approached the WMMS. He reported his movements and his studies and sent an assurance of his adherence to Methodist doctrine and discipline. In London the challenge could no longer be resisted. Thomas Farmer, the Society's Treasurer, was an enthusiast for the project and renewed a very generous offer of financial support. Two young ministers, William Beach and Josiah Cox, said they were ready to go to China. So it was that they were ordained and sailed in 1853, accompanied by Piercy's fiancée, Joan Wannop. They carried a parchment certifying Piercy to be ordained, albeit without imposition of hands, and a set of instructions putting him in charge of the mission. In mid-year, George and Joan were married. In December, the three men held a Synod. No doubt Joan made them tea; but, although Wesleyan Synods then were strictly for the ordained, she must have been party to their plans, problems and prayers. She had spent the years of her engagement at Westminster College and within months of her arrival she started a girls' school. It began with just three pupils – her husband's boys' school was a little bigger – but in 1858, after a period of exile in Macau, she opened what was said to be the first boarding school for girls in China.

Reviewing their first few months in China, their daily attempts to proclaim the gospel at street corners in halting Cantonese, their little schools, the Synod was realistic about the task on which they had embarked. They knew that Robert Morrison and the LMS colleagues who subsequently joined him had between them baptized just ten converts in twenty-seven years. Their report warned the Committee at home not to expect many converts for a long time. Nothing daunted, they began preaching tours of the countryside around and Piercy tackled the translation of catechisms and hymns. To help in the task the LMS lent him the services of Liang Fa, one of Morrison's converts and the earliest Chinese Protestant preacher.

As the quartet were getting into their stride, southern China was convulsed by the Taiping rebellion. The Taiping ('Great Peace') Heavenly Kingdom was proclaimed in 1851 by Hong Xiuquan, who had been deeply affected by some pamphlets Liang Fa had written many years earlier.[3] As a result of his reading

---

[3] See P.R. Bohr, 'Liang Fa's Quest for Moral Power', in *Christianity in China: Early Protestant Missionary Writings*, ed. S.W. Barnett and J.K. Fairbank, (Cambridge, Mass,

he thought he had made sense of a vision in which he had seen God the Father and God's son, Jesus, and had been anointed as Jesus' younger brother, 'God's Chinese Son'.[4] He had gathered disciples and formed a Christian sect with a strict moral code and a grand ambition to convert the Chinese people and overthrow the decadent Manchu dynasty. Missionaries – both the Wesleyan novices and others with a longer view – at first had high hopes of the movement. Cox, who became friendly with Hong's cousin, wrote

> When I came to China I felt all around me the gloom of midnight darkness; now the clouds seem to be breaking, and I know not what the day may bring, but I hail the glimmering dawn.[5]

Hong's zealous band of converts rallied other dissident groups to their cause and soon he raised an army of several hundred thousand which swept through the southern provinces with spectacular success and in 1853 took the city of Nanjing, which he made his capital, proclaiming himself the Taiping Emperor. But the missionaries were eventually disillusioned by his messianic claims, his dogmatic misuse of the Bible and the bloodshed which cost millions of lives in a dozen years.[6] The Bible without further instruction had proved dangerous indeed.

Years of bitter struggle were ended by an unlikely alliance of the Qing and a British officer corps under the command of Charles Gordon. Nanjing fell in 1864, Hong died from unknown causes and the Taiping Dynasty was over. In the 1850s meanwhile, the British took advantage of the turmoil to demand even better terms than they had obtained in the 1842 Treaty. When the Emperor refused their demand, they found a weak excuse to bombard Guangzhou and so the Wesleyan mission, by then doubled in strength, was evacuated in 1856 to Macau. Hostilities were interrupted by the Indian Rebellion in 1857, but at the end of that year an Anglo–French expedition occupied Guangzhou. By 1860 they had routed the imperial army, enforced a new treaty which opened up more ports, obtained the right of foreigners, including missionaries, to travel throughout the interior, burned the Summer Palace in Beijing and thoroughly humiliated China.

Piercy and his band made the most of their exile in Macau. They had taken some of their pupils with them, reopened their schools and soon had much larger classes. Five years after his arrival in China, Piercy conducted the first three Wesleyan baptisms. He then travelled to various parts of south-east Asia, preaching to Chinese emigrants, before it was safe to return to their ruined homes in Guangzhou and start again. Under the occupation life was much easier for them.

Harvard University Press, 1985), pp. 35–46.

  [4]   J.D. Spence, *God's Chinese Son: The Taiping Heavenly Kingdom of Hong Xiuquan*, (New York, W.W. Norton, 1996).

  [5]   Letter of 4 June 1853, published in *Missionary Notices*, 1853, p. 138.

  [6]   Some estimates suggest there were more deaths, many from famine and plague, than in either of the World Wars of the twentieth century.

Piercy ministered to the troops for a while and reported the conversion of thirty soldiers in the space of six weeks. But in the province of Guangdong there were thirty million people. For the time being the mission focused its work on the city and its suburbs, acquiring several plots of land, building churches, schools and residences and instructing the handful of Chinese converts – seventeen members were recorded in 1860. One by one local preachers were formed, some of whom became paid catechists; in 1877 two became the District's first Chinese ministers.

Piercy was now well known in Wesleyan circles and was consulted on several occasions about the work of the Chinese mission in Australia. His view was that two years of language and culture training in China would prepare a minister for the mission in Victoria better than any local training could do. When in 1868 James Caldwell, a probationer newly arrived in Australia, volunteered for the Chinese work he was sent to study with Piercy. He spent six hours a day on Cantonese and also learned a good deal about the strength of family and village ties in China. His insights and skills would have been invaluable in Victoria, but after just four months, on an expedition with Piercy, he slipped, fell into a river and drowned.

Thomas Selby arrived in 1868 and after a period of orientation went to Foshan[7], a city of half-a-million people and the earliest outpost of the District beyond Guangzhou. He was a forthright character who did not waste time; he could provoke the Chinese, try the patience of his colleagues, defy the Committee in London and exasperate the British consul. On one occasion, told by the consul to leave due to anti-foreign riots, he retorted 'I love the Queen, God bless her, but I'm hanged if I will pay attention to her consular officers!'[8] After furlough in 1877 he pioneered an area 200 miles upriver in Hakka country. The Hakka dialect differed from Cantonese in that they used tones differently, which was confusing but not a totally new language. No-one would let a house to a foreigner, so Selby lived on a houseboat along with 'a Chinese preacher, a colporteur and the skipper with his family and farmyard'.[9] Colporteurs and Biblewomen, poorly educated but devoted to their Lord, were the vanguard of the church in China, taking Bibles and tracts to villages far and wide. The team travelled up and down the river and the Hakka church grew steadily and, by Chinese standards, rapidly.

Joan Piercy died in 1878, after twenty-five years of devoted service. Piercy himself and Selby were both invalided home in 1882. Piercy then started a Chinese mission in London's dockland and preached in Cantonese for another thirty

---

7   Transliterated until 1958 as Fatshan.
8   Rose, pp. 45–6.
9   Rose, p. 47.

years.[10] Selby became a prolific writer whose books were widely acclaimed.[11] Among those who took up the baton were Charles Wenyon and Roderick Macdonald. For both, the prefix 'Revd Dr' meant they had medical as well as ministerial qualifications. Wenyon heard the call to be a medical missionary as a young minister in Lancashire and somehow combined his circuit work there with qualifying at Queen's College Dublin. In 1880, taking his wife and three children, he travelled to China via Marseilles where she became ill and they missed the boat – a boat which sank a few days later with the loss of all on board. How easily those long nights of study might have proved in vain. Instead he spent sixteen years in Foshan, building up what became a major hospital complex, before he returned to London in 1896, later becoming the minister of Wesley's Chapel. After using the Foshan preaching-house as a dispensary for a while, he was able to rent a building and convert it into a hundred-bed hospital. He saw a hundred patients on the day it opened and 6,000 within the space of a few months. Before long he had enrolled seven medical students and registered the Wesleyan Medical College from which over a hundred doctors graduated in the thirty years it functioned.

Hong Kong was still a sparsely populated island when Piercy arrived in 1851. By the unequal treaty of 1858 Kowloon on the mainland was ceded to the British colony and by the 1880s a seaport was developing fast. It attracted migrant workers including three Local Preachers who opened a small meeting room and two schools in 1882. Charles Wenyon, in his other capacity as District Chairman, obtained grants from the Hong Kong government which enabled the educational work to develop successfully, but only in 1889 did the little fellowship get a minister. Leong On Tong had worked among the Chinese in Melbourne.[12] Josiah Cox spent eight weeks in Australia en route from furlough in 1871 and examined

---

[10]　'Further down the road towards the West India Docks there is a quaint inscription in four Chinese characters. It signifies that here is the Chinese mission-house. This is open twice a day for general purposes. The missionary, the Reverend George Piercy, lived thirty years in China, and he has gained much renown and respect among the Chinese of all classes. In Limehouse the old and the young, the residents and the new-comers, look upon him as the father, the friend, and the adviser of all who are in difficulty or trouble. Chinamen who have been unjustly accused of crimes and offences, a thing which is not uncommon, and crews which have refused to work under some misapprehension, have owed their liberation to his kindly offices and many young boys and girls of the colony have to thank him for advice and help. On Sunday evenings, about six o'clock, you will see in the mission-house a table laid for a score or more of young Chinamen who under the presidency of Mr. Piercy, will regale themselves with tea, bread and butter cakes and biscuits. It is a homely gathering. The missionary chats with all, answers questions and imparts information on every subject.': G.R. Sims (ed.), *Living London*, (London, Cassell & Co., 1902), pp. 81–2.

[11]　See T.G. Selby, *Chinamen at Home*, (London, Hodder & Stoughton, 1900), *As the Chinese See Us*, (London, T. Fisher Unwin, 1901), *The Chinaman in his own Stories*, (London, Charles H. Kelly, 1905).

[12]　See p. 41.

Leong in Chinese, since his English was poor. On Cox's recommendation he was received as a probationer and subsequently ordained. He came to Hong Kong in retirement and did sterling work. Meanwhile successive missionaries ministered briefly to the English-speaking civilians and soldiers, who were mostly on even shorter-term appointments. Eventually Charles Bone, who had already been eighteen years in China, moved to Hong Kong, took charge of both the Chinese and English churches and built them up over a further seventeen years' ministry.

The life of the District, along with all Christian mission in China, was overshadowed throughout the period by the international treaties imposed on the Chinese. On the one hand it benefited from and, on the other, it was undermined by, the 1858 Toleration Clauses. These placed not just the missionaries but all Christians under the protection of the foreign powers. While that made persecution less likely, it was a situation open to abuse. There were those who joined the church in the hope of material advantage or of winning the backing of a foreigner, whom in truth they despised, in some local dispute. But most Chinese viewed westerners as oppressors and had no way of distinguishing missionaries from the rest. Christianity was a foreign religion and converts were taunted with the slogan 'One more Christian, one less Chinese'. Around 1898 the members of a secret society called the 'Righteous Harmonious Fist' began attacking foreign importations such as railways, telegraph lines and Christian missions. In the course of the Boxer Rebellion, which lasted until 1901, 230 foreign missionaries and over 32,000 Chinese Christians lost their lives. It was ultimately quashed by an international force drawn from eight nations commanded by a British officer. The uprising never spread to the south but its slogan 'Defend Chinese Religion and Get Rid of Foreign Religion' reflected the widespread xenophobia the missionaries had to contend with everywhere.

Central China[13]

In 1860 Josiah Cox, on furlough in England, received two letters on the same day. One was from his friend, the Taiping Emperor's cousin, inviting him to Nanjing, the other from Piercy recommending him to accept the invitation, which he duly did. He had been excited by the potential of the Taiping project and was still well disposed to the movement. But when he reached Nanjing in 1861 he found it had descended into anarchy, heresy and self-indulgence. He was cold-shouldered and had to abandon hope of establishing a mission there. So he took a boat up the Yangtze to the next great city on its banks, Hankou, one of the new treaty ports, to ascertain what opportunities central China held. Hankou is at the confluence of the Yangtze and Han rivers, facing Wuchang across the first and Hanyang across the second: a triple city with a huge population.[14] Reaching Hankou in 1862, Cox was

---

[13]   See G.A. Clayton, *Methodism in Central China*, (London, Charles H. Kelly, 1906).
[14]   The three now constitute the mega-city of Wuhan.

welcomed and encouraged by Griffith John of the LMS, who had arrived the year before. Cox decided to buy a property on the spot. He knew that Piercy was keen to exploit the strategic potential of Hankou, so acted on his own authority, risking the wrath of the Committee. William Arthur was one of the Secretaries at the time, however; he had seen enough of Cox to give his unqualified approval to the venture. History now repeated itself. Just as the LMS had seconded Liang Fa to assist Piercy in Guangzhou, so now John offered the services of his first convert in Hankou to Cox. Chu Shao Ngan's immediate task was to teach Cox Mandarin, for Cantonese was of little use; he went on to become the first Wesleyan minister in China.

Josiah Cox prepared a detailed and costed plan of action which he submitted to London. Not all his proposals could be implemented, but his particular request for a medical missionary was met. Dr Porter Smith was his first colleague in Hankou and the first male lay missionary appointed by the Society. Smith started work in 1864 with a little rented dispensary, with the Chinese characters *P'u Ngai I-Yuen*, Hospital of Universal Love, at the door. He learned the language, got a small hospital built, wrote leaflets about hygiene and sanitation and began a programme of health education. He lived up to the hospital's name, treating mandarin and beggar alike. He served for six years, as did his successor Dr Hardey. In 1865 Cox welcomed two ministerial colleagues, William Scarborough and David Hill.[15] At this time central China was severed from the South China District due to the vast distances and became the Wuchang District, since Wuchang was the official capital of Hubei province. Scarborough spent twenty years in China and Hill thirty, the one leaving heartbroken at his wife's untimely death, the other, who had chosen celibacy for the gospel's sake, dying exhausted at the age of 55.

David Hill's thirty-year ministry was outstanding. He had no ear for music and struggled to distinguish the different tones that are a vital element of Mandarin pronunciation, but with dogged perseverance he gradually made himself a fluent communicator. He had an ascetic lifestyle and although on his father's death he inherited a considerable sum he spent little on himself. His prayer times were his daily bread, never neglected whatever the demands on his time and energy. He ministered first in Wuchang and then downriver where he occupied two rooms in a house in Wuxue and covered hundreds of miles on foot, preaching and selling Christian literature. Then in 1877 came a cruel famine in the north of China, leaving seventy million people starving and ten million dead. Hill contributed liberally to the relief fund, but for him that was not enough.[16] He obtained leave of absence and set out for the north. At this time he resolved to adopt Chinese dress and to wear his hair in a queue, a practice he followed to the end of his life. He joined a team of relief workers headed by the Baptist missionary, Timothy Richard. They did all they could amid the most terrible destitution and desperation, which even

---

[15]   See W.T.A. Barber, *David Hill, Apostle to the Chinese*, (London, Wesleyan Book Room, 1906); G.R. Senior, *David Hill, Missionary in Central China*, (Oxford, Wesley Historical Society, 2008).

[16]   Senior, *David Hill*, pp. 16–19.

Figure 9.1   David Hill distributing famine relief, Shanxi, 1878

drove some to cannibalism. Hill spent two years in Shanxi province. Shortly after returning to his District, he went on furlough for the first time in sixteen years. He was the executor of Joseph Race,[17] a colleague who died of typhoid at the age of 32, and accompanied his family home.

Hill's furlough was as momentous as his ministry. He spoke all over Britain and his impact was comparable with David Livingstone's earlier and Bill Platt's later. He made the case for lay missionaries, still a rarity for the WMMS, though increasingly employed by the China Inland Mission (CIM). The Society's unwillingness to follow suit did not deter him. He appealed for volunteers to serve wholly or partly at their own expense and inspired the 'Central China Wesleyan Lay Mission' which sent out a succession of valuable agents over the last two decades of the century. He founded the Central China Prayer Union, with just one condition of membership, to pray every day for the District; he began a regular prayer letter which continued to be circulated bi-monthly long after his death. He lost no opportunity to vent his outrage at Britain's complicity in the opium trade and published, at his own expense, a series of sketches by a Chinese artist, with the title *The Rake's Progress*, which depicted the downfall of an opium eater. To his dying day he prayed and worked for an end to the opium trade, which he considered the chief obstacle in the way of Christianity in China.

---

[17]   See S. Race, *The Two Worlds of Joseph Race*, (London, Souvenir Press, 1988).

After two years' absence Hill arrived back in China in 1882 and when Scarborough left he reluctantly took over the District Chair. Under his leadership schools, hospitals, orphanages, a school for the blind and a stream of Christian literature made their appearance and Chinese preachers ventured into the neighbouring province of Hunan.[18] Then in 1895 another crop failure brought a flood of refugees to the gates of Wuchang. Hill wore himself out ministering to them, caught typhus and collapsed after celebrating Easter 1896. His death was sorely felt and yet the expansion of the District continued apace.

Hunan was vehemently anti-Christian and at a general China Missionary Conference in 1890, which Hill chaired, Timothy Richard had warned that the inflammatory posters and propaganda coming out of Hunan would lead to violence. The very next year the lay missionary William Argent was killed in an outbreak of violence in Wuxue.[19] The CIM and other Societies had hitherto failed to establish a base in Hunan. But a brave Wesleyan preacher, Tsang Yih-tze, undertook three journeys into the province between 1892 and 1896. He reported that opposition to the gospel came from a clique and not from the general population and urged the formation of a China Missionary Society to promote the evangelization of Hunan. It was duly begun, with its first principle that no foreigner should contribute to its funds. This Society had sent three Chinese missionaries by the turn of the century and three English missionaries made a preliminary tour of reconnaissance, but the enterprise was interrupted by the Boxer rising of 1900. European staff were called in from the outstations, their families were evacuated to Shanghai, the Chinese Christians had to lie low. But before long evangelistic activity resumed, converts were made, churches planted and a separate Hunan District came into being in 1907.

North, East and West[20]

Methodism in north China was of two varieties, American and British. The Methodist New Connexion launched its mission in the port of Tianjin 1861 and concentrated its activities in Shandong province, while the Americans were based in Beijing.

On the east coast the United Methodist Free Churches began work in 1864 at the suggestion of Hudson Taylor, who later founded the CIM. The son of a local preacher in the Wesleyan Reform Union, he had worked for six years in the treaty port of Ningbo and recommended it as a suitable base. The UMFC wisely restricted its work to a small area around Ningbo but in 1878 started a mission in Wenzhou, another treaty port 200 miles to the south. They were administered as two separate Districts.

---

18   See M. Sheaff, *From Tortoise Hill*, (Leominster, Orphans Press, 2007).
19   See p. 264.
20   See chapter 12.

In the far west, again at Hudson Taylor's instigation, the Bible Christians settled in Zhaotong in 1887. Yunnan province is home to many ethnic groups speaking mutually unintelligible languages and at first the Bible Christians could only preach to the Chinese-speakers, with little result. Yet their labours were preparing them for the day in 1904 when members of the Miao people would seek them out and large numbers would clamour to hear the gospel.[21]

---

[21] See Pritchard, *Methodists and their Missionary Societies 1900–96,* chapter 6.

Chapter 10

Advance in Africa

Most of Africa was yet to be explored when the nineteenth century began. Until 1885 it was a continent largely without national borders. One by one European nations laid claim to and fought over territory of which they knew little beyond the coastal towns where they had settled. Inland, feudal-like societies predominated: some of them extensive kingdoms with powerful monarchs and opulent palaces, many of them little chieftaincies where allegiance was confined to the village, the clan or at most the tribe. Even the smallest communities were connected by trade: almost all of West Africa, for example, formed a 'cowrie zone'[1] where cowrie shells were the currency of a flourishing market economy. In the south there was less stability; whole peoples were on the move long after Dutch and British settlers had made themselves at home. In the heart of Africa, such men as Livingstone, Stanley and Speke were tracing the courses of the Zambezi, the Congo and the Nile, charting the Great Lakes and, more importantly, meeting the people and learning about their ways, their stories and their tribulations.

Livingstone's objective, as he famously declared in 1857, was to 'go back to Africa to make an open path for commerce and Christianity'. Soon the continent's potential as a market and as a source of mineral wealth would result in what *The Times* called 'the scramble for Africa'. The frontiers were determined by European statesmen at the Congress of Berlin, 1884–85; but they had little to do with natural ethnic and linguistic boundaries as perceived by Africans. Africans became subjects and had to be subdued. The expansion of the British Empire was, in the eyes of the public, a glorious enterprise, 'the biggest collective adventure of all, even if it had to be enjoyed by proxy'.[2] Africans had a different perspective. The Emperor of Ethiopia said, 'I know their game. First, it's traders and missionaries. Then it's ambassadors. After that, they bring the guns.'[3] A critical Englishman, in the year of the Congress, took the same view:

> The explorer reconnoitres the ground, and the missionary prepares the soil, the trader 'works' it. The time is then ripe for protectorates and annexations.[4]

---

[1]   B. Davidson, *The Story of Africa*, (London, Mitchell Beazley, 1984), p. 154.

[2]   Thomson, p. 206.

[3]   Davidson, p. 167.

[4]   Ernest Belfort Bax in William Morris's socialist journal *Commonweal*, quoted in Davidson, p. 173.

It is too facile to charge missionaries collectively with aiding and abetting the colonial enterprise and with profiting from it to advance their evangelical cause. In contrast with the merchants, hardly one was in Africa for the sake of personal gain. In contrast with the settlers, hardly one was there in the hope – even if the hope was vain – of a comfortable and prosperous life. In contrast with the armies, their objective was not to subjugate Africans but to open their hearts and minds to the truths that they themselves embraced and in which they found joy and peace. For most missionaries, home life in England was impecunious and hard and they expected nothing else in Africa. What they had not bargained for, especially in West Africa, was the dispiriting effect of isolation from their compatriots, especially believing compatriots. The maladies, on the other hand, they knew of and risked. Until quinine began to be used in the 1850s, malaria was rife, sending even more to the white woman's grave than to the white man's. The link between malaria and mosquitoes was first tentatively made in 1881 but only proved in 1898. Not every missionary death was due to disease; some were lost at sea, others in childbirth, others from dysentery. The overall mortality rate was terrible; but the result of their work was considerable.

The Gambia[5]

'The term Western Africa,' wrote William Moister, 'is generally applied to that part of the vast continent which lies between the Great Desert on the north, the Equator on the south, the Atlantic on the west, and the river Niger on the east.'[6] The Gambia, where Moister had served, was the most westerly of the Wesleyan missions in Africa. Work there was begun in 1821. In 2009 it was the last overseas District to become an autonomous Methodist Church, when its membership, which had reached 800 in the first thirty-five years, still numbered barely 2,000. The Gambia is the smallest country on mainland Africa and consists of a narrow strip of land astride the River Gambia, stretching 200 miles inland and never more than twenty-five miles wide. By the Treaty of Versailles in 1783 the French ceded the river to Britain and the military post of Bathurst (now Banjul), founded in 1816, was at first governed from Freetown as an adjunct to Sierra Leone. Governor Macarthy, a good friend to the WMMS during his seven years in the colony, drew The Gambia to the Society's attention and in 1821 John Morgan was sent to the little settlement the British had established on St Mary's island, a few miles upriver from the estuary. Bathurst was home to hardly more than 1,000 people, chiefly rescued slaves. Morgan, soon joined by John Baker from Freetown, was commissioned to work among the indigenous Mandinka, Fula and Wolof people.

---

5   See B.B. Prickett, *Island Base*, (Banjul, Methodist Church Gambia, 1969) and M.T. Frederiks, *We Have Toiled All Night: Christianity in the Gambia 1465–2000*, (Zoetemeer, Uitgeverij Boekencentrum, 2003).

6   Moister, p. 94.

They found that the Mandinka were Muslims who, literate in Arabic if at all, abhorred Roman characters which they regarded as a European *gris-gris* or fetish. Clearly the missionaries were ill-equipped to work among them. They were also suspect because in African eyes every European was associated with the slave trade and slavery was still practised over the border in French Senegal. They were unwelcome, had difficulty procuring food and building a house and inevitably fell ill. The rigours of the Gambian climate were such that of 397 British soldiers sent to Bathurst in the course of 1825–26, only 120 survived for nineteen months. Though neither of the pioneers died in The Gambia, each had to withdraw, broken in health – but not before Morgan had buried two new colleagues within months of their arrival.

Morgan eventually persuaded the Society that they must make their base in Bathurst, among the Aku-speakers. Aku is a much-adapted form of English, similar to the Krio of Sierra Leone. It was much easier for the missionaries to pick up than indigenous tongues and the Aku were potentially receptive to the gospel. There was also a settlement 150 miles upriver, founded in 1823 and named Macarthy's Island, where Morgan lived for a short time. In these two places, very slowly, the church took root. Thirty members in 1825 grew to 812 by 1860, but then declined. The work was inhibited by the rapid turnover of missionaries. A handful of schools were opened but they too suffered from the lack of consistent management. Robert McBrair, a linguist who had served in Alexandria and Malta, was sent expressly for translation work and stayed long enough to get a grasp of Mandinka; when he in turn was obliged to return to Britain he was accompanied by a Mandinka interpreter and between them they published a grammar and a translation of St Matthew. William Fox, exceptionally, survived ten years in The Gambia and before he left in 1844 wrote: 'Send us sufficient help, and, ere many years have elapsed, you will, I trust, have a missionary at the great emporium of Africa, Timbuctoo.' His assessment was over-optimistic and in any case his plea was vain. The helpers arose among the Gambian Christians themselves. Cupidon, Salah, Juff and others had been slaves of French proprietors in Senegal and had slipped across the frontier into freedom. A succession of African ministers from Sierra Leone also came to stand in the breach.

Islam was a minority religion in The Gambia in the first half of the century but as the years went by the numbers of Muslims rose steeply while Christianity spread very slowly. The missionaries and their African colleagues had little knowledge of Islam and no preparation for working among them. Their approach tended to be abrasive and counter-productive. Conversions were few and it was with joyful excitement that Richard Cooper wrote in 1859 about the conversion of a Wolof Muslim *marabout*:

> He is a Jaloof and received his early education training in our day school to which he often refers with feelings of grateful remembrance. After leaving school he was sent by his parents to the Maraboos (priests) to be prepared by them for entering the Mohammedan priesthood ... His love of Arabic led him

to apply to us about 2 years since, for the loan of an Arabic Bible ... After that I lost sight of our Maraboo friend, until last Christmas when he called upon me in much distress. The cause was that while he had been sojourning on the mainland and was crossing a river, the canoe had upset and his treasure was lost. He begged me to supply him with another ... Upon my asking if he believed the Lord Jesus died for his sins, he replied: 'No, He did not die for all, only for those who believe in Him and I do not believe. I am a Maraboo.' ... I next enquired how he hoped to be saved if he did not believe in the Son of God as his Saviour. 'O,' he replied, 'The Bible says all religions are good, Mohammedanism as well as Christianity', but he could not tell me where to find this statement. Desirous of bringing him to decision, I found him Gal. 1:8v. 'But though we, or an angel from heaven, preach any other gospel unto you, than that which we have preached unto you – let him be accursed.' He read it slowly and thoughtfully, paused, appeared perplexed, a shade came over his intelligent countenance, his bright eyes filled with tears as he looked at me and said in English 'Sir, I do believe in Jesus.' Then resuming his own tongue, further confessed: 'I would renounce Mahomed, only by doing so, I should lose caste, my friends would become my bitter enemies. I should lose all my earthly all and die of want.' I endeavoured to comfort and assure him, with the loving words of Jesus and asked him to read the 3rd chapter of John. And slowly and thoughtfully and prayerfully he promised to do so and departed. On Monday ... he called again and then professed to have found the Messiah ... He further confessed to me, that he had in his heart renounced Mahommedanism and was engaged, as far as he dared, in preaching against it and proving from Scripture that Jesus is the Christ. On this account, he is much persecuted; particularly the Maraboos and his own family who declare that he has disgraced himself and them – that the white minister and his Koran have turned his head ... He has now only one wife and has very willingly given me his greegrees ...[7]

Such rare instances kept alive until the 1920s unrealistic hopes of conversions *en masse*, but all efforts proved futile.[8]

In mid-century it occurred to the French that this slip of land jutting right into their Senegalese colony was an irritating anomaly they could do without and so, in 1866, they formally proposed an exchange with Britain in return for territory, to be defined, elsewhere in West Africa. The idea was pursued in desultory fashion over some years. Governor Kennedy in Freetown was enthusiastically for the plan; the missionaries were not. At their annual meeting in 1871 – a mini-Synod, for which the Chairman came from Freetown – they 'respectfully but earnestly request[ed] the Wesleyan Missionary Committee to use its influence' to prevent the exchange. The Committee did not exert itself greatly, either then or when the

---

[7]   Letter to WMMS, 20 April 1859: SOAS, MMS/West Africa/Correspondence/Gambia/FBN5.

[8]   Frederiks, pp. 231–2.

proposal was revived in 1874. The Gambia was as marginal to their designs as to the Government's. But in the end the plan came to nothing.[9]

For practically all this time The Gambia mission was administered from Freetown; all too often the needs of Sierra Leone took priority and missionaries who were fit enough to remain in Africa were recalled there. In the early 1890s the staff consisted of two African ministers and no Europeans. The station on Macarthy's Island, which had been erratically staffed at best, was abandoned. Ralph Williams, who arrived in 1894, stayed for eight years, ministering effectively in Bathurst but no further afield. By the end of the century the total membership was still less than had been recorded in 1860.

Map 11   West Africa, from The Gambia to Liberia

Sierra Leone

After several false starts, an enduring mission to Sierra Leone began in 1811.[10] As elsewhere, missionaries tended to stay the course for no more than a few years and some lives were cut short in a matter of months. But steady church growth was

---

9   For a full account of this long drawn out affair, see Darch, pp. 144-171.
10   See chapters 2 and 5.

recorded among the Krios of the Freetown peninsula. Samuel Brown, who lasted a little more than two years[11] having lost his wife after seven months, saw a hundred new members and wrote as he departed early in 1819:

> I have sown in tears, but now we reap in joy. Thank God! this is an ample recompense for every sigh, every tear, every shaking ague, every burning fever, every bereavement, every restless and sleepless night, I have had to endure since I came to Africa.[12]

The church in Freetown, however, was neither founded by nor accustomed to white ministers. The Nova Scotians had a tradition of independency which sat ill with the authoritarian leadership role assumed as a matter of course by missionaries. As a result the Rawdon Street congregation whose preacher had requested help in 1807[13] went its own way in 1821. This chapel was later to be the focus of the disputes which brought the 'West African Methodist Church' into being and the United Methodist Free Churches into Sierra Leone.[14]

Three Wesleyan missionaries stayed for longer than the average. Thomas Dove and Henry Badger arrived in Freetown in 1837. Dove served until 1845, Badger to 1847: both lost their first wives there. Dove's great achievement was founding a High School and a Training Institution at King Tom's Point, a former naval depot which he acquired and adapted.[15] The need for African ministers was urgent, given the swift turnover of missionaries, and, for thirty years, the institution trained teachers and catechists, a few of whom went on to ordination. Joseph Wright and Charles Knight[16] had both been rescued from slave-ships in their childhood and brought to Freetown; Wright was sent to England and trained at Hoxton, Knight was trained at King Tom. Dove also set up a printing press and produced a monthly religious newspaper. Badger remarried Mrs A.L. Gordon, a teacher who had moved to Freetown following eleven years on St Kitts in the Caribbean, at first with her missionary husband and for another ten years after she was widowed. There were as yet no Wesleyan women missionaries other than those who accompanied their husbands and her reason for coming to Freetown remains to be unearthed. She was devoted to the education of African women, a cause in which her marriage gave her extra influence, both in Sierra Leone and then when Badger was transferred to The Gambia, where she died in 1851.

---

[11]   Almost forty years later, he returned to Sierra Leone as a supernumerary and had a longer stay of three years.

[12]   *Missionary Notices,* July 1819, p. 108.

[13]   See p. 47.

[14]   See p. 196.

[15]   King Tom was the Temne chief who sold the land on which Freetown was built.

[16]   http://www.dacb.org/stories/sierraleone/knight_charles.html [accessed 31 October 2012].

The third long-serving missionary was Benjamin Tregaskis, who came as Chairman in 1864 after a quarter of a century in the Caribbean. He was renowned as a strict disciplinarian and he often clashed with both British and African colleagues. The Secretaries in London received regular letters of complaint from them. But he has better claims to fame. His opposition to the hut tax which the Governor decided to levy was influential. An annual charge of five shillings per house, irrespective of the age or income of the occupants, was a crushing burden for the poor, but their protests were ignored. Tregaskis took their part and contacted Sir William M'Arthur, an MP who subsequently became Treasurer of the Society. The result was that the Governor was removed, the tax abolished, the danger of revolt averted and a thanksgiving service attended by some 5,000 grateful worshippers. Secondly, Tregaskis was a fierce advocate of education and training. He sold the King Tom site for a good price and obtained one in a better location where a new High School and Training Institution were built.[17] Nonetheless he created such disharmony that the Committee prevailed upon him to return to Britain in 1874. Charles Knight who replaced him as Chairman was the first African to hold such a position; it was seventy-five years before there was another.

The first Principal of the High School was Claudius May, whose father, a rescued Yoruba slave, had become an 'assistant missionary' in 1829 and was still working as a supernumerary in 1891. Claudius May spent twenty-five years of his ministry at the Boys' High School.[18] By 1899, when it celebrated its first quarter-century, over 1,000 pupils had passed through the school. Thirteen of them had become ministers, four were doctors, another three barristers and others held a variety of civil service appointments. One of May's protégés was Orishatukeh Faduma, the son of a Yoruba couple who had been captured in Nigeria, rescued in mid-Atlantic and converted in Demerara where they were taken to work on a sugar plantation. The family eventually re-crossed the Atlantic and settled in Waterloo, a village on the peninsula where the young Faduma attended the Wesleyan primary school. He was 19 when in 1876 he embarked on six years at the High School while working for the Principal as a live-in kitchen boy. Next he went to Wesley College, Taunton and on to London University, where he was the first West African to pass the intermediate B.A. Returning in 1885, he taught at the Wesleyan Boys' High School and distinguished himself not only as a teacher but also as a community leader. He started a movement for cultural reform that aimed to foster attitudes and practices more attuned to African heritage and identity and became a member of the Dress Reform Society which sought to establish a form of dress more culturally and environmentally appropriate for West Africans than the Victorian attire – the Religion of the Frock Coat and Tall Hat – which many Krios associated with the attainment of Christianity and civilization. He later joined the AMEC, studied at Yale, became a Congregational minister in the United States and was one of the architects of the West African Congress which had as its objective 'to secure for

---

[17]   Findlay and Holdsworth, vol. 4, pp. 99–100.
[18]   http://www.dacb.org/stories/sierraleone/may_jc.html [accessed 31 October 2012].

West Africa a recognition of those social, political, and national rights, which the representatives of Great Britain in the colonies have not infrequently denied us'. He is remembered as an evangelical Pan–African whose theology accommodated the findings of modern scientific scholarship. Already in the nineteenth century he was formulating ideas that would become influential in the twentieth. He called for a greater respect and appreciation of non-Christian religions and cultures; the indigenization of Christian ritual and personnel; the disassociation of mission efforts from Western racial, cultural, political and religious chauvinism; a renewed emphasis on the service and social dimensions of the mission enterprise; a call for ecumenical and co-operative efforts; and an end to the paternalistic relationship between the older and the younger churches.[19]

Until 1892 the District's activity was confined to the Freetown area which formed the Sierra Leone colony. Adjoining territory was not under British rule, though increasingly drawn into the British economic sphere. The colonial government made treaties of friendship with neighbouring rulers and gradually acquired jurisdiction over the coastline, but the hinterland came into British hands only once the Treaty of Berlin had defined the frontiers with French and Liberian territory. In 1896 the country beyond the coastal colony was declared a British Protectorate. Already in 1892 the Wesleyans were at work in the interior. Matthew Godman, who promoted and pioneered this development, had served for four years in The Gambia and thirty in South Africa before coming to Freetown. He was Chairman of the District for the last five years of his ministry and came to regard them as the most fruitful period of his life. He found the Krio circuits insular and self-satisfied, not at all mission-minded. He began to visit the chiefs down the coast; his colleagues and successors followed suit and as the years passed covered a steadily widening area. First Sherbro Island, then Tikonko and Bandajuma in the heart of Mende-land, became centres of Methodist activity. Expansion was facilitated by the railway to the Liberian border which began to be built in 1895.

The Mende people, however, did not understand the concept of a Protectorate. They had not asked to be protected. They saw no reason to pay taxes on trade which they had hitherto carried on freely. And when the administration brought in the five shilling hut tax which had been so unpopular in Freetown, dissatisfaction turned to revolt. Troops from Freetown were dispatched to quell the trouble. The savagery that ensued in 1898 became known as the Mende war, though they were joined by some of the Temne and other ethnic groups. All aliens, both European and Krio, were targeted and the only missionary who escaped with his life was Charles Goodman of the UMFC at Tikonko.[20] A congregation assembled to open a new chapel in the Sherbro circuit was attacked and over 200 members were killed. The uprising was soon put down; the destruction wreaked by the malcontents was compounded by the troops burning scores of villages to the ground. The

---

[19]   http://www.dacb.org/stories/sierraleone/faduma_orishatukeh.html [accessed 31 October 2012].

[20]   See p. 196.

Protectorate was devastated, the hut tax was retained. Within a year, however, the Chairman reported that 'extensive building operations are being carried on' and the Mende chief of Bandajuma was writing to the Governor to ask for missionaries

> for the Christianization of my people, with a school, that our children may have a religious teaching. I have already consulted most of my headmen concerning this and they unanimously promised to do their utmost to erect small buildings both for divine worship as well as residence for a teacher.[21]

The Mende mission was under way; it was until 1951 administered directly from London and known as the 'Committee Area' while the churches of the colony were answerable to the District Synod.

Gold Coast

Between Freeman's first and second visits to Kumasi,[22] the WMMS summoned him to England for a fund-raising tour. He was accompanied by William de Graft, who had deputized for him in Cape Coast during his three months away in Ashanti. In Bristol, de Graft preached to a congregation that included the widow of Captain Potter, who had conveyed the Bibles and the missionary to Cape Coast five years earlier. De Graft reported that she wept for joy, saying 'Once we sent missionaries to Africa, but now here is an African ... preaching Christ Jesus unto us' – words not often heard before the 1970s. Although Wesleyans had only just dipped deep in their pockets for the 1839 Centenary Fund, they raised almost £5,000 for the Gold Coast work. At the end of 1840 Freeman and de Graft returned with five more missionaries, three of them married. When four of these eight died within a year and a fifth was forced to leave by ill-health, Governor Maclean wrote to the Society in frustration:

> These deaths have [not] been caused solely by the climate ... each of the lamented individuals in question had passed safely through the seasoning fever ... with sufficient prudence and care, their lives might have been preserved ... when persons have arrived at a certain age, their habits and opinions on the subject of health become generally fixed, and they will not readily forego those habits and opinions, however earnestly urged by those who are much better acquainted with the country and climate, than they can possibly be ... young persons should, if possible, be elected for the work of the Mission in this country... they would become more readily and easily acclimated, than persons more advanced in life;

---

[21]   Nano (or Momo) Kaikai, 5 September 1899: SOAS, MMS/West Africa/Correspondence/Sierra Leone/FBN6.

[22]   See p. 50.

and they would more willingly listen to, and adopt, the suggestions of persons
more experienced than themselves.[23]

Maclean's confidence in youth is open to question; in any event, the only enduring
ministry which ensued was that of Henry Wharton, who, like Freeman, was of
mixed parentage. At home in Grenada he had been encouraged and mentored by
the much-travelled William Moister and on entering the ministry he was Moister's
colleague in St Vincent. After meeting Freeman when on furlough, he decided that
the Gold Coast was where he was called to work and served there from 1845 to
his death in 1873. He took charge of the seminary which Freeman had established
in Accra, training schoolteachers and catechists. From among their number able
African ministers soon began to emerge and by 1856 nine were active.

There were by that time enough circuits to make good use of them all. Churches
were planted among the Fante along the coast and inland and then among the Ga
around Accra, though the Ashanti mission was for long periods unstaffed. It was a
great strength that the people looked upon these churches and the schools that were
built alongside them as their own creation and their own responsibility. Teachers
were trained either at the Institution in Accra or by an in-service programme in
Cape Coast. A government report in 1856 recorded thirty-one Methodist schools
with sixty-one men and nine women teaching 914 boys and 315 girls. By then
Freeman had also set up two schools in Dahomey and two in Nigeria as well.
Girls' schooling was pioneered by Elizabeth Waldron. Freeman claimed that 'all
the influential women of the time were trained by her in their youth'. The daughter
of an Irish father and an African mother, she was recruited by George Wrigley in
1837 to run the school in Cape Coast which his late wife had started. By 1840 she
had eighty girls on the roll and later she took in boarders – for which she negotiated
with the church an allowance of £55 per annum to accommodate twelve children.
Boarding establishments were tried at some of the other schools in an attempt to
secure more regular attendance, for the children were all too often taken away to
assist in plantation work.[24]

But Freeman had underestimated the cost. His vision and enthusiasm could
not atone for his administrative and financial incompetence. The District's
expenditure in the period 1854–56 exceeded income by over £10,000 and at length
an exasperated Committee sent Daniel West and William West to redress the
situation. Daniel West was to conduct an inquiry and report; William West, with
twenty-one years' experience in the Caribbean, was to be the financial secretary
of the District. Daniel was taken ill and died as he was returning to England but
his report was written. Although it spoke of 'good chapels and school houses,
large and attentive congregations and greatly increasing societies', Freeman was
charged with 'a reckless disregard of the instructions of the Committee in respect
of finance' and 'a persistent disregard of advice and direction'. There was no

---

23   *Missionary Notices,* December 1841, pp. 616–17.
24   Bartels, pp. 21, 64–5, 72.

question of embezzlement or seeking private gain; nothing other than his zeal for Christ and his love of the people drove him. But inevitably he was deposed as Chairman. He left the ministry for fifteen years, but he retained his membership and continued to serve the church in the Gold Coast with the same enthusiasm while not on the payroll.

William West assumed the chair and did three tours of duty, until in 1870 his sight failed and he had to retire. During all thirteen years he never had more than two colleagues, except in 1863–64 when there were four. The Committee expected him to consolidate the rapid expansion of the Freeman years, but it was no easy task with so little support. Despite his frustration there was a very positive side to the situation, for the leadership of the local churches and seven circuits and the day-to-day management of the schools were in African hands. The foundations of a strong African church were being laid. The training of leaders, however, continued to be problematic. When in 1861 West was put in charge of all Methodist work from The Gambia to Lagos, the Accra Institution was closed and all training of teachers and preachers was centralized at King Tom Point in Freetown, which had less inadequate facilities than anywhere else.

There were three social concerns which deeply troubled the leaders of the young church: human sacrifice, domestic slavery and polygamy. Freeman had encountered the first in all its gory horror when he arrived in Kumasi in 1840. He was welcomed with an ostentatious parade, at which quantities of gold and silver and ornate carvings were displayed. He described them in his journal and continued:

> I saw what was calculated to harrow up the strongest and most painful feelings – the royal executioners, bearing the bloodstained stools on which hundreds, perhaps thousands of human victims have been sacrificed by decapitation, and also the large *death-drum* which is beaten at the moment when the fatal knife severs the head from the body, the very sound of which conveys a thrill of horror.[25]

A few days later the drum began to beat. The Asantahene's brother had died and a ritual killing to provide him with servants in the spirit world was under way. The Asantahene sent a message to Freeman asking him not to go out into the town, since he knew that Europeans did not like to see human sacrifice. Forty victims were slaughtered for that funeral ceremony. Missionaries in the Gold Coast, as elsewhere, used every endeavour to secure the abolition of this horrific custom.

Domestic slavery was another long-established practice. The chiefs who sold their captives to European slave-traders at the coastal forts kept slaves of their own and, while the ending of the transatlantic trade lost them a profitable business, it did not disrupt their lifestyle. This was another iniquity to which the missionaries and all who came to share their faith were implacably opposed.

---

[25] Freeman, p. 47.

Polygamy was a more thorny issue. While nobody could be received into the church without renouncing human sacrifice and domestic slavery, to refuse baptism to everyone in a polygamous marriage was a questionable policy. Yet any other course might suggest that the church condoned polygamy. Some took a hard line and even denied baptism to the children in polygamous households, holding that their parents were in no position to keep the promises they were required to make in the baptismal service. Others could not deny baptism to an innocent child and many were ready to baptize the wives, since the woman had only one husband. The most intense debate, which continued throughout the nineteenth and twentieth centuries, was about the polygamous men who professed their faith. On what conditions, if at all, might such a person be baptized? To say he must first dismiss all his wives but one was too facile a solution, even if he retained only his aging first wife and not the latest, nubile and fertile. For to dismiss his wives was to condemn them and their children to destitution – a fate far worse, for most, than the spouse rivalry and half-sibling rivalry they endured as co-wives. As the church grappled with the problem, not only Wesleyans and not only in the Gold Coast, the choice appeared to be between denying him baptism and baptizing regardless of his marital state. For those who held that to die unbaptized led to eternal damnation, denial was harsh. For those who held that baptism is a sign of God's prevenient grace and not a reward for learning the catechism and obeying its precepts, the alternative was theologically acceptable and the apparent condoning of polygamy would have to be addressed through education. Agreement on which course to follow consistently eluded mission societies and denominational policy-makers, missionaries and national church leaders.

In 1875 the Gold Coast Synod took a stance against extravagant marriage ceremonies and the payment of so-called 'dowries' by which a bride was in effect purchased from her family. Ten years later it prescribed that no church member may marry a 'heathen', that no woman church member may marry someone already married and that no man with more than one wife may be admitted as a church member. The Synod minutes did not refer explicitly to baptism, which was not normally synchronized with entry into membership. In 1893 the Synod went so far as to insist on the Christian rite of marriage as a condition of membership and persuaded the government to license many chapels for marriage and increase the number of registrars.

The problem of polygamy was widespread; whereas it was in Ashanti particularly that slavery and human sacrifice were prevalent. One Ashanti chief said, 'The Fantis can do without polygamy and without slaves, but we cannot.'[26] The challenge could not be ignored, so William West endeavoured to re-activate work in Kumasi. In 1862 he made the difficult journey himself and was welcomed with honour. After the same long delay that Freeman had experienced, the Asantahene summoned him and agreed that missionaries and Christian teachers

---

[26]   *Missionary Notices*, 1876, p. 195, extract from a long letter from Picot dated 3 May 1876.

could return. But West's efforts were in vain. Missionaries were not forthcoming and the African agent who was sent was allowed little freedom and no influence. For some years he was cut off from the churches on the coast, while relationships between the Ashanti and the colonial government deteriorated. From 1863 the country was in a state of unrest. There were no defined boundaries; there were both British and Dutch forts on the coast; the Ashanti and the coastal Fante were historic enemies and there were repeated skirmishes. In 1871 Britain purchased the Dutch Gold Coast, including the fort at Elmina to which the Ashanti laid claim. The Ashanti invaded the new British protectorate, provoking a war which ended in 1874 when British troops captured and burned Kumasi. British armaments manufacturers had supplied both sides and the government refused to interfere with their commercial interests. The arms trade, every bit as monstrous as the slave trade and the opium trade, was destined to long outlive them as a legitimate business activity.

The war left chapels and schools in ruins and congregations scattered. But the members' faith was not discouraged and they set about energetically rebuilding, repairing and recruiting new Christians. In 1873 Freeman returned to full-time ministry; he was stationed at Anomabo where the church was growing so fast that at one point he conducted over a thousand baptisms in six months. He described one 'baptismal service in the open air, under the shade of the trees near the chapel. The candidates for adult baptism were formed in rows and answered the usual questions. They then knelt down, and I passed along each kneeling rank and baptized each person. The total number was 207...'.[27] A new Chairman, Thomas Picot, succeeded Henry Wharton who died that year. His responsibilities still extended to Lagos and there was more than enough to keep him occupied in the south, where fifty new stations were opened in three years. Yet the challenge of Kumasi could not be ignored and he in turn visited the city in 1876. It was no longer the opulent capital of Ashanti that had impressed earlier visitors; its tumbledown houses and overgrown streets bore the scars of war. The reigning Asantahene, having imposed the customary long wait for an audience, proffered assurances of goodwill but his interest lay in how far missionaries could be useful go-betweens in his relations with the government. He adamantly refused to allow a school.

> Ashanti children have better work to do than to sit down all day idly to learn 'hoy! hoy! hoy! hoy!' They have to fan their parents, and do other work ... It is a tradition among us that Ashantis are made to know that they are subjects, altogether under the power of their king, and they can never be allowed liberty of conscience. The Bible is not a book for us ... It is your religion which has ruined the Fanti country, weakened their power, and brought down the high man

---

[27]   Quoted by Findlay and Holdsworth, vol. 4, pp. 173–4.

on a level with the low man. The God of the white man and of the Fantis is different from the God of the Ashantis, and we cannot do without our fetishes.[28]

But in 1884, with a new ruler on the Royal Golden Stool, the Synod made yet another attempt and perseverance was eventually rewarded. Kumasi would eventually become a major centre of Methodist work. It was 1896 before a permanent station was opened at Kumasi itself, but many of the towns in Ashanti were now receptive to the gospel and their overlord no longer had the power to prevent them. One local chief was obliged by his people to swear that he would abolish human sacrifices and maintain a mission station.

Education beyond the elementary school level proceeded by fits and starts. In 1876 Picot began a High School in Cape Coast which laid the foundations – insecure though they were at first – of the renowned Mfantsipim School, which boasts Kofi Annan, the seventh Secretary–General of the United Nations, as one of its alumni. Its original purpose was to take the brightest elementary school leavers and turn them into elementary school teachers. William Cannell, who spent a breathtaking five years in Cape Coast from 1882, was appointed to educational work but took a broad view of his remit. He was amazed to find that there were no Fante Bibles and that African preachers translated from a King James Version as they went along. Without any record of their sermons, one can only imagine the variations of the Bible story that emerged from the process. There were no Bibles because Fante was not a written language. Cannell studied Fante assiduously, as few of his predecessors had done, and succeeded in developing a script and publishing a grammar and dictionary. Then, with the assistance of a Fante minister, Andrew Parker, and Joseph Brown, head of the Wesleyan Primary School in Cape Coast, he made a translation of the gospels which was published by the British and Foreign Bible Society. In 1883 he founded the Book Depot which soon became an important business in terms both of its service to Christian education and of its turnover. He started out with a stock worth £20 and made a loss of £8 in the first year, but within a decade sales exceeded £1,000 per annum and there was sufficient profit to make generous grants to the church. By 1895 the Book Depot was in a position to invest in a printing press and produce its own literature. Wesley Girls' High School in Cape Coast was also his creation. In its first year, 1884, the twenty girls paid £29 in school fees and the schoolmistress received a salary of £24. All this Cannell achieved while serving as the headmaster of the High School.

Cannell recognized the shortcomings of the teacher training and ministerial training available locally, so in 1886 two young men, W.F. Penny and S.R.B. Solomon, who had worked with him as assistant masters, were sent to England to study at Richmond College and attend lectures at Westminster College. They led worship in London churches and, as the 1888 annual report noted, 'conducted themselves with great propriety'. On their return they exchanged the anglicized

---

[28]   *Missionary Notices* 1876, pp. 194–5, extract from a long letter from Picot dated 3 May 1876.

Figure 10.1   Standfast Hall, Cape Coast

'Christian' names they had been given – either at baptism or when starting school – for their African names, Egyir Asaam and Attoh Ahuma.[29] They set a trend that was widely (though not invariably) followed. They had grasped – and demonstrated – that Christianity and Englishness are not one and the same.

In 1887, when Cannell had to leave for health reasons, Denis Kemp arrived. He was equally keen on education and concerned that it should be practical as well as academic. He feared that young Africans were beginning to despise manual work and so began a technical school. Among the trades on the curriculum the most popular was printing, making good use of the Book Depot's press. The High School, Technical School and Book Depot were all accommodated in Standfast Hall, a building originally acquired by Dunwell in 1835. It was gradually expanded to provide living quarters for missionaries, classrooms and workshops and the headquarters of the District until they moved to Accra in 1925. Somehow Kemp also made space for twenty boarders; among the first was Kwegyir Aggrey, aged 17 in 1892, who became the most influential African educationist of his generation.

Kemp was a controversial character. His work to promote opportunities for young people was outstanding. But as Chairman he was a dictator, who worked hard *for* Africans but not *with* them. An exasperated group of African superintendents

---

[29]   www.dacb.org/stories/ghana/attoh_ahuma_s.html [accessed 31 October 2012].

complained to London about his high-handedness following the 1894 Synod. Amongst other things, he had insisted on examining missionary probationers in an all-white Synod and not in the full Pastoral Session of Africans and Europeans. Later that year came news of remarks he had made while on furlough in 1893. In an address to the students of Richmond College he had deplored the fact that African ministers did not take their meals with their wives. Andrew Parker, the doyen of the African ministers and Kemp's senior by nineteen years, took strong exception, since it was not the custom for wives to eat with their husbands. Kemp had not taken on board the underlying reasons why African names were being adopted. His curt riposte was that, as Parker 'had adopted an English name, English dress, and was not above using English food and furniture, he might be allowed to borrow English ideas about home life'.[30] Kemp was not unusual in maintaining, as he did to the Committee, that Africans were not 'on an equality – intellectually – with the white race' and that his colleagues were 1,500 years behind English Christians. The 1895 Synod broke up in disarray. Somehow an uneasy truce allowed Kemp to complete his term to 1897, but there was no reconciliation.[31] The episode redoubled the confidence of the African church leaders and reinforced their self-assertion. They wanted white colleagues but not white control. What they sought for the church they sought also for the state; sixty years later the state got there first and the nation of Ghana was born.

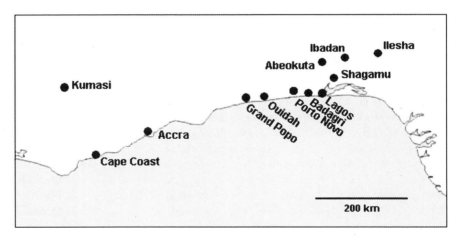

Map 12   West Africa, from Ghana to the Niger

30   Bartels, p. 140.
31   Bartels, pp. 136–7.

Lagos

It is no more appropriate to speak of Nigeria than of Ghana in the nineteenth century. When the Gold Coast District was split into two sections in 1877, the eastern part was known as the Yoruba and Popo section, the town of Grand Popo being situated on the coast at the border of present-day Bénin and Togo, while the Christians in the territory which became western Nigeria were mostly Yorubas. However Lagos, where the eastern section was administered, was a fast-developing city and in 1886 it was fully separated as the Lagos District. Colonial boundaries agreed the previous year had made Togo a German colony and Dahomey French – though France only seized control from the traditional kingdom of Dahomey in 1894 – while the territories which in 1914 were unified as Nigeria were British. So maintaining relations between the church and the colonial authorities was a constant headache. The territory east of the Niger delta, where Primitive Methodists began work in 1893, was known from 1891 as the Oil Rivers Protectorate – named for its palm-oil, not the fossil fuel discovered later – and from 1894 as the Niger Coast Protectorate.

The territories Freeman visited on his pioneering 1842 journey were entirely under African rule. There was no British administration as in Freetown, no European fort and trading station as on the Gold Coast. The vast Yoruba nation had three distinct clans who were often in conflict: the Egba, Ijebu and Ijesha. The Egba of Abeokuta were almost permanently at war with Dahomey, especially in the reign of King Gezo. During Gezo's long rule over Dahomey from 1818 to 1858 he waged a military campaign every dry season, selling his prisoners of war into slavery. Although the British West Africa Squadron was patrolling the seas to enforce the ban on slave traffic, Portuguese, Spanish, Italian and Arab vessels still frequented the slave harbours of Popo, Ouidah, Badagry and Lagos. The price of a male slave on the American market was $360 in 1850, at least ten times the price in Africa, which made the risk of interception by the navy well worth running.[32] Gezo told Captain Winniett of the U.S. navy that he took about 9,000 captives annually.

> 'The slave trade,' he said, 'has been the ruling principle of my people. It is the source of their glory and wealth. Their songs celebrate their victories and the mother lulls the child to sleep with notes of triumph over an enemy reduced to slavery. Can I, by signing ... a treaty, change the sentiments of a whole people?'[33]

British naval officers tried to persuade Gezo that palm-oil could be just as lucrative, but he was not enticed. The Egba did their share of slaving too, but in 1848 they sent a petition to Queen Victoria asking for a new road from Abeokuta to Lagos so that they could take up lawful commerce. Lagos was the busiest of the slave

---

[32] H. Thomas, *The Slave Trade*, (New York, Simon & Schuster, 1997), p. 808.
[33] A.H. Foote, *Africa and the American Flag*, (New York, D. Appleton & Co., 1862), p. 82, quoted in Thomas, p. 697.

ports, closed to missionaries who, WMMS and CMS alike, were still making slow progress in Badagry and Abeokuta. A second petition from Abeokuta in 1851 asked Her Majesty to occupy Lagos and bring the country peace. This time Palmerston, the Foreign Secretary, authorized action. The ruling chief in Lagos, a usurper, was ousted and his uncle was reinstated. 'At a single stroke a great export centre of the slave-trade was shut down, Dahomey was deprived of its most powerful ally and Abeokuta given a security it had not before enjoyed.'[34] A treaty negotiated with the reinstated chief included a clause to the effect that

> Complete protection shall be afforded to Missionaries or Ministers of the Gospel, of whatever nation or country, following their vocation of spreading the knowledge and doctrines of Christianity, and extending the benefits of civilization ... nor shall any subject of the King and Chiefs of Lagos who may embrace the Christian faith be, on that account, ... molested or troubled in any manner whatsoever.[35]

In 1854 Freeman made a second tour from Ouidah to Lagos, accompanied by Henry Wharton, and Ebenezer Gardiner was installed as the first European missionary in Lagos. Lagos was formally annexed by Britain in 1861. In that year Thomas Champness,[36] after three years in Sierra Leone, was posted to Abeokuta. His stay was short-lived; his wife died and he returned to an influential ministry in England. Abeokuta was now a prosperous but still a troubled town. The Egba probably suspected that they, like Lagos, were about to lose their independence. They feared that a proposed new road to the interior, by-passing Abeokuta, would bring economic ruin. They accused the missionaries of being in cahoots with the new government. In October 1867 they turned on the missions, looting their premises and expelling the foreigners with nothing but the clothes they were wearing. For years thereafter the church in Abeokuta depended almost wholly on Yoruba ministers and teachers, many of whom had grown up in Freetown. It was 1880 before expatriates were able to return.

Wesleyan ambition was not restricted to Yorubaland. John Milum, first Chairman of the separate Lagos section, not only built up the church in Lagos itself but set his sights on 'a Central Africa mission'. He was encouraged – but unsurprisingly not financed – by the Committee. Michael Elliott, who joined Milum in 1879, was sped on his way from London with the parting words, 'Remember, Lake Chad!' The lake, however, was 800 miles, in a straight line, from Lagos. Milum succeeded in planting a church in Nupé country 300 miles up the Niger and stationing an African agent, Allahura Sharpe, where he was joined

---

[34]   C.P. Groves, *The Planting of Christianity in Africa*, (4 vols, London, Lutterworth Press, 1948–58), vol. 2, p. 56.

[35]   A.C. Burns, *History of Nigeria*, (London, Allen & Unwin, 1929), Appendix C.

[36]   See pp. 202–3.

by Elliott. But Elliott almost died in 1886 and had to leave Africa. The station was eventually handed on to the CMS.

John Halligey, who had earlier served in Sierra Leone, was the first Chairman of the fully fledged Lagos District. From 1887 he was asked to administer the Gold Coast District as well and he moved his base to Cape Coast in 1889 until he retired in 1891, but he was a natural itinerant and spent months at a time on his missionary journeys. The long arduous route marches, the uncomfortable nights, the malarial fevers daunted him no more than the burden of caring for the churches, encouraging the local leaders and winning over backsliders. On one of his first journeys he was caught up in yet another Egba–Dahomey war. His party was attacked at Abeokuta, their provisions taken, four of his companions carried off on suspicion of being Dahomey agents and Halligey himself detained. Only through the intervention of the Governor in Lagos were they all released. But cheering messages came from other Yoruba towns distancing themselves from the Egbas' actions and requesting Halligey to return and plant mission stations. So the next year he took the alternative route through Ijebu country and settled agents in a number of centres, not least in Ibadan which was one of the biggest cities in Africa at the period. The first chapel there, serving a population of 200,000, consisted of a mud parapet wall about a metre high, with a thatched roof and a metre-wide gap for ventilation between the eaves and wall.

Figure 10.2   Lagos District Mission Boat, a gift from John Halligey's friends in York, 1886

Two days after getting back from this long tour he set out again, this time travelling west to Porto Novo and Popo. This section had brought little reward and agents of the mission had often been imprisoned or expelled. Bernasko, the agent stationed in Ouidah, obtained an interview with Gezo's son Glele in 1860 and Glele stated that his people would not be permitted to become Christians, because they would become cowards and refuse to go to war. Nor would he allow children to attend mission schools. Later Milum travelled by dug-out along the lagoons as far as Grand Popo, where he appointed Ellis Williams, a missionary, and Aaron Franklin, an African minister, to work together in the German sphere of influence. Bryan Roe, Halligey's colleague and one of his successors in the chair, spent two spells in Togoland; the first was cut short when he almost died of blackwater fever. He returned in 1891 and found that 'congregations, schools and finances all show very gratifying progress'. However the French and German governments now insisted that teaching in the schools should be in the language of the occupying power. The difficulties this created were to some extent resolved when two German Methodists, Johannes Muhleder and then Karl Ulrich, worked on the Togo side while Henri Arnett was the first of many French ministers to serve in Dahomey.

Meanwhile Yoruba work continued to spread. In 1892, when Ijebu Remo was annexed to the Protectorate, the new Chairman, Dawson Sutcliffe, accompanied by a Christian merchant who was a scion of the royal house, visited the king and was given land in Sagamu. In 1894 the merchant, Prince Ademuyiwa visited England, spoke at the WM Conference and addressed missionary meetings around the country. On his return he busied himself in evangelistic work and within three years Ijebu Remo reported seven congregations, two ministers, six lay agents and fifty-two members. In another decade membership had grown ten-fold. In Ijesha the king, who had become a Christian while living for a time in Sierra Leone, repeatedly asked for a mission to his capital Ilesa. In 1898 at last a local fund in Lagos made it possible and Frederic Martin, an African minister, was posted there. As happened everywhere, there was opposition from the partisans of traditional religious practice, but the king's influence thwarted them. Though he lived and died a polygamist and never became a church member, he insisted on a Christian funeral and when the time came in 1901 the old rites were not performed. Both Ilesa and Sagamu were destined to become major centres of Methodist activity.

In the usual fashion elementary schools, in the most basic of classrooms, were built wherever the church was firmly established. Most of the first teachers were themselves poorly educated, but their diligence – albeit with exceptions – produced a gradual rise in standards. The Lagos High School was built in 1878 and by 1890 had an African headmaster, W.B. Euba. From 1893 to 1902 the head was Jacob Samuel, who had been trained in England at Richmond College. He resigned from the ministry in 1902 when he was appointed the first Secretary of the Egba United Government, the first attempt to establish democratic local government in the Yoruba area. He took his Christian values into public service and proved an astute administrator. Euba returned as head of the High School from 1902 to 1913, by which time it was fully self-supporting and oversubscribed.

Mrs Milum's sister, Sarah Smith, came to Lagos in 1879 to start a girls' high school, but within weeks Mrs Milum died and Sarah's own health and grief caused her early departure. The school eventually opened under African leadership, but its results were too poor to qualify for government grants and it was closed for a time in 1890. More suitable classrooms were built at the end of the century.

By 1900 Methodism was firmly rooted in West Africa and new Christians were joining the church at a steady, if not spectacular, rate. The numbers recorded gave no inkling of the amazing growth Nigerian Methodism was to see in the twentieth century, but the seeds were being planted. At the same time Islam was attracting more and more followers. For every African who forsook fetish for the Bible, another turned to the Qu`ran. Hausa traders took their faith to market along with their wares. Missionary literature described 'a powerful revival of Muslim fanaticism', called Islam 'the Antichrist of this continent' and declared that 'the march of Muhammad must be arrested without delay. A new and holier Crusade is called for.'[37] Religious people and religious zeal, as Nigeria knows too well, can be hateful as well as loving and compassionate.

South Africa

The second half of the nineteenth century saw Wesleyan activity extend eastwards into Natal, Swaziland and Mozambique and northwards to the Transvaal and beyond. At the same time the work centred on Cape Town and Grahamstown continued to grow. The numbers joining the church were much greater than in West Africa. Membership grew from 8,000 to 20,000 between 1856 and 1882 and from 20,000 to 73,000 in the next decade. Stations were opened in Port Elizabeth, Bloemfontein and East London when they were still insignificant places; they became the bases for evangelization in far-flung rural areas. Disagreements with the Committee far away in London were frequent. In 1878 James Scott, a future President of the South African Conference, sought to change the rule which barred from membership those who did not attend class meeting, on the grounds that it prevented good men from holding office. A sub-committee of the Society reacted fiercely: the scheme was 'utterly subversive of all that is distinctive of Methodist organization'.[38] (Scott's proposal related to white congregations in places like Bloemfontein; the committee was perhaps influenced by the opinion of John Milum, from his very different situation in West Africa, that 'Our class system gives us a great hold upon the people and enables us to keep a purer Church than we otherwise should.'[39])

---

[37] Findlay and Findlay, p. 202 – the language is not untypical.
[38] Cragg, p. 137.
[39] Milum to George Perks, a WMMS Secretary, 10 April 1877: SOAS, MMS/West Africa/Correspondence/Gold Coast/FBN12.

Tribal warfare continued in the Transkei and Peter Hargreaves, at Clarkebury among the Thembu from 1857 to 1881 and at Mfundisweni among the Mpondo from 1882 to 1901, played an influential and sometimes risky part in defusing critical disputes, mostly over cattle-stealing. The 3,000 square miles of Pondoland were annexed by the Cape Colony in 1894; that the annexation took place by treaty and not by conquest was largely due to the mediation of Hargreaves, trusted by the Mpondo chiefs and the colonial government alike.

The visit of William Taylor, a noted American Methodist evangelist, in 1866, had a powerful impact. He was welcomed by his fellow-Methodists:

> His unassuming manners, his scrupulous delicacy in abstaining from any interference in local church affairs, his shrewd observations, and his intense devotion, won their affection, and they honoured the gifts of God in him.[40]

He made no great impression in Cape Town, but as he moved eastwards his preaching began to have a profound effect. At first his message had reached English-speakers only, but at King William's Town he was joined by Charles Pamla who proved an able interpreter and a dynamic evangelist.[41] Their joint ministry produced at least 6,000 new Christians. Missionaries worn out with the struggle to hold congregations together in violent times, exhausted by the task of rebuilding ruined churches, despondent and apprehensive of further attacks, found their hopes and their ardour revived. Men and women, both black and white, were changed, as Henry Dugmore reported:

> Leaders in vice have become champions in defence of the religion they had reviled. Men of profligate lives, with bitter shame, made confession, and are endeavouring to repair the evil of their former courses … Drunkards, who were the terror of their families and the pests of their neighbourhood, have renounced the use of intoxicating liquors … Profane swearers are shuddering at the recollection of their favourite oaths and blasphemies. Frauds and wrongs have been acknowledged, and restitution made. Long-standing family discords have been healed …[42]

Charles Pamla had grown up in a Methodist family in Annshaw, a mission station which bore the name of William Shaw's partner in ministry. From an early age he wanted to be an *umfundisi* (minister). While herding sheep he would practise public speaking by preaching to the trees. At the time he met Taylor he was a

---

[40]   J. Whiteside, *History of the Wesleyan Methodist Church of South Africa*, (London, Elliot Stock, 1906), p. 265, quoted in Groves, vol. 2, p. 252.

[41]   See Millard, pp. 61–3; D. Balia, 'Charles Pamla and the 1866 Revival' in P. Denis (ed.), *The Making of an Indigenous Clergy in Southern Africa*, (Pietermaritzburg, Cluster Publications, 1995).

[42]   *Missionary Notices,* 26 December 1866, p. 7.

candidate for the ministry and in 1867 he was accepted for training at the new theological institution at Healdtown. Ordained in 1871, he proved a faithful minister for over forty years.

Three others were trained with him at Healdtown. These were the first black South African ministers. By the time they started their training there were already twelve African ministers in West Africa. In South Africa there had not at first been the same emphasis on education. Healdtown, situated north of Grahamstown, was named after one of its benefactors, James Heald, the first Methodist MP. It had opened modestly as an industrial school in 1852 and developed with the encouragement of the Governor of Cape Colony, Sir George Grey, who secured a grant for the buildings of £3,000. After Grey's departure in 1861 policy changed, government grants ceased and one by one industrial schools closed. Healdtown however was re-invented as a teacher-training and theological college and quickly became one of South Africa's foremost institutions of learning. Its purpose was to produce graduates who, as Christians, would cultivate and practise enlightened approaches to community development and it successfully transformed the lives of many people across the Eastern Cape. Westminster College in London, which also owed much to James Heald's support, regularly provided staff and for a century Healdtown enjoyed the reputation of being the largest and one of the most advanced African residential schools in the country.[43] Ministerial training was transferred in 1880 to a new institution at Lesseyton and at the end of the century to Lovedale, a Presbyterian campus, from which developed (in 1916) the University of Fort Hare.

John Kilner, when as a WMMS Secretary he visited South Africa in 1880, was scathing about the Wesleyans' educational provision. He contrasted what he saw on his tour of the Districts with his experience in India and Ceylon.[44] There, he wrote, 'every Missionary actively interests himself in teaching the youth of the land; here there is scarcely a case in which the Missionary uses this lever'. Not long afterwards a 5,000 acre plot was bought by the Transvaal District which became its educational centre and was named Kilnerton.

Natal became a British colony in 1843. It combined the coastal town, then spelt D'Urban, and the short-lived Boer Republic of Natalia with its capital at Pietermaritzburg. William Holden was sent to Durban in 1847 and for a time he was the only minister of any denomination in the town and the Wesleyan chapel was the only place of worship. His pastoral duties were almost wholly to Europeans; but his evangelistic vision encompassed the warrior Zulus whose territory adjoined Natal until it was annexed in 1897. From 1850 onwards thousands of settlers, including many Methodists, moved into Natal and congregations with ready-made local preachers and class leaders sprang up. The growth of the church was so rapid that in 1855 Natal was made a separate Methodist District. In 1860

---

[43]   Later alumni were Seth Mokitimi, the first black President of the South Africa Conference, and Nelson Mandela.

[44]   See p. 95.

the demography of the territory was again reshaped with the arrival of indentured labourers from India, brought over to work on the sugar, coffee and cotton estates. The WMMS promptly appointed Ralph Stott, a minister with eighteen years' experience in Ceylon[45] who spoke both Tamil and Hindustani, to work among them. He was joined by his son Horner, also a minister; between them they made the rounds of eighty estates. Their success in terms of converts was unremarkable; their energetic service among a Hindu community was ahead of its time.

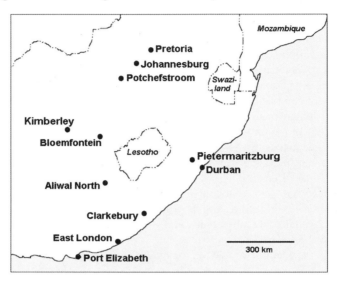

Map 13   South Africa: new centres in the north and east

In 1866, when Taylor and Pamla held meetings in Natal, 500 new members were made in a short space of time. The revival inspired a spontaneous movement aimed at evangelizing the Zulu kraals. It was named *Unzondelo*, meaning 'desire', and was eventually institutionalized as the 'Wesleyan Native Home Mission'. Whites and 'natives' belonged to the same District of the same Church, but in church life as in daily life there was a minimum of interaction – except that the white members of the Native Home Mission, though outnumbered, kept a tight rein on its activity and funds.

The discovery first of diamonds and then of gold transformed South Africa. The first diamond was found on the banks of the Orange River in 1867 and within a few years the Kimberley mine was attracting thousands of European prospectors and African mineworkers. The church saw a need and seized the opportunity. In 1872 the Diamond Fields Circuit was set up with two English ministers. As security against the theft of precious metals, the African miners were housed

45   See p. 94.

in compounds, crowded together, restricted in their movements, far from their families. It was an unsavoury existence, but it did afford the preachers easy access to people from remote areas they could never have visited. There were miners who, at the end of their contracts, returned to the village with a new faith that they introduced to families and neighbours and the seed of the gospel took root.

Methodism across the Vaal river originated in the ministry of David Mogatla[46] – or Magatta, as Wesleyans wrote his name. Magatta's remarkable story included being captured by an Ndebele raiding party and kept as a domestic slave by the Ndebele chief, Mzilikazi. When the Boers finally drove the Ndebele from Transvaal he escaped and eventually arrived in Thaba 'Nchu where he was converted, learned to read and became a wandering evangelist. He spoke six languages. He settled in Potchefstroom, a town founded by the voortrekkers in 1838 and the first capital of the Zuid-Afrikaansche Republiek. He gathered an African congregation, started a school and provoked the wrath of the Boers who were incensed by the very idea of a black preacher. He was flogged and banished from the town. But he had the good fortune to meet with the Boer commander Paul Kruger who heard his story, took his part and authorized him to return and resume his activities. He built up the congregation and formed the people into Methodist classes. At length the church caught up with him, if only nominally; in 1865 a Potchefstroom circuit was listed on the stations, with 'One earnestly requested'. Then, towards the end of the decade, small gold deposits were found and the character of the area rapidly changed. In 1872 'Potchefstroom (Gold Mines)' became a circuit with three missionaries appointed.

This was the prelude to the gold rush of 1886 when far richer deposits were discovered on the Witwatersrand and the city of Johannesburg sprang up. By then the church was established in Transvaal, which became a separate District in 1880 with Owen Watkins as Chairman. Watkins's missionary service had been put on hold by illness while at Richmond College and he came to South Africa on medical advice. He was first stationed at Pietermaritzburg but after four years the Natal District released him as part of its contribution to developing the Transvaal work. It was, however, 1882 before he was able to take up his duties, as all the ox-carts had been requisitioned by the army in support of military action first against Cetshwayo's Zulus and then in a ten-week war with Kruger's Boers. Civilians were unable to travel until peace was restored. The British incurred heavy losses at the hands of the Boer forces and the outcome was continued Boer self-government, until the lure of gold provoked the better-known – and much more costly – Boer War in 1899.

Watkins made his headquarters in Pretoria, which had become the capital of the Zuid-Afrikaansche Republiek in 1860. Here in northern Transvaal there were already, as in Potchefstroom, churches founded by local initiative. Watkins was delighted to discover that for nine years Klass Oliphant had been preaching in a hamlet called Aapjee's River, supporting himself and well respected by the

---

[46]   See Millard, pp. 45–6.

local community.[47] There were some ninety people in the congregation, most of whom were waiting to be baptized. Another self-made evangelist was Hans Apie, converted while living at the Cape and now back home at Makapan's kraal where he had gathered over 200 worshippers.[48] He joined Watkins and others on preaching tours further afield. Much further north in Soutpansberg, Samuel Mathabathe had also come home. In the 1860s he went to Natal to find work, met up with Methodists and was converted. There he learned to read and write, to farm efficiently and to preach. Arriving back in Soutpansberg, he was told by the chief, 'If you hold meetings to talk about the 'new Chief' [Jesus] you will have to leave the tribe or I will put you to death.'[49] Undeterred he followed his calling and persevered in spite of opposition. More than once he saw the church he had built with his own hands pulled down and each time began again. He sent two of his converts to study with the French missionaries in Lesotho. They walked 700 miles to get there and 700 miles back again two years later. When Watkins found Mathabathe and saw the hostility he had to endure, he bought a farm where the little Christian community settled, which became known as the Good Hope Mission. Both Mathabathe and Apie became candidates for the ministry; they proved unable to cope with the studies but went on serving as beloved evangelists.

The origins of Methodist work in Mozambique lie in the activity of yet another unofficial evangelist, Robert Mashaba.[50] Born around 1850 at Ntembi's Place, near Delagoa Bay (now Maputo Bay), he too travelled to Durban in search of work. He had never been to school but in Durban he attended basic evening classes run by missionaries. In 1875 he moved to Port Elizabeth to improve his prospects and there began attending Wesleyan services. It was as a result of a repeated vision and a voice commanding him to pray that he joined the church. He saved £40 and went to study at Lovedale. In 1885 he returned to Mozambique and started a church and school. Though there were no other Methodist Christians in the country, he insisted that his church was Wesleyan. It grew to 200 members with four local preachers and a class leader by 1893, when he was visited by George Weavind. Weavind had become Chairman of the District when Watkins moved north to Mashonaland. Again, the possibility of entering the ministry was raised but shelved. Later Mashaba was falsely accused of complicity in a revolt against the Portuguese and deported to Cape Verde. The Methodist network came to his rescue; the intervention of Robert Moreton, the long-serving missionary in Portugal, secured his release but he was prohibited from returning to Mozambique. He entered the ministry and worked on the Witwatersrand and in Swaziland until his death in 1935. He translated 100 hymns into Tsonga, his native tongue, for the

---

[47]   D. Crafford, *Trail-blazers of the Gospel: Black Pioneers in the Missionary History of Southern Africa*, (Pretoria, ISWEN, 1991), pp. 125–6.

[48]   See Millard, p. 4.

[49]   W.G. Mears, *Methodist Torchbearers*, (Rondebosch, Methodist Missionary Department, 1955), p. 16.

[50]   See Millard, pp. 33ff.

benefit of the many migrant workers who came to the mines from Mozambique and north-east Transvaal.

From 1886 a new challenge arose at the heart of the Transvaal District. Johannesburg was born and fast became a teeming city. The first Wesleyan church soon proved too small and within three years no fewer than eleven were built as more neighbourhoods sprang up. In the beginning one missionary served both English and African congregations; by 1895 there were three missionaries assigned to English work and another, along with three African ministers, to African work. The Africans included not only mineworkers but domestic servants in white households. Visitation was not easy but numbers grew apace. There were setbacks of all sorts. The world's largest dynamite facility was close by and when a trainload blew up it left a crater 250 metres wide and thirty metres deep, around a hundred people dead and 2,000 injured and many properties destroyed, including the brand new Fordsburg church and manses.[51]

Then the outbreak of the Boer War[52] led to the expulsion of missionaries, the disruption of church life and the destruction of buildings. But the African ministers held the flock together, to such good effect that the membership of the District increased by 30 per cent, from 8,794 in 1899 to 11,165 in 1903.

From 1883 only the Transvaal and Swaziland District remained under the British Conference. As early as 1860 William Shaw had suggested that there should be a central executive of all the Districts, which were reporting separately to London. The Committee rejected the proposal, but in 1873 a triennial General Meeting of representatives from all five Districts – Cape of Good Hope, Graham's Town, Queen's Town (as those places were spelt at the time), Bechuana and Natal – was instituted. By its third meeting there was a groundswell in favour of unifying them in a provincial Conference after the North American and Australian model. WMMS secretary John Kilner made a tour of the Districts and then chaired the Meeting. He was not overly impressed with what he found. Besides his views on educational provision, he had other criticisms of the missionaries and he authorized the ordination of over fifty evangelists whom they had failed to advance. But he recognized the argument for 'home rule' and drew up a draft scheme which was adopted by the Meeting in 1880, somewhat modified by the Committee in 1881, agreed by the Conference in 1882 and effected in 1883. The new Conference continued to receive grants-in-aid for twenty years, but from £14,000 in 1882 they reduced to nothing by the war's end. The Transvaal District was by mutual agreement excluded from the new Conference. It was wiser to administer work in the Boer Republic from London than from Cape Town or Durban; and the District was still in its infancy. In 1889 Watkins and Weavind attended the South African Conference to discuss transferring Transvaal to its care, but it was still premature and the District remained under the WMMS until 1932.

---

[51]   A graphic eye-witness account of the explosion is in a letter quoted in F. Clemmow, *Days of Sorrow, Times of Joy*, (Kibworth, Matador, 2012), pp. 201–4.

[52]   See B. Nasson, *The South African War 1899–1902*, (London, Arnold, 1999).

Rhodesia

Cecil Rhodes arrived in South Africa in 1870 at the age of 17. Within twenty years he had made a fortune out of Kimberley diamonds. He was an adventurer and set his sights on a land north of the Limpopo river where he judged there were more fortunes to be made. He had to negotiate with Mzilikazi's son Lobengula, now settled in the area which became known as Matabeleland; but his objective lay further north in Shona country. He formed the British South Africa Company and in 1890 set out with 117 wagons, 180 pioneers and 300 armed police to protect them. To steer clear of Lobengula's kraal they slowly cut a new road to a place they named Fort Salisbury in honour of the British premier. The column avoided the Ndebele *impis* (warriors) on their slow journey, but in 1893, ignoring the pact Lobengula had made, the *impis* made war on the settlers. It was a short but bloody war, which ended in defeat for the Ndebele. They revolted again in 1896 when rinderpest destroyed their herds of oxen and they attributed this hitherto unknown plague to the coming of the white man; but they were speedily put down.

The Society, and in particular Watkins, had already shown a cautious interest in advancing northwards. A Finance & General Purposes Committee minute early in 1890 expressed its 'heartfelt sympathy … with the desire' of the Transvaal District 'to extend the sphere of our operations and carry the Gospel further into the interior of Africa, but … in the present position of the Society's funds it is impossible for the Committee to find any money …'. Watkins was not to be put off; he persuaded Rhodes to offer £100 per annum to support a Wesleyan minister in the new country. The Committee hesitated no longer and in 1891 Watkins himself made the arduous journey to Mashonaland, accompanied by Isaac Shimmin who had been working at Kilnerton. Their first service 'was held in a store. The reading desk was a barrel, a few soap boxes were the pews, and a congregation of four men crowded in.'[53] Watkins did not stay long. His chief role was to persuade Rhodes to allocate to the Society three farms and a prime site in the town. He had intended to resume his responsibilities in Pretoria but was desperately ill on the journey back and had to return to England.

With the distance so great and the travel so difficult, it made no sense to administer the new work from Pretoria and in 1894 the Mashonaland District was separated. There was the usual twin focus to the work: on the one hand a ministry to the European community in Salisbury and Bulawayo, the city built on the ruins of Lobengula's kraal, and on the other the establishment of strong centres for African work. The first of these were at Nenguwo, Kwenda and Epworth in Mashonaland and Tegwani in Matabeleland, each with enough land on which to build major institutions in the twentieth century. African work was headed initially by ten Basotho and Xhosa evangelists from South Africa. Two of them were killed in a Shona revolt in 1896.[54] James Anta and his congregation of eighteen worshippers

---

[53]   C. Thorpe, *Limpopo to Zambesi*, (London, Cargate Press, 1951), p. 43.
[54]   See pp. 259–61.

were speared to death after a midweek service. Modumedi Moleli was killed at Nenguwo, where he had begun to develop a church and school, after going to the rescue of a white farmer who had been wounded in an earlier attack.[55]

The use of workers from South Africa was not long continued. It was argued that 'the expense of this arrangement, and the uncertainty that such workers would remain for any length of time'[56] made it unworkable, ignoring the fact that the same objections could be raised to the use of far more expensive British ministers. In any event it was urgent to train local Christians and in 1900 John White – whose value to Rhodesia was infinitely greater than his cost to the Society – opened a seminary within sight of Moleli's grave. This institution was subsequently developed with a benefaction from the Bradford philanthropist Joshua Waddilove and took his name.

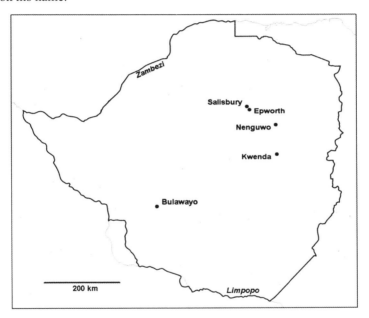

Map 14   Zimbabwe: the first stations in Rhodesia

The ambivalent relationship between European and African in the nineteenth century can be illustrated by two quotations from the pioneer Isaac Shimmin. Shortly after his arrival he wrote that he rejoiced that 'the more I see of the natives, the more do I rejoice at the possibilities before us ... they are likely to make sound and intelligent Christian believers'. Yet he retained ingrained assumptions which contrast

---

[55]   See B. Graaff, *Modumedi Moleli*, (Harare, Mambo Press, 1988).
[56]   Findlay and Holdsworth, vol. 4, p. 389.

with that assessment. His words could have come from many a missionary not only in the nineteenth century but well into the twentieth:

> These people with centuries of barbarism behind them, and with the bias of their own moral nature so set against godliness, are at first incapable of comprehending even those plain religious facts which appear so self-evident to every Christian child.[57]

> Men, women and children listened eagerly to the strange gospel, but the simple truths of the Bible were utterly beyond them. I had clever interpreters and as clearly as I could, I told them the 'old old story' of redemption, but even this was above their grasp. I spoke of sin, repentance and forgiveness; they only smiled and looked puzzled. They knew that this religion must be very good, for it was the creed of the superior strangers, but they complained that it was all very difficult to understand.

> These people are so dense that nothing seems to make an impression and they must be taught slowly, 'line by line, precept upon precept, here a little and there a little'. Their centuries of inherited barbarism must not be forgotten.[58]

A deep sense of disappointment underlied these words. Missionaries to Africa were often in despair both at the lack of conversions and at the quality of converts' lives. Disillusionment was shared by secular administrators as well. They feared criticism from those at home and wondered whether they were wasting their time and the church's or the public's resources. Communications from the WMMS Committee did sometimes reveal impatience at paltry results. Missionaries were not likely to accuse themselves of inadequacy and fell back on two excuses. One was that they were never provided with enough resources, enough funds or enough personnel to do a proper job. The other was the patronizing racist explanation so forthrightly expressed by Shimmin.

The truly remarkable thing was not that African Christians were so few but that they were, by the century's end, so many.

---

[57]   *Work and Workers in the Mission Field*, February 1893, p. 59.
[58]   *Work and Workers in the Mission Field*, October 1893, pp. 432–3.

Chapter 11
Islands in the Sun

Thousands of miles apart, the West Indies and the South Pacific were both regions where Christianity became the dominant creed in the course of the nineteenth century, though in Guyana as in Fiji indentured labourers from India brought their own religious beliefs and practices. In both regions, churches were planted and flourished. Slavery and its aftermath shaped Caribbean society for ever, whereas Pacific cannibalism, episodic and practised largely in the context of warfare, left a less enduring mark once those localized wars were brought to an end. For the purposes of this chapter, the 'islands' in the Caribbean sun include three coastal territories of the American mainland, Honduras, Panama and Guyana.

The Caribbean

The 1833 Act for the Abolition of Slavery provided 'for promoting the industry of the manumitted slaves and for compensating the persons hitherto entitled to the services of such slaves'. Compensation to the tune of £20 million – 40 per cent of the government's annual expenditure – was paid out; the transition from slavery to industrious liberty was to be managed via a compulsory period of 'apprenticeship', during which the freed slaves were obliged to remain in their master's employment, albeit as wage-earners. The six years specified in the Act were reduced to four and in August 1838 they were at last liberated from this bond-service; there was renewed rejoicing and more celebrations in church. Unsurprisingly most field-workers soon deserted the plantations. They complained of the small wage that the planters offered: it was as little as four pence a day in some instances. In Jamaica the planters began to turn the people off their lands, destroying their huts and cutting down the fruit trees their former labourers had planted. The ill-will on both sides and the planters' lack of tact and patience drove the labourers from the estates. Some drifted to the towns, many set up as independent small-holders on hitherto unoccupied land. From the Virgin and Leeward Islands there was a tide of emigration to the expanding colonies of Trinidad and Demerara. Only in Barbados were the labourers content to remain on the plantations.

The results were devastating. Gradually the large estates decayed and many were abandoned. Their decline was compounded in 1848 by Britain's termination of sugar-duties in the interests of Free Trade, which meant that the island colonies could not compete with slave-grown sugar from Cuba and Brazil. Later, beet-sugar production in Europe made matters still worse. In 1850 less than 15 per cent of the world's sugar-trade was in beet; by 1900 it was two-thirds.

Other factors detrimental to the life of the islands and consequently to church life included: the frequent hurricanes, the occasional earthquake and volcanic eruption, epidemics of cholera – 32,000 died in Jamaica when it made its appearance in 1850 – smallpox and yellow fever and the disruption caused by the American Civil War of 1861–64 which had a dire effect on trade, especially in the Bahamas. These were disasters over which the islanders had little control – though the insanitary conditions in which many lived were responsible for the heavy toll of disease. The provision of schooling, on the other hand, was something which might have been much better done. Schools for their slaves had never been high on the planters' agenda and emancipation made no difference; they were not ready to sponsor the village schools which would have brought education to the masses. The valiant efforts of the churches and the limited investment of government funds were quite inadequate to the task. In the first few years Wesleyan expenditure on education grew tenfold, thanks to the Special Fund raised in Britain and to parliamentary grants amounting to £10,000. Twenty-four new schools were opened, but that achievement was no more than a drop in the Caribbean bucket. Thousands of children would have slipped through the net, but the combined efforts of church and state did not so much as produce a net to slip through. They remained unschooled. Yet for the Wesleyan Districts and the WMMS, the cost of maintaining non-fee-paying schools was an ongoing and crippling financial burden.

For all that, membership grew apace for a decade after emancipation. Across the area some 32,000 Wesleyan members in 1833 grew to 54,000 in 1844. It was, except in the Bahamas, a predominantly black membership; white members tended to transfer their allegiance to the established church. Jamaica, much the largest District, saw its numbers double in seven years, despite the difficulty of ministering to those who had scattered to remote smallholdings and despite a series of contentious internal disputes. There was a long-running argument about wearing gowns in the pulpit: dignified according to some, pretentious in the eyes of others. There were serious differences between Thomas Pennock, the Chairman,[1] and John Corlett, his successor. Their feud led to two rival Synods being held in 1834 and Pennock's secession in 1838, taking 3,000 dissident Wesleyans with him. Corlett too got into trouble. He overspent recklessly on new chapels to accommodate the swelling congregations and was moved on from Jamaica, only to repeat his extravagance on other islands. Nonetheless Corlett, a powerful Manx preacher and indefatigable worker, spent almost fifty years in the Caribbean and was warmly welcomed back when he was again stationed in Jamaica in 1866.

Robert Young, who had worked in the old Jamaican capital of Spanish Town in the 1820s, was sent back by Conference in 1843 to inspect the work and encourage the workers – a mission he undertook again in the Pacific eleven years later.[2] Young reported in glowing terms on the developments brought about since emancipation. An old black woman encapsulated the contrast with the conditions

---

[1]   See pp. 195 and 208.
[2]   See p. 42.

he had known before, when she crouched down with her hands over her eyes and said, 'In the old days we stood so; but now' – raising herself erect and opening her eyes wide – 'we stand so!'[3]

Membership increase was most remarkable in Barbados, where the birth-pangs of the new era were less traumatic: 383 in 1833 became 1,887 in 1847 and over 4,000 by 1855. The growth in Barbados in the 1850s was counter to the general trend, for total membership in the West Indies peaked at 57,000 in the mid-1840s and then began to decline. The losses can be attributed to a variety of causes. To some extent they arose from migration: members who left one island were not necessarily enrolled when they arrived somewhere else, especially if they went to Panama where the church followed them only belatedly. To some extent they arose from disenchantment with the church's rigid attitude to marriage. Slavery had often torn couples and families apart; where they remained together it was without the benefit of any ceremony save perhaps one of their own devising. For missionaries it was a paramount duty to insist on monogamy and marital faithfulness. At first only a mutual pledge was demanded by Wesleyans; the Anglican clergy reserved to themselves the right to celebrate marriage and black nonconformists were unwilling to seek an Anglican blessing. One by one however the island legislatures extended the prerogative to other denominations. In 1838 an Act – drafted by Richard Matthews, the Methodist barrister[4] – retrospectively afforded legal recognition of the existing marriages of former slaves even where no religious ceremony had taken place and authorized non-Anglican clergy to officiate at weddings and register them.[5] But many couples could not afford the expense of a wedding on a budget which struggled to meet life's bare essentials, even though Wesleyan fees were much less than those demanded by the Established Church. They co-habited happily, but the disapproving eye of the missionaries alienated them. Others drifted or were driven from the church because their lifestyles were incompatible with Christian discipleship; in reaction to the oppression of former years, they substituted idleness for toil or made their liberty into licentiousness. Some again were captivated by *obeah*, a syncretistic African religion which was revived noticeably in mid-century when Cuba-bound slaves were intercepted by the navy and landed in Jamaica.

In spite of these setbacks thousands of Christians witnessed faithfully to their growing families and to their neighbours. But the church struggled to answer the calls made upon its meagre resources. David Barley returned to St Vincent in 1861 after a twelve-year absence and found

---

[3] SOAS, WMMS/West Indies/Jamaica/Correspondence/Various Papers/FBN47.

[4] See p. 63.

[5] It was 1898 before the same provision for non-Anglican officiants was enacted in England.

a half-empty instead of a crowded chapel; the poorer members gone; the mass of the humbler classes who once belonged to us, no longer with us; pew-rents, class and ticket-moneys, Society-membership – all reduced by much more than half.[6]

The ministerial staff was insufficient for the task. Young, in 1843, had recommended that a Theological Institution be opened for young West Indian preachers, but it did not materialize for thirty years. There was no increase in the number of ministers over the quarter-century from 1846 to 1871. Finding stipends was usually problematic and one of the financial issues was whether locally-recruited ministers should be on the same pay-scale as missionaries – a contentious issue for the Committee, wherever a local ministry emerged, for many decades to come. The first black minister in the Caribbean was John Hodge of Anguilla, who was ordained in 1822 and spent much of his ministry on his home island. At the time he began, Synod raised the question of a differential scale and the Committee rejected the idea. Forty years later when the cash-strapped Secretaries wanted to introduce differentials, it was too late. Parity of stipend was now the long-accepted practice and it would have been unjust and injurious to abandon it. Then the Secretaries suggested that the time had come for the West Indian Districts to demonstrate their maturity and reduce their dependency on the Society by meeting the costs of the ministry locally. To this Jonathan Edmondson, the long-serving Chairman of the Jamaica District, replied in forthright terms. He was highly experienced and greatly respected. The Secretaries, he argued in a succession of letters in 1863, were out of touch with reality, for even well-to-do Kingston families had fallen on hard times:

> It is not unusual to find the inmates of what was once a large, commodious dwelling compelled to retreat from one part of the house to another – from the upper storey to the lower storey, from the lower-storey to the out-rooms or what was once the servants' apartments, there to nestle together for years in a room only a few feet square, while the stately mansion falls piecemeal into dust and rotten lumber.[7]

The debts of the District, incurred by ambitious church- and manse-building projects in the boom years, were still outstanding when the slump came and creditors, having heard of the Society's proposed change of policy, were pressing their claims.

> The Missionaries cajole and badger and shame their people for money in every possible way, *ad nauseam* … We feel quite discouraged. We do what we can to

---

6   *Missionary Notices*, October 1861, p. 207.

7   Edmondson to Boyce, 8 December 1863: SOAS, WMMS/West Indies/Jamaica/Correspondence/FBN50.

raise money, and can never give satisfaction ... we never get one cheering word from the ink of the Mission House ...[8]

The tension and frustration were acute on both sides of the Atlantic. In the islands there were needs unmet, opportunities lost, personal hardships, national calamities. In London the Society's income had fallen by 20 per cent through the Reform crisis and the focus of missionary enthusiasm had moved on once the anti-slavery cause was won. In the West Indies there was now a well-established church with thousands of members, whereas in Asia and Africa there were handfuls of Christians attempting to evangelize millions of people. The Committee assumed that, as in England, the West Indian Districts would have competent laypeople who should be encouraged to take a greater role in the church's affairs. They did not appreciate how few had received more than the most elementary education and how ill-equipped they were to be Circuit and Society Stewards.

It was therefore in a mood of doubt and discouragement that the Jamaica Synod met in 1864. In the past seven years its membership had fallen by 7,000 and the signs of revival in 1860 had proved superficial and short-lived. But a crisis of another sort was looming. The griefs of the black population – who outnumbered white Jamaicans in the ratio of 32:1 – boiled over. Three years earlier the island of St Vincent had been convulsed by riots, strikes, arson and then outright rebellion. While only a few hundred engaged in lawlessness, they had general support; exploitation, bullying and insults on the part of tyrannical estate managers were a common experience. The revolt was subdued after three weeks and the activists received savage floggings. It was many years before racial animosity cooled down. Missionaries were reviled not only for their colour but for their insistence, no matter where their sympathies lay, on obedience to the law. Thousands deserted the church on St Vincent. The Morant Bay uprising of 1864 in Jamaica had similar causes. It was confined to the south-east of the island, but men died – and the reprisals were as brutal as those inflicted in India upon the mutineers and rebels of 1858.

Relations between the Jamaican planters and the labouring population had become increasingly embittered. Since 1861 the American Civil War had been raging and food imports from America were very dear. From 1863 a severe drought had begun to afflict Jamaica. In October 1864 some 2,000 labourers led by Paul Bogle, a Baptist who enjoyed considerable influence in the neighbourhood, marched into the town of Morant Bay and demonstrated in front of the Court House. The volunteer militia were called out and fired on the crowd and in retaliation Bogle's men set fire to the building. Some of those inside were killed while trying to escape. Martial Law was proclaimed and the revolt was put down with brutal and indiscriminate severity. Over 1,000 huts were burnt; nearly 600 people, Bogle included, were shot or hanged and a large number of men and women were flogged. In 1866, a Royal Commission found that 'the punishments inflicted during Martial Law were excessive; that the punishment of death was unnecessarily frequent; that

---

[8] Quoted by Findlay and Holdsworth, vol. 2, p. 364.

the floggings were reckless, and at Bath positively barbarous; and that the burning of 1,000 houses was wanton and cruel'.[9] The governor was recalled and dismissed from the Imperial Service. The Jamaica Assembly renounced its powers and the island became a Crown Colony.

This brought about a change in Jamaica's fortunes. There was no further desertion of the church in the manner of St Vincent's sorry experience. The new régime taxed the people as heavily as ever, but they began to see value for their money. George Sargeant, who became Chairman of the District in 1872, compared what he found on his return with the Jamaica he had left thirteen years before. He noted social and economic progress – the development of agriculture and commerce and the absence of the sullen discontent of the masses which he had known formerly. He now saw no insuperable obstacle to the creation of a West Indian Conference. Home rule would encourage local responsibility. This pronouncement, purely personal though it was, was music to the ears of the Committee in London. They had been pressing the point from the time of Young's 1843 deputation and all the more since the autonomous Conferences of France, North America and Australia were set up in the 1850s. But what was right for Jamaica was not necessarily right for the other Districts.

There were now five Districts in all.[10] The Antigua District comprised the Leeward and Virgin Islands, the St Vincent District the Windward Islands, Trinidad and Tobago and the British Guiana District that part of the South American coastal belt which became Guyana. The Bahamas were the fifth District. Haiti was at various times a separate District or administered from Jamaica, while work across the border in the Dominican Republic was part of the Bahamas District from 1855 to 1879. Work in Honduras and later in Panama was linked with Jamaica. Each of these Districts had a chequered history.

Antigua, the birthplace of Caribbean Methodism, suffered a series of painful quarrels among missionaries which ought to have been no more than storms in a teacup but which resulted in a haemorrhage of members between 1844 and 1864; in the Antigua circuit from 2,700 to 1,700 – far fewer than when Coke first landed there – and in the District as a whole from 14,000 to 9,000. A hurricane in 1871 caused £3,000's worth of damage on Antigua alone and was followed by a four-year drought to compound the island's misery. Later, when the Society's grants were being cut, the Chairman, Thomas Chambers, wanted to reduce the number of missionaries rather than cut back on the expense of chapels and schools. The Synod took the opposite view, judging that deliberate understaffing was a suicidal policy. The ministers present at the Synod even agreed to take a cut in their allowances to maintain the numbers. But the Chairman, while reporting the Synod's request,

----

     [9]   *The London Quarterly Review*, 1866, p. 125.
     [10]   A District structure was put in place as early as 1806, not long after it was introduced in Britain; the number and the boundaries of the Districts were changed periodically during the pre-Conference period.

privately advised the Committee to reject it. The indignation when no-one was sent and his action became known can be readily imagined.

Such traumas do not of course constitute the whole story. Between the recurrent upsets there were fruitful periods. Other islands in the District – St Kitts, Nevis, Montserrat, Dominica, Tortola, St Eustatius (the Dutch island, where slavery was at last abolished in 1863), St Bartholomew, St Martin and Anguilla – also had their joys and griefs. St Kitts survived a fire in 1867 which swept through Basseterre, the capital; the hurricane of 1871; and a tragic flood in 1880 when 200 perished, the manse was swept away and the District's records were lost. Chambers, superintendent on St Kitts for twenty years, held the circuit together and both St Kitts and Nevis made great strides towards self-support.

While *St Vincent* Methodism was plunged into disarray by the 1861 uprising, the other islands in the District – Barbados, Trinidad, Tobago and Grenada – pursued their own course. The distances between the islands meant that they had little contact with one another; within Trinidad most Methodists were migrants from other islands, widely scattered and hard to reach. While competent and dedicated laypeople gradually assumed greater responsibility, their horizons were restricted. The suggestion of a Caribbean-wide training institution for locally-recruited ministers did not capture the imagination and the Theological College opened at York Castle in Jamaica in 1875 – an adjunct to the new High School there – was far too distant. Barbados was visited in 1860 by the American evangelist William Taylor and 'a blessed influence and glorious results' were reported.[11] Throughout the islands Methodists worked alongside Anglicans, Roman Catholics and others, but in contention rather than co-operation. Opposition from Anglican clergy was a thorn in the flesh; irksome enough to be recorded by Methodist historians, but beneath the notice of their Anglican counterparts.

In the South American colony of *Demerara*, William Claxton, a former slave from Nevis, had established a Society based on Methodist principles in 1811. The Treaty of Utrecht in 1814 ceded to Britain the Dutch colonies of Essequibo, Demerara and Berbice, which had been occupied by British forces since 1803; these were eventually consolidated as British Guiana in 1831. The treaty opened the door for Thomas Talboys, the soldier–minister from Trinidad,[12] to take up residence in Georgetown, which at the time was the most populous city in the entire Caribbean region. The membership was almost entirely Afro–Guyanese, the majority of them slaves. Before long Talboys was accused by slave-owners of preaching sedition and the mission house was subjected to repeated attacks. The Governor took offence at a Connexional quarterly membership ticket in 1816 which carried the text, *The Kingdom of God suffereth violence*; it appeared 'like a rallying-sign for the slaves'. Talboys was arrested for defamation of character and given legal notice to quit the colony. But Claxton and his fellow-Methodists were not deterred.

---

[11] Findlay and Holdsworth, vol. 2, p. 406.
[12] See p. 45.

Work began in Essequibo (known as the Arabian Coast) in 1835, when the government agreed to a resident minister and a church building on condition that a Methodist school was built, and in Berbice in 1854. The Demerara District was separated from St Vincent in 1836, recombined in 1855 and detached again as the British Guiana District in 1862.

After emancipation and despite immigration from West Indian islands, the rapidly developing colony experienced a shortage of labour, so labourers from Asia were imported to meet the demand. The government paid their passage and they served one or two five-year terms of indentured labour. Many then took advantage of a free return passage, but many stayed. An appeal in the *Missionary Notices* in 1848 referred to 'the thousands of coolies who are being brought here from India'.[13] The writer suggested that, far from home, 'caste must to a great extent have been destroyed, and thus the great obstacle to their conversion must have been removed' – a complete misunderstanding of the power of caste distinctions. But among the new arrivals was an intelligent young Hindu from Trincomalee in Ceylon, where he had been to the Wesleyan school. In Georgetown he was converted and took the baptismal name of Samuel Johnston. He began to translate Bible passages into Tamil and sent a letter, signed by a number of 'his countrymen', to the Committee asking that a missionary be appointed for their special benefit.[14] The missionary James Bickford supported their request. Thus it was that in 1852 John Williams, a Tamil-speaker not long returned from Ceylon, was appointed to Guyana. The government of the day was glad to subsidize his appointment and use him as its Tamil interpreter, but he fell ill and died the next year. It was 1860 before Henry Bronkhurst, an Anglo–Ceylonese minister, took up the mantle. He gave long service but in terms of conversions its result was small; the almost accidental focus on Tamil work had no impact on those Hindus and Muslims who spoke other tongues.

Another great disappointment was the failure of an imaginative scheme for a teacher-training college in Georgetown. A building was erected, a government grant secured, students selected, but Warder, the young, well-qualified but inexperienced missionary Principal appointed by the Society in 1859 – against the advice of the local committee – proved inflexible and intolerant. The experiment was an ignominious failure; when he left, the college was closed and the buildings re-assigned. Not a single teacher had graduated. Twenty years later the District was rocked by another scandal. John Greathead was Chairman from 1874 to 1883. He was not only spendthrift and un-businesslike; he borrowed to meet his debts and secretly borrowed again on worse terms to cover the first loans. These underhand transactions were known in the colony and reported to London from 1877, but only in 1881 did an investigation uncover the extent of the irregularities. His profligacy

---

[13]   William English, letter dated 3 December 1847, in *Missionary Notices* 1848, p. 61.

[14]   J. Bickford, *An Autobiography of Christian Labour, 1838–1888*, (London, Charles H. Kelly, 1890), p. 83. 'Countrymen' presumably refers to ethnic Tamils rather than just Ceylonese.

cost the District £12,000. Astonishingly, at the point when he was recalled to Britain he was offered and accepted an Anglican curacy in Georgetown and then attempted to win over his former flock to his new parish. In view of the Society's failure to exercise adequate control over Greathead, it took responsibility for repaying some of the debt, but the balance weighed heavily on the District for years.

In spite of these vicissitudes, 'It would be wrong to suppose that the misdoing or inefficiency of those in high places nullified all the faithful toil of the missionary staff'[15] – or indeed, of the Guyanese Christians whose standard of living was barely at subsistence level but whose faith and discipleship were unswerving. Their commitment to evangelization led to new work among the East Indians and Capoey Amerindians being developed in the twentieth century.

The advent of Methodism in *Haiti* was due to the recommendation of a ship's captain, Francis Reynolds, whose vessel docked briefly at Port-au-Prince in 1815. He obtained an invitation from the President of the infant republic, which had wrested independence from France in 1804; the embryo – not yet infant – WMMS responded with two missionaries within a year. However, a change of régime drove them out less than two years later. But a small group of Methodists, sometimes having to meet in secret at the home of Mme Antoine Bauduy, persevered. Meanwhile a rival government, based at Cap Haitien in the north of the island, allowed in a different pair of missionaries in 1820, but a combination of ill health and political pressures compelled their departure too within months. It was 1828 before a missionary returned to the island and 1835 before work recommenced at Cap Haitien.

The one who returned in 1828 was a Haitian: St Denis Bauduy, Mme Bauduy's son, who had spent four years in England and was trained under the direction of Jabez Bunting and his colleagues. For seven years he was the only minister on the island; he went on to give, in all, thirty-five years' ministry to his homeland. The Society recognized Haiti as a District in 1834. The first Chairman, John Tindall, who had clashed with Bauduy, suffered a breakdown and departed abruptly in 1840. He was succeeded by two men of stature who between them served for seventy-six years: Mark Baker Bird from 1840 to 1879 and Thomas Picot from 1879 to 1916.

Bird miraculously survived a devastating earthquake in 1842, which destroyed Cap Haitien as comprehensively as the earthquake of 2010 destroyed Port-au-Prince. Then he shepherded the District through a series of political upheavals between 1844 and 1850 which saw the eastern half of the island permanently separated from Haiti as the Dominican Republic and placed severe restrictions on work in the rural areas. Because of these restrictions 'Wesleyan Methodism (became) a small élitist minority ... This was a consequence of a narrow concentration of effort into urban schools and dealing with bourgeois congregations.'[16] The schools which Bird started played an important part in church development; when the

---

[15]   Findlay and Holdsworth, vol. 2, p. 415.
[16]   L.J. Griffiths, *History of Methodism in Haiti*, (Port-au-Prince, Imprimerie Méthodiste, 1991), p. 72.

troubles died down a boarding department was added to the secondary school in Port-au-Prince which not only benefited children from the interior but enabled Bird to maintain contact with places from which he was excluded.

The church, however, failed to grow. A promising group of lay leaders and potential ministers dwindled, as one was dismissed for immorality, two became Baptists, another joined the Episcopalian Church, one died at the age of 24 and only Othello Bayard emerged to give valuable service, first as a teacher and from 1859 as an ordained minister.[17] Then in 1862 Bauduy resigned after a series of disagreements with missionary colleagues and two years later Bayard, unable to care for his family on the reduced stipend the Committee in London imposed on local ministers, broke the rules by engaging in trade to supplement his income. For that he was compelled to leave the ministry, though he continued to work loyally for the Methodist cause for another twenty years. Along with these disappointments the numbers of local preachers, class leaders and Sunday school teachers dwindled as well.

The woes of the mission increased when in 1860 the Haitian government signed a Concordat with the Holy See which brought an influx of Roman Catholic clergy and religious and a substantial contribution from the national exchequer towards their upkeep; and again when in 1869 the Port-au-Prince premises were razed to the ground, along with much of the city, in the course of civil war. The Secretaries, who had had many a harsh exchange with Bird on questions of finance and policy over the years, contemplated abandoning Haiti but asked George Sargeant to go over from Jamaica and assess the situation. Sargeant's conclusions were unexpected:

> … our work in Hayti has taken a much broader, deeper, firmer hold upon the people than any mere tabulated results can indicate. True our numbers are but few among the masses of Port-au-Prince and more insignificant still among the population of the country, but many of them are among the most intelligent of the community, and the most influential too …

> Mr Bird has secured the affection of our people, and the confidence of all classes with whom I have conversed, and it is thought that no better man can be found to meet the present need.[18]

The premises were rebuilt, the school re-opened and government grants were obtained.

Bird remained in office for ten years more, but his health deteriorated and in 1879, at the age of 71, he retired to Jersey. Thomas Picot's Chairmanship did not begin well. Three French-speaking missionary reinforcements died within a few

---

[17]   Griffiths, p. 103.
[18]   Letter from Sargeant, 9 July 1870, quoted by Griffiths, p. 130.

short years. A smallpox epidemic which ravaged the island prevented the Synod from meeting in 1881. Civil strife continued to pit black against mulatto Haitians. The advent of a West Indian Conference did nothing to make Picot's task easier.

It had seemed in 1844 as though the West Indies might soon be ready for autonomy, but then the church's fortunes began to decline. On a visit in 1878–79 Marmaduke Osborn, one of the WMMS Secretaries, having toured the area, concluded that the time had not yet come – most members were both too poor for self-support and ill-equipped for self-government. George Sargeant, who accompanied Osborn on his tour, was disappointed; most of the missionaries were relieved. But by 1883, the year an autonomous South African Conference was established, Osborn had changed his mind. In January the Synods were sent a draft scheme; by the time the British Conference met, the scheme had been revised and was adopted. Recognizing that the cost of travel was bound to be a burden, it provided for a triennial Conference, overseeing two parallel annual conferences: Western, comprising Jamaica and Haiti, the Bahamas and Honduras, and Eastern, comprising everywhere else, with around 23,000 members in each. The scheme was parachuted into the West Indies without any of the consultation that had marked the creation of other Affiliated Conferences. The principle of autonomy was never put to the Synods, but only the details. The Antigua and Bahamas Synods declined to debate them and when in 1884 the scheme was put into effect the Bahamas and Honduras remained outside it, continuing as Districts of the British Conference and reporting directly to the WMMS.

The *Bahamas* work was well established. It was begun in 1800 by the Barbadian William Turton who had already pioneered the work in Tobago and St Bartholomew. At first linked with Antigua, in 1812 the Bahamas became a separate District. The islands were distinctive in many respects: located in the Atlantic rather than the Caribbean; much less dependent on sugar (cotton cultivation was attempted but the soil proved too poor); the Methodist community, reflecting the demography, included far more white members than on the other islands; although severe restrictions were placed for a time on religious activity among slaves, from 1820 many injustices – other than slavery itself – were removed by the colony's legislature. The church grew apace, both before and after emancipation. The capital, Nassau, prospered during the American Civil War, but it was prey to hurricanes; in 1866 the newly-completed Trinity chapel was demolished by one, as were church buildings and manses at Spanish Wells, Eleuthera, Harbour Island and Andros. The Society gave far more generous assistance to their reconstruction than it did in the Caribbean; it is difficult to escape the conclusion that this was due to the presence, influence and pressure of a significant number of capable white Bahamians. When they were presented with the autonomy proposals, they deemed it folly to throw in their lot with Jamaica and Haiti and successfully argued for retaining their British connexion. The District continued to thrive and was spared the responsibility of contributing resources to the new Conferences.

Queen's College in Nassau, founded in 1890 to replace an earlier High School, soon acquired a reputation for excellence which it retained into the twenty-first century. The High School was begun by Henry Bleby, the missionary who was tarred and feathered within days of his arrival in Jamaica back in 1832.[19] Bleby spent forty-six years in the West Indies, the last ten as Chairman of the Bahamas District. For a third of his time he had worked in Jamaica; he had also served as Chairman in St Vincent and Demerara and had written several books including the widely-read *Death Struggles of Slavery* (1853).[20] His journeys as Chairman took him to the Dominican Republic too; it was in the care of the Bahamas District because of the animosity between francophone Haiti with its periodic convulsions and the Hispanic Republic in the other half of the island.

Like the Bahamas, the *Honduras* mission was geographically remote from the Caribbean island colonies and won its appeal to be excluded from the new Conference. The first missionary, Thomas Wilkinson, had arrived in Honduras in 1825, at the invitation of an English businessman. He found an embryonic society in Belize; he undertook a three-week tour up-river on the Committee's instructions, meeting and preaching to the gangs of mahogany-cutters; he had his knuckles rapped for overspending on the property he acquired to serve as a chapel and manse, though it later proved a sound investment; and then he succumbed to the climate. The Committee asked his successors to extend their sphere of activity further into Central America, but the venture was ill-conceived. Only on the coast, in Belize city and a short distance to the south, did the work take root, until 1860 when a missionary was first placed on the Bay Islands. The mission was inevitably hampered by the turnover of personnel, which meant that none became proficient in either Spanish or the local Maya tongue before Richard Fletcher arrived. He spent the years 1855–60 in Belize and then moved ninety miles north to settle in Corazol. In 1860 Honduras was detached from the Jamaica District and Fletcher became the Chairman. For twenty years he administered the District from Corazol, at the same time translating three gospels and other texts into Maya. Gradually other societies were formed in British Honduras, but hopes of extension into neighbouring countries – other than the Bay Islands, which were ceded by Britain to the Honduras Republic in 1860 – were always thwarted.

The antipathy between Honduras and Jamaica was likened by one missionary to that between Jews and Samaritans. There were no regular sailings between the two colonies; it was necessary to travel via New York. Letters took four weeks, whereas a letter from Belize to London took only eighteen days. It was thus impractical, as well as distasteful, for Honduras to be part of the new Western Conference. Yet there was very little benefit from the continued relationship with Britain. The development of railways across the Honduras Republic and Guatemala opened up many opportunities and invitations, but the District was starved of both human and financial resources. A circuit around San Pedro del Sula, in the Republic, was eventually established, but soon afterwards left unstaffed by all but a dedicated schoolmaster. At the century's end a WMMS Secretary, William Perkins, paid a

19   See p. 65.
20   Bleby, 1853.

useful visit to the District which removed many misunderstandings and a new Chairman, James Lord, was able to develop the work by small increments over the next decade.

Meanwhile the autonomous West Indian Conference was sailing through troubled waters and perilously close to shipwreck. George Sargeant, the long-time advocate of autonomy, was its first President. He had begun his ministry in Jamaica in 1847, returned to England for a decade in 1860 and came back to Jamaica as Chairman. He had opened the York Castle High School for boys and envisaged a Theological Institution that would serve the West Indies as a whole. He had fulfilled various commissions beyond Jamaica and travelled widely. From 1880 to 1884 he was again in English circuit work and a member of the WMMS Committee where his influence was instrumental in bringing the new Conference to birth. He returned from England as President and based himself in Barbados, which was a pivotal location for shipping from Britain and on to the other colonies. The Presidency was a full-time post, underwritten by the Society, entailing many voyages. Sargeant exercised his duties with dignity and authority, cheerfulness and unflappability and with an exceptional understanding of West Indian life. He served for six years, during which membership of this Conference area grew by 4,000 and new work was begun among the migrant labourers in Panama.

But Osborn had been right in his original assessment of the situation. The circuits were hard-pressed to meet the stipends of their ministers. Missionaries were frequently obliged to beg for theirs and one, after thirty-seven years' service, said he was 'at times without means to procure a dinner, or even to buy a postage stamp'. Before long their numbers were depleted as sheer physical necessity forced their return to Britain. There were too few local candidates of the calibre to replace them and so new recruits were sought from Britain. Many of these had been candidates for the ministry who had fallen at the last hurdle and were not accepted by the British Conference. The loss of experienced ministers left disciplinary matters to men of unreliable judgement, creating predictable personality clashes. The West Indian Conference was burdened from the outset with considerable debts on its properties; when it came to repairing or rebuilding them after hurricane or earthquake, or indeed because of the rapid decay of wooden buildings in such a humid climate, debt inevitably accumulated. The annual and triennial Conferences were unavoidably costly and after 1894 the General Conference no longer met. In 1897 the Eastern Conference sent an urgent message to the Society, as did the Western Conference the following year:-

> Unless something can be done to cheapen the present expensive system of Church government, and unless aid be given from the parent Missionary Society, many of the Stations will have to be abandoned ... We have done our best to

work efficiently, economically, and loyally the system you imposed upon us in 1885 … but the experiment has failed![21]

… a sense of weariness in the strife has settled upon the minds alike of the Ministers and the membership. So far we stand alone, not unpitied, but unhelped, in this day of our calamity.[22]

These lamentations induced the Society to arrange a four-month deputation in 1898–99. Ripley Winston, formerly of Ceylon and Burma, and Major John Smith of the Mission House staff investigated thoroughly and recognized the validity of the pleas. They mapped out a scheme for financial relief from the Society, together with adequate financial control. It was not enough. In 1904 the Committee bowed to the inevitable and the Wesleyans of the West Indies reverted to the care of the Society in London.

Pacific Islands

The island Districts in the Pacific became part of the Australasian Conference in 1855 and their ministerial staff were no longer accountable to the WMMS. They were, however, still first- or second-generation 'colonials'. Some had originally been appointed by the Society; others had migrated from Britain and been ordained – or indeed converted – in Australia or New Zealand.

One of the latter was George Brown, born in County Durham, who after a colourful youth sailed to Auckland in 1855 at the age of 19. He was kindly received by his uncle and aunt, a missionary couple. Under their influence he experienced a conversion, became a local preacher and in 1859 offered himself for missionary service. Newly married and newly ordained, he was appointed to Samoa where he worked from 1860 to 1874, learned the language and wrote about Samoan culture. His early experience in a doctor's surgery and chemist's shop and a brief career as a sailor had given him practical skills which served him well. He saw the importance of training Samoans for the ministry and was instrumental in the establishment of Piula Theological College. He established good relations with the white beachcombers living on the islands, but the activity of German traders, who were selling arms and ammunition to the natives, alarmed him.

After fourteen years he was ready for a new challenge and he led a team of Fijian and Samoan teachers to the Bismarck Archipelago (New Britain, New Ireland and the Admiralty Islands) off New Guinea. When he called en route in

---

[21]   Memorial to the Missionary Committee from the Eastern Conference of 1897, quoted by Findlay and Holdsworth, vol. 2, p. 404.

[22]   Memorial to the Missionary Committee from the Western Conference of 1898, quoted by Findlay and Holdsworth vol. 2, p. 405.

Fiji, all eighty-three students at the training centre at Navuloa volunteered to join him; nine were selected. As they were preparing to board the *John Wesley*, the authorities intervened, thinking the Methodist Church had forced the students to go. Aminio Baledrokadroka spoke on behalf of the volunteers and said:

> Mr Brown told us all ... about the character of the people, the unhealthiness of the climate and the dangers we will probably have to encounter. No one appointed us to go. We were simply asked whether we would volunteer ... we have fully considered this matter in our hearts; no one has pressed us in any way; we have given ourselves up to do God's work and our mind today, sir, is to go with Mr Brown. If we die, we die. If we live, we live.[23]

Whereas in Samoa there were many professed Christians when Brown landed, this was a very different and dangerous assignment among people who were still constantly fighting among themselves. In 1878 a group of islanders attacked and killed some of the teachers, including four of the Fijians. Brown called a meeting of the white residents, the native teachers and some of the chiefs, to decide how to react.

> I determined that as some action was unavoidable, even if not desirable, it was the best plan to enlist the sympathies and help of all the well-disposed natives on our side, rather than to array them against us; and let the punishment of the murderers come from the natives as much as from us. The murder of Sailasa and the teachers, it must always be remembered, was not in any way connected with their position as Christian teachers, nor was it caused by any enmity against the lotu. They were killed simply because they were foreigners, and the natives who killed them did so for no other reason than their desire to eat them, and to get the little property they had with them.[24]

In a punitive expedition three villages implicated in the massacre were burnt down and some of the murderers were killed. Brown said he was determined to demonstrate that 'roast missionary' was 'too expensive a dish to indulge in'. But this 'Blanche Bay affair' caused an uproar in the Australian press. *The Australian* said:

> If missionary enterprise in such an island as this leads to wars of vengeance, which may readily develop into wars of extermination, the question may be raised whether it may not be better to withdraw the Mission from savages who show so little appreciation of its benefits.[25]

---

[23]   G. Brown, *George Brown, pioneer missionary and explorer: an autobiography*, (London, Hodder & Stoughton, 1908), pp. 79–80.

[24]   Brown, p. 258.

[25]   Brown, p. 277.

Brown was however defended and supported by the Australian WMMS, continued his work and began to see its fruits in baptisms before he returned to Sydney in 1881.

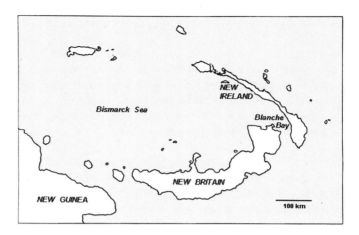

Map 15   New Guinea: The Bismarck Archipelago

Having experienced the German traders in Samoa and lived on an archipelago which became a German Protectorate in 1884, Brown took a negative view of their presence in the Pacific and wrote a series of anonymous articles in the *Sydney Morning Herald* affirming the necessity of British control of the islands. This was a matter in which the Committee in London had long taken a more than arm's-length interest.

The Fijian chief Cakobau,[26] who was at last baptized in 1857, had earlier taken the title *Tui Viti*, 'King of all Fiji'. The title was disputed but he was recognized by 80 per cent of the chiefs and by the French and US governments – the Americans were pursuing a compensation claim for damage to property at the time and it was in their interest to fix the claim on him. In 1858 Cakobau exercised the doubtful right to offer the islands to Britain, in the person of the first British Consul in Fiji, W.T. Pritchard.[27] His motive was to secure for himself a powerful overlord who would bolster his authority and defend him from the excessive American claim. James Calvert, for whom Cakobau had a high regard, was an enthusiast for British annexation and before he returned to Britain in 1855 had encouraged Cakobau to think in those terms. The Colonial Office sent Lt Col W.J. Smythe to advise on the desirability of annexation; Joseph Waterhouse, the Wesleyan Chairman, acted as his personal translator. Smythe recommended that the offer be refused, which disappointed the missionaries. Nonetheless they could take heart from his

---

[26]   See pp. 75–6.

[27]   The uncomfortable relationship between missionaries and consular officials is examined in Darch, pp. 84–9.

judgment that Fiji's future lay in 'a native government aided by the counsels of respectable Europeans' – an undoubted reference to the missionaries, of whom he wrote in glowing terms. They deplored what they saw as a lost opportunity,[28] but got on with their work. They even got Cakobau to write to London – not, for some reason, to Australia – to request reinforcements to the staff as the Methodist community was now growing rapidly.

But in the 1860s Fiji, like Samoa, saw an influx of beachcombers and unscrupulous traders, described by one historian as 'the derelict scourings of the ports of the Old World'.[29] Thanks, ironically, to the missionaries' success, they were no longer deterred by the prospect of being killed and eaten. With their arrival the 'respectable' Europeans began to lose their influence and in 1869 the WMMS reported:

> Viewing the matter in the light of past events and experience of other lands, New Zealand especially, we confess to the deepest anxiety for the future of our Mission in Fiji.[30]

Calvert had now returned as Chairman and had influential contacts in Britain – particularly William M'Arthur the MP who was later Treasurer of the Society and William Boyce, who was now one of the Secretaries. One occasion on which he made use of them was when John Thurston, a coconut planter, became acting British consul in 1869. Previously a sheep farmer in Australia, Thurston had been shipwrecked on Rotuma, rescued by Calvert and brought to Fiji in 1866 aboard the *John Wesley*. But Thurston was adamantly opposed to annexation and Calvert manoeuvered to have him removed. For a few years he was sidelined, but his competence and his facility in Fijian made him indispensible and he was soon back in office. Then in 1872 M'Arthur, well briefed by Calvert, moved in Parliament the establishment of a British protectorate over Fiji. The motion was lost, but M'Arthur maintained the pressure. Smythe re-entered the lists to declare that a change of conditions over the previous twelve years had changed his mind. A Fiji Committee was organized in London to lobby for annexation in which the WMMS Secretaries, Boyce and Arthur, played an important part. After several more parliamentary debates, a commission of enquiry and a new formal invitation from Cakobau, Fiji became a Crown Colony in 1874. The primary reason for the long-delayed annexation was humanitarian; it was the only way of controlling the white planters who had no respect for indigenous Fijian authority and the labour recruiters whose methods often amounted to kidnap. It was an outcome for which most of the missionaries had long hoped, brought about in no small measure by the efforts of the Secretaries and their allies in London.

---

[28] See the *Annual Report* of the WMMS for 1862.
[29] R.A. Derrick, *A History of Fiji*, (Suva, Government Press, 1946), p. 37.
[30] 1869 *Annual Report*, p. 109, quoted in Darch, p. 90.

Tonga was a different case. King George Tupou, the Local Preacher, consolidated his authority and in 1875 made Tonga a constitutional monarchy. In 1880 he appointed a Methodist missionary his prime minister. This was Shirley Baker, another emigrant from England. Baker, born in London in 1836, went to Australia at the age of 16 as a stowaway. He worked as a farm hand, miner and apothecary's assistant and became a local preacher. He offered for missionary service in 1860 and, despite his meagre education, was ordained by the Australian conference and posted to Tonga. In due course he became the Chairman of the District and he was the King's trusted advisor.[31] He designed the national flag. But he was a controversial figure. Unlike Brown, he had pro-German sympathies, which led to a treaty in 1876 by which Tonga's independence and Tupou's sovereignty were recognized. His political activity made him unpopular with British officials and with the Australian WMMS officers, who recalled him in 1879. He defied them and accepted the office of prime minister. Baker concurred with Tupou's determination to assert Tongan independence and his dispute with the Wesleyan authorities was among the factors which led Tupou to proclaim, 'Tonga should have an independent church ... the missionaries and the whole world should see that I am determined to have the separation.' They established a self-governing Free Church of Tonga in 1885 and most Tongan Christians transferred their allegiance to the new body.

The few remaining Wesleyans were led by James Moulton, a minister whose scholarship matched that of his brother William, founding headmaster of The Leys School in Cambridge. James had offered to serve in China but was appointed to Fiji and studied Fijian on the voyage to Sydney in 1863. On reaching Australia, however, he became a minister of that Conference and was in 1865 stationed in Tonga at the behest of the King. He served church and people well, re-translating the Bible, writing many hymns, serving as the first head of Tupou College and eventually as Chairman of the District. But he became embroiled in disputes with Baker which played no small part in prompting the split. Now the Wesleyan rump suffered discrimination, in violation of the 1875 constitution by which religious freedom was guaranteed. Baker survived an assassination attempt in 1887, in which his son and daughter were wounded; Wesleyans were suspected and many were deported to Fiji. George Brown, now Secretary of the Board of Missions in Sydney, visited Tonga in 1888 to assess the situation and try to heal the breach. He was unsuccessful – it was not until 1924 that Queen Salote effected reunion under the name Free Wesleyan Church of Tonga. But in 1890 Thurston, now Sir John, Governor of Fiji and High Commissioner of the Western Pacific, visited Tonga and, Tongan independence notwithstanding, deported Baker at short notice to Auckland for being 'prejudicial to the peace and good order of the Western Pacific'.

Baker pursued his business interests, not very successfully, until he retired to Tonga in 1900 and died in 1903. King Tupou died, not far short of 100, in 1893

---

[31]   See N. Rutherford, *Shirley Baker and the King of Tonga*, (Melbourne, Oxford University Press, 1971).

and was succeeded by his son, Tupou II, who signed a Treaty of Friendship with Britain in 1900 under which Tonga became a British-protected self-governing nation. Thurston remained Governor of Fiji until his death in 1897. George Brown outlasted them; he continued as Secretary of Missions until 1907 and died in 1917. His friend Robert Louis Stevenson, with whom he had sailed to Tonga, offered to write his biography, but he declined.

Chapter 12
Parallel Missions

The Methodist Churches which united in 1932 each had overseas work, all of which then became the responsibility of the new Methodist Missionary Society. The Methodist New Connexion, Bible Christians, United Methodist Free Churches and Primitive Methodists, whose founders all acknowledged their debt to Wesley's inspiration but fell out with his successors, were just as enthusiastic as the Wesleyans about worldwide evangelization.

The Methodist New Connexion

The MNC was formed in 1797, after Alexander Kilham had been expelled by the Conference for his advocacy of lay representation in Methodist affairs at every level. Kilham was reluctant to go, but could not accept the terms of the 1795 Plan of Pacification for the organization of post-Wesley Methodism. Five thousand Methodists, 5 per cent of the total membership at the time, chose to secede, including sufficient able preachers to ensure that the new body survived Kilham's death, aged 36, in the following year. The growth of the MNC was slow and impeded by litigation over the ownership of chapels and by the lack of preachers able or willing to exist on the paltry allowances the Connexion could afford to pay. But in 1836, 'firmly believing it to be our duty to take a part in the great cause of Foreign Missions'[1], the Liverpool Conference of the MNC appointed its first missionary.

In the wake of the Wesleyans, Primitive Methodists and Bible Christians, John Addyman sailed for Canada, where he worked for eight years. The year 1841 was a time of unrest and division for Canadian Wesleyans and some of them transferred their allegiance to the MNC. No fewer than thirty-six Irishmen served the MNC in Canada; the Gundy family alone, emigrating *en bloc* in 1842, supplied five, William and four sons. Each made his mark: three became District Chairmen, two were Presidents of the Conference and one was expelled for intemperance.[2] The Connexion concentrated its activity on the larger towns and its membership grew to over 8,000 by the 1870s. But the divisions which loomed so large at home made no sense in Canada and in 1874 the MNC and Wesleyans united – one of a succession of unions which brought Methodists together and eventually produced the United Church of Canada. The MNC brought to the union twenty-four chapels, eighty ministers – mostly recruited in Canada – and 8,312 members.

---

[1]   MNC *Minutes* 1836, p. 46.
[2]   Taggart, 'The Irish factor', pp. 3–4.

MNC work in Australia was even more short-lived. A first missionary was sent to Adelaide in 1862, another to Melbourne in 1865. In neither place were there ever more than two or three congregations and with a sensible recognition that it was not viable to pursue a separate course they united in 1887 with the Bible Christians in Adelaide and with the Wesleyans in Melbourne.

Map 16   China, showing the centres of activity of all four denominations

In 1859 the MNC was caught up in the missionary fervour of the time and took the decision to start work in China. John Innocent[3] and William Hall[4], both from the Scotland Street chapel in Sheffield, landed in Shanghai while the Taiping rebellion was still troubling the country and remained there for a time, studying Chinese and investigating possible places to make a start on their mission. They eventually settled in Tianjin, a port city with a population of over half a million, 100 miles from Beijing, where they arrived in 1860. They sensibly hired a Chinese Christian, Hu Enti from Shanghai, to work with them. He proved an invaluable partner in the enterprise. Nowhere in China were conversions rapid or numerous in the nineteenth century, but Hu Enti's witness produced ten new Christians in two years. Five of them became preachers and one, Chang Ch'ih San, was later ordained

---

[3]   See G.T. Candlin, *John Innocent: A Story of Mission Work in North China*, (London, United Methodist Publishing House, 1909).

[4]   J.T. Wilkinson, in Davies, George and Rupp, (eds), *History*, vol. 3, p. 168, wrongly calls Hall William Nettlethorpe.

and became the first Chinese principal of the Preachers' Training Institute.[5] Hu Enti himself was the first Chinese minister to be ordained by the MNC, but that did not happen until 1880, not long before he died. In 1862 the missionaries agreed to supervise the BFBS's colporteurs, the itinerant Bible-sellers in the region.

In 1866 a second station was opened, at Chu Chia, 150 miles from Tianjin in Shandong province, as a result of a call from an elderly farmer known as 'Old Dreamer' who gathered a congregation from his own and nearby villages. Hu Enti was posted there and prepared fifty people for baptism. Hu's wife, who was baptized in 1866, long survived him; she spent thirty-nine years in Chu Chia working among the women until she died at the age of 97 in 1905.

In 1869 William Hodge, another member of the missionary team, travelled by boat from Tianjin to Shandong in the company of James Williamson of the LMS. The boat was attacked by robbers, Williamson was killed and Hodge was left for a while a nervous wreck. But worse was to befall the mission. In 1870 a terrible massacre was perpetrated in Tianjin. Rumours had spread that foreigners, especially Roman Catholic sisters, were kidnapping children and gouging out their eyes and hearts to make magic medicine which they used to get more converts. A mob attacked the cathedral and the hospital across the river, butchering missionaries and Chinese Christians alike. Although Catholics were the primary targets, other missions were not immune. A Chinese preacher, Liu Tu Ya, was beaten viciously in the MNC chapel and died of his wounds a few weeks later.

William Hall was on furlough in 1874 and the Conference authorized him to launch an appeal to fund the building of a Training Institution. He raised £3,208 and on his return to China he oversaw its construction. For thirty years the Institution regularly had between ten and twenty students. The building work, however, was interrupted by the famine of 1877 which ravaged Shandong and Henan provinces as well as Shanxi.[6] Relief funds had to be distributed largely by missionaries, who wore themselves out physically and emotionally. Hall succumbed to typhus and died in 1878, the year the building project was completed. Innocent's other colleagues were unfit to carry on and he was left for a while alone. Among those who came to join him was Dr David Stenhouse, fulfilling at length Innocent's long-held dream of starting medical work. Stenhouse began work in Laoling in mud-built shacks. Within a few years he was handling 4,000–5,000 visits annually. A better building was erected in 1881 but it was destroyed by fire the next year. A more substantial hospital was built in 1883 and enlarged in 1889. This was wrecked in the Boxer uprising of 1900. The indemnity paid to the mission subsequently enabled a new hospital to open in 1905. Among those who followed Stenhouse and extended the medical work, most came via the Edinburgh Medical Missionary Society. An exception was John Robson, who had the private means to be a self-supporting missionary. Not long after he arrived in China, after serving in several

---

[5]   G.R. Senior, *The China Experience*, (Peterborough, Methodist Publishing House, 1994), p. 5.

[6]   See pp.126–7.

English circuits, he was so impressed by the health issues he found that he took study leave and obtained his MD qualification in America. On his return he was assigned to 'Evangelistic and Medical Itineration'.

The Innocents endured many trials. They sent their son George to England for his education when he was just seven and their daughter Annie at the age of fourteen. Within five years Annie had been called to missionary service in her turn and was accepted. She was appointed Principal of a new Girls' School in Tianjin and her parents looked forward with excitement to her arrival, but she was taken ill and died before she could sail. A year later, in 1882, George returned. He had been absent for sixteen years. He had received his own call to the ministry and been given permission by the MNC to undertake his training and serve his probation in China. He was ordained in 1887 and was soon respected for himself and not just for his name and parentage. But in 1891, returning from furlough, newly-wed, he like his sister was taken ill and died before they reached Hong Kong. In spite of their grief the Innocents, like so many others, carried on faithfully if wearily. One of the last things John Innocent did in China was to draw up a Code of Rules for the mission which gave Chinese Christians a say in its administration. Until then no Chinese held any post of authority; there was no fixed stipend rate for Chinese workers; every decision was taken by the missionaries. What they practised was in complete contrast with the principles for which Kilham had stood a century earlier. With the new Code in place, Innocent left China after thirty-eight years of missionary service and on reaching England was immediately made President of the 1897 Conference. By this time North China boasted eighty-nine chapels, six missionaries, thirty itinerant Chinese preachers and 2,092 members and probationer members. The MNC did not delay ordaining its full-time workers; John Hedley, creditably but at the time exceptionally, listed many of his Chinese colleagues by name with a short profile of each.[7]

The missionaries survived the Boxer uprising but most of the mission property was destroyed and members suffered severely. Li Fu, a preacher, was terribly maltreated:

> They surrounded the chapel, and broke down the doors and windows. My wife was dragged out by the hair, carrying her child of two months old. She had been struck in the eye with a pistol barrel, and the blood was trickling down her face. My little boy, Joseph, followed her out. His right arm and his back had been hurt with a spear. I saw my little girl, nine years old, being pulled along, her face all dyed with blood, and her hand thrust through with a knife … They dragged us all to a temple at the east end of the village, where the Boxers drilled, and bound us all to trees. They then commenced beating me fiercely over the head with the handle of a sickle. I called out to the Lord several times, when they exclaimed: He still calls on the Lord! Beat him! Beat him! Beat him! They only stopped beating when I had fainted away. I recovered consciousness to still find

---

7   J. Hedley, *Our Mission in North China*, (London, Geo. Burrows, 1907), pp. 58–9.

myself bound hand and foot ... I was aware of my little babe lying beside the road crying. They had flung the child there when they bound my wife ... My left thumb nail was taken off with a sword, I was beaten about the shoulders with a spade ... I could only sigh, and beseech the Lord to take me soon. Then they commenced burning my right eye, and also both shoulders with a torch ... At this time, thanks be to God, a strange peace filled my heart. I had not the least fear. I forgot my bonds and my wounds, and felt that we should soon be in a new world I smiled on my wife, and asked her if she was at peace. She restrained her tears, but made no reply.[8]

Li Fu was released after sixty days and resumed his ministry. A list of other martyrs to the Boxers was said to hang 'in every Church vestry in the Connexion'.

The Bible Christians

William O'Bryan's difficulties were local rather than connexional. He was twice expelled from Cornish circuits for indiscipline: his call to preach took precedence over Methodist regulations and restrictions and his independence annoyed his superintendent. His followers, calling themselves Bible Christians, held their first Quarterly Meeting in 1816 and the first Conference 'of the Preachers in Connexion with William O'Bryan' in 1819. O'Bryan ultimately left the Bible Christians and the prime mover of the Connexion was James Thorne of Shebbear in Devon, who had been his associate from the first. The west country was always the heartland of the movement, though congregations of Cornish emigrants and other sympathizers began to materialize further afield and the third Conference in 1821 formed a Missionary Society 'for the purpose of sending Missionaries into dark and destitute parts of the United Kingdom and other countries, as Divine Providence might open the way'. By 1865 this Society had received over £70,000 and Thorne claimed that 'for every pound which had been given a soul had been saved'.[9]

In 1831 two preachers were sent to North America. John Glass went to Canada and Francis Metherall to Prince Edward Island, where within two years he had established thirty-six preaching places. Some time later he was able to revive a Wesleyan cause which had not seen a preacher for five years. Scrupulously conscientious, he wrote to Richard Knight, the Chairman of the Wesleyan District, to say he had been able to re-establish class meetings and to ask for a pastor to come. Knight magnanimously and with realism replied, 'As God has blessed the labours of the Bible Christian ministers, the souls gathered belong to their Church.' Metherall spent forty-three years on the island, where he died at the age of 84 in 1875.

---

8   Candlin, pp. 272–3.
9   Bourne, p. 98.

On mainland Canada, John Hicks Eynon had a ministry comparable to Metherall's. He married Elizabeth Dart, the earliest woman preacher employed by the Bible Christians, who had been instrumental in his conversion – the employment of women itinerants was debated and agreed at the founding Conference and was a feature of the movement's early years. The Eynons sailed in 1833 and exercised a joint ministry until she died in 1857. They were often parted as she preached and visited in the neighbourhood of Cobourg on Lake Ontario where they made their home, while he ventured further and further afield. He soon had a circuit of almost 200 miles to cover and in 1845 he drove another 600 miles westwards to visit frontier communities. As a result new stations were opened which within a few years became self-supporting circuits. The ebb and flow of membership returns was due to the constant migration of settlers, leaving the missionaries to follow in their wake. But in the decade to 1850, membership in Canada grew from 318 to 1,267, or 12.7 per cent of all Bible Christians. The number of preachers had increased from three to sixteen, including one in Ohio and one in Wisconsin. In the next decade membership rose to 3,986 and F.W. Bourne, the leading light of the connexion for many years, was convinced that this number would have been far higher if more ministers had been stationed in Canada rather than 'in such places as Yaxley, Dymock, and two or three mountain villages a few miles from Penrith, which were afterwards abandoned'.[10] Eynon worked on until he retired to Exeter, Ontario, where he died in 1888. In 1854 the British BC Conference, after some hesitation, authorized Canadian Bible Christians to hold their own Conference and manage their own affairs. It was no coincidence that this was the same year that the Wesleyans became autonomous. Thirty years later they united; on such a grave matter the Bible Christians still sought the permission of their home Conference but when it was withheld they went ahead anyway.

Cornish farmers and miners in South Australia sent a request for pastoral care in 1850. James Way, who had been President of the 1847 Conference, and James Rowe responded to the call and William Hicks, a Cornish Methodist friend, generously helped to defray the costs with £100. Some of the emigrants in Adelaide had already thrown in their lot with the Wesleyans and told Way, 'You did not come soon enough'. Way was not a poacher and gave them his blessing. His first pulpit was in a butcher's shop. When he asked if he could hold services there, the reply was, 'I don't think it will do to sell meat in the morning and have preaching in the afternoon'. Way agreed; Sunday trading ceased and services began. A small chapel was soon built but within a year huge numbers deserted South Australia to prospect for gold in Victoria, among them circuit stewards and local preachers. Way and Rowe persevered and against the odds they had recruited 8,000 members in South Australia and Victoria within seven years. Small ventures were also begun in Queensland and New Zealand. In due course all entered Methodist unions, which came about much more readily in the dominions than at home.

---

10   Bourne, p. 365.

Serena Thorne, O'Bryan's grand-daughter, began to preach at the age of seventeen and was known as 'the sweet girl gospeller'. From 1865 she began to make a name for herself in Queensland and Victoria and in 1870 she was invited – by Way's son, a barrister, and other leading citizens – to Adelaide. Over 2,000 listened to her first sermon 'with breathless attention'; hundreds were turned away. She preached, too, in suburban churches and in the country. On night visits to Adelaide prostitutes, she influenced some to enter a Female Refuge. In 1871 she married the Shebbear-educated minister and social reformer, Octavius Lake, but only after she had drawn from him an avowal that he approved of women preachers. She believed sexual equality to be 'the original design of the Creator' and enthusiastically supported votes for women. Speaking on suffragette platforms in South Australia and New South Wales, she combined logical argument, wit and evangelical passion. She drove her buggy long distances across country, gaining hundreds of members, male associates and suffrage petition signatures. Her efforts epitomized the contemporary influence of evangelical religion. Confident that women 'possessing that sword – the ballot' would curb the 'abominable liquor traffic', she campaigned on temperance society platforms too.[11] Her husband also had a prominent ministry, but she did not live to see him President of the now united Australian Methodist Conference in 1915.

One of the most momentous Conferences in Bible Christian history was held in 1884, when Hudson Taylor, the founder of the China Inland Mission (CIM), was invited to speak. It was the year when Bible Christians in Canada forewent their identity for the sake of union; and at home 'the question on every hand was, Is it God's will that we should have a mission to the heathen proper in place of our first colonial mission?'[12] It was. Twelve months later Samuel Thorne, O'Bryan's great-grandson and scion of the Shebbear family, and Thomas Vanstone were commissioned and embarked on an eight-month journey to Yunnan in south-west China. They began work in collaboration with the CIM, which supplied all the help and encouragement they could wish for in the early years, including wives for some of the missionaries. The two pioneers were soon followed by Francis Dymond and Samuel Pollard, ministers' sons, schoolfellows and life-long friends. Before making the perilous journey up the Yangtze and across the mountains to Yunnan, they spent nine months at the CIM Training Home in Shanghai, where Pollard proved a brilliant student. After three months he managed to take evening prayers in Chinese. 'They said they understood but so polite are they that you could never find a Chinese who would tell you otherwise,' he reported.[13] Vanstone's fiancée spent some months at the Training Home for Ladies. When at last they set out for Yunnan the journey proved perilous indeed. On the upper Yangtze their

---

[11]   *Australian Dictionary of Biography*, http://adb.anu.edu.au/biography/lake-serena-13037 [accessed 31 October 2012].

[12]   Bourne, p. 491.

[13]   G.R. Senior, *Samuel Pollard*, (Emsworth, World Methodist Historical Society, 1999), p. 6.

junk overturned in rapids and the whole party was fortunate to escape with their lives, albeit without most of their baggage.

They established two bases for their work in Yunnan, at the provincial capital of Kunming and at Zhaotong in the north-east corner of the province. They divided their days between language study and evangelism and spoke in the open air on a daily basis. Pollard wrote:

> One was often surrounded by a thousand people gathered together to see what the foreigner was like … The experience of being in the centre of a curious, gaping crowed [could be] most unpleasant. On the other hand, when one was out for preaching, it was an asset of considerable value to be able to attract an audience just by standing still.[14]

A baptismal service in Kunming in September 1888 brought the Bible Christian Church in China to birth with three members, but that was a rare event. After ten years' hard work there were twenty-eight members and three chapels. Thorne died in 1891. His wife Lois, previously a CIM missionary, came back to Britain and was instrumental in starting a BC Women's Missionary League before returning to China in 1893. About this time a newly-ordained minister, Lewis Savin, began medical training. Once he had qualified he joined the team at Zhaotong and later moved to Kunming.

The Boxer troubles disrupted the work for a while. In Zhaotong hostile elements even petitioned the Prefect for permission to attack the foreigners; the Prefect warned Pollard to watch his back. Later, the mission premises in Kunming were attacked, looted and destroyed. The missionaries were unharmed, but they were all obliged to leave. When Pollard announced their departure, sixteen catechumens asked him to baptize them. Then for nineteen months the church in Yunnan was entrusted to Chinese leadership. When the terror subsided, all the missionaries returned to their stations. Little did they know what great opportunities would soon open for them among the Miao people up in the mountains.[15]

The Primitive Methodist Church

John Wesley was used to preaching in the open but his successors were more staid and expelled Hugh Bourne and William Clowes, preachers in the Potteries, for holding 'camp meetings'. By 1811 they and their supporters had become a distinct community which issued its own class tickets. The name they adopted was inspired by Wesley's farewell address to his preachers in Chester:

---

[14]   W.A. Grist, *Samuel Pollard, Pioneer Missionary in China*, (London, United Methodist Publishing House, 1920), p. 37.

[15]   The mass movement among the Miao is described in Pritchard, *1900–96*, chapter 6.

Fellow labourers, wherever there is an open door enter in and preach the Gospel: if it be to two or three, under a hedge or a tree, preach the Gospel; go out quickly into the streets and lanes of the city, and bring in the poor and the maimed and the halt and the blind ... and this is the way the primitive Methodists did.[16]

Stoke and Hull were the earliest centres of the movement and the first Conference was held in Hull in 1820. The following year the first Missionary Meetings were held and a resolution was passed about 'the dark and benighted villages of the Peak of Derbyshire' as well as mission in foreign lands. In 1825 a General Missionary Society was formed, but for another eighteen years it existed in name only. Then in 1843 a Missionary Committee was appointed which had oversight of both home and foreign missions and a magazine, *Advance,* was begun which covered both.

In 1829 four missionaries sailed for New York and two to Philadelphia. They included the first single women missionaries from any branch of Methodism, Ruth Watkins and Anne Wearing. They suffered many hardships and the societies they founded in New York City struggled. Ruth Watkins wrote several pitiful letters home complaining of the lack of support she was receiving either from England or in America. On the back of one an unknown hand wrote 'As it could not be officially answered, no answer was sent'.[17] In parts of Pennsylvania, however, the societies attained considerable strength. Up to 1840 the societies in the United States constituted a 'Mission under the control and partial support of the British Conference'. But the customs and methods of the old world were not suited to the conditions of the new world and, as the British Conference insisted upon maintaining its old world methods and rules in America, the Americans resolved in 1840 'that we consider ourselves from this time, distinct from, and, unconnected with the English Conference'.[18]

One by one other colonial missions were planted. In 1830 Nathaniel Watkins, Ruth's brother, was appointed to Toronto where a class was already meeting. He was energetic and enthusiastic but barely literate. He stayed in Canada only a year and then went south where both he and his sister soon disappear from the records. But the Canadian work was begun and was under the care of the Hull circuit until the General Missionary Committee took responsibility in 1843. A Canadian Conference was formed in 1854 and brought to the Union of 1883 8,223 members, 99 travelling preachers, 246 local preachers and 239 chapels. Under the guidance of the new Committee, work was begun in Australia and New Zealand. Robert Ward reached New Zealand in August 1844 and, though he learned some Maori, the church remained a small and mostly *pakeha* body, with barely 3,000 members by the end of the century. Joseph Long and John Wilson landed in Adelaide the same winter and joined a well-established society which had held

---

[16]   W.E. Farndale, *The Secret of Mow Cop*, (London, Epworth Press, 1950), pp. 43–4.

[17]   Ruth Watkins to William Clowes and John Flesher, March 1835: held at MARC.

[18]   H.B. Kendall, *The origin and history of the Primitive Methodist Church*, (2 vols, PM Publishing House, 1906), vol. 2, p. 438.

its first Quarterly Meeting in 1841, when it could boast a church building, sixteen members and no fewer than seven local preachers. The arrival of the missionaries heralded expansion and in later years societies were formed in New South Wales, Victoria and Queensland. In 1858 a little band of Primitive Methodists from East Anglia held a camp meeting at Launceston in Tasmania, formed a class and raised £60 to bring them a missionary. A church in Hobart followed, founded by E. Cook Pritchard, who had a vibrant ministry of over twenty years and spoke at many camp meetings in both Tasmania and New South Wales, with attendances as high as 800.[19]

It is not always long-serving ministers who have powerful ministries. Hugh Gilmore spent a mere two years in Adelaide, where he went in the hope of improving his health after twenty-four years in English circuits. He was a Christian Socialist who wanted to serve in the city slums but was sent to minister in a pleasant residential area where his preaching quickly attracted a congregation of very diverse degrees of wealth, education and political attachment. The chapel soon had to be enlarged with a gallery. Within a year Gilmore found himself elected President of the Primitive Methodist Conference of South Australia and then presided over the first 'intercolonial' Conference of the connexion in Australia. But he is best remembered for his passionate speaking on social evils, his critique of capitalism, his support for the unions in the Great Strike of 1890 and for the suffragettes, as well as for the Christian Commonwealth movement which he began in April 1891. Membership of the movement was open to all Christians whatever their religious attachments. Its purposes were to give relief to the poor, to offer friendship, accommodation and employment to strangers, to redeem the lapsed and depraved and to address political and social questions. Gilmore, however, was unable to pursue his evangelical and political vision. Australia did not improve his health and he died in October 1891.[20]

Primitive Methodists entered Methodist unions in Canada in 1883, in Australia in 1900 and in New Zealand – where they declined to join until the Australian and New Zealand Conferences had separated – in 1913.

Primitive Methodism celebrated the year 1860 as its Jubilee, commemorating the first Class Meeting in March 1810. At the Jubilee Conference it was decided that part of the Jubilee Fund should be devoted to establishing a mission in South Africa, but it was 1870 before a station was opened. In Aliwal North, 300 miles from the coast on the Orange River, lived a farmer, Mr J.D. Lindsay, who had once been greatly moved by a PM mission in Ireland. He wrote to the PM President in 1869 requesting 'a young minister to serve 50 Europeans, 100 Kaffirs and 50 Hottentots.' As a result Henry Buckenham was sent to work there and with Lindsay's co-operation a room for worship was found, a Sunday school begun, an evening class and then a day school opened and at length a church and parsonage

---

[19]   See E.C. Pritchard, *Under the Southern Cross*, (London, W.A. Hammond, 1914).

[20]   *Australian Dictionary of Biography*, http://adb.anu.edu.au/biography/gilmore-hugh-3618 [accessed 31 October 2012].

built. He pastored separate black and white congregations, neither very large. He was joined in 1874 by John Smith, who was presented with £200, a substantial gift (worth £13,000 at the turn of the millennium), from the Yarmouth Circuit to meet the cost of sending him and his family to South Africa. Buckenham left the next year to resume work in England, but his heart was in Africa and for a short period he served on Fernando Po. There he lost his first wife and was himself repatriated, terribly emaciated by repeated bouts of malaria. However, he recovered, remarried and responded to a fresh challenge.

Smith recognized that there was an ample supply of churches in South Africa and saw no likelihood of greatly developing the work at Aliwal North. He knew that in 1885 the French missionaries nearby in Lesotho had begun to evangelize the Lozi people north of the Zambezi. They suggested that the PMs should undertake a similar mission to their neighbours, the Ila. When Smith returned to England in 1888 he put the idea of a Central African Mission to the Conference. His proposal was accepted and the Buckenhams, with two colleagues, sailed in April 1889. It took them four years and eight months to reach their destination.

They prepared their wagons at Aliwal North – three large tented wagons, each drawn by a team of eighteen oxen, which would be their homes on the way and an open cart pulled by six. Their goods from England were delayed by a dockers' strike in London and almost a year had passed before they were able to set out from Kimberley. On good days they travelled at two miles per hour following the tracks made by a few earlier wagons. They frequently had to extricate wagon-wheels from the mud and sometimes had to replace exhausted oxen or repair broken spokes or axles. Repair they managed; replacement was almost beyond them. None of the party were wheelwrights, the timber yard was the forest and they did not have the proper tools. On one occasion it took ten days before the wagon rolled again. Crossing the Zambezi meant dismantling the wagons and floating them over, while the goods were ferried in dug-out canoes and the oxen had to swim across. The river was over half-a-mile wide and the crossing took six days. The longest delays were waiting for permission from the Lozi chief to pass through his territory and they remained for many months at the Paris Missionary Society station at Sefula. After many machinations they set out on the last leg of their journey, which involved crossing seventeen rivers. Three of them flowed through deep gorges and they had to build strong log bridges. The convoy arrived in Ila territory[21] at the end of 1893 at the height of the rainy season and in the most trying circumstances they built a mud kraal and began their work.[22]

Although the first little mission station at Nkala became a regular meeting place for people from a wide area and though they enjoyed the singing, it was seven years before the gospel message began to reach their hearts as well as their ears. In 1896 Buckenham had said his farewells and set out for England,

---

[21]   Then known as Mashukulumbweland, in what is now southern Zambia.

[22]   For a fuller account see A. Baldwin, *A Missionary Outpost in Central Africa*, (London, PM Young People's Missionary Department, 1914), pp. 14–35.

but he got no further than the Zambezi before he died. It was another costly venture. Every missionary family knew bereavement. Arthur Baldwin, who wrote a graphic account of the long expedition and the early years, fell ill a few months after the first signs of spiritual awakening appeared and had to leave; he recovered but within a week of reaching Aliwal North his wife succumbed. By then reinforcements, both English and African, had arrived. Robert Moalosi, one of several Sotho evangelists from Aliwal North, served among the Ila from 1897 to 1922 and was invaluable as teacher, preacher, carpenter and bricklayer. A second station was opened at Nanzela, a short distance from Nkala, in 1895 and a third at Nambala, 100 miles further away, in 1905. Moalasi went to Nambala and was the mainstay of the station, left at times in charge when Europeans were on furlough.

John Smith became Secretary of the General Missionary Committee in 1894. His son Edwin, born and bred at Aliwal North, entered the ministry in 1897, served his first appointment in his birthplace and then from 1902 to 1915 worked among the Ila. He produced a Handbook of the Ila language and, with collaborators, an Ila translation of the New Testament and became a distinguished anthropologist.[23]

A rapidly-organized mission in West Africa began at the same time as the long-contemplated South African venture. In 1869 a merchant ship trading between Liverpool and West Africa called at the island of Fernando Po (subsequently known as Bioko). The captain and the ship's carpenter, both Primitive Methodists, discovered a handful of leaderless African Christians and did their best to encourage them. Captain Robinson returned with a letter addressed 'To the General Secretaries of the Primitive Methodist Society, London':

> Sirs – The object of my addressing you now is to crave your help and sympathy in behalf of the inhabitants of this island. The place was once occupied by the Baptist Missionary Society, but they were expelled after the arrival of the Romish Church on the island, in 1858. Happy to state, that the present laws of Spain have granted liberty of worshipping God according to the Protestant creed to everyone of her subjects in all her colonies, and the people here have the same liberty given them, and may invite a minister of any denomination to come and settle with them … Fortunately, one of your local preachers, who is the bearer of this letter to you, arrived here and preached to us … and every individual in the place was greatly blessed by his labours, therefore I am requested by the inhabitants to apply to your Committee for a missionary to come and direct them in the way that leads to eternal life.[24]

The Committee received the letter as a call from God. Richard Burnett and Henry Roe volunteered forthwith and landed at Santa Isabel just as Buckenham was arriving in South Africa. They were welcomed with joy. They led worship in the home of Mamma Job, a redeemed slave, that very evening. The little class

---

23   See W.J. Young, *The Quiet Wise Spirit*, (London, Epworth Press, 2002).

24   N. Boocock, *Our Fernandian Missions*, (London, W.A. Hammond, 1912), pp. 7–8.

comprised English-speakers from assorted West African territories and one who
was able to interpret for his local Bubi people. A splendid site in Santa Isabel
(much later Malabo, the capital of Equatorial Guinea) was acquired, overlooking
the harbour. One morning Peter Bull, the interpreter, came to Henry Roe with tears
running down his cheeks and in broken English told how he had not slept because
all night long God had been telling him he was unfit to do God's work. Roe led
him to unreserved Christian commitment and observed that from that day on there
was a marked improvement in his translations. It was however difficult to muster a
regular congregation, because so many made their living by trading in the interior
of the island and were absent from the fellowship for weeks at a time.

Official goodwill was notable by its absence; not only the day-school but the
Sunday school too were shut down from time to time; on occasion singing in church
was forbidden. In 1879 there was a dispute over the boundary of the mission property.
The governor first ordered a new fence to be built, then claimed it encroached on
the public road, had it pulled down and banished the missionary involved, William
Holland. When the report reached Madrid, however, the governor's actions were
disowned. Holland was able to return and the schools reopened.

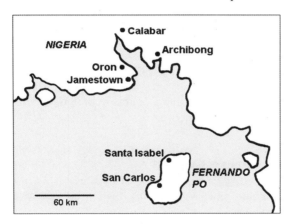

Map 17   Fernando Po and eastern Nigeria: Primitive Methodist stations

Burnett and Roe visited other parts of the island but did not have the resources
to maintain permanent missions, except at San Carlos thirty-five miles along the
coast. Rather than travel through the densely wooded interior they used dug-out
canoes to get around. In 1888 the ladies of Hull raised £425 towards the total cost
of £600 for a steam launch which was much quicker, safer and more comfortable.
It served the purpose well for several years.

A name to conjure with in Fernando Po over several generations was Barleycorn.
William Napoleon Barleycorn was the first, converted shortly after the missionaries
arrived. He was sent to Barcelona for two years to get teaching qualifications and
ran the San Carlos school before entering the ministry in 1880. His sons went to

school in Birmingham. Another influential worker was Mamma Job, who was probably in her sixties when she welcomed Burnett and Roe and not far short of 100 when she died. She was a woman of both prayer and action. In the course of her long life she brought up scores of orphans at her own expense. She was faithfully at worship and class meeting and visited every member of her class each week. She was killed when a tornado hit her house after the Easter service in 1896.

The mainland nearby was visited from the island in 1893 and a new mission was opened at Archibong, on the disputed frontier of what became the German colony of Cameroon and the Niger Coast Protectorate. Marcus Brown was the first to be stationed there; in little more than eighteen months he built a church, formed a society, began a Sunday school and baptized the first convert. By the century's end the congregation had grown to nearly 200, a day school had opened with sixty pupils and there was a Sunday school of ninety scholars. Frontier issues were a problem however and the focus of the mission moved to Jamestown and Oron at the mouth of the Cross River. In the twentieth century it became a District extending for great distances inland.

H.B. Kendall, who wrote *The origin and history of the Primitive Methodist Church*, concluded in 1905 his account of PM foreign missions:

> Africa looms large before the Connexion, but there is a growing conviction that, while our mission on this vast continent must be vigorously pursued, it is high time we turned our attention to India or China.[25]

His suggestion was not pursued; the Committee preferred to concentrate rather than disperse its resources and energy.

The United Methodist Free Churches

In the first half of the nineteenth century there were further secessions from mainstream Wesleyanism.

> There was an increasing opposition to ministerial absolutism [and a determination] to secure … a real measure of self-government within the circuits and churches, together with a controlling Conference which should be composed of elected representatives, ministerial and lay.[26]

The Protestant Methodists from 1827, the Wesleyan Association (WA) from 1835 and small groups in Scarborough and Derby, Wales and Scotland had all come together by 1839 and groups in Jamaica, Tasmania and Nova Scotia joined them. Under the banner of the WA and in the wake of emigrants, 'missions were begun

---

25   H.B. Kendall, vol. 2, p. 506.
26   Davies, George and Rupp, *History*, vol. 2, p. 313.

in Ireland, in Hamburg and Australia (1839), in Prince Edward Island (1841), New Brunswick (1842) and Wisconsin (1845)'.[27] A new and much the largest rift followed the fly-sheets controversy.[28] In five years after 1849 the Wesleyans lost 100,000 members, some to other denominations, others to the Wesleyan Reform Union (which remained outside the twentieth century Methodist reunions), some lost to the Christian church altogether and many to the Reform movement which linked up with the earlier bodies in 1857 as the United Methodist Free Churches. The UMFC inherited the WA's foreign missions from the outset and from 1865 one of the highlights of its year was the big Missionary Meeting at Exeter Hall in London.

The Jamaican branch of the UMFC[29] came about when Thomas Pennock, the chairman of the WM District, resigned in 1838. A majority of his colleagues took exception to missionaries marrying black Jamaicans; he defended them. A black candidate for the ministry was turned down by the Committee in London, who would only accord him the inferior status of 'assistant missionary'; Pennock took his part. Over 3,000 disaffected members went into the Wesleyan Association with him. He remained a divisive figure however and in 1845 left the Association along with half of its members. In spite of the assiduous ministries of such men as William Griffith, who served the UMFC in Jamaica for fifty years, the numbers never recovered. Other blows included the destruction of seventeen chapels by a hurricane in 1880. But the little church retained its missionary enthusiasm. At the end of the century many Jamaicans migrated to Panama where the Canal was under construction and while the Wesleyans followed them to the isthmus, the UMFC opened a station on the offshore island of Bocas del Toro.

British UMFC links with Australia were sporadic until a handful of missionaries arrived in the 1850s. Relationships with the Wesleyans were unpredictable and there were constant comings and goings of ministers and congregations between the two. Eventually two autonomous Districts were created, vast in size but small in numbers, one serving Victoria and Tasmania, the other Queensland and New South Wales. In 1902 when the Methodist Churches in Australia reunited, the UMFC brought 1,875 members to the unified body. In New Zealand the UMFC had an even briefer independent existence, from 1859 with seven members to 982 at Methodist Union in 1895.

Within a few years of coming together, the United Methodist Free Churches embarked on missions in Africa and China. In 1859 some Krio Methodists in Freetown, whose independent West African Methodist Society dated back thirty years, decided to join the Free Methodists. The missionaries who volunteered to go and work among them met with the same afflictions as the pioneer Wesleyans long before; the first, Joseph New, died after three years at the age of 27 and his colleagues were invalided home by 1864. They had wasted no time, however, in setting up ministerial training and the first African UMFC ministers, W.H. During

27   Ibid., p. 318.
28   See p. 87 and Beckerlegge, pp. 30–39.
29   See Birtwhistle, 'Methodist Missions', p. 75.

and William Leigh, were appointed in 1875. In the 1880s the work expanded into the protectorate. Charles Goodman was in Tikonko when the Mende War, provoked by the hut tax, broke out in 1898. He went into hiding but was betrayed and seized and marched to the rebel King Gruburu in his underwear. He escaped execution only because there were Mende people who interceded for him. The king finally agreed to spare his life, saying 'You do not fight; you teach the children book; you are kind to all women; you mend people who are sick. That is all good; there is no bad in it; you shall not be killed ... the King will care for you till the war is done.'[30] Nonetheless Goodman remained in danger. He was kept in filthy conditions and went down with blackwater fever; he owed his life to the man who, some weeks later, brought him his Bible, his pith helmet and his supply of quinine. As the British punitive expedition gained the upper hand the rebels began to surrender and Goodman was released, bizarrely, when Gruburu sent him to the British camp as his messenger to announce his submission.[31] It was not long before, by popular demand, missionaries both Wesleyan and UMFC were back in Mendeland. In the Freetown area, UMFC membership was small and its concerns parochial; although adhering to the United Methodist Church in 1907, many seceded following the 1932 union and became once again the West African Methodist Church.

In 1860 the UMFC Missionary Committee met with Dr Ludwig Krapf from Germany. Krapf's vocation was to bring the gospel to the Galla people of East Africa, believed at the time to be far more numerous than they really were. He had spent five years in Ethiopia and seven in the Mombasa region, where he compiled the first Kiswahili dictionary, before poor health forced his return to Europe in 1853. Back home, he wrote *Travels, Researches and Missionary Labours,*[32] a book which greatly impressed Charles Cheetham. Cheetham, a Lancashire mill-owner who later became the UMFC's connexional treasurer, introduced it to friends and the meeting was set up. The Committee's enthusiasm was aroused and they resolved to begin work in East Africa. They asked a re-invigorated Krapf to lead a party of two UMFC ministers and two Swiss, which arrived in Zanzibar in 1862. Three of them, however, could not cope with the climate and returned within months and it was left to Krapf and Thomas Wakefield[33] to establish a mission station. They settled at Ribe, some fifteen miles inland from Mombasa, not far from a CMS station Krapf had pioneered at Rabai. Then he too returned to Europe.

Wakefield, on the other hand, stayed for twenty-seven years. Life was hard; he buried his first wife, his infant son and three colleagues at Ribe. The gospel was slow to make an impact in a region which had long been predominantly Muslim

---

[30]   Beckerlegge, pp. 84–5.

[31]   See W. Vivian, *A Captive Missionary in Mendiland*, (London, Andrew Crombie, 1899).

[32]   J.L. Krapf, *Travels, Researches, and Missionary Labours During an Eighteen Years' Residence in Eastern Africa*, (London, Trübner & Co., 1860).

[33]   See B. Wolstenholme, *Not Dear to Themselves*, (Loughborough, Teamprint, revised edn, 1998).

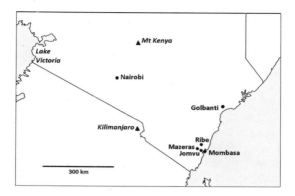

Map 18   Kenya: United Methodist Free Church stations

and it was ten years before the first baptisms. He made translations into Kiswahili and into Galla, for he shared Krapf's belief that the evangelization of the Galla would open the way to the conversion of the continent. Although he did not travel as widely as his colleague Charles New, he made four journeys from Ribe into Galla areas and each was the subject of an article published by the Royal Geographical Society. He was highly regarded not only as a missionary but as an explorer and botanist. He avidly collected botanical specimens for Kew and became known for his unique method of gathering geographical data from members of native trading caravans, which resulted in compiling *A Map Showing the Routes of Some Native Caravans from the Coast to the Interior of Eastern Africa*. Until the East African slave trade was abolished, long after the Atlantic trade, the routes he described were trodden by thousands of shackled Africans. At the end of 1874 Charles New wrote:

> Wherever I go, I see and hear the same horror that prevailed years ago; chained gangs, manacled and fettered individuals; the clank, clank of irons ... the thud of the stick, the screams of the afflicted fall upon the ear every day. Unmentioned cruelties are perpetrated and the victims suffer, bleed and die; yet England is congratulating herself upon her wonderful philanthropy and persuading herself that slavery is no more.[34]

Although the Sultan of Zanzibar was persuaded to close the Zanzibar slave market, it was 1890 before trading was abolished along the coast (and slave-holding remained legal in Zanzibar until 1907 and in mainland Tanganyika until 1927). Meanwhile the Free Methodists concerned themselves with freed slaves, runaways, liberated at sea or in some cases bought directly from dealers. Some of their stations and CMS stations were known as 'colonies', administered by the missionaries on the Freetown model. They were at risk of reprisals from the slavers

---

[34]   Quoted in Z.J. Nthamburi, *A History of the Methodist Church in Kenya*, (Nairobi, Uzima, 1982), p. 21.

and the British consul warned that harbouring fugitives could lead to bloodshed and their expulsion from the Sultan's dominions. Only with the establishment of the East African Protectorate in 1895 were they able to operate in more security.

Charles New had joined Wakefield in 1863, shortly after his brother Joseph died in Freetown.[35] New spent months at a time exploring the interior, seeking to locate peoples to be evangelized and to identify suitable bases for the work of evangelization. Although none were to be found at the summit of Kilimanjaro, New is the first person known to have reached the snowline. Obsessed with the mountain which on a clear day loomed large in the distance, he neglected his missionary work for long enough to climb it and he sent a list of the vegetation he found there to the Royal Geographical Society. He was a careful observer and took detailed notes on his travels which he wrote up while on furlough.[36] He died in 1875 returning from a fruitless expedition to establish a mission in the foothills of Kilimanjaro.

In view of the high missionary mortality rate, the Committee wanted to deploy African ministers 'who by constitution and colour would be suited to the climate',[37] and in 1879 W.H. During was seconded from Sierra Leone. After spending some time at Ribe acquiring Kiswahili and Galla, he was appointed to pioneer work in the Galla country that Wakefield had been exploring. He set out with Matthew Shakala and Aba Shora, two of the first converts who were now respected Christian leaders. Together they opened a base on Lamu island and then proceeded to Golbanti, near the Tana River, where they acquired land and built a mission house and chapel. During then returned to his family in Ribe and his place was taken by a couple from England, John and Annie Houghton. They too had spent some time in language study at Ribe, before moving to Golbanti at the start of 1886. Tragically, only a month after they arrived, a Maasai raiding party attacked Golbanti and Aba Shora and three other Christians were among the dead. Then in May, when they had been just four months at their station, the Houghtons in turn fell to Maasai spears along with most of their congregation.[38]

Wakefield's distress can be imagined. He endured many trials and sorrows in the course of twenty-seven years. In 1887, at last, he returned to England, where he was made President of the UMFC Assembly in 1888 and a Fellow of the Royal

---

[35]   See R.E. Kendall, *Charles New and the East Africa Mission*, (Nairobi, Kenya Literature Bureau, 1978).

[36]   C. New, *Life, Wanderings and Labours in Eastern Africa*, (London, Hodder & Stoughton, 1873).

[37]   E.S. Wakefield, *Thomas Wakefield: missionary and geographical pioneer in east equatorial Africa*, (London, Religious Tract Society, 1904), p. 158. Esther Wakefield was Wakefield's second wife.

[38]   See R. Brewin, *The Martyrs of Golbanti* (London, Andrew Crombie, 1888).

Geographical Society in 1889. His place at the head of the mission was taken by Thomas Carthew, who arrived from four years' service in Sierra Leone.[39]

Carthew was in every sense a strong man. He had a powerful frame and it is told that he once lifted a chest that four Africans could not lift and carried it to its place. He was strong-willed too and gained the nickname *samba* (lion) for the fierce and fearless way any slave-traders who crossed his path were sent packing. He was incensed by the policy of the Imperial British East Africa Company, founded in 1888 to represent and develop British interests in the area. The Company's policy, like that of the East India Company long before, was to do nothing that would have an adverse influence on trade and the missionaries were warned that in the Sultan's dominion they must not disregard the Sultan's law; removing slaves from their legal owners could not be tolerated. So Carthew ransomed slaves from his own pocket and settled them in one or other of the colonies at Ribe, Jomvu and Mazeras. But he was a harsh administrator of these ex-slave settlements. He ruled by decree and was not above inflicting severe corporal punishment when his decrees were not obeyed. It must have been difficult for the former slaves to see any difference between the life they had escaped and their new-found, so-called freedom. Carthew insisted on punctuality at daily evening prayers and

> If some unfortunate proved inattentive while Carthew was proclaiming the Gospel in Church, the preacher had an unfailing method of recalling wandering wits. A book was invariably at hand, and Carthew was never known to miss.[40]

Carthew died of blood-poisoning following an accident in 1896. Robert Ormerod also died in service. His ministry in Africa lasted from 1892 to 1899. Stationed in Golbanti, he grew increasingly frustrated by the lack of responsiveness exhibited by the Galla people. In 1895 he undertook a three months' tour of the Tana River area, noting in each place the number of its inhabitants. He realized how greatly exaggerated were Krapf's and Wakefield's estimates of the Galla population. In that area there were hardly more than 5,000, whereas their neighbours the Pokomo were three times as numerous. Besides, the Galla were nomadic pastoralists while the Pokomo were settled agriculturalists for whom both school and church had some attraction. In time the mission acquired 6,000 acres to farm commercially in order to fund its activity, as well as to offer training in agriculture; the loss of this tract of ancestral land aroused the resentment of the Galla.[41] The end result was that the Galla mission, the basis on which the UMFC had begun its work in East Africa, was abandoned in favour of the Pokomo and, a few years later, of the Meru in the foothills of Mount Kenya.

---

[39] See J. Kirsop, *Life of Thomas H. Carthew, Missionary to East Africa*, (London Andrew Crombie, 1897).

[40] A.J. Hopkins, *Trail Blazers and Road Makers*, (London, United Methodist Publishing House, 1928), p. 6, quoted in Nthamburi, p. 19.

[41] See J. Kirsop, *Life of Robert Moss Ormerod, Missionary to East Africa*, (London, Andrew Crombie, 1901).

But Ribe remained the centre of UMFC operations. From time to time visitors would arrive at the mission compound asking for a missionary. Stations were established among the Chonyi and the Duruma in 1873 and were served by African workers. John Mgomba began work at Ganjoni in 1873; when the property there was burned down in 1883, in all probability by arson, he took over Samburu. In 1885 Thomas Mazera rebuilt the Ganjoni station. These two became the first indigenous UMFC ministers. Mazera's ministry was so highly regarded, indeed, that the name of Ganjoni was changed to Mazeras; when the railway from Mombasa to Uganda was built Mazeras became a well-known station in a new sense of the word. A deputation from England in 1902 described the devotion of Mgomba, Mazera and Shakala – who survived the massacre at Golbanti and was still at work on the Tana River – as 'above praise'.[42]

Missions to Sierra Leone from 1859 and East Africa from 1861 were followed by a new venture in China in 1865. Robert Eckett, who was the chief architect of the WA's constitution in 1840 and the second President of the UMFC in 1858, was instrumental in the launch of the overseas missions, though he died in 1862 and did not see his China project realized. Charles Cheetham was the other prime mover and benefactor. He invited Hudson Taylor to meet the Committee. Taylor had returned from six years in Ningbo, on the coast south of Shanghai, and suggested that Ningbo would be a suitable centre for a new mission. The bold decision was taken, though a beginning could not be made until the Taiping turmoil was ended by the fall of Nanjing. It was a stuttering start, but the arrival of Frederick Galpin in 1868 brought stability to the enterprise. Although for several years he was the lone missionary, he was assisted by Chinese preachers and saw more and more people take an interest in his message. He spent thirty years in China. In 1874 he was joined by Robert Swallow, who served for a similar period and reported on one occasion that he had baptized seven converts in a Buddhist temple.[43] Swallow became convinced not only of the need for a medical ministry but of his own call to take a share in it; he devoted his second furlough to medical studies. Later he was able to study further in San Francisco and became fully qualified to practise as well as to preach. His service in China was interrupted when he contracted blood poisoning while operating. On returning home, he was almost immediately elected President of the 1897 Conference. He returned to China as a medical missionary after seven years in English circuits.

After ten years in Ningbo, Galpin explored the possibility of another mission in Wenzhou, 200 miles to the south, and work began there in 1878. When William Soothill[44] arrived in Wenzhou in 1882, he worked for the first nine years without a colleague. In 1884, while China was at war with France, all the mission buildings

---

[42]   Nthamburi, pp. 35–8.

[43]   34th *Annual Report*, 1890, p. 6.

[44]   J.T. Wilkinson in Davies, George and Rupp, *History*, vol. 3, p. 173, wrongly describes Soothill as a medical missionary; he was a minister and scholar.

Figure 12.1   William Soothill, 1861–1935

were destroyed by a rioting mob. The government paid compensation and Soothill took charge of the rebuilding. Ten years later his wife Lucy recalled:

> Incompetent foremen, dishonest contractors and bad workmen all combined to make the building period one of great disquiet and constant unpleasantness.[45]

The role of architect and clerk of works was not Soothill's forte; he was relieved when he could turn his attention again to evangelism and scholarship. He produced a New Testament and hymn-book in the Wenzhou dialect. He developed a school which began with a few boys and simple equipment and in 1906 became a College with 200 students enrolled. Lucy Soothill opened a school for girls and introduced the very controversial rule that girls should have their feet unbound. In the quarter-century Soothill led the church in Wenzhou and its environs, it grew from a congregation of thirty to 10,000, including thirty Chinese ministers and 200 local preachers. There were 200 places of worship and a hospital, opened in 1897 under the direction of Dr Alfred Hogg, the UMFC's first medical missionary. In 1907 he moved to be Principal of Shanxi University.[46]

---

[45]   *Missionary Echo,* August 1894, p. 121.
[46]   http://www.bdcconline.net/en/stories/s/soothill-william.php [accessed 31 October 2012].

James Heywood served for longer than them all. He worked first in Wenzhou, then moved to Ningbo where he succeeded Galpin as superintendent of the mission. In sixteen years he saw the number of churches increase four-fold. He then returned to Wenzhou and gave in all forty years of his life to China. These Districts – known locally as the English Methodist Free Church Mission – proved more fertile ground for the gospel than elsewhere in China and the remarkable increases were recorded in spite of the disruption caused by the Boxer Rising at the turn of the century.

Joyful News

For a few years at the end of the century there was a parallel mission within Wesleyanism. The Joyful News evangelists were not in the employ or under the discipline of the WMMS, but they worked in circuits and institutions for which the Society was responsible. They were recruited and appointed by Thomas Champness, a man of many projects. He made great efforts to train people to be better local preachers who had not had the opportunity of much education in their youth. In 1883 he began a newspaper called *Joyful News*. It sold for a halfpenny and had a wide circulation among people who could not afford any other paper. It was profitable and the proceeds were used at first for the Worn-out Ministers' Fund and to finance Joyful News Missions in rural England. Champness had spent the first six years of his ministry in West Africa and, after returning for his health's sake, he was briefly on the WMMS staff, as assistant to Dr George Osborn during Osborn's first Presidential year. Evangelization abroad remained dear to his heart, but he came to feel, as did others, that the Society was unduly extravagant and that a simpler, less expensive type of missionary service could be organized. It was from this perspective that he engaged in the missionary controversy of 1889–90 alongside Hugh Price Hughes.[47] He showed himself forthright but fair and not above admitting errors of fact or judgement when he was shown to be mistaken.

A year or so before the controversy was ignited, Champness sent evangelists of his own training, David Pilgrim and George Chisnall, to Zululand. Before long he had a team working alongside missionaries in South Africa, Nigeria, Ceylon, Central China and the South Seas. Most of these appointments were short-lived, but one or two were outstanding. J.T. Whittome was sent to India in 1891 and spent five years running the industrial school in Karur.[48] He brought it up to the standard necessary to secure government funding; he himself had qualifications which entitled him to receive half his salary from the government. The school was inspected regularly and the quality of the teaching and the efficiency of the management remained high. Others did not do so well. Two men were posted to

---

[47]   See pp. 113–15.
[48]   See p. 99.

Ibadan in Nigeria in 1890, but neither lasted long and one, who joined the Baptists, caused more trouble than was necessary on departing.

The most fruitful field of work proved to be China, where the encouragement of David Hill made the difference. The Joyful News evangelists tended to be older than the ministerial missionaries and found the language more of a struggle, but those who survived did sterling work. The first two, A.C. Tollerton and S.J. Hudson, sailed in 1888; one died of smallpox in 1891, the other of dysentery in 1894. They were followed in 1890 by William Argent and Ernest Cooper; Argent was killed by a mob in 1891,[49] but Cooper went on to be ordained and continued to live and work in China beyond his formal retirement in 1916. When the news of Argent's death reached England four more evangelists were sent out to continue his work, supported through the generosity of Argent's mother who kept none of the compensation paid by the Chinese government for herself. In 1892, another four followed, including Champness's own son. Seymour Champness and two of his companions were eventually ordained in China; they had outlasted the Joyful News project.

The project contained the seeds of its own undoing. It was too dependent on the personality and resourcefulness of its founder and when he died in 1905 the organizing genius was lost. And, regrettably, the evangelists were looked on as second-class missionaries. They may have struggled to acquire the language, but most succeeded. As time went on, however, they found themselves serving, not under a David Hill with all his vision and empathy, but under superintendents who were younger and less experienced than they, men who had less command of Chinese and less sound judgement, but who had the authority of their ordination. It was an ordeal shared down the years by all too many laymen and women.

---

[49]   See p. 264.

Chapter 13
The Century in Retrospect

As the century drew to a close, the statistics[1] recorded 21 Bible Christian members in China, 1,180 PM members in Africa and 1,618 MNC members in China; the UMFC had 3,495 members in Jamaica and Panama, 2,808 in Sierra Leone, 1,455 in China and 412 in Kenya; the longer-established and more numerous Wesleyans numbered 1,614 in China, 5,449 in the Bahamas and Honduras, 6,653 in Transvaal and Rhodesia, 10,635 in the Indian subcontinent and Ceylon and 16,945 in West Africa. The WM figures were less than half those recorded fifty years previously, for several of the overseas missions had 'grown up and left home' in the interim. Yet the membership in China and India, where that had not yet happened, was tiny in comparison with the returns of some other Protestant Societies. The number of missionaries too was small and at any one time some of those included in the figures would have been on furlough or at sea. There were seven BC ministers, two women workers and a layman serving in China, nine PM ministers in Africa, six MNC ministers and two lay missionaries in China and in all twenty-one ministers, one woman and one layman appointed to the UMFC overseas stations; scattered across the twenty-five WM overseas Districts still under the care and direction of the British Conference there were 145 ministers, seven deaconesses and forty-two women workers. Thus there were 188 ministers, fifty-four single women and four laymen from the various British Methodist connexions working in 'the foreign field' at the end of the nineteenth century.[2]

There is more to evaluating the accomplishments than counting heads, however. There were all the scripture translations, the lives illuminated by schooling and the suffering relieved by medical care. Some of the overseas Churches had become self-governing, directing their own affairs, no longer frustrated by slow communications with London. In Canada and Australasia, where the membership consisted almost wholly of European emigrants, Wesleyans established autonomous Conferences in mid-century and by the century's end the overseas branches of all the Methodist denominations had joined together and pooled their resources. The Australasian Conference included the Pacific islands, where the Australian MMS had taken the reins from London. In South Africa too there was an autonomous Conference, with a growing black membership but with its leadership firmly in white hands. Its fief did not, however, extend to Transvaal, under Boer rule until 1900; here the District (which also included the kingdom of Swaziland) was still under British

---

[1]   The figures are those returned for 1896.

[2]   The numbers of wives and children are excluded from the tally solely because it is impossible to arrive at accurate figures.

authority. In the Caribbean, with a primarily black membership but again with a white hierarchy, the experiment in self-government was faltering in 1900 and would soon be aborted.

Alongside these ecclesiastical achievements and disappointments, the missionary presence – not by any means exclusively Methodist – had in the course of the century contributed to far-reaching social transformation. To some extent this resulted from quite deliberate attempts to effect change: not only requiring converts to renounce polygamy, traditional sacrifices and fetishes and to adopt European 'Christian' names and clothing, but equally through the introduction of settled agriculture to nomadic peoples. In other respects transformation took place simply because missionaries lived, as far as possible, in the manner to which they were accustomed. Some of their ways appealed to their indigenous neighbours, who began to copy them insofar as their means allowed – 'cotton dresses, brass bedsteads and window panes' were coveted. The calendar was another innovation: in places the seven-day week was a radical novelty, for market-day occurred every fourth, fifth or sixth day and vernacular vocabularies did not necessarily include seven different day-names. Weekly classes, Quarterly Meetings and annual feast-days marked the passage of time.

> In his first letters from the field, [Samuel] Broadbent had complained that, for Tswana, 'every day was alike.' In less than a year, he noted with pride, Sunday in Matlwasse had become as quiet and still as in England.[3]

The Comaroffs, in their monumental study of the encounter between British missionaries and the Tswana, also pointed to the Methodists' role in the transformation of the economy, which they attributed to John Wesley's attitude to money. In his much-quoted sermon on the subject, he saw it as a precious 'talent': the injunction to 'gain all you can, save all you can, give all you can'[4] spurred Methodist missionaries to encourage the development of a cash economy, 'ushering the African into a world of money, manufactures and wage work' – and collections were 'a prominent feature of Methodism'.[5]

While Sunday observance was an essential element of the Christian message, other innovations were incidental, prompted not by explicit directions from London but by assumptions about how missionaries would live, both in contexts where they were likely to consort with other Europeans and in situations where compatriots would be few. It is necessary to distinguish between Africa and the Pacific Islands, territories where missionaries launched a full-scale assault on indigenous culture,

---

[3]   Comaroff, vol.2, p. 300, quoting S. Broadbent, *A narrative of the first introduction of Christianity amongst the Barolong tribe of Bechuanas, South Africa*, (London, Wesleyan Mission House, 1865).

[4]   J. Wesley, *Sermons on Several Occasions*, vol. 4, (Bristol, J. Grabham & W. Pine, 1760), Sermon XLIV, (4th edn, London, Epworth Press, 1944), pp. 576–88.

[5]   Comaroff, vol.2, pp. 215, 170.

on the one hand and on the other India, where by 1890 the Society was committed to 'withstand carefully the Anglicizing tendency that is always operating more or less powerfully in the native church'.[6] In China there was no such tendency; western ways were abhorrent in Chinese eyes and missionaries strove to couch their message in Chinese forms. In the Caribbean, with its slave history, a western cultural veneer prevailed, whatever the beliefs, emotions and customs it cloaked. The missionaries themselves were not fully aware of the multifarious by-products of their activity, as they materialized gradually over the century. The administrators at the Mission House and the supporters in the circuits, primarily concerned about results in terms of conversions, could only be dimly aware of the far-reaching changes for which their labours and funds were partly responsible.

At the Mission House

The WMMS's Centenary Hall in Bishopsgate was no longer fit for purpose by the end of the century. The Wesleyan Conference in 1886 and 1887 had contemplated selling it and buying more suitable premises, but it was not a financially viable proposition at that time. A decade later, however, much of the building was demolished and rebuilt, with a lift to serve its five floors, re-opening in 1903. The Society's offices occupied the top three floors and the rest of the building was let. At the same time a property nearby in Carlisle Avenue was leased to serve as a warehouse; it soon became the offices of a growing Home Organization Department, publishing regular magazines and other missionary literature and producing magic lantern slides for use at missionary meetings. The cost of all the property developments was easily recouped by the commercial lettings at Bishopsgate. The smaller branches of Methodism, embarking at a later date on their foreign missions, had no other mission headquarters than the head office of the denomination.

The Secretaries were often men of considerable distinction. Not a few served as President of the Conference, beginning with Jabez Bunting, who is remembered as an autocrat after the style of John Wesley. He was the dominant figure in the connexion for a generation, with a high view of the ordained ministry and a very high view of his own place within it. There was an occasion, early in his ministry, when a church resolved in his absence to give no more money for foreign missions until its own finances were on a sounder footing. Bunting took the minute book and wrote underneath, 'This minute is rescinded.'[7] He came to the fore at a time when the itinerant preachers had begun to be called ministers and he was instrumental in generalizing the practice of ordination by the imposition of hands, hitherto reserved for those proceeding overseas. He was insistent that ministers must be adequately equipped, pushed through a controversial plan to provide residential

---

6   WMMS, p. 332, quoted more fully below.
7   C.J. Davey, *The March of Methodism*, (London, Epworth Press, 1951), p. 72.

training and became President of the first theological institution at Hoxton in 1834. Holding this office alongside the WMMS Secretaryship reinforced the power he exercised within the connexion and was bitterly resented by some. He was not a man to brook opposition. His trenchant style is evident in the letter addressed by the Secretaries in 1837 to the Wesleyan societies in Jamaica:

> Mr Pennock[8] and those who have seceded with him retain few principles in common with the discipline of Methodism ... You will see through the invidious designs of those who tell you that you would still continue to be Methodists were you to join their party; and you will act accordingly. Those who have so signally failed to destroy our beloved Connexion at home would rejoice to have their agitating plans and endeavours crowned with success in Jamaica ...[9]

When the five anonymous *Fly-Sheets* of 1846–49 attacked Bunting and his coterie he reacted with pique and his heavy-handed treatment of the suspected authors led to the exodus of many Wesleyans and the formation of the UMFC (to which the Jamaican secessionists eventually adhered). The favourite theme of the *Fly-Sheets* was the accumulation of power in the hands of a few ministers who no longer itinerated but stationed themselves permanently in London, particularly the Mission House Secretaries, Bunting, Alder, Beecham and Hoole

> whose power is falsely assumed to be so necessary, not to say vitally important, to the right management of our missionary and other interests ... There is an incongruity between the location of ministerial secretaries and the Christian ministers sent forth on foreign missions; implying separate calls to the same apostolic office; sending forth others, while luxuriating at home themselves ...[10]

Mission House extravagance was another complaint: the appropriation of so much of the 1839 Centenary Fund for Bishopsgate displeased some of those who struggled to keep British circuits solvent. Like his Queen, Bunting was not amused. The Society's own financial position was dire, as he explained in a letter inviting the Scot, Thomas Chalmers, to preach at the annual Anniversary meetings of 1841:

> Our funds are quite exhausted; we are greatly in debt already; our expenditure annually much exceeds our income; our Missionary progress is arrested, though our calls & openings for usefulness are multiplied; and some new & powerful impulse is wanted, to extricate us from our present embarrassments ...[11]

---

[8]   See p. 195.
[9]   Quoted by Findlay and Holdsworth, vol. 2, p. 335.
[10] Davies, George and Rupp, vol. 4, pp. 472–3.
[11] Ibid., p. 456.

The root of the problem lay not in extravagance but in a failure to calculate the cost of maintaining the earlier missions while still embarking on new ventures. The Secretaries and the Committee forged ahead in faith that the Methodist people would provide the means and at times their ambition proved over-optimistic. The anti-Bunting agitation of the 1840s made matters worse for a time; the reformers campaigned to 'stop the supplies' to the Society with the aim of bringing him down.

Yet Bunting deserves to be remembered as a first-rate administrator and organizer. Not only was he a prime mover of the Society's foundation, its later development owed much to his creative mind, far-sighted vision and competent management. He was a gifted orator and debater and a man of prayer.[12] One of his principal critics had no shortage of good words to say for him: James Everett, expelled in 1849 and the first President of the UMFC, wrote earlier:

> All acquit him of selfishness; all unite in giving him credit for the purest motives; and when his proceedings are viewed in the aggregate, he will be found to be generally philanthropic in his views, feelings and purposes ... How has he obtained such ascendancy in the body? Not by fraud, not by misconduct; but by lending his superior talents to promote the best interest of the Connexion.[13]

None of Bunting's successors had quite the same influence over WMMS policy. John Beecham was the architect of the Affiliated Conferences scheme – he died not long after returning from an exhausting visit to North America to negotiate the formation of the Canada and Eastern British America Conferences. The Irishman William Arthur, with an intellect comparable to Watson's, wrote – as had Watson – a major treatise while in office: *The Tongue of Fire* (1856), on the subject of the Holy Spirit and Christian Holiness.[14] His thinking on a wide range of topics, including education, pan-evangelicalism and philosophical theology had wide influence. Marshall Hartley, a third-generation Wesleyan minister whose thirty-one years in office are the second-longest on record, had, like Bunting, a great breadth of interest; he was as dictatorial as Bunting and, Bunting-like, managed to be Secretary of the Conference as well as a Secretary of the Society in 1895–1902.

The Secretaries' wives had their part to play. Elijah Hoole, a Secretary for thirty-eight years, married Elizabeth Chubb (of the locksmith family) a year after he took office in 1834. At that time the Mission House still served as a hostel for missionaries about to sail and the Hooles's hospitality was proverbial. Elijah had innumerable duties to preoccupy him and it was Elizabeth who took care of those who stayed with them. She was a prodigious correspondent and maintained contact with missionaries all over the world. She was a founding member of the Ladies' Committee in 1858 and was for many years its 'Foreign Correspondent'.

---

12   See the testimony of Matthew Johnson, *UMFC Magazine* 1863, p. 150.
13   J. Everett, *Wesleyan Takings*, (London, Hamilton Adams, 1841), p. 11.
14   W. Arthur, *The Tongue of Fire*, (London, E. Stevenson & F.A. Owen, 1856).

Luke Wiseman *père,* who was one of the founders of the *Methodist Recorder,* became a Secretary in 1868 and died in office in 1875. Nine months before he died – and shortly after his year as President of the Conference ended – he married Caroline Shum, then in her fortieth year. Automatically she became a member of the Ladies' Committee, about to become the Ladies' Auxiliary.[15] She was the dominant figure in the Auxiliary for over thirty years and the prime mover of its expansion. In 1876 she took over from the ailing Mrs Hoole as the Foreign Secretary. She transformed the organization. She took charge of preparing the business meetings so that priorities for action were determined in an informed, rather than haphazard, manner. She travelled up and down the country, enthusing audiences with the accounts she relayed from missionaries' letters. She was closely involved in selecting agents. Those who were considered particularly promising were invited to stay with her for a week. They were given various tasks such as doing the accounts, visiting the sick or playing the harmonium. When they were not so occupied Mrs Wiseman was reputed to watch closely what books they read and what other occupations they found for themselves. When in 1888 she made a five months' visit to India and Ceylon, her welcome everywhere was tantamount to a royal visit. But she saw beyond the banners of greeting, the speeches and demonstrations, to the sparse conditions of everyday life, both of those she called her 'girls' and of the women among whom they worked.

Fourteen years later, she travelled again; again to India and on to China. Such was her care for her girls that when she saw the insalubrious street along which a young missionary in Hankou had to make her way to school each day and the jeering crowds who tormented her, she went so far as to have a sedan chair made and ordered her to use it. A highlight of her tour was to be a guest at the opening of a new hospital in Medak, a direct result of the activities of Emilie Posnett and Sarah Harris.[16]

Mrs Wiseman returned from her travels to undertake a strenuous round of missionary meetings, bringing her eye-witness accounts of what was being achieved in Asia. Now in her 70s, she broke her self-imposed rule of speaking only to women and occasionally addressed meetings with men present. She poured her energy into preparations for the Jubilee of the Auxiliary in 1908: it was marked by a splendid exhibition in London and by an appeal which raised £27,000. Part of this sum formed the basis of a much-needed pension fund, now that long-serving single missionary women were surviving into retirement. After this, she was gradually obliged by growing infirmity to renounce her travels, but she still dictated letters and went to committee meetings until a month short of her death in 1912, at the age of 78. Her thirty-six years at the helm of the Auxiliary had seen its activity, its income and its impact multiplied many times over.

In addition to the Secretaries the Society was served, on an honorary basis, by a ministerial treasurer from 1814 to 1912 and a lay treasurer from 1815

---

[15]   See pp. 251–3.
[16]   See pp. 101–2.

onwards. John Scott, twice President of the Conference and the first Principal of Westminster College, and James Rigg, likewise twice President and Scott's successor at Westminster, both held office for many years. Thomas Farmer was the lay treasurer from 1835 to 1860. He was an industrialist and philanthropist and also the treasurer of the Theological Institution. His wife Sarah was the first President and Treasurer of the Ladies' Committee. Sir William M'Arthur, MP and Lord Mayor of London, was another distinguished treasurer. A passionate humanitarian, he had a prominent role in the British and Foreign Bible Society, the Anti-Slavery Society, the Aborigines' Protection Society and the Evangelical Alliance. Advised by missionaries in Fiji, he led a long campaign for the annexation of the islands by the crown; finally successful in 1874, he was congratulated by Gladstone with a grudging tribute to 'the real, but sadly deluded, philanthropy of my hon. friend'[17] – which did nothing to dampen his ardour.

Funding the Enterprise

Each of the Missionary Societies began with a flourish. Wesleyans expanded their field of operations rapidly in the 1820s. The New Connexion and later the Bible Christians went to China on a tide of enthusiasm, as did the UMFC to East Africa. Primitive Methodist missions to Africa were launched not before time, given that a Missionary Committee had been established twenty-five years earlier. It is impossible to assess the volume of prayer which supported the enterprise, but it is reasonable to suppose that the income of the Societies reflected the enthusiasm which their ventures aroused. Wesleyan support waxed and waned over the century. In 1813 contributions for foreign missions amounted to £5,550; by 1846 they had reached £94,000. There had been a brief interruption to the steady increase in 1835, when Samuel Warren's differences with Jabez Bunting took around 17,000 members away from mainstream Wesleyanism. Much more serious, from every point of view, was the reform agitation which saw the departure of some 100,000 Wesleyan members in five years from 1849. Income was inevitably and drastically affected; in 1851 it had fallen to £78,000, but it then increased steadily to £125,000 twenty years later. After that it began to decline again and in the wake of the controversy over missionary lifestyle in 1889–90 it was down to £102,000.

The reasons for the increases included the growth in membership of the connexion and, conversely, a decline in membership was a reason for falling income. But that is far from the whole picture. Missionary meetings, especially when speakers were just home from abroad with enthralling stories to tell, regularly aroused Methodist ardour. From time to time there were lucrative special appeals, though they were usually to wipe out debts accumulated during lean years – one produced a sharp upturn in contributions in 1882, only to fall just as steeply a year later. The fluctuations did not particularly reflect the economic climate. The 1830s

---

[17]   Darch, p. 106.

were hard times yet income continued to rise; at the 1863 Jubilee of the Society substantial donations to the Jubilee Fund came from Lancashire, just at a time when the American Civil War had virtually closed down the cotton industry.

The doubts raised by Henry Lunn's accusations, though they were not upheld, clearly had a deleterious effect, but by the time he made them, giving had been falling gradually for nearly twenty years. Enthusiasm for foreign missions was waning and the controversy he aroused was symptomatic of a growing coolness, not its cause. There was no single cause for the downturn; several factors were influential.

One of these was theological. The belief that the unconverted faced an eternity in the torments of hell, which motivated earlier generations of missionaries and assured them of support, was no longer as widely shared as before.[18] Indeed, William Impey, the Chairman of the Grahamstown District in South Africa, resigned in 1878 declaring that he could no longer believe in the 'literally ceaseless, conscious and eternal torment' of the impenitent. The expectation that the end-times were near weakened, reducing the sense of urgency which had been a dominant motive up to and beyond the mid-century. A new imperative – the depths of human need – spurred a new and controversial emphasis on mission both at home and abroad. Hugh Price Hughes said in a sermon in 1887, in answer to a complaint that he was not sufficiently concerned with saving souls:

> I might have settled the matter by saying that I had no disembodied souls in the congregation, but that I had souls incarnate, souls attached to bodies, and that we must deal with man as a complete being. If I had a congregation of disembodied souls with no physical wants and no connection with London, I might take a very different course. But there is too much truth in the saying I have often quoted of late that 'some very earnest Christians are so diligently engaged in saving souls that they have no time to save men and women'.[19]

Despite Hughes's vigorous criticisms of the WMMS, he did not fault the Society and its missionaries on that score. But those who complained of Hughes complained of them in the same vein.

Secondly there were major appeals for other elements of the connexion's activity which diverted funds. In particular mission in Britain itself, as an enterprise over and above the ongoing work of local churches and circuits, had enthusiastic advocates. Passionate in their concern for the heathen at home, especially for mission in the city slums, they adopted the well-tried fund-raising methods of the Missionary Society, with circuit and church Home Mission secretaries and treasurers, collecting boxes in homes and special meetings and services. In places

---

[18]   See p. 233.
[19]   Sermon on 'Jesus Christ and Social Distress' preached at St James' Hall, 6 November 1887 and published in H.P. Hughes, *Social Christianity*, (London, Hodder & Stoughton,1889).

the protagonists of home and overseas missions competed for funds all year round, in keen rivalry which, friendly or not, persisted for a century.

A third factor was disappointment at results. Year after year the numerical returns revealed the paucity of conversions. Methodists were particularly methodical in recording statistics and diligent in publishing them. Inevitably they became a yardstick by which progress was evaluated and by which missionaries were judged. Excitement and optimism waned. The knowledge that the life of the missionary consisted not in daily adventures but in 'the daily round, the common task' left some disillusioned. Letters home, printed in the Wesleyans' monthly *Missionary Notices* which were published from 1812 to 1904 and in *Work and Workers in the Foreign Field* (1892–1904), became more mundane because they reflected reality and it became harder to cultivate the thrill of living vicariously the adventure of foreign mission. People were thrilled when the seed fell on good ground and bore fruit; they were disheartened when the returns demonstrated how small the harvest was. They were unhappy with the realization that the life of the missionary was not all heroism in the face of danger, 'encounters with cannibals and Kafir hordes … hairbreadth escapes and cruel imprisonments and desperate hardships'.[20] They looked back at a time, well within living memory, when foreign missions constituted a glorious and glamorous enterprise, when 'there were giants in the land'; they bewailed the lack of success in more recent years. It was easy to become weary in well-doing. And this had a circular effect: less income, more retrenchment, fewer advances, little to reinvigorate cooled hearts. Westmore Smith in Haiti, complaining of the diminishing grants to the West Indian Conference in 1893, wrote to the Secretaries:

> I know it is useless to apply to the Committee for anything except sympathy and good wishes – you evidently imagine we can paddle our own canoe. Well praise the Lord we have not yet gone under although sometimes we feel it really rough work especially now that you are cutting off by degrees the blade of our paddle.[21]

Notwithstanding these setbacks, the Society, with its zealous Women's Auxiliary, stuck to the task. The majority of their supporters were not deterred by any of these developments. By 1900 there was a new upturn in giving, funding a constantly growing number of missionaries and more and more institutions, educational and medical, under its care.

Ireland

Thomas Coke found the Irish Conference, over which he presided on twenty-three occasions, a fruitful recruiting ground. In his lifetime, Ireland supplied nineteen

---

[20]   Findlay and Findlay, p. 216.
[21]   Griffiths, p. 192.

WM missionaries: sixteen went to the Caribbean, James Lynch and George Erskine to Ceylon and John McKenny initially to Cape Town. In addition the Irishman Adam Clarke, three times President of the British Conference, described himself as one of Methodism's 'first missionaries' after serving in Jersey in 1786; in 1790 he was one of those appointed to the first Missionary Committee to share with Coke the oversight of the West Indian missions.[22] Between 1814 and 1900 just twenty-five more Irish missionaries were appointed, eighteen ministers and seven single women. Besides this small number, Irish-born ministers and laypeople played a considerable part in the spread of Methodism, though MEC Bishop Janes was exaggerating when he claimed in 1866 'that wherever English-speaking Methodism existed out of England, it had been planted by Irishmen'.[23] In Canada alone in the nineteenth century over 230 Methodist ministers and probationers – BC, MEC, MNC, 'Primitive Wesleyan Methodist' and WM – had Irish roots.[24]

At the same time the WMMS did not ignore mission opportunities *within* Ireland. Between 1799 and the early twentieth century the Society promoted, directed and bore much of the cost of the body known as the Irish Mission (IM). The IM, with its schools, teachers and missionaries, worked in Ireland among both Irish-speakers and English-speakers, including Roman Catholics, often in areas beyond the reach of normal circuit life in Irish Methodism. The Irish circuits contributed to the funds of the Society through the 'Hibernian Auxiliary', but throughout the century the Society expended more on the IM than it received from the Auxiliary.

Successive failures of the potato harvest, leading to the 'Great Famine' of the mid-1840s, accounted for the large numbers of Irish emigrants who took their place in the North American churches. Around two and a half million people left Ireland in the decade 1846–55.[25] In 1849 the Address of the British Conference to the Irish Conference spoke of 'emigrant witnesses for Christ' rendering 'a blessing beyond all calculation'.[26] Those who emigrated were people with initiative and drive. Thomas Waugh told the Annual Meeting of the WMMS in 1847 that 'hundreds and thousands of our very best and most industrious people have fled to America'.[27] Their departure meant that able ministers for the Irish connexion were in short supply and was a factor in the small number of Irish missionaries recruited by the WMMS after William Arthur in 1839.

---

[22] See p. 19.

[23] *Irish Evangelist*, April 1866, pp. 47–8, quoted by Taggart, *The Irish*, p. 6.

[24] Taggart, *The Irish*, pp. 194–201.

[25] D. Fitzpatrick, *Irish Emigration 1801–1921*, (Dublin, Dundalgan Press, 1984), p. 3.

[26] *Minutes of the Irish Conference*, 1849.

[27] *Missionary Notices,* June 1847, p. 126, quoted in Taggart, *The Irish*, p. 39.

Missionary Preparation

Preparation for service overseas was not a significant call on the budget until 1843, when Richmond College in Surrey was opened. In the days of Wesley and Coke missionaries received little instruction, apart from the regular epistle from one or the other to which they were expected to reply just as regularly. The chief criteria for selection were their abilities to preach and travel. With the establishment of the Society, for some years they received, at most, a smattering of guidance from the Secretaries while they spent a few weeks at the Mission House waiting for a passage. From 1834 they spent longer in training, at the 'Wesleyan Theological Institution for the Improvement of Junior Preachers' at Hoxton, which left them better educated but only marginally more prepared for the task which awaited them. The principal guidance they received was enshrined in the *Instructions Delivered by the Committee to the Wesleyan Missionaries,* drawn up in 1820 and printed in every Annual Report of the WMMS until 1861. Its nine paragraphs filled four-and-a-half pages and contained these injunctions:

I.   We recommend to you. *in the first place, and above all things,* to pay due attention to your personal piety...

II.   We wish to impress on your minds the necessity and great importance of using every means of mental improvement ... You are furnished with useful books ... Let the Bible be your book...

III.   We exhort you, Brethren, to unity of affection, which will not fail to produce unity of action...

IV.   Remember, always, dear Brethren, that you are by choice and on conviction Methodist Preachers ... *You have promised to preach, in the most explicit terms, the doctrines held* as scriptural, and therefore sacred, in the Connexion to which you belong...

V.   We cannot omit, without neglecting our duty, to warn you against meddling with political parties, or secular disputes...

VI.   You will, on a foreign station, find yourselves in circumstances very different from those in which you are at home ... On your arrival at your stations, you will be instructed what steps to take in order to obtain the protection of the local government...

VII.   [Particular instructions for the West Indies, which were amended in 1835 and 1839 following the abolition of slavery]

VIII. It is *peremptorily required* of every Missionary in our Connexion to keep a Journal...

IX.   It is a positive rule amongst the Wesleyan Methodists, that no Travelling Preacher shall 'follow a trade'...

Armed with this text-book, which they had sufficient time to study on their outward voyages, they embarked on their mission. But it was not enough and the Committee knew it. The 1839 connexional Centenary appeal raised £221,939 (including 500 guineas contributed by students of the Institution) out of which

£70,000 was allocated to the Society and £71,609 for ministerial training. This funded two new colleges,[28] in Manchester and Richmond, which replaced Hoxton; the first Theological Tutor at Richmond was the autodidact Thomas Jackson, who in 1813 in Leeds had moved the resolutions which paved the way to the WMMS. The Society eventually bought Richmond, for the sum of £37,500 – part of the £180,000 raised by its own 1863 Jubilee appeal – and in 1868 appointed one of its Secretaries, George Osborn, as Theological Tutor. The students, unsurprisingly, were not consulted about the changes; their vigorous but vain protest was led by the young Hugh Price Hughes. Not all Richmond students would go abroad,[29] though from 1868 to 1885 only students preparing to work overseas went there. The names of those who became missionaries were recorded on a series of boards, together with the date of their death which sometimes ensued swiftly: not simply their memorial but a challenge and a warning to their successors.[30] The departures date from 1844 to 1938 when the practice ceased, management of the college having reverted to the Ministerial Training Committee in 1931. The deaths recorded on the boards date from 1846 to 1968.

Figure 13.1   Richmond College

---

[28]   They were at first called 'branches of the Wesleyan Theological Institution' because the word 'College' was viewed with suspicion.

[29]   MARC holds a register of students' names, at both Hoxton and Richmond, noting which leavers proceeded overseas.

[30]   The boards were hung at the Marylebone Road Mission House when the college closed in 1972.

Despite its vested interest in Richmond, the Society had a cavalier attitude to the training it offered and often withdrew its students to go abroad long before the end of the three year course. In 1870 all Richmond's final year students were withdrawn; in 1875 less than half completed the course. From 1885 it was judged better to distribute missionary candidates among the four colleges – by then Richmond in London, Didsbury in Manchester, Headingley in Leeds and Handsworth in Birmingham – rather than segregate them. The syllabus remained fundamentally biblical and theological; students 'might have been told something about tropical medicines, about customs and religious beliefs in the various fields, about learning languages and school management'[31] but were not. It was late in the century before that essential requirement, book-keeping, was introduced.

Another issue for the Secretaries was the reinsertion of those who returned from abroad into a home circuit. They naturally expected to be redeployed. In 1832 the newly-appointed WMMS Secretary John Beecham addressed the issue: 'Missionaries come home with families and want houses and are obliged to be sent to circuits where young married preachers would otherwise be employed', which was a burden on the Contingent Fund it would not otherwise have had to bear. It was even put to him that they should not benefit from the Contingent Fund because, unlike the preachers at home, they had not been begging on its behalf in their circuits. Beecham was a diplomat and his solution, that the Society and the Fund should share the burden, was agreed – a solution which, as he said, would 'promote the oneness of the home and mission work'.[32]

The other branches of Methodism likewise offered little in the way of specific preparation. Indeed, none had any college for ministerial training at all until the 1860s; then the Methodist New Connexion opened Ranmoor College in Sheffield in 1864, the Primitive Methodists opened Elmfield in York in 1865 and moved it to Sunderland in 1868 and the UMFC opened Victoria Park in Manchester in 1872. Shebbear School was the Bible Christians' only seat of learning; it was all the formal education even such a scholar as Sam Pollard received before sailing. For him, as for countless others, it was the nurture of a Christian home and a local chapel that did most to equip him for ministry and mission.

Continental Europe

In 1848, three years before he became a WMMS Secretary, William Arthur expounded the view that there were three dimensions to the Society's activity: mission to the heathen, to the colonies (by which he meant the settlers' countries, destined to become British Dominions) and to Europe. At the turn of the century, with 'colonial' Methodism now autonomous, the twenty-five WM overseas

---

[31]   F.H. Cumbers, *Richmond College 1843–1943*, (London, Epworth Press, 1944), p. 63.

[32]   Beecham to Bunting, 22 March 1832, quoted in Porter, p. 134.

Districts were to be found in the Bahamas, Honduras, six in Africa, thirteen in Asia and four in Europe. Arthur, whose own missionary service in India had been cut short due to his poor eyesight, vigorously promoted work in Europe. In France, the small Methodist Church established its own Conference in 1852 – the first self-governing offshoot of British Methodism since the MEC in America in 1784 – but it continued to rely on financial support from Britain until its merger with the Eglise Réformée de France in 1939. The slightly larger German church merged with the MEC's German work, which was much more extensive, in 1897. But small missions in Italy, Portugal and Spain had taken root.

In 1860 Arthur resigned as a Secretary of the Society for health reasons and before resuming office a year later he travelled in *Italy*. Italy was not yet unified, though thanks to the cunning diplomacy of the wily Camillo Cavour its resurgence – *risorgimento* – was well under way. Arthur wrote up the conversations he had with some of those he met and published them in *Italy in Transition*.[33] Within months of his return the first two missionaries had begun work. One was Richard Green, later the founder and first President of the Wesley Historical Society; poor health compelled his return to England after only two years. The other, Henry Piggott, gave forty years' ministry to Italy and lived in Rome in retirement for another fourteen. In 1863 Thomas Jones arrived; he spent practically forty years in Naples, while Piggott superintended developments in the north. The Italian mission worked initially out of Ivrea, north of Turin, but this was a region where the Waldensian Church was active. Piggott had no intention of competing with other reformed Christians. Indeed, he favoured 'combining into a single, national organization all the agencies at work for the evangelization of the country'[34] – Waldensians, British and American Methodists and others – but to no avail. From Ivrea he moved his centre of operations to Milan in 1862 and then, after the liberation of the north-east from Austrian rule in 1866, to Padua. Italian reunification was completed in 1870 with the fall of Rome – ironically Pius IX lost temporal control of the Papal States in the very year he proclaimed, as the first Vatican Council ended, the dogma of papal infallibility – and in 1872 Piggott established his headquarters there.

Although Arthur had found evidence of a widespread antipathy to the Roman Catholic Church and a corresponding interest in other forms of Christianity, Piggott was swift to realize the hold the old faith had on the people and in September 1862 he wrote:

> For years yet everything must go on slowly in this land … It is not at all true that is currently said in England of the rupture of the Italian mind from the Roman faith. Nothing, indeed, could be more extreme than the vituperation and ridicule which, just at this crisis, are poured upon the Pope and the priesthood; but the

---

[33]   W. Arthur, *Italy in Transition,* (London, Hamilton, Adams & Co., 1860).

[34]   T.C. Piggott and T. Durley, *Life and Letters of Henry James Piggott,* (London, Epworth Press, 1921), p. 102.

Italians distinguish, or try to distinguish, between Popery as a system of religion and the men who administer and abuse it.[35]

It was realistic to suppose that only small numbers, here and there, would be attracted by a Methodist gospel and, while he saw the importance of a foothold in the foremost urban centres, there were little Alpine villages where, under the influence of his Italian colleagues, Methodism took root. From the outset the Society supported and encouraged the ex-priests and seminarists who had embraced an evangelical faith and offered their services to the mission. Piggott saw his chief task as training and nurturing them.

The first of these was Bartholomeo Gualtieri, whose ministry in Florence predated the missionaries' arrival and who was given a small allowance from the Society. Later a Franciscan monk, Francesco Sciavelli, joined the team. After working in Parma and then in partnership with Thomas Jones in Naples, he moved to Rome and inaugurated Methodist work in the new capital. Salvatore Ragghiati was a priest who was excommunicated as a consequence of his vocal participation in the struggle for independence. He had shed his ecclesiastical dress, donned the red shirt worn by Garibaldi and his followers and drew the crowds with political speeches as stirring as his preaching had been in the days when he was known as Father Gabrielle. After Garibaldi's victory he had withdrawn from public view but Jones sought him out and he became a powerful Methodist preacher. At first the Italian preachers were recognized as evangelists, but Piggott was in no doubt of the importance of an Italian ministry and in 1869 eight of them were received as probationers. The first ordinations followed four years later. There were other men of calibre whose offers to engage in full-time ministry could not be taken up purely for lack of the means to support them.

A secondary school for girls was opened in the early days in Milan and transferred to Padua, where it was registered as 'the Evangelical International Institute', an alternative to the schools run by nuns. Notable citizens sent their children to it and by popular demand it became a co-educational school. The Society, which all too often obliged the Italian mission to curtail its work for lack of resources, made the school a priority both for funds and for missionary teachers. It closed however when educational resources were concentrated in the seaport of La Spezia, which was known as a Methodist 'stronghold' even though church membership barely reached three figures. For church growth was proving as slow as Piggott had forecast.

Leo XIII succeeded Pius IX in 1878 and the Roman Catholic Church, which had for a time been demoralized by the loss of the Papal States, began to reassert itself. Any ambitious thoughts Protestants may have entertained of a thorough-going Reformation in Italy were seen to be misplaced. The Wesleyan leaders realistically concluded that their vocation was to establish small centres of Christian life to leaven Italian society. By the end of the century these were dotted from the

[35]   *Missionary Notices*, October 1862, p. 189.

Alps to Sicily and there was even an Italian Mission to Egypt with a minister in Alexandria. Both Piggott and Jones retired in 1902 and William Burgess, formerly of Hyderabad, was appointed General Superintendent of the entire field.

In *Spain*, where intermittent sorties from Gibraltar repeatedly came to nothing, a modest venture in Barcelona was launched in 1868. It was prompted on the one hand by the 'glorious revolution' which deposed Queen Isabella II and heralded a time of greater religious toleration and on the other by an offer of service from one of the Society's own employees. William Brown was a clerk at the Mission House who had learned Spanish and used it among Spanish sailors in the Port of London. For a decade he distributed scriptures in and around Barcelona, gathered a little Methodist society comprising three preaching-places and twenty-three members and started a school. In 1879 he was ordained and transferred to Minorca in the wake of some of his congregation. He and his successors there lacked the resources to work the Balearic Islands effectively and the station was closed in 1896, leaving 124 members to be visited as occasion offered from the mainland. An attempt to establish a church in Madrid, where the Bible Society agent in 1884 was a Wesleyan, was abandoned in 1893. But in Barcelona, despite the untimely death of two of the ministers appointed to develop Brown's work and despite very inadequate premises, the tenacious little society maintained its witness. Two-thirds of the population of Spain were illiterate and Methodist schools had no difficulty in attracting more would-be pupils than they could accommodate. By 1900 there were sixteen little schools with eighteen teachers in all and 708 scholars.

Methodism was introduced to northern *Portugal* by Cornish miners who met in class from 1853. Then in 1868, the same year that Brown went to Barcelona, James Cassels began preaching in Porto, Portugal's second city. He was an English businessman. He devoted himself to building a little chapel and took pastoral care of those who joined him. For this unlicensed activity he was sentenced to six years' banishment, a ruling that was overturned on appeal but convinced him that his work needed to be put on a more secure footing. He approached the WMMS and in 1871 Robert Moreton was sent to Porto. Moreton, who was born in Buenos Aires, remained for forty-three years. Cassels worked with him for a while but was not comfortable with the role and eventually returned to his Anglican roots. Moreton visited the Palhal mines in the nearby district of Aveiro and took the miners under his wing. It was nearly thirty years before he acquired a ministerial colleague. Alfredo Henrique Da Silva had started attending services as a boy and experienced hostility and vilification in consequence. But he remained steadfast; Moreton trained him first as a local preacher and then for the ministry. He was ordained in 1899. It was in the same year that an initiative in Lisbon was prompted by Julio d'Oliveira who had returned from Brazil where he had been converted. After only a few years that work was to be relinquished and it was 1986 before Lisbon again appeared on the stations. Methodist work continued to be based in Porto and concentrated in the north.

The Encounter of Civilizations and Cultures

In Europe, the Society worked in the context of a civilization which had been impregnated with Christianity ever since the gospel first reached the west. The century saw many challenges to inherited beliefs, which caused dispute and doubt. From science came Charles Lyell's *Principles of Geology*,[36] making a nonsense of the traditional calculation of the age of the world by reference to biblical data. Charles Darwin published his treatise *On the Origin of Species* in 1859.[37] Equally disturbing was David Strauss's *Life of Jesus*,[38] translated from German by George Eliot in 1846; he cast doubt on the literal veracity of the Bible, characterizing the miraculous elements in the gospel narratives as mythical (albeit without equating 'myth' and 'falsehood'). Liberal Christian thought had little difficulty in reconciling these revelations with honest Christocentric belief, though Matthew Arnold detected 'the melancholy, long withdrawing roar' of the Sea of Faith.[39] Other Christians rejected scientific insights and biblical criticism alike and some were doubtless glad to escape to foreign climes where, whatever the privations and dangers, they would not be faced by such awkward issues.

Beyond Europe's shores, the religious and social context was utterly different. In Europe, missionaries were not attempting to civilize as well as convert people. In the non-western world, on the other hand, their evangelistic objective could not be disentangled from the transformation of society and of lifestyle. Their concern for literacy naturally had an overriding motive and the Bible, or a portion of it, was the first book published in many tongues; but literacy opened a lot of other doors. They demonstrated better building techniques in the first place because they wanted comfortable homes for themselves, but they earnestly wanted others to enjoy greater domestic comfort. They sought to develop more efficient and nutritious agriculture, even if in places they did not pay sufficient attention to local knowledge. Their critical attitude to native dress, in hot climates where there was very little of it, arose from a sense of decency which has been castigated as Victorian prudery, but which upheld the standards they embraced for themselves. Their faith made them humanitarians. William Shaw, giving evidence to a Select Committee of the House of Commons in 1836, was asked whether he knew 'any class of missionary who, in their attempts to instruct the natives in Christianity, combine the principles of Christianity and civilization'. He replied that this was 'precisely the plan in which the missionaries of the Wesleyan Society endeavoured to act'.[40]

The Select Committee on Aboriginal Tribes (British Settlements) was set up in 1837 at the instigation of the anti-slavery campaigner Thomas Buxton, whose concern now was the way indigenous people were treated by white settlers.

---

36 C. Lyell, *Principles of Geology*, 3 vols, (London, John Murray, 1830–33).
37 C. Darwin, *On the Origin of Species*, (London, John Murray, 1859).
38 D.F. Strauss, *Das Leben Jesu kritisch bearbeitet*, (Tübingen, 1835–36).
39 *Dover Beach,* probably written in 1851 but published in 1867.
40 Porter, p. 146.

The Frontier disputes in South Africa, the treatment of native Australians, land-grabbing in New Zealand, unscrupulous trading in weapons, liquor and women and dishonest trade in other commodities, all revealed a heinous disregard of the rights and dignity of people who were entitled to ask, in the catchphrase of the abolitionists, 'Am I not a Man and Brother?' The Select Committee's report described 'the effect of European intercourse' as a calamity; only missionaries were exempt from that damning judgement, as they did not act out of self-interest. They could and should be instrumental in establishing harmonious race relationships.

> Piety and zeal, though the most essential qualifications of a missionary to the Aborigines, are not the only endowments indispensable to the faithful discharge of his office … it is necessary that with plans of moral and religious improvement should be combined well-matured schemes for advancing the social and political improvement of the tribes and for the prevention of any sudden changes which might be injurious to the health and physical constitution of the new converts.[41]

This was a welcome public endorsement of the missionary movement. Colonial officials were now expected to afford assistance and protection to missionaries; colonial governments were urged to make grants-in-aid to mission schools. But with hindsight it was easy to see how the colonial enterprise and the missionary enterprise became entangled. Yet for most of the nineteenth century there were few colonies other than the West Indian islands and the territories which were later known as the dominions. When the crown replaced the East India Company, Indian affairs were administered by a new India Office rather than the Colonial Office and in Africa there was great reluctance to extend colonial territory beyond coastal Sierra Leone, the Gambia and the Gold Coast trading posts. The systematic colonizers of Africa were the French and Germans and only at the Conference of Berlin in 1885 did Britain stake major territorial claims. In the Pacific the century was well advanced by the time Britain established Protectorates designed to guard the islanders from unscrupulous traders and labour-recruiters. Protectorates, leaving a territory with its own ruler and a degree of self-government, were preferred to annexation in the hinterland of Sierra Leone and in Uganda too.

Protection for the inhabitants was welcomed by missionaries. But the assertion of former Colonial Secretary Earl Grey in 1853 that the British crown 'assists in diffusing amongst millions of the human race, the blessings of Christianity and civilization' was a mixed blessing. Individual missionaries did not on the whole confuse evangelization and colonization, but for many of those millions the Bible and the flag appeared to be two sides of the same coin. There was an inevitable ambiguity about mission in the context of Empire. Andrew Porter's conclusion to a magisterial study of the subject was that 'Although missions could not avoid empire, they were determined to put it in its place.'[42]

---

41   Select Committee Report pp. 80–81, quoted in Porter, p. 144.
42   Porter, p. 330.

The relationship of Boyce and D'Urban in South Africa and that of Watkins and Rhodes later were exceptional in the Wesleyan story, though such associations looked normal enough in South Africa where the Dutch Reformed Church and the Afrikaner leadership enjoyed an intimate connection. The Wesleyans' close ties with government led them, alone among the nonconformist missions, to lend their overt support to the British cause in the Boer War. In China the missionaries had no special influence with either the Chinese or the occupying powers, but in times of trouble they could always benefit from the protection afforded by the foreign concessions. Only the few Chinese with personal knowledge of missionaries could know that they were in any way different from other 'long-noses'. In India there was a large and long-standing British community with which missionaries had a natural affinity. They tended to socialize with their compatriots – and many lived in the same élite neighbourhoods. It was one of Henry Lunn's charges in 1889 that they did not mix socially with their Indian colleagues. The reply of the Wesleyan missionaries did not deny their preference for European company and lifestyle; on the other hand it demonstrated a shrewd awareness of the difference between gospel and culture. They did not feel able to live as Indians – they knew how the health of those who had tried was undermined and they relied on the yearly escape to the hills to preserve their own. But they saw the folly of encouraging Indians to adopt a European lifestyle.

> We Englishmen find it hard to present to the people of India a Christianity free from Western accessories and appendages; and in proportion as we connect Western habits and manners with the Gospel that we offer, we make it hard for Hindus to accept our offer. To spread the idea that becoming Christian means becoming English is to make the task of evangelizing India infinitely harder than it need be. Yet it is difficult to avoid spreading this notion. For not only do we ourselves find it hard to distinguish between the essentials of Christianity and the accidentals that our Western upbringing has connected with them, but many of our native Christians also, by a natural process, tend to become imitators of us not only in our beliefs and religious practice, but in outward things, such as dress and manner of life. In proportion as they do so, they spread among the heathen the feeling that by becoming Christians they will lose their nationality and have to give up everything that is familiar to them. To avoid this most injurious misconception, we have to withstand carefully the Anglicizing tendency that is always operating more or less powerfully in the native church; and nowhere have we to withstand it more carefully than among our native ministers, to whom and their successors we look as the chief hope of the evangelization of India.[43]

Those who sought to civilize the barbarian did not foresee the threat to their cause already simmering on the home front, where western civilization was soon to implode in bloody barbaric conflict. The first 'world war' broke out in 1756,

---

[43]   WMMS, p. 332.

when Britain and France fought in Europe, North America, Africa and India. Another, more localized but much bloodier, was imminent. The unification of Germany and Italy in the nineteenth century brought new players onto the colonial scene. Spain's power declined with the loss of its Latin American colonies, Turkey became the 'sick man of Europe' and the Habsburg Empire was falling apart, but the newly created nation states now entered the competition for industrial, military and colonial might. The quest for land, labour, export markets and control of the high seas led both old and new nations – with Britain and Germany, the countries that, America apart, boasted the largest number of Protestant missionary societies, at the forefront – to raise armies, build battleships and develop the weapons of mass destruction that would unleash the 'Great European War' and set a giant question mark against the right of Europeans to preach to the rest of the world.

Chapter 14

The Life of the Missionary

Missionaries were not necessarily or usually the vanguard of the enterprise; they were rarely, even at first, lone pioneers; but their role, particularly in the early history of the overseas Churches, was of immense consequence. Generalizations are well-nigh impossible, yet the question 'What did they do?' cannot be ignored.

> General histories that embrace a region, a nation or a continent must always remain abstractions, true possibly for everywhere but not true of everywhere, built out of many local studies without being invalidated by local exceptions. The historian is not a scientist, constructing a theory from detailed local experiments and then continually checking it against the latest local finding to ensure its continuing relevance, but rather works as an artist assembling a great mosaic. Each little piece has its own validity, and if patterns subsequently emerge, so much to the good, but that does not mean that patterns should or must emerge. The mosaic created by thousands of local studies has its own validity as confirmation of the unique validity of each historical circumstance.[1]

The difficulty is compounded when the survey covers not only five continents but two centuries of rapid social and technological change. The scope of this chapter extends into the twentieth century, in order to reflect the scale of those changes. Voyages lasting months at the start of the period became flights taking hours by the end. Letters awaiting reply for as much as a year developed into instant communication by telephone and e-mail. And crucially, the role of commanding officer gave way to that of overseas partner under indigenous direction; in 1995, somewhat belatedly, missionaries were formally renamed 'mission partners'. Nineteenth century missionaries in some places were effectively settlers, returning to Britain or Ireland rarely if at all. By the end of the twentieth century it was not unusual to take home leave every year or two. At first Missionaries were invariably ordained men, usually with wives who did not bear the name but shared the vocation; from the mid-nineteenth century there were also single women; then greater numbers of laymen, at first doctors and teachers but a gradually expanding list of roles requiring many different skills.

Let the generalizations begin with the ordained, whether physically by the laying on of hands or, in some early cases, 'virtually' by the vote of Conference and letters of ordination. Some spent their entire ministry abroad, some eventually

---

[1]   E. Royle, 'Writing the Local History of Methodism', in *Methodism and History*, (Oxford, Applied Theology Press, 2010), p. 14.

returned to serve in home circuits, some went overseas after itinerating for a time in Britain or Ireland. For years they and they alone were the Missionaries with a capital M. When George Warren went to Sierra Leone in 1811, he was accompanied by three schoolmasters.[2] They outlived him, yet Freetown was deemed to be without a Missionary. The schoolmasters' names are known from correspondence, but were not recorded in official documents of the Conference or of the embryonic Society. Yet many of the generalizations can be applied to them and to the laymen and laywomen of later years, as much as to the ministers.

What Did They Do?

Their activities and priorities depended on their circumstances and personalities. But first and foremost, unquestionably, they prayed. Whether at home on the mission station or travelling, personal, family and public devotions were prominent features of the missionary's life and witness. Only that constant attentiveness to God made each day liveable. Thomas Birch Freeman recorded in his journal how, on a journey in the Gold Coast, tired and hungry, his sleeping-place 'was a very bad one, into which an Englishman would scarcely place a pig; but I laid me down with humble confidence, and slept in peace'. He concluded this entry by quoting the hymn:

> How do thy mercies close me round!
>   For ever be thy name adored!
> I blush in all things to abound;
>   The servant is above his Lord.
>
> Inured to poverty and pain,
>   A suffering life my Master led;
> The Son of God, the Son of Man,
>   *He* had not where to lay his head.
>
> But lo! A place he hath prepared
>   For me, whom watchful angels keep;
> Yea, he himself becomes my guard,
>   He smooths my bed, and gives me sleep.[3]

A hundred and fifty years later to the day, British and Irish Methodists at home and abroad using their Prayer Handbook – for the first time jointly produced with the Home Mission Division – prayed in the words of another missionary pioneer, Ignatius of Loyola:

---

    [2]   See p. 47.
    [3]   18 April 1839: Freeman, pp. 64–5.

Teach us, good Lord, to serve you as you deserve; to give and not to count the cost; to fight and not to heed the wounds; to toil and not to seek for rest; to labour and not to ask for any reward, except that of knowing that we do your will …[4]

Vernon Stones spent his last months in China interned and in solitary confinement before he was deported in 1951. His Bible and hymn-book were taken from him and he was not allowed to sing, so that he thought himself worse off than Paul and Silas. But he spent much of the time praying for every minister whose face he could remember. He said later that he was able to put a name to every face bar one. The attitudes, the language, the content of prayer varied with the times and the persons, but prayer is the prime constant in this history.

Secondly and no less vitally they needed to survive. The sheer business of survival could be so engrossing and exhausting that there was hardly any time left for the work they had come to do. 'Travelling, obtaining supplies, arranging the dispatch of mail, gardening, digging irrigation canals, ensuring your daily meal … let alone having babies, coping with illnesses, and learning a language'[5] took almost every minute of the week and every ounce of energy. The priority of survival, however, was not only a basic human instinct but vital to the task in hand. As the long-serving LMS missionary Griffith John, who spent nearly sixty years (1855–1910) in central China, concluded, 'The cheapest mission is the mission which can keep its missionaries the longest, and get out of them the best service which they are capable of rendering.' This meant that they had to be 'properly fed and housed' and so provided for that they were 'able to work without distraction'.[6] J.L. Barton, also writing at the start of the twentieth century, argued:

It is the missionary's duty to invest his life in the way that will bring forth the largest and most permanent results, and experience has proved that, as a general thing, these results are not obtained by starving the body or misusing it by unnecessary hardships, or causing it to carry unnecessary burdens, and thus wearing it out early in his career.[7]

These observations, based on the premise that the call to missionary service was a life-long call, were born of bitter experience, after a century in which all too many failed to survive. The twentieth century saw the gradual emergence of very different expectations. Very few died on active service, but it became common to

[4]   *Catch the Flame: Sharing in God's Mission through Prayer 1988–89*, (London, MCOD, 1988), p. 37.

[5]   A. Hastings, *The Church in Africa 1450–1950*, (Oxford, Clarendon Press, 1994), pp. 269–70.

[6]   John, pp. 214–15.

[7]   J.L. Barton, *The Missionary and his Critics*, (New York, Fleming H. Revell Co., 1906), p. 164; Barton was Secretary of the American Board of Commissioners for Foreign Missions.

give less than a decade of life to working overseas. At the same time expectations of what it meant to 'work without distraction' rose. The rationale adopted by some amounted to an assertion that:

> ... the most effective missionary was, beyond doubt, the live one; the live missionary was the healthy one; the healthy one was the comfortable one; the comfortable one was the one whose way of life when abroad most closely approximated that to which the missionary was accustomed back home.[8]

It was a dangerous argument. It could only widen the gap between missionaries and those among whom they worked, compounding the cultural and linguistic differences by great economic disparities. The issue of affluence and lifestyle, already at the root of the missionary controversy of 1889, was again the subject of lively debate in Methodist circles a century later.

The business of surviving and the practice of prayer were the constant, indispensable context of the life of the missionary. Their activities, lifestyle and attitudes, however varied, were shaped by their physical needs and their spiritual discipline.

The Pioneers

The hopes and fears with which early missionaries set out and the prayers of those who watched them depart were versified in a hymn written by the Irish evangelical Thomas Kelly (1769–1855) around the time when the WMMS was begun:

> Speed Thy servants, Saviour, speed them;
> Thou art Lord of winds and waves;
> They were bound, but Thou hast freed them;
> Now they go to free the slaves:
> Be Thou with them, 'tis Thine arm alone that saves.

> Friends, and home, and all forsaking,
> Lord they go at Thy command,
> As their stay Thy promise taking,
> While they traverse sea and land:
> O be with them; lead them safely by the hand.

---

[8]   J.J. Bonk, *Missions and Money,* (New York, Orbis Books, 1991), p. 33; the two preceding references were cited by Bonk.

When they reach the land of strangers,
And the prospect dark appears,
Nothing seen but toils and dangers,
Nothing felt but doubts and fears,
Be Thou with them, hear their sighs and count their tears.

When no fruit appears to cheer them,
And they seem to toil in vain,
Then in mercy, Lord, draw near them,
Then their sinking hopes sustain:
Thus supported, let their zeal revive again.

In the midst of opposition
Let them trust, O Lord, in Thee;
When success attends their mission,
Let Thy servants humbler be:
Never leave them till Thy face in Heav'n they see.

There to reap in joy forever,
Fruit that grows from seed here sown;
There to be with Him, who never
Ceases to preserve His own;
And with gladness give the praise to Him alone.[9]

It is difficult in the age of jet-aircraft, electronic banking, international direct dialing and e-mail to envisage how it felt to embark at Gravesend in the nineteenth century. Some features of the experience can however be imagined.

The voyage would be long and hazardous. It would be expensive too and there would, health permitting, be no early return to Britain. Those proceeding to the colonies with their settler population had hardships enough, but what follows relates primarily to those who landed in Asia and Africa, in some parts still as pioneers in the late nineteenth and early twentieth centuries. On arrival the missionary would have to fend largely for himself – or, if married, they would fend for each other. They would need to rely on their own wits, practical skills and resourcefulness. Life would be simple, food basic, domestic comforts few – fewer even than those with which most of them had grown up at home. In the event of illness, medicine would be at best rudimentary. They inevitably expended more energy on surviving than on evangelizing. The good will of the local people was imperative for survival and getting to grips with the local language was a priority. Relationships were built primarily in the course of daily living. There might well be other Europeans around and sometimes they were hospitable, even life-saving

---

[9]   T. Kelly, *Hymns on Various Passages of Scripture,* (Dublin, Marcus Moses, 1820 edition).

companions. Others were unsavoury characters and to associate with them did nothing to advance the cause of the gospel. Letters from home arrived infrequently if at all. Margaret Cargill wrote from Fiji in January 1837 to thank her mother for her letter dated August 1835 which had just arrived; Joseph Dunwell, whose ministry in Cape Coast began and ended in 1835, felt his isolation keenly:

> A sense of loneliness and isolation seized him now and again. The first occasion was when he said goodbye to Captain Potter on 5 January. There were several others when no letters came from home. He wrote to his sister … his parents, Francis May, the missionary secretaries and others, yet he received no letters at all. True, ships called rather infrequently; nevertheless he could not but feel miserable and lonely when the only communications he ever received were the January and February numbers of the *Methodist Magazine* and some newspapers, on 2 June, three weeks before he died.[10]

Asian experience was different. There had been European contact with India and Ceylon for much longer. Expatriate and Eurasian communities existed. There was an established structure of social relationships and the missionaries accommodated themselves to it. In 1816, at the first embryonic synod in Ceylon, they agreed that it would be improper for 'native assistant missionaries to live under the same roof or eat from the same table as the missionaries themselves'.

The Caribbean was different again. There were Europeans on all the islands but many were slave owners until 1833 and hostile to missionaries. From the outset it was expected that stipends be paid out of local giving and not sent from London, though married ministers received allowances for their wives. Itinerancy was practised as in Britain, with frustratingly frequent changes of station. 'It is a painful thing to be moved about so and I do most conscientiously believe that it works against Methodism in this part of the world,' wrote Thomas Hyde in his journal, saying that it was impossible either to get to know a widely dispersed flock or to win the confidence of the civil authorities in a short time.[11] John Brownell attacked the system as early as 1800 on five counts:

> Firstly, because of the great and needless expense which [frequent moves] cause especially in time of war;

> Secondly, the anxiety which they occasion both to the preachers and people who have perhaps just begun to know and love each other properly, and

> Thirdly, they prevent the exertions of a preacher who knows not that he shall stay to finish anything, and therefore begins nothing.

---

[10] Bartels, pp. 16–17.

[11] D.U. Farquhar, *Caribbean Adventures. Extracts from Missionary Journals*, (Boston, Mass, Mt Prospect Press, 1999), p. 37.

Fourthly, there being no trustees, nor stewards who will take care of the chapels, or finances, or be responsible for any debt contracted, the change of course causes much confusion in temporal affairs.

Fifthly, the disagreeableness and danger of travelling in small vessels undoubtedly hastens many preachers to England.[12]

Shipwreck or warfare could easily interfere with communications. In places more remote than the Caribbean, the missionary would perhaps learn that the Conference, meeting some months before, had directed him to move elsewhere. This might seem quite unreasonable and sometimes it was possible to ignore the direction, but generally he got on with making the arrangements.

There was usually some building work going on – a house, a church, an institution. The missionary, whether or not he was working on the building himself, would have to oversee the local builders. It was as well that most early missionaries came from a working background and had practical skills. Even those who sailed in their early twenties had several years of work experience in agriculture or learning a trade behind them. William Fox in The Gambia described a missionary's occupations, essentially his own, in the third person:

In addition to frequent preaching and pastoral duties, he had to superintend a number of mechanics, being architect and builder too; besides which he had on the 600 acres of land sometimes seventy day-labourers preparing it for cultivation, with about as many head of cattle. He had also to act as a magistrate; and no small time was spent in dispensing medicines … he was a kind of ambassador-general to most of the petty chiefs and kings for some hundred miles east, west, north, and south.[13]

When Wakefield and New arrived in Ribe, Kenya, in 1862, they set about improving the buildings they occupied.

First they went with axes into the nearby woods, and cut down branches and felled trees. Then together they dragged the timber to the site and prepared it for building use. After many days of labour, they were able to erect rough, pole frames, and fix doorways and windows.

For the foundations of the building they could do little more than mix clay and water, for no cement or stone was obtainable. By trial and error, they formed shuttering of rough boards, filling in the interior space with mud, and tamping down by hand. Several times the walls collapsed and had to be rebuilt. 'We are such novices that we have to pull down on the second day what we have put up

---

12   Ibid., p. 5.
13   Quoted by Findlay and Findlay, p. 71.

on the first, and then erect it again on the third. This involved three times the
labour; and we need a great deal of patience.'[14]

In those early days few missionaries died of old age; their wives and children were
even more vulnerable. As time went by, the mortality rate lessened; but many
have been moved, as was Dietrich Bonhoeffer, by the boards at Richmond College
recording the names of students with dates revealing in how many instances their
date of departure did not long precede the date of death.[15] It was only with the
confirmation in 1897 that malaria was carried by the anopheles mosquito that life-
saving preventive measures reduced the toll in West Africa.

But the privations endured by missionaries were as nothing compared with
the human need and misery in a host of forms that surrounded them. They did
whatever they could to alleviate it. A concern for the spiritual needs of people with
no knowledge of the gospel was the primary motivation which led them abroad,
but they rapidly became conscious of elementary physical needs on every hand.
As best they could they taught, they comforted, they treated sickness and injury
and frequently they made representations to the authorities, whether indigenous
or colonial.

What for some was, at first, impossible, was the conduct of public worship; it
might take years before they gathered a congregation. In those circumstances they
would invite whosoever wished to come to their family prayers and they would
gather a crowd of the curious, sometimes largely children but often of all ages,
and sing. The hymns they sang and taught were in English; they depended on an
interpreter to whom they would painstakingly explain the meaning of the words
and hope they were passed on intelligibly. As their familiarity with the language
developed, they would attempt street-preaching, which drew many a laugh at their
mispronunciations but also the first glimmers of understanding of their message.

As soon as they were competent, a primary task was to translate the gospels
and eventually the whole Bible. For those with the ability (not necessarily the
academic training, for many had very little formal education) this entailed plenty
of desk work as well as extensive discussion with people whose mother tongue
they were working on about the vernacular terms to use. In some instances –
notably James Evans in Cree and Samuel Pollard in Miao – they had first to devise
a script in which the vernacular text could be written down. This collaborative
work often forged close bonds and led to their collaborators becoming preachers
and even ministers.

The importance of their linguistic work cannot be underestimated. Their
primary purpose was to proclaim the Word of God and although dedicated lives
and deeds of love spoke louder than words they needed to give a reason for their
presence and their way of life. So their primary tool was necessarily the language
the people understood. Moreover, those who mastered the language began to

---

[14]   R.E. Kendall, p. 74.
[15]   See p. 216.

appreciate and enter into its cultural context, realize why people thought, acted and reacted as they did, empathize more closely with them, recognize the ways in which the gospel and the culture were in harmony as well as the areas where they were discordant.

Time spent on the mission compound, building, translating, gathering a little flock and praying with them, writing letters and journals, telling children the stories of Jesus and administering first aid when possible, had to be balanced with time spent further afield. Going on trek was essential to the evangelistic and pastoral ministry. Travelling was on foot, perhaps with porters or bearers or with an ox-cart, horse or donkey; sometimes by dug-out canoe. Eventually there were bicycles; it was a long time before motor vehicles became available.

There were two essential components to their preaching. First, they would tell the stories of Jesus, the heart of their message, over and over again. Second, they appealed to their hearers to 'decide for Christ', abandon their old ways, receive baptism. As Methodists, they believed with John Wesley that all need to be saved and all can be saved from 'the wrath to come'. As missionaries, their calling was to bring men and women to 'the throne of grace'. Within those parameters, some took the strict view that the souls of the unconverted were irrevocably destined for the torment of hell-fire – a view which gave urgency to their preaching, but risked and often incurred the response: 'In the after-life I wish to be with my ancestors, and if you are telling me they are in hell then that is where I will join them, thank you very much.' For others, as for John Wesley himself, 'The idea that an angry God could condemn vast numbers of human beings to eternal punishment without so much as an offer of salvation was … morally offensive.'[16]

As the nineteenth century drew to an end, 'the ghastly argument drawn from the appalling picture of the future misery of the heathen' was abandoned. T.E. Slater, an LMS missionary in India, spoke for an increasing number of his contemporaries in rejecting it, although in 1882 he was premature in proclaiming its demise. He was well ahead of his time in wrestling with the consequence: 'If the heathen are not perishing, why trouble to rescue them? If they are not rushing into hell, why hasten to them with the tidings of salvation?'[17] For the early missionaries, these questions may not have been an issue, but in practice they were facing them, in two different ways: one evangelical and one political. In the first place, they served a God of love; God's loving character, as revealed in Jesus, was central to their message and took precedence over the angry vengeful God of their theology. They had found joy, peace and confidence in following Christ; they earnestly wanted those whom they labelled pagans or heathen to know the same joy and peace. They did not necessarily forge close loving relationships with these others; sometimes they kept them very much at arm's length. They did not 'go native' in housing, nor totally in diet and least of all in clothing. In adopting a style of life which imitated

---

16   Hempton, p. 42.

17   T.E. Slater, *The Philosophy of Missions: A Present-Day Plea*, (London, James Clarke, 1882), pp. 25–6, quoted in Cracknell, pp. 111–16.

as closely as possible what they knew at home, they erected barriers, both physical and mental, between themselves and those to whom they were sent. Yet it was out of love that they administered first aid and medicine where they could, out of love that they gave such a high priority to literacy and learning and above all out of love that they sought to lead others to the Christian faith. Whatever the after-life might hold, they wanted the best for men and women in the here-and-now.

Out of love – but also out of an unquestioning sense of superiority, not merely the superiority of their religion but of their culture. Their assurance that theirs was the true faith, not just superior to other religions but the final and absolute revelation of truth and virtue, was unshakeable. They saw themselves too as ambassadors not only of Christianity but of civilization. Some made a close study of the indigenous culture, but their judgments were largely negative. Converts had to take a 'Christian' name, which meant a European name. They were required to adopt the European pattern of family life and renounce polygamy. They were expected to sing their hymns to European tunes and for years indigenous melodies and instruments were outlawed. And they were expected to wear clothes designed for a very different climate. Missionaries were particularly obsessed with nudity, whether because of Jesus' commendation in the parable, 'I was naked and you clothed me'[18] or more likely because loincloths and beads were seen as quintessentially pagan and naked breasts a sure sign of depravity. Nevertheless William Shaw in South Africa, perhaps untypically, showed appreciation if not approval of the Xhosa dress code.

> One day I said to a certain petty chief, 'I wish you would try to dress yourself.' 'Dress myself?' he replied with evident surprise. 'Don't you see that I am dressed? Don't you see that I have got a new *inguba*? And do you not see that it is lined with tiger skin?' This was undeniably true and his calling my attention to it betrayed his pride of birth, none but chiefs being allowed to put tiger-skin facings on their cloaks. And he added with much animation, 'Don't you see that I have been well-greased and smeared with ochre?' … He called my attention also to the singular and careful manner in which his hair had been dressed that morning … He continued by referring to the string of beads around his neck and the brass wire bracelets that covered his forearms, and concluded by saying, 'I am dressed just as we dress to go to a wedding feast or dance, and you tell me to try and dress myself. I don't understand you.'[19]

An un-named missionary's wife in the Caribbean was also taught a lesson when a black servant boldly rebuked her:

---

[18]   Matthew 25:36.

[19]   C. Sadler, *Never a Young Man: Extracts from the Letters and Journals of the Rev William Shaw*, (Cape Town, HAUM, 1967), p. 63; Shaw's original account was first published in 1860.

'No, Ma'am, anything will not do for black people, because black and white are the same.' 'How do you know that black and white are the same?' 'Because I read in my Testament, that God hath made of one blood all nations of men to dwell on all the face of the earth.' 'Then do you think the blood of white people and black people the same?' 'Yes, the blood is the same; it is only the skin that is different.' Holding out a penknife, which she happened to have in her hand, Mrs D said playfully, 'Do you really think so? Let us each cut a finger, and see.' 'Yes, Ma'am,' archly replied Matty, 'if you will cut yours first!'[20]

Had Rebecca Wakefield lived longer she might have repented of her journal entry for 14 January 1871. Landing at last on the African mainland after some time in Zanzibar, she was encumbered with a lot of baggage and a small daughter. Her disapproval of what ensued displayed a prejudice which was not only common in her time but which was reiterated for generations beyond the age of the pioneers. Of the luggage she recalled, 'The people obstinately refused to take up the loads, or to touch a single thing, except we would promise them an exorbitant payment for their trouble'. And of her little girl: 'Nobody offered to take her even for a few minutes to relieve me, though I was completely worn out. This I have since discovered results from their extreme laziness. It is a matter of principle with East Africans, never to do a scrap more work than they are compelled to do, *lest they should feel tired!*'[21] Quite oblivious to the incongruity, she then described in the next sentence how they were carried to their destination by four bearers in a chair with two poles attached.

Cultural attitudes and opinions inevitably seasoned the missionary addresses they gave when they came home on furlough. After long spells abroad, furlough might well last many months, but they were not devoted to rest and relaxation. There was a constant round of missionary meetings to sustain the enthusiasm and financial support for the enterprise. They told their stories with pathos – the word 'pathetic' in its original, complimentary sense appears again and again in reports of such meetings. Whatever the theological basis of their sermons and addresses, it was self-evident that those Kipling called 'lesser breeds without the law' ought not to be left in the miserable state in which the missionary had found them. With that evangelical conviction they returned to their stations and new volunteers found themselves called by God to accompany them.

Later Generations

After the pioneers came the consolidators. In ancient Corinth, Paul 'planted, Apollos watered, but God gave the growth … The one who plants and the one

---

[20]   Moister, pp. 92–3.

[21]   Brewin, *Mrs Wakefield,* pp. 115–16.

who waters have a common purpose.'[22] So it was as the nineteenth century gave way to the twentieth and missionaries were most likely to go to places where the church was well established in order to build on the foundations laid by their predecessors. By the mid-nineteenth century already the North American and Australian Methodist Churches were largely self-sufficient and missionaries proceeding to the Caribbean found settled though not yet self-supporting churches organized in circuits such as they knew at home. On the other hand, there were areas where, well into the twentieth century, the primary task of missionaries was still to seek out unevangelized villages and tell the gospel story for the first time. The era of the pioneer and the era of consolidation cannot be neatly separated.

Consolidation meant more construction. Mission compounds were often building sites. Schools were expanded, dispensaries opened, dedicated places of worship erected where classrooms had hitherto served the purpose. The early mission houses were replaced with more sturdy, more spacious accommodation; more houses were built for native teachers, catechists and nurses and for additional missionaries. Dispensaries and clinics grew into hospitals. Hostels were added to schools. Much of the labour and some of the materials were supplied locally, but the charge on mission funds was bound to be considerable; authorizing expenditure, negotiating with contractors, eking out the resources, were part and parcel of the job. The experience of Wakefield and New in the early days of the UMFC mission to East Africa had a familiar ring for many in the years that followed; they

> engaged a Swahili carpenter from Mombasa, who with his three young assistants, became the nucleus of the building team. Local men were employed for manual labour, but it was an entirely new experience for them to work for certain hours each day with regularity and to receive a daily wage.

> About twenty people were engaged on the building and one gains the strong impression from the records that the workers found New to be a forceful, tireless and perhaps impatient task master. He in turn complained bitterly of their small appetite for hard work and over-eagerness for wages.

> It became clear as the work proceeded that the carpenter's assistants were his slaves, and he eventually withdrew his compulsory labour because of dissatisfaction with the payment. With a new burst of energy they set about finishing the work themselves.[23]

What was to be done when the costs outstripped the Society's grants? In India William Goudie, later to be one of the WMMS Secretaries, held that in every village where he administered baptisms a school and a teacher's salary were needed. He wrote in 1896:

---

22   1 Corinthians 3: 6, 8.
23   R.E. Kendall, pp. 74–5.

I am most anxious that you should understand that we are not recklessly ... committing the Society to increased expenditure. When you have said your last word on economy, the fixed nature of our grants, and the necessity of keeping within our budget, it is impossible not to allow us some discretionary power, and we should show ourselves unworthy of the trust which you have reposed in us, did we not under certain circumstances set aside your written instructions and act on the counsel which we know you would give us were you cognizant of the new facts that have arisen. Regarding this principle I am possessed of the conviction that in this circuit I have nowhere entered on a responsibility which you would not have justified and shared to the full, had you been here observing the conditions and listening as I have listened to the call of the people.[24]

Goudie wrote not only to the Society. An Indian colleague recalled finding him writing begging letters to England at midnight and recorded that as he put each letter in its envelope, he offered a prayer before he sealed and stamped it.

Accurate accounting for money was imperative and missionaries had to be inducted into the system of double-entry book-keeping and trial balances. Not all mastered the intricacies, not all were conscientious, some insisted that they were called to be evangelists not administrators. As time went by, lay accountants were appointed, but they were generally responsible for the books of the District and needed competent colleagues in the circuits. Where schools were in receipt of government grants or where staff were liable for tax or social security contributions, competent book-keeping became even more important. It was not unusual for ministers to be school managers, sometimes (like Goudie) with a large number of schools to oversee, staff to pay and student fees to keep track of. However much they pored over their ledgers, few avoided every pitfall.

Alongside material construction, the church was being built of 'living stones'. The task of identifying those in their congregations with the potential to be preachers, teachers, catechists and ordained ministers – and of caring for those who thought they had the aptitude but did not – lay heavily upon a missionary. Some of the finest indigenous church leaders were spotted young and while still at school taken into the manse where they earned their keep with household duties, shared in family prayers and were nurtured in their faith by a man or woman who became both guru and role-model. It was in this phase of church growth that V.S. Azariah, subsequently the Anglican bishop of Dornakal, appealed to the Edinburgh 1910 World Missionary Conference for more profound and unpatronizing personal relationships

Through all the ages to come the Indian Church will rise up in gratitude to attest the heroism and self-denying labours of the missionary body. You have given

---

[24]   J. Lewis, p. 89.

your goods to feed the poor. You have given your bodies to be burned. We also ask for love. Give us Friends.[25]

Intimate friendships of that kind were not common, however. One percipient observer noted that in photographs of a missionary and an Indian in a brotherly attitude, 'it was always the Englishman's arm which was around the Indian's neck, never the converse position, and he could not help longing that we should sometimes see something of that too'.[26] At times of relaxation missionaries were more likely to enjoy the camaraderie of fellow-expatriates. In both India and China they would retreat from the hot season for several weeks in the hills, where their indigenous colleagues rarely followed them. C.C. Pande, who became Chairman of the Bengal District in 1950, said that only after independence did he feel able to call his missionary colleagues anything but 'Mr'.

The life of the missionary was now much less isolated than in the early days. Several might live on the same compound; anyone living at a distance would be able to cover the distance with more speed. In these new circumstances, the authority of the one in charge was enhanced. He set the tone of the station, circuit or District and if, as sometimes happened, he behaved in an autocratic manner, his subordinates, especially probationers and women missionaries, felt the strain. Or he, with experience and wisdom, might find his patience strained by them. Little expatriate groups thrown together in a foreign land had to work hard at their relationships. Team working and community living came naturally to some but not to all. John White, as Governor of the Waddilove Institution (while Chairman of the Rhodesia District and later), used to invite his fellow missionaries, by turns, to supper and a game of billiards on Monday evenings.

After twelve years in China David Hill decided to identify more closely with the people and began to wear Chinese clothing, with his hair in a queue. In this, as in many respects, Hill was exceptional. In marked contrast, missionaries to India were expected to conform to the ways of their secular compatriots. A frock coat still figured on the outfit list issued by the MMS in the 1930s and dinner jackets, which were required nightly on board ship, were *de rigueur* whenever one dined in company. One Chairman's wife roundly rebuked a young minister who arrived for lunch in the heat of the day without a jacket. The same minister, David James, was taken aback when, arriving at last at his first appointment by train from Bombay, he was instantly introduced to his Urdu language teacher and to his servant 'to

---

[25]   The full text of Azariah's address on 'The Problem of Co-operation between Foreign and Native Workers' is in the official record of the World Mission Conference, *The History and Records of the Conference, together with Addresses Delivered at the Evening Meetings,* (Edinburgh & London, Oliphant, Anderson & Ferrier, 1910), vol. IX, pp. 306–15.

[26]   Quoted in Cracknell, p. 204.

wait on me at table, run my errands, clean my cycle, etc.'[27] If David Hill was exceptional, so, at the other extreme, was North India.

Language study everywhere was now on a more organized footing. Many would spend months at a language school – probably managed jointly by several mission agencies – before they could begin their work. Others had individual tuition on the job. In several countries there were language exams to be passed in the first, second and third years of missionary probation – which was not the same as, but might be concurrent with, ministerial probation. Senior missionaries sometimes served as language examiners, for while native speakers made the best teachers they could not, some felt, be necessarily trusted to make sound judgments on their pupils' progress.

Some appointments made heavy demands on physical fitness. John Fell deserved the nickname *Sianguzu*, meaning 'man of strength' given him by the Batonga; he reported in 1914 that:

> the tremendous heat of the Zambesi Valley makes it almost impossible to do very laborious work, to undertake long journeys, or to display great energy in our tasks. Fortunately this year the thermometer has not registered more than 114 in the shade. This being so we have been able to do more than if it had been hot ...[28]

Robert Harrison, in China in the 1930s, walked sixty miles each way once a month from his home in Changsha to help revive work in Liuyang which had been disrupted by the Red Army's revolutionary activity a few years before. 'This was no hardship,' he recalled half a century later, 'as the country through which I passed, with its interesting villages, valleys of rice paddy, delightful streams among wooded hills was always a joy'.[29] But times were changing: 'I was the first person to cycle from Changsha and mine the first bike most of its residents had ever seen, but they soon learned to ride ...'. Before long China became a nation of cyclists.

As they built on the foundations laid by their pioneer predecessors, some missionaries began to glimpse a day when their successors would not be replacements from home but their indigenous colleagues. The vision of a self-governing and self-supporting church which would propagate the gospel on its own initiative illuminated the thinking and planning of the more far-sighted missionaries. Local ministers had to be competent theologians and preachers, of course, but they also had to be trained in financial and administrative skills. This was not just the responsibility of those appointed to theological institutions; it was

---

[27] D.W. James, 'The hand that guided, the heart that planned', privately circulated memoir.

[28] Kanchindu PM Station report, in United Church of Zambia archives (file 609), Kitwe.

[29] R. Harrison, 'Incidents Illustrative of Two Terms in Hunan, 1930–43', privately circulated memoir.

one of the priority tasks of the circuit ministers. By the 1940s it was inescapable because, as one wrote,

> We missionaries were constantly being made aware that, though we were needed and indeed valued, we could no longer assume that we were in charge, or that a missionary-minister was necessarily more effective in a circuit than an Indian minister, not forgetting that our standard of living was such that we were a lot more expensive![30]

Lay Ministries

It was not until 1864 that the WMMS began sending laymen as missionaries. Previously anyone who was commissioned was automatically ordained, even if – as for example in the case of George Piercy in China – ordination was by letter rather than by imposition of hands. The terminology did not regard laymen or ministers' wives as missionaries, though that is what they were in all but name. The schoolmasters who accompanied Warren to Sierra Leone in 1811, Gogerly the printer sent to Ceylon in 1818, Tindall the blacksmith who accompanied Lawry to Tonga in 1822, were responding to a need and a call every bit as much as Richard Lyth FRCS, the first missionary doctor, who was ordained before sailing for Tonga and Fiji. Whatever their trade or profession, they were first and foremost agents of the gospel. They brought their skills, convinced, in the words of the Methodist Covenant Service, that 'Christ has many services to be done' – to enlighten ignorance, to heal the sick, as well as to preach. But the offer of salvation was paramount. The schools were begun for no other reason. Children taught to read could read the Bible for themselves; and although that was a target many failed to reach, they imbibed Bible stories in the classroom, they discovered how to pray as Christians pray, they learned to sing the praises of Jesus. Locally-hired schoolmasters may have had a superficial faith at best, but they taught the Three Rs while the minister or evangelist would provide the Christian teaching: in town schools almost daily, in villages whenever they visited.

To open schools was policy from the outset. Medical work began more spontaneously. Basic medical chests and first aid boxes were a vital part of the missionaries' kit, for their own good. But in the face of injury or fever, they unselfishly brought out whatever they possessed in order to administer treatment. It would not be long before sick people began to come to the mission station in greater numbers, though often they arrived only when all else had failed – when they had tried the traditional remedies, consulted the fetishes, made the customary sacrifices, to no avail. As ad hoc treatment grew into little clinics and dispensaries and in places great hospitals, the opportunity to tell of Christ the healer was not lost. The day began, in Outpatient Departments around the world, with prayers –

---

[30]   James, 'The hand that guided'.

at which the staff, the sick and the accompanying family members alike formed a captive congregation. There were regular prayers on the wards too. These times usually included an element, however short, of preaching. A minister or evangelist would sometimes be in charge; often a member of staff was responsible.

It was to such institutions that most lay missionaries, men and women, came. The women took the initiative; the parent Society saw their wisdom and followed suit. The first Ladies' Committee agent went to Belize in 1859; five years later Dr Porter Smith was sent to China as an unordained medical missionary. The number of laymen on the Societies' books was never large, when compared with the number of ministerial or women missionaries or with the numerous lay Methodists who worked abroad in the civil service, in business or industry.[31] Some of the women were engaged in evangelistic work, as for a short while were the Joyful News lay missionaries,[32] but for a hundred years the great majority were in either education or medical work. They included, especially in the late twentieth century, administrators, engineers and librarians as well as surgeons, matrons and teachers. It is noteworthy that most missionary headmasters and principals, until they were succeeded by nationals, were ministers, with lay missionaries in supporting roles. The Wesleyan tradition guarded ministerial prerogatives jealously and leadership of educational institutions was one; the practice remained widespread long after Methodist union. Girls' schools were different and often had women heads; only at a later stage were the distinctive gifts of professional laymen recognized and utilized. By then there was a tendency for teachers to return to Europe after a relatively short overseas career and by the 1970s this was the norm for most laypersons, as employers increasingly and mistakenly viewed a period away from the British scene and its in-service development opportunities as a disadvantage rather than an asset.

---

[31] In 1896 there were, from all branches, 188 ministers, 54 single women and 4 laymen; in 1946 there were 327 ministers, 230 single women and 60 laymen; in 1996 there were 19 ministers (8 of them women), 10 single laywomen and 18 laymen.

[32] See pp. 202–4.

Chapter 15
Women Workers

While Ruth Watkins and Anne Wearing, sent to New York by the Primitive Methodists in 1829, were probably the only Englishwomen (of any denomination) to be formally appointed as missionaries before 1837, many women played a prominent part in early Methodist history. The first Methodist class-meeting in America was started in 1766 at Barbara Heck's instigation. In the Caribbean women like Sophia Campbell, Mary Alley and Mary Gilbert in Antigua, Ann and Christina Gill in Barbados, maintained a Christian witness with and without missionary leadership. Of the women who went overseas from Britain and Ireland, by far the most numerous were married women accompanying missionary husbands. Few missionaries took the line of Francis Asbury, who remained single on the grounds that:

> I could hardly expect to find a woman with grace enough to enable her to live but one week out of the fifty-two with her husband; besides, what right has any man to take advantage of the affections of a woman, make her his wife, and by a voluntary absence subvert the whole order and economy of the marriage state, by separating those whom neither God, nature, nor the requirements of the civil society permit long to be put asunder?[1]

In 1858 Wesleyan women formed their own organization and began sending and supporting single women; a further source of personnel appeared with the creation of a Deaconess order at the end of the century.[2] The other branches of Methodism too eventually established their own women's sections.

The Wives

Many of the wives of the early missionaries did not live long enough to make their mark, but they were exceptional people. In some cases they knew almost as little of the man they married as of the land for which they immediately set out; it was a shared calling which had brought husband and wife together. Others went, after much heart-searching and with much apprehension, their doubts often fuelled by their parents, to be with the man they loved. In later years an unsurprisingly

---

[1]   F. Asbury, *Journal*, (New York, N. Bangs & T. Mason, 1821), vol. 3, p. 128: 27 January 1804.

[2]   The Wesley Deaconess Order is discussed in Pritchard, *1900–1996*, chapter 2.

high number of single women missionaries sooner or later became missionary wives. Some of them indeed were engaged by the time they disembarked after their first voyage, while in other instances a widower with a small child was swift to propose. While early missionaries succumbed all too frequently and all too quickly, their wives were at even greater risk, since the perils of childbirth were greater than at home and the maternal mortality rate was markedly higher – hence the widowers with small children. These women were brave as well as devout.

The role of the missionary wife, throughout the nineteenth century and for most in the twentieth as well, was two-fold: bearing and raising children, running the home, cooking and cleaning (with or without domestic help) on the one hand, sharing actively in her husband's vocation on the other. The first, inevitably but not only when there were young children around, took precedence. Men would have liked more assistance but could rationalize the situation with the argument that an exemplary domestic life was a crucial element in the task of evangelization. Women were often unhappy as 'organ blowers to the musicians'.[3] They felt guilty that they could not do more mission work; they felt equally guilty if they failed to provide the comfort for which a husband craved.

Home tuition for school-age children was usually a mother's responsibility, delivering her own syllabus in the early years and using formal schemes later on. Occasionally there were local schools children could attend daily; in India there were boarding schools in the cool of the hills for expatriate children; many, sooner or later, returned to Europe to complete their schooling. A common solution was to send the children, when they became teenagers if not before, to Kingswood School in Bath (WM), Elmfield College in York (PM) or Ashville College in Harrogate (UMFC) and to a relative for the school holidays. The Society helped with school fees and eventually (in the late twentieth century when the practice was less common) with fares to ensure that the family had some time together every year. But children as young as six might be shipped home if they were returning along with older siblings. This ensured they received a good education and enabled a mother to give more time to mission work, but the emotional strain of such partings was enormous for all concerned. Sometimes a woman, obliged to make the invidious choice between saying goodbye to her children in order to stay with her husband and being wrenched from her husband for the children's sake, would go home with them.

The women, as did single men, had some household assistance – an *ayah* or *amah*, bearer, cook, 'sweeper',[4] houseboy (rather more staff, as a rule, in North India than elsewhere). Many, unused to servants at home, found supervising their domestic workers one of the most stressful aspects of daily life. But it enabled

---

[3]   The phrase was used by Bessie Price of the LMS: U. Long, ed., *The Journals of Elizabeth Lees Price, written in Bechuanaland, 1854–1883*, (London, Edward Arnold, 1956), p. 105.

[4]   A euphemism employed in India for one who not only swept the yard but manually cleaned out the latrines.

them to give more time to Christian service in the community. This however did not necessarily eliminate the demands of home. Henry Piggott reported on the conditions in which he began work in Italy:

> I have a vivid picture of how ... I found my wife, insufferant by instinct and habit of dirt, crouched with bent knees on a chair, and gazing in despair on the floor, on which no pail of water had ever been poured since the cement that covered it had been laid down.[5]

Some wives had professional skills, in education or health care, which they could put to good use – not a few schools and clinics began life on a manse veranda. However it did not take a trained nurse to nurse a sick person. Mary Calvert, who before her marriage had visited from home to home in Buckinghamshire during a cholera epidemic with medicines and comfort, had no sooner arrived in Fiji than she found herself nursing the desperately ill daughter of an important chief. The girl recovered her health and became a Christian. The news spread and soon Mary's home seemed more like a hospital ward than a living room. Wives were able to approach local women much more closely than could their husbands and shared the Christian message with them in both informal and organized groups as well as in casual conversation. The missionary wife, especially in a rural area where she was more often than not the only white woman, soon became a well-known figure at the market and, if language skills allowed, would engage in 'gossiping the gospel'. It is told of Mrs Johnston[6] that in Dominica in 1810

> She embraced every opportunity of instructing the poor female slaves and their children, privately. Gathering them around her by stealth, in her own home, she taught them of Christ ... Leaving to her husband the more public work of the mission, she went in and out ceaselessly among the female population, striving to raise, civilise, Christianise, and refine them, by teaching, 'in season and out of season', the Gospel of Christ, and its kindred lessons.[7]

For both women and men, the separations were hard to endure. Men might often be away from home, touring a far-flung circuit or attending a synod or committee, as Calvert and Lyth were in Fiji when their wives threw caution to the winds and intervened in preparations for a cannibal feast and Boden and Protheroe in China when their wives were viciously attacked.[8] In circumstances less dramatic but still traumatic, a child's sickness or a servant's rudeness could compound the stress of

---

[5]   Quoted by Findlay and Holdsworth, vol. 4, p. 479.

[6]   Her husband served in the West Indies from 1808 to 1821 and was Chairman of the Jamaica District when he died. She died in 1811 after four active but frustrating years.

[7]   E.R. Pitman, *Lady Missionaries in Foreign Lands*, (London, S.W. Partridge, n.d.), pp. 69, 75.

[8]   See pp. 75 and 264.

separation. Douglas Gray, who would spend five weeks at a time on trek in the Rhodesian bush, wrote with feeling:

> It is the women who pay the price of missionary work ... the wives who stay at home in utter loneliness, and grapple with all the problems of a big station, and bear the burden of everything.[9]

The lengthier separations when couples found themselves continents apart were sacrificially and painfully borne. Sometimes they lasted much longer than planned – separated wives shared the fears of servicemen's wives as World War Two dragged on. Such fears were occasionally justified. Lilian Burgess went to England to visit her children and her parents, expecting her husband to follow; he was persuaded to prolong his time in India and so she set out to rejoin him, but was drowned on the voyage.[10] In 1938 Ida Goldsworthy was in England with her children when her husband was murdered in China.

Wives did not always terminate their service when they became widows. Mrs Gordon remained in St Kitts as a teacher for ten years after her husband died; then in 1845 she went to teach in Sierra Leone and at length remarried.[11] Mrs Roberts in Madras likewise remained at her post for a decade.[12] Thomas Jenkins worked among the Mpondo in the Transkei from 1845 to 1868; when he died, his widow stayed on in Mfundisweni for twelve years more and was buried beside him. Clara Ellis, whose husband was the Chairman of the Gold Coast District when he died, could not settle back in Britain. Appalled by the lack of education available to girls, she returned in 1900 at her own expense to restart the school in Cape Coast which had been set up in 1836[13] and later became the prestigious Wesley Girls' High School. In Rhodesia, when Richard Mayes was killed in a road accident in 1969, Joan remained for another nine years, as District administrator and secretary to Andrew Ndhlela, the first black Chairman of the District, until an autonomous Zimbabwe Conference came into being.

Both on furlough and after their definitive return to Europe, many missionary wives and widows were as keen and able as their husbands – if not more so – to speak about their experiences and make the case for more money, more women and constant prayer. They were much in demand at women's meetings and their letters from abroad were regularly read out to such gatherings. One, describing from a woman's perspective the life of a Victorian missionary in Kenya, was written by Annie Houghton:

---

9   S.D. Gray, *Frontiers of the Kingdom*, (London, Cargate Press, 1930), p. 93.
10   See p. 101.
11   See p. 136.
12   See p. 111.
13   See p. 140.

We are now settled down in a good six-roomed house with a very large garden ... We have some very beautiful flowers all around us ... We have, too, the prettiest little chapel in East Africa, and a number of excellent rooms for joiner's shop, stores, etc. We are very comfortable, and should like you to see our house with its pictures (minus frames) antimacassars, etc. and piano. The piano was the first Mrs. Wakefield's, but the rats have eaten the inside away. We have varnished it and made a pretty piece of furniture of it, on which we put our musical box, which plays 'Grandfather's Clock,' to the no small amusement of our African friends ... Ribe is as bonny a place as you would wish to see. It is on a hill, and from our front verandah we look across ... right to the sea, and it is possible to see ships near the coast, as they sail along. There are not many people here, for the famine last year has decimated the inland countries for hundreds of miles. We hope for better things with this year's harvest.[14]

The Single Women

In 1821 a Bristol woman sent £26 to the Mission House, urging the formation of a Female Association to help 'poor infatuated females in India'. It was nearly forty years later before it came about. In the absence of such an association Mary Twiddy, a minister's daughter with a missionary vocation, went to Ceylon in 1841 under the auspices of the *Society for Promoting Female Education in China and the East* (which had been formed in 1834). She became governess to the widowed Peter Batchelor's son and soon married the father. They spent most of the next twenty years in South India. As well as raising a family, they had a shared ministry with education at its core. In spite of opposition, she started a school for girls in Negapatam. But running it single-handedly was difficult alongside maternal duties, especially if a child was ill. So in 1858 she wrote to a friend in London, whose father, Thomas Farmer, happened to be a Treasurer of the WMMS, stating the case for young women teachers to reinforce the work that she and other missionary wives were doing.

The letter had results she could never have expected. It was read to the Committee, which at once gave its blessing to the proposal, resolving:

That the subject of female education in India is regarded by this Committee with lively interest. They rejoice in the help that has been afforded by many Ladies' Working Societies in London and elsewhere, and look favourably on the project for organising these societies more extensively for the extension of female education in India and in other parts of the Mission field.[15]

---

[14] Brewin, *The Martyrs*, p. 58.

[15] General Committee minute, 13 October 1858: SOAS, MMS/Home/General Minutes/FBN2.

Promptly at the end of 1858, therefore, a group of enthusiastic women met at the Mission House to plan their activities. They would publish Occasional Papers with letters from missionaries – Mary Batchelor was quick to supply the first. They would continue the practice of those informal ladies' societies, sending packages of useful articles to missionaries, not to mention warm clothing for Inuit women in the arctic climate of the Hudson's Bay Territory. And they would raise funds to train and support single women missionaries: twenty-five young women swiftly came forward, though funds allowed only a handful to be selected. All this, it was resolved, would be managed by *The Ladies' Committee for the Amelioration of the Condition of Women in Heathen Countries, Female Education, etc* – no doubt an amalgam of competing suggestions for a name.

The Ladies' Committee's earliest appointments were short-lived. The very first, Susannah Beal, was given six months' training at Westminster Normal College, still in its infancy. The Ladies' Committee found £11 for her fees, £4 for books, £10 for her outfit and a first-class passage to Belize. But she survived only a few months before she died of yellow fever. Mary Gunson, who had been the first woman to study at Westminster and completed her training before she offered herself to the Committee, was sent to China to support Joan Piercy in her work among women. The Committee had already sent Mrs Piercy some materials for her Dorcas Society, a woman's group making clothes for the poor, and some money for her girls' school, but after Susannah Beal's death they were hesitant to send a young woman to an equally dangerous environment. On the other hand, Joan Piercy was managing to raise a family and yet remained fully immersed in mission work; so they took the risk. It did not pay off. Mary Gunson contracted tuberculosis and after nine months was compelled to return to England, where she died within another year. Meanwhile Mary Batchelor thought she had got her wish when Mary Scott was sent to join her. Miss Scott, however, succumbed to a different fate. She did not even get as far as Negapatam before meeting and marrying Robert Stephenson, a minister in Madras. She was not the last …

But the Ladies' Committee would not be discouraged. By 1862 they had sent eleven agents – not being ordained, the Society would not officially recognize them as Missionaries – to Belize, China, India, Fiji and South Africa. Of these eleven two died, three married and only two of the others completed as much as seven years' service. One of them was Eleanor Lamb, again Westminster-trained, who was sent to Verulam in South Africa. The last twenty miles of the long journey to her appointment were on horseback from Durban; riding lessons had not been part of her training and she had never ridden before. She was soon in her element, however. The little school she found grew until she had sixty pupils in the morning and another sixty in the afternoon. Two dozen boarders were somehow accommodated in the mission house. She taught the girls crochet and needlework, while her minister colleague taught woodwork to the boys. The Natal government was impressed and helped to provide purpose-built classrooms for these practical subjects. But Eleanor's pleasure in these achievements was far surpassed by her joy when, after long waiting, a first group of young people made their professions of Christian faith and the first school prize-giving was complemented by their baptism.[16]

Before long the Committee could rejoice in much longer-serving women, such as the Irish sisters Charlotte and Anna Beauchamp. Charlotte taught in South Africa from 1869 to 1896 and Anna (always known as 'A.M.') in India and Sri Lanka from 1869 to 1905, with only a three year break of service. Charlotte described her initiation in March 1870, after 'nearly a month ... on the road, being delayed first by heavy rains, then by impassable rivers'. Describing the school to which she was appointed and revealing her own culture shock, she wrote:

> I am sorry to say, not one child at the school has what we call clothes, viz, dresses, petticoats, trowsers, &c; they are all wrapped up in blankets ... Most of the girls come with babies fastened on their backs ... When a baby cries, or is fretful, I send the girl out while she quiets it.[17]

Annie Wood, from Ireland like the Beauchamps, worked in China from 1885 to 1904, even though for a time there was such unrest and anti-western feeling that she was obliged to keep a boat moored at her back door in case it should be necessary to slip away downriver. Earlier, from 1866 to 1878, Catherine Radcliffe, had pioneered women's work in Guangzhou, as a teacher and teacher-trainer on her first tour and on the second 'to resume her former work, and extend her influence more widely by visiting the native women in their own homes'.[18] In a letter dated 28 June 1876 she wrote:

> The last few weeks my women's meetings have been very well attended. At this season of the year women from the country come to spend a few days with their city friends, and are brought by them to see the foreigners, as one of the sights of the neighbourhood, I suppose. By this means people from a good distance come within hearing of the Gospel for once in their lives ... One of them inquired, 'Have you any wonderful things you could let us see?' Some coloured pictures illustrative of Scripture history, pleased them greatly, and also afforded an opportunity of telling them something of Bible truths ...
>
> I was inquiring the other day how it happened that people care to go to so much trouble to have their slave girls taught, while others are so indifferent about the education of their own daughters ... 'It is all about money. When people have no children, they sometimes buy a slave girl or two, and when they are grown

---

[16]   Webb has chapters on Batchelor, Beal, Gunson and Lamb, culled from their letters home and other information published in the Occasional Papers.

[17]   Letter dated 5 March 1870, published in *Ladies' Committee Occasional Paper 45*, July 1870, p. 88.

[18]   *Ladies' Committee Occasional Paper 72*, April 1877, p. 320.

up marry them [off] for secondary wives: then, if they are able to read, that increases their value ...'.[19]

Catherine Radcliffe was commended by Josiah Cox in a letter of 1874 for 'her discretion, sound judgement, strong sympathy and patient diligence' – characteristic marks of the effective missionary, in which the Ladies' Committee could justly take pride.

In the same letter Cox, Chairman of the Wuchang District, raised the issue of how the Committee's agents and those of the parent body, the WMMS, should work together. His suggestion was

> that your teachers, with our worthy wives, should form a Girls' School Committee, administer your funds, and exercise almost full control over this department. The office of the Superintendent will be, I suppose, to encourage, help, and advise both you and them.[20]

The expression 'almost full control' was indicative of a determination to ensure that the life of his District should be properly managed and ultimately under his direction. The relationship between ministerial and women missionaries was a delicate matter to handle, both at headquarters and in the local situation, and was not always handled delicately. A 'Women's Sub-Committee' of the Synod was in time formed in many Districts and often the men and women worked in respectful partnership, but there were also many instances over the years of ministers who ruled the roost over their female colleagues in an oppressive manner. Women missionaries had to be strong characters, if they were not to be under the thumb as well as under the eye of the ordained man, who might well be younger and far less experienced than they were themselves.

Nonetheless, women missionaries were challenging stereotypes in an unprecedented way. Far from the constraints of their native culture, working unchaperoned, they discovered and realized their potential and they developed a self-confidence which helped them to withstand the pressures of overbearing men as well as to tackle the many demands and opportunities which confronted them.

> When they took on the agenda of justice and began to question the cultural norms which meant that women's feet were tortured and bound in China, that widows were killed in India, that twin-children were slaughtered in Africa, that girl children were forced into prostitution and grown women into zezana harems, they challenged a world which had been established by men for the convenience and servicing of men, whatever their religious tradition. Islam,

---

[19]   *Ladies' Committee Occasional Paper 71*, January 1877, p. 306.
[20]   Quoted by Finday and Holdsworth, vol. 4, p. 35; all original correspondence with the Ladies' Committee and Women's Auxiliary is missing.

Hinduism and the African religions were judged and found wanting; but then so too was Christianity.

This was why the connections which the missionary women began to make made them a dangerous force within Christianity. The very freedom they professed to proclaim, the gospel message itself, turned round and hit them in the face and demanded that they too become accountable to the Lord of history. When they named the outrage they felt as they witnessed the violation of women's human rights, they raised difficult questions about the place of women in any society, including their own. When they called for change, they were demanding change for themselves as well. When they freed women by ensuring that they should have education, they challenged the entire social structure which, traditionally, had restricted it to men. In a most moving way the journey of the missionary women was a journey into freedom.[21]

This made them pioneers at home as well as abroad. Not the least of their achievements was opening eyes, both male and female, to the strengths and abilities of women waiting to be released. As Annie Wood pointed out, people who were reluctant to have a woman doctor themselves were enthusiasts about sending them to Eastern women.[22] The impact was unforeseen; whether indirectly or militantly, they made as big a difference to the culture of the west as in the east.

The Ladies' Committee responded imaginatively to changing circumstances and soon decided to abbreviate its name. In 1874 it became *The Ladies' Auxiliary for Female Education,* a title making clear its relationship to the WMMS. In 1882 it became simply *The Ladies' Auxiliary,* reflecting a broader remit, and in 1893, for reasons which in more recent times might have been termed 'political correctness', it was changed to the *Women's Auxiliary* (WA).[23]

As well as sending its own agents abroad, it responded positively to the suggestion, first made from Mysore, that local women be recruited. The idea was not a complete novelty; thirty years earlier in the Gold Coast, Elizabeth Waldron had successfully built up a primary school at Cape Coast.[24] She was still at work until 1880 and the school was then called the 'Wesleyan Girls School and Training Home'. Its aim was to give the girls basic education with an emphasis on domestic science, to prepare them for marriage to the élite gentry.

In India, Ceylon and China the Committee took responsibility for recruits who were known as Biblewomen. The earliest, Sanjivamma in Mysore,[25] was appointed

---

[21]   L. Byrne, *The Hidden Journey,* (London, SPCK, 1993), p. 11.

[22]   Taggart, *The Irish,* p. 66.

[23]   It became the *Women's Department* of the WMMS from 1927 until 1932 when Methodist union brought about *Women's Work,* a term that had long been used in publications.

[24]   See p. 140.

[25]   Webb, pp. 65–9.

in 1868. She was a courageous young Hindu woman who had refused, first, to be 'dedicated to the temple' (in other words, become a sacred prostitute) and, second, to marry the man of her parents' choice. Instead she married a fellow-convert to Christianity. Her gifts as a story-teller and preacher were recognized and she justified the faith the missionaries put in her with forty-eight years' outstanding service. Biblewomen's work was not primarily educational but more directly evangelistic. They would tour villages and converse, in their own tongue, with the women as no man could do. They could obtain entry to the zenanas of India, the quarters of a prosperous Hindu home in which women were secluded. Although some were barely literate, they could entrance their hearers with the Bible stories they retold with passion. Later on, the WA began to fund local schoolmistresses as well as Biblewomen. At one time (1912) it supported above 300 locally enlisted women.

Visits to zenanas, by missionaries as by Biblewomen, had a simple evangelistic purpose, but results in terms of conversion were rare. One of the rare instances aroused a hail of opposition. Muttu Lakshmi in Mysore had been deeply affected by her conversations with several visitors and under the influence of Helen Dunhill she resolved to put her faith in Christ and seek baptism. Her parents did their utmost to dissuade her and even threatened legal proceedings, but she was of age and of sound mind and her baptism took place in 1888. Hindu feelings were so bitterly aroused that for some while all zenanas, in Mysore State and beyond, were closed to Christians and the attendance of girls at Mission schools declined sharply. A 'Hindu Tract Society' was formed to publish anti-Christian literature and missionaries and their colleagues had to endure abuse both in print and in the face. Muttu Lakshmi and her mentors were unashamed.

In the 1880s, the WA lent its support to an 'adoption' scheme which, yet again, sprang from a proposal from India. To begin with, sponsorship at the rate of four or five pounds a year was sought for destitute children in orphanages; subsequently the policy was extended to the support of village schools and of Biblewomen and to the provision of hospital beds. All these would naturally be in situations where missionaries could oversee the use of the funds, for there were as yet no areas outside direct missionary control and the questions about sponsorship debated a century later did not arise.

In 1882 the Auxiliary extended its remit to include medical work as well as education. In cultures which would not allow a man access to a sick woman, the solution was obvious. The WA Committee was exercised as to how much training would be necessary for health care workers and initially prescribed two years of study and a year in hospital. Agnes Palmer, the WA's first medical agent, had no more than this basic medical training when she was posted to Madras in 1884, but there she was able to train further, alongside her workload, at the Madras College of Medicine. The next year, Louisa Sugden was sent to Hankou to meet Cox's repeated appeal and almost immediately declared her work impossible unless she had a hospital. The request was a daunting one for the WA, with its many commitments, but a heroic effort, especially on the part of Caroline Wiseman, its indefatigable organizer-in-chief,[26] resulted in the opening of the Hankou Women's Hospital in 1888. Here the Auxiliary's first fully qualified doctor, Ethel Gough, was appointed in 1895 – and although ten years later she married a minister and therefore ceased to receive any salary, she continued to work in China for the rest of her days, dying in Wuhan in 1941. In a letter from India in 1898 Mrs Wiseman was exhorted by William Goudie:

> Strengthen your medical work everywhere; do not be discouraged by past disappointments … Avail yourselves of facilities offered in Edinburgh, and never be without two or three students in training. A large order, do you say? Then have large faith, and give the women of Methodism no rest.[27]

Goudie never tired of importuning Mrs Wiseman and was generally persuasive.

As with the men and the couples, the pattern of single women's lives varied immensely. There were full-time teachers with a regular time-table, hospital staff with rotas and emergencies and village workers taking the gospel, along with new skills such as needlecraft, to women's groups of unpredictable size, often meeting in the open, never assembling until the missionary appeared. Others ran orphanages or 'colonies' for victims of leprosy.

The whole operation was funded by the efforts of women many of whom were doubtless also giving to the general funds of the WMMS and contributing their pennies to JMA collectors. In the 1880s Wesleyan women in Manchester proposed to collect 'Christmas pennies' for the work of the Auxiliary. Caroline Wiseman had a better idea and Easter Offerings were begun in 1883. They were a major resource long into the twenty-first century. The WA also promoted 'Busy Bees', working parties for children and young people, usually girls, sewing, knitting and stitching articles to be sent abroad; a list of what was received was published each quarter. But 'Busy Bees' were not always girls' groups. In 1885 a Miss Gurney in Richmond started one for boys, so popular that an evening a month soon became a weekly event:

> At one table would be boys employed in sawing, filing or painting, preparing wood to make work-boxes or picture-frames etc, and duly painting their own coats as well as the work. At another table would be younger boys cutting out pictures, making swap books or working perforated card. During this time we used to read aloud, always a missionary book or magazine, so as to keep our object in view … The boys always liked to have a voice in the matter of the destination of the box.[28]

---

[26] See p. 210.
[27] J. Lewis, p. 82.
[28] *WA Quarterly Paper*, January 1896, pp. 24–5.

The Primitive and United Auxiliaries

The other branches of the Methodist family formed women's units as well. In 1907 three of them were brought together as the Women's Missionary Auxiliary of the United Methodist Church (UMC). The Bible Christians had launched their Women's Missionary League in 1892. It undertook to create support groups in every circuit, to organize Busy Bees where children sewed and made items of use in China and to maintain correspondence with the women missionaries. For a while that meant the married women, but, by the time the UMC was formed in 1907, a dozen single women had gone to serve in Yunnan. In 1899 the MNC in turn established its Women's Auxiliary. A plan to start it in 1890 had fallen through when the woman they planned to support, Annie Holt, was taken ill and unable to take up her appointment, but a forthright Conference resolution in 1899 challenged the women of the Connexion to take up the active role they had observed women assuming 'in some of the Missionary Societies'. By the time of union the MNC had sent just three single women to North China and two of them had married there – but their letters stimulated the enthusiasm of the women at home. In the UMFC, Ladies' Missionary Auxiliaries (LMA) had been started in Yorkshire in 1897 and they spread quickly. But the Foreign Missionary Committee was disparaging. The LMA was scornfully called the 'Leave Men Alone' Society – to which the women's riposte was to sing the hymn 'The Master praises, what are men?'. The Committee finally approved a central LMA structure in 1905. Although it sent no unmarried woman abroad, its slogan 'Deeper interest; closer knowledge; harder work; constant prayer' reflected the commitment to the missionary cause it brought to the UMC just two years later. A United Methodist, Mrs Henderson, became the first President of Women's Work in 1932.

In 1907 the Primitive Methodist missionary secretaries called for a Women's Missionary Federation to be founded. The first single women PM missionaries, Ruth Watkins and Anne Wearing, had sailed back in 1821; the first of the twentieth century, Amy Richardson[29] and Annie Langley, a minister's widow, were already working in Nigeria by the time the 1909 Conference set up the Federation. Mrs Mary Leuty was its first Secretary; when in 1931 a hospital was opened at Ituk Mbang in Nigeria it was at first named after her.

---

[29]　Webb, pp. 102–12.

Chapter 16
Missionary Martyrs of the Nineteenth Century

Many missionaries died on active service, but no Methodists were martyrs in the classic sense that they were executed for refusing to renounce their faith. Almost all those who met a brutal death did so either as victims of anti-foreign, rather than anti-Christian, terror or else for the sake of their goods, murdered by robbers. But whatever the immediate cause, it was their devotion to their Lord which led them to the place where they were murdered. Lest we forget, there were besides the missionaries many indigenous Christians who died a martyr's death; only a few can be honoured in the paragraphs that follow.

In Africa

The first Methodist missionary to come to a violent end (if Robert Gamble in St Vincent be discounted[1]) was William Threlfall.[2] Still only 26, he had already found himself near to death more than once during his short spell of missionary service. Born in 1799, at the age of 17 he heard the call to missionary service and, believing God needed him in Madagascar, began to study French. In due course he became a minister, but the proposed Madagascar mission had to be abandoned for want of funds and he was sent to South Africa in 1822. After a few weeks in Cape Town with Barnabas Shaw and a few months in Albany with William Shaw, the opportunity arose to take the gospel to Delagoa Bay (now Maputo Bay, Mozambique): a free passage on a British survey ship. As this took him nearer to Madagascar, he did not hesitate. William Shaw wrote: 'The cheerfulness with which he left us, to face every danger and difficulty, showed he was getting into his proper element.' He was put ashore in July 1823, 500 miles from the nearest mission station. He was welcomed by the local chief and provided with a hut. He was unperturbed by the fact that the locals had murdered some Portuguese settlers a few years earlier. But his isolation and deprivation were extreme. With only a few words of Zulu at his command, he ventured into the interior, only to collapse with

---

[1]   See p. 61.
[2]   T. Cheeseman, *The story of William Threlfall, missionary martyr of Namaqualand, with some account of Jacob Links and Johannes Jager*, (Cape Town, Methodist Publishing Office, 1910); N.A. Birtwhistle, *William Threlfall: A Study in Missionary Vocation*, (London, Cargate Press, 1966).

fever. Back at the coast, he sank into a delirium which lasted for several days: 'I wrote a note to anybody on board the English vessels in the river to come and see me ... Pray sir do come on shore and bury me, for I died last night.' He survived, but for five months malaria plagued him and he had no option but to leave. He took passage on a ship bound for Madagascar, still believing it was his destiny to work there, but at sea the whole crew suddenly fell prey to fever and the captain decided to head south instead, bound for the Cape. It was a terrible voyage. The first and third mates and eleven others succumbed to the epidemic, out of a crew of thirty. Threlfall read the funeral services as each was committed to the deep. The captain became sick and the second mate was no navigator. Threlfall himself had to take over the management of the ship which eventually made port in April 1824; the weather was the only thing in their favour. The ship was quarantined and, though weak and emaciated, Threlfall could not disembark for a month. When at last he recovered enough strength to walk and ride a horse again, he joined Barnabas Shaw at Leliefontein to recuperate. At the start of 1825 he wrote to the Missionary Committee to report that the 'salubrious air of this elevated station' was already improving his health and to say that he was still willing to proceed to Madagascar.

But Threlfall's next, and last, missionary journey took him north across the Orange River into territory which eventually became Namibia. He set out in June 1825 with two African colleagues, Jacob Links and Johannes Jager. This time there would be no language problem. Links, the same age as Threlfall, was a literate Namaqua who knew the Khoi language and could write in Dutch – in fact he wrote the first letter the WMMS Committee ever received from an indigenous convert. He acted as Shaw's interpreter and in 1822 was made a 'native assistant missionary'. He made several journeys with another Methodist missionary, James Archbell, on one occasion sailing up the coast to Walvis Bay. Jager was a more recent convert. At a love-feast in Leliefontein in January 1825 he told how he had heard the gospel from a Namaqua woman called Delia. He and Links became firm friends and before long he too was able to read. Jager yearned for a missionary to his own clan in the barren Karee hill-country, but, at Links's behest, he was the one to become a missionary (though he would not have recognized the term, for missionaries were Europeans). The trio's plan was to make contact with the San people beyond the Fish River and leave Jager there until a 'real' missionary could be made available; Threlfall's frequent illness precluded him from settling there. Their first letter, on 4 July, brought good news. The expedition was going well and they had found a guide to take them further. A further brief message announced that they had reached Warmbad. After that there was silence for many months. Not until the following March was the LMS missionary Schmelen[3] able to ascertain what happened that August.

At Warmbad the party had at first been unable to find a guide to the Fish River, since it would be a hazardous journey, supplies were low and game would be scarce. They set out nonetheless, but failed to find water for their oxen and were

---

3   See p. 52.

obliged to return to Warmbad for fear of being stranded in the desert without transport. They bought fresh oxen and finally found a guide, whose name was Nauwghaap. He may well have been tempted by Threlfall's possessions, meagre though they were. A night or two after their departure they stopped at a San kraal where they ate, prayed and slept. At midnight Threlfall was aroused by a gunshot. Jacob Links had been shot and Johannes Jager had been killed by San arrows. Threlfall was beaten and stoned to death. The bodies were stripped and left unburied for the vultures and hyenas, while the assassins divided the spoils and fled. Nauwghaap was eventually caught still wearing Threlfall's clothes and handed over to the Colonial Government.[4]

The tragedy sent a thrill of horror through British Methodism and his story was told from missionary platforms all over the land. In 1987 a memorial was erected at the scene of the crime with the inscription:

In Memory of
The Rev William Threlfall
Wesleyan Missionary in South Africa
Who – with two native converts, devoted to the same Service and
Sacrifice for the sake of their countrymen – was treacherously
Murdered by their guide and his accomplices, on their way
To carry the Gospel into Great Namaqualand
August 1825

In the course of the Cape Frontier Wars[5] missionaries were often at risk and their work was seriously disrupted but no life was lost. However, shortly after the wars were brought to an end, James Thomas, who had ministered in South Africa since 1839, was murdered. In 1855 only two missionaries were left in an area where there had formerly been seven and Thomas found himself in charge of five stations. One of these, Clarkebury, was constantly without an adequate water supply, so Thomas searched for a better location. He had barely found a place and named it Beecham Wood when cattle raiders attacked and Thomas received three assegai thrusts which killed him.

Thirty years later John and Annie Houghton of the United Methodist Free Church Mission to Kenya met the same fate. John Houghton had started work in a hat factory in Denton, near Stockport, at the age of eleven and eventually married the sister of one of the partners in the firm. By then he had served in two UMFC circuits and, when in 1883 there was an appeal not only for £1,000 for the East African mission but for men to work there, he responded. The newly-wed couple sailed for Africa in October 1884. They were both assiduous letter-writers and told how at Aden their vessel took on board over eighty black children who had been rescued from slavery by a British gunboat in the Persian Gulf. They were met

---

4   Birtwhistle, p. 137.
5   See pp. 54–6.

by Thomas Wakefield and spent five months with him at Jomvu near Mombasa, the largest of the three main UMFC stations. In February 1885 Wakefield and Houghton undertook the difficult journey to Golbanti on the Tana river, beset (as Houghton wrote in a letter for publication in *Welcome Words*) by 'millions of mosquitos'. Golbanti was in Galla country; W.H. During, the West African missionary seconded from Sierra Leone, with a handful of converted Gallas from the coast, had established the station there at Christmas 1883 and had begun to gather some candidates for baptism. This was the post for which the Houghtons had volunteered, but first they were to spend the rest of 1885 at Ribe, continuing their Kiswahili study alongside their ministry. They transferred to Golbanti in January 1886; During left for Ribe after a few days to rejoin his family. Annie Houghton was the first white woman ever seen in the area and wrote 'It is very lonely here'; they were, however, delighted to receive the *Illustrated London News* and Manchester and Stockport papers, even though their Christmas post arrived only in April.

Less than a fortnight after During's departure there was a Maasai raid on Golbanti. Such raids were common, though this was the first for some years. Four of the Galla Christians were killed on that occasion. A second raid early in the morning of 3 May began with an attack on the mission compound. Annie and John Houghton were speared and many other Golbanti people died, either at Maasai hands or when making their escape in an overcrowded canoe which sank in the river. The survivors buried the dead. The Houghtons's missionary service was even shorter than Threlfall's: fourteen weeks in Golbanti, seventeen months in Africa.

Later, two missionaries died in the Transvaal. Fuller and Fanny Appelbe were sent to Mafikeng (the Setswana name was mis-spelt Mafeking by British settlers) when in 1884 a British Protectorate was proclaimed over Bechuanaland following years of unrest and anarchy. Arriving in 1885, they found that throughout the troubles the Rolong Christians had kept the faith and worshipped Sunday by Sunday. Their leader Molema[6] had died, but his brother Montsioa, the Rolong chief, though not himself baptized, was friendly. He was also unreservedly on the British side in their struggle with the Boers and in recognition of his loyalty Sir Charles Warren, commander of the British force, had a Wesleyan chapel built. Warren and Montsioa laid the foundation stones and Appelbe oversaw its completion. The church grew apace. In 1890 the Appelbes moved to Johannesburg where they ministered to the English-speaking community. Fanny kept open house and offered a cheerful, sympathetic welcome to the lost and lonely of the big city. The manse was of course alcohol-free and the missionaries campaigned vigorously against the liquor trade. Getting drunk was – apart from going to church – almost the only leisure activity available to the migrant gold miners and the African hostels were liberally and illicitly supplied with cheap liquor by white profiteers. The police generally colluded with them. When in April 1899 Fanny

---

6   See pp. 57–8.

Appelbe was viciously attacked on the street and died of her injuries, a Colonial Office report claimed

> There can be little doubt that the outrage is an act of deliberate revenge on the part of liquor dealers for efforts made by the Ministers to expose their nefarious trade.[7]

George Maddison was also killed on the street. He went to South Africa in 1904 after two years in circuit in Nottingham and was posted to Johannesburg in 1905. Returning on his bicycle from a meeting one evening in 1906, he went to the help of a European who was being assaulted by a group of Africans and in the ensuing scuffle was stabbed in the neck. An operation on the wound could not save him and he died in hospital. He was buried on his thirty-third birthday. The murderers, apprehended and condemned to death, declared that they had been under the influence of drink and on the eve of their execution sent a message to the Synod urging the Methodist community to use every endeavour to bring the illicit trade to a halt.

The birth-pangs of Rhodesia at the end of the nineteenth century accounted for the death of two more African missionaries. The arrival of the 1890 pioneers was at first greeted with suspicion, but not hostility, by the Shona people. The white presence might afford some protection against the depredations of their Ndebele neighbours. But they soon revised their opinion. The British South Africa Company assumed the right to allocate land to settlers regardless of Shona claims and it was not long before it began to levy a hut tax. The settlers saw themselves as infinitely superior to the local people.

> In the field of administration (they) assumed that the rough bush justice meted out by the white man was in the main fair; that the individual white man had the right to administer that kind of justice against which appeal procedures were not necessary; … that more progress would be made by making the Shona do what the white man saw was good for him than by spending valuable time and money on explanation and persuasion.

> On the moral and cultural level it was held that the Shona was a cowed race who understood force more than reason; that they had no long remembered tradition; that they were hardly, if at all, capable of creative activity; that they were morally and religiously degenerate.[8]

The Shona had never taken arms against the pioneers and had not been defeated in war. But the imposition of the hut tax amounted to defeat. Their resentment was compounded by the Company's thoughtless use of Ndebele police and messengers to collect the tax, which, failing cash, was payable in the form of livestock. Then in

---

7 Quoted by Findlay and Holdsworth, vol. 4, p. 353.
8 Graaff, pp. 92–3.

1896 rinderpest, previously unknown, infected their cattle. It destroyed nearly half the cattle in southern Africa. The administration ordered every infected herd to be shot in order to limit its spread. The intention was good and the plan was sound; but it meant the loss of many Shona livelihoods and the blame fell squarely if not fairly on Company rule.

Resentment and resistance became revolt when an influential traditional spirit-medium, Kagubi, spread the word: I have heard a voice from the rocks and trees saying, 'Kill the white man but do not take his things.'[9] Paramount chiefs and petty chiefs alike heard the call to arms. They turned not only on the white farmers – a tenth of the European population were killed – but on all who associated with them, especially if they were foreigners.

A handful of foreigners, Sotho and Xhosa evangelists from the Transvaal, had volunteered to work alongside the Methodist missionaries in Mashonaland. James Anta, a Xhosa who was fluent and literate in Zulu, was one of these. He had been placed at Hartleyton, to the north of Salisbury, as a teacher and preacher. Single-handed he built a rough mud structure to serve as school and church. One of his students recalled that 'he used small Xhosa/Fingo spelling books for teaching spelling. He taught counting one to ten and beyond in English. The children used slates. Anta read from the Zulu Bible, doing his best to translate into Shona. There were no games.' Trouble arose when in 1894, during a patrol to enforce payment of the new hut tax, a soldier was killed at a nearby kraal. A police detachment, sent from Salisbury to investigate, arrived in Hartleyton on a Sunday, when James Anta was leading a church service attended by most of the villagers. All the chiefs present were ordered to step forward and four of them were then murdered in cold blood. This action shattered such trust as the locals had vested in the missionaries; many suspected that Anta had been part of a plot to gather the chiefs together. So when the Shona uprising started, relatives of the dead chiefs took their revenge. In June 1896 the little chapel there was surrounded, just as a mid-week service came to an end, and James Anta and his family were murdered, as were eighteen members of the congregation who tried to protect him.

The elderly Modumedi Moleli was another victim of the uprising. In 1892, on an exploratory tour, he had come to Nenguwo, south-east of Salisbury, looking for an opening to start a school. He had been well received and when the missionary Isaac Shimmin visited the area the next year, the chief and people sent a deputation to ask for a teacher. Shimmin reported:

> Not only would they send their children to school, but they would also come themselves and learn the right way. I promised to do my best for them, and should meanwhile leave one of the teachers in the village.

He left Moleli, continued his trek and after 18 days returned to Nenguwo.

---

9   Graaff, p. 98.

... my astonishment was great when the teacher started them singing, and they went through several tunes fairly correctly, evidently enjoying the novel performance ... By means of songs the teacher had first won their confidence and awakened their interest, and they were now thirsting to know more. I ... asked if they still wanted the teacher to remain. Their response was clamorous, no other word is fitting.[10]

Moleli settled in Nenguwo and his wife and family came from the Good Hope Mission[11] to join him. They endeared themselves to the people, though distanced from them both by race and custom and by their Christian mode of life. When the war broke out a nearby farm was attacked and the farmer, James White, was left for dead. On hearing the news, Moleli set out at once to investigate and found White wounded but alive. Well aware he was being observed, he found an ox-cart and brought White back to the mission. As they arrived, the attackers struck. Both men were shot; then the killers turned on the family. Mrs Moleli, beaten unconscious, somehow survived, but four out of six children in the household died. After a sixteen-month war the Shona chiefs surrendered to the Company's forces in 1897.

The Hut Tax War in Sierra Leone in 1898 claimed the lives of five African workers.[12] The UMFC had extended its operations eastwards and a few Krio Methodists from the Colony were working among the Krio communities that had settled along the line of rail. After the establishment of the Protectorate in 1896 there was a tendency among the Mende people to regard all Krios as collaborators with an oppressive British government and when the uprising began many were killed. Among the dead were the Revd and Mrs J.C. Johnston and their lay colleagues, Timothy Campbell and Theo Roberts and his wife. Neither *The Missionary Echo* nor the UMFC *Annual Report* made mention of these martyrs, although fully covering the narrow escape of the missionary Charles Goodman[13] and publicizing William Vivian's 'thrilling account of Goodman's wonderful deliverance from death: and his strange experiences during the Sierra Leone rebellion' which could 'be had for a few pence'. Vivian, a former General Superintendent of the UMFC Mission in Sierra Leone, did however place on record their deaths.[14]

---

[10]   Shimmin's report dated 7 July 1893, quoted in Graaff, pp. 56–7.
[11]   See p. 156.
[12]   See p. xxi.
[13]   See p. 196.
[14]   Vivian, *A Captive Missionary*. Johnston suffered posthumous indignity: the first three post-1932 editions of *Hill's Arrangement*, in which the names of UMFC ministers (and other UM and PM ministers) were listed alongside Wesleyans, correctly recorded his details, but in subsequent editions he unaccountably became John C. Johnson who purportedly died in 1932.

In the Pacific

Although the early years of European contact with the islanders were fraught with danger, it was only in the 1860s that any missionary was murdered. Thomas Baker from Sussex was taken to New South Wales with his parents at the age of eight. Converted in his youth, he entered the Wesleyan ministry in 1859 and went to Fiji. His last station was at Davuilevu, on the main island of Viti Levu, where already there was a training institution which later developed into the Methodist Theological College. In July 1867 he set out, with Setareki Seileka, a Fijian minister and some of the students, to visit a number of Fijian teachers who had recently been stationed inland in villages where there were new converts. He spent a week visiting these outstations and then decided to make his way through unknown territory to the northern coast and return home by sea. This, as he wrote to his wife, was a journey he had been contemplating for some time. Accompanied by Seileka, two Fijian teachers and six students, he came to the village of Nabutautau.[15] They were given a hut for the night, but they found the atmosphere of the village menacing and left early in the morning. Barely a hundred metres from the village they were attacked by armed men, led by the village chief, and were all killed apart from one teacher and one student who somehow managed to escape.[16] A reason for the attack given in some accounts was that the chief had borrowed Baker's hat. Baker tried to take it back without knowing that to touch a chief's head was taboo and punishable by death. The explanation is unlikely: Baker had been eight years in Fiji and must have been aware of such things. He knew he was in dangerous country and would not have acted in such a brazen manner. A different account suggests that rivalry between local chiefs prompted the attack; a Christian chief felt slighted by Baker's choice of a meeting-place and asked the Nabutautau chief to kill him.

The Baker party thus perished at the hands of pagan Fijians on the request of a Christian convert. The European Missionaries in Fiji, while they were often reviled and threatened in the early decades of their mission, seem to have been largely immune from direct attack, but the same was not true of their Fijian converts, many of whom were killed by followers of Fijian religion, particularly after Christianity began to take hold and to threaten the authority of chiefs and priests.[17]

What is known is that Baker was roasted and eaten: almost certainly the last act of cannibalism in Fiji. 'We ate everything but his boots,' claimed one of the villagers; one boot, teeth marks and all, is in the Fiji Museum in Suva.

John Whiteley from Nottinghamshire entered the ministry in 1832 and with his new wife Mary Ann sailed directly for the Bay of Islands in New Zealand. He

---

[15]   Some accounts name the place Navosa or Nagagadelavatu, but it was the villagers of Nabutautau who in 2003 held a ceremony of apology to a group of Baker's descendants.

[16]   E. Susu, *The history of Methodist Theological education in Fiji until 1973*, (Suva, Fiji, Pacific Theological College, 2009).

[17]   J. Ryle, *My God, My Land: Interwoven Paths of Christianity and Tradition in Fiji*, (Aldershot, Ashgate Publishing, 2010), p. 65.

became a fluent Maori speaker and concerned himself with all aspects of Maori welfare. He encouraged chiefs on the west coast of the North Island, where he was stationed from 1839 to 1855, to sign the 1840 Treaty of Waitangi and in 1847 he joined protests against Colonial Secretary Earl Grey's instructions to the governor to treat unoccupied land as Crown land and sell it to settlers. Whiteley argued that all land in the country had customary claimants and that if the Crown took unoccupied land it would contravene the letter and spirit of the Treaty of Waitangi. He continued to protest long after his Wesleyan superiors had decided to let the matter rest.

In 1856, after a brief appointment in Auckland, Whiteley was sent to the troubled district of Taranaki, where he did much to smooth the tensions between Maori and Pakeha. As time went by he came to believe that the settlers had a just case. He let his views be known to both settler and Maori alike. He believed that armed opposition to the sale of land was rebellion against the Crown and when a new Land War broke out in 1860 he supported the government. From 1858 he acted as an unsalaried commissioner for native lands, as well as serving the government as a translator and adviser on Maori affairs.

In the 1860s the Taranaki tribes fought amongst themselves and Whiteley did his utmost to prevent these conflicts. Then war with the government broke out again. It was to be the last of the Land Wars which disturbed North Island between 1845 and 1872. One of the Maori leaders bore the name Hone Wetere (that is, John Wesley). On 13 February 1869 Whiteley, now 62, rode out on a regular visit to the military outpost at Pukearuhe. He had no idea that the little garrison had been massacred earlier in the day by Wetere's war party. Suddenly a hidden voice called sharply, 'Hokia! Hokia! Go back! Go back!' He answered in Maori, 'Why should I go back? My place is here.' A shot was fired that brought down his horse. Kneeling in prayer beside the animal Whiteley was shot again and again. He died because he insisted on performing his pastoral duty. His murderers were never brought to trial. The government granted an annual pension of £100 to his widow.

William Hill from Wolverhampton studied for three years at Richmond College and was sent to Ceylon in 1850, but was invalided home in 1853. He was next stationed to the very different climate of Newfoundland, but before he could sail his designation was switched to Australia. Robert Young, on his lengthy tour of the South Seas,[18] had identified an urgent need occasioned by the influx of migrants to the goldmines of Victoria and the Australian churches were ready to pay the passage and meet the stipend. Hill's health held up during a succession of appointments and in 1869 he was stationed in Melbourne for the third time. In May that year he went to visit prisoners in Pentridge stockade prison. In one cell, as he knelt in prayer, he was murdered in cold blood by the prisoner with a piece of iron which he had torn from his bedstead.

---

[18]   See p. 42.

In China

William Argent, an evangelist who went to China under the arrangement between David Hill's Laymen's Mission and Thomas Champness's Joyful News Mission, was the first Methodist martyr in China. The arrangement took effect in 1888 and Argent was the third evangelist to arrive. One of his predecessors, Alfred Tollerton, died of smallpox in 1891 and the other, S.J. Hudson, died of dysentery while on furlough in 1894. William Argent was based in Hankou on the Yangtze but not long after his arrival he was sent downriver to care for the sick Tollerton at the Mission House of Rest in the hills above Wuxue. David Hill had lived in Wuxue for six years from 1870; the townsfolk were accustomed to the presence of missionaries, who had never been troubled. But it was an unsettled time along the Yangtze valley. Anti-Christian literature was being circulated and there were incidents of violence against missionaries in a number of places. One night, shortly after Tollerton's death, while Argent was waiting for a boat back to Hankou, a riot broke out in Wuxue. A man came into the town carrying two baskets, one suspended from each end of a pole slung across his shoulders. When people asked him his business he said he was taking the children in the baskets to the Roman Catholic Foundling Hospital.

Some of those who heard him must have remembered rumours about missionaries who mutilated bodies and gouged out children's eyes. In no time an angry crowd collected around the man and he was dragged off to the *yamen*. When the mandarin found no substance in the story they were all sent away but the fury of the crowd did not die down. A general stampede followed in which a child in one of the baskets was crushed to death. The crowd then made its way to the mission houses and threw stones at them.[19]

The resident missionaries, Boden and Protheroe, were away. Their wives, the Protheroe children and a visiting missionary's wife, Mary Warren, were inside when a stone came through a window, overturned an oil lamp and set both houses on fire. The women ran from the burning houses with the children and were viciously beaten as they escaped. Bruised and bleeding, they survived because the crowd suddenly turned its attention to two men who appeared on the scene. William Argent and a customs officer who was also waiting at the landing-stage had seen the blaze, realized it was the mission houses that were burning and rushed to help.

Unknown to the women, William Argent was struck on the head and fell on the steps of the mission chapel. He died instantly. Mr Green in desperation ran into a pond and stood up to his neck in water but even there the people threw stones at him. At last an official arrived and ordered him out of the water, promising him protection. The crowd, however, was beyond control and the official could do nothing. The people fell upon Green and he too was killed.[20]

---

[19]   Sheaff, p. 32.
[20]   Sheaff, p. 33. Sheaff was Mary Warren's grand-daughter.

While not martyrs in the 'Recant or die' sense, Argent and Green died because of the wave of hostility and unfounded suspicion of Christians. It was an instance of the blood of the martyrs proving to be the seed of the church. As a direct result of this tragedy, an Imperial edict was posted on the walls of 1,400 cities, to the effect that Christianity was one of the tolerated religions in China, that Christian missionaries should be allowed to go about their business unhindered and that converts were not to be persecuted. Argent's mother at first declined to accept the compensation that was paid to the dead men's relatives, but was persuaded to change her mind on condition that it should be used for Christian mission in China. Four more Joyful News evangelists were appointed at once.

Roderick Macdonald[21] wanted to be a doctor but when he left Woodhouse Grove School his father, who was the Chairman of the Scotland District, placed him in a Glasgow bank. However his uncle, Sir John Macdonald, was an inspector of naval fleets and hospitals and offered to help pay for his medical training and get him a nomination for the Royal Naval Medical Service. His studies in London and Edinburgh went well and after two years in a large rural practice in Cornwall he obtained his MD – but by then he felt called to missionary service and offered to go wherever he was needed. The WMMS Committee wanted him in China, but they also wanted him to be ordained. At this Macdonald demurred; he was a preacher but did not feel worthy to be a minister. After much hesitation, however, he bowed to the Committee's wishes and was ordained, without any

Figure 16.1   Boats in San Ui Creek, South China, drawn by Roderick Macdonald

---

[21]   See M. Macdonald, *Roderick Macdonald MD, a servant of Jesus Christ*, (London, Robert Culley, 1908) by Macdonald's widow; Rose, pp. 78–82.

formal theological training, in August 1884. He proceeded to Guangzhou (Canton) and after six months of orientation he was placed in charge of the hospital in Foshan which had been opened by Charles Wenyon in 1881. Dr Wenyon was away organizing medical work on the battlefields of the nine months' Sino–French war and subsequently combined medical work with his wider duties as Chairman of the South China District. Macdonald was not only new to China but still new to medicine and recorded with relief in his diary: 'My first cataract case can see, and the second also!' Another 1885 entry revealed the atmosphere of suspicion in which these pioneers worked: 'Placards up about our taking children's eyes and brains. They connect photography with this.' However he was not deterred, either by solitude, illness or opposition. In 1886: 'Started on famine relief expedition: visited nearly thirty villages … Pitiful sights on every hand. I can never forget the horror of it all.'[22]

In 1890 Macdonald was sent to Shaoguan, where a newly-graduated Chinese doctor had opened a dispensary, with the aim of developing it into a hospital. But when human remains were unearthed as the foundations were dug, the project was arrested for many years. He went on furlough, came back to Foshan, went down with pulmonary tuberculosis and had to return to England again. His service in China seemed to be over, but by 1897 he was fit enough to resume work and was appointed to Wuzhou, a recently opened Treaty Port, 250 miles up the Xi river west of Guangzhou. Again the intention was to start a hospital, which eventually opened in 1904. But at first he lived, with his wife Margaret and their baby, on a tiny houseboat. Several times it was almost wrecked by storms before they found a home on dry land. He acquired a site for the hospital but first built a house, working alongside the local builders. They moved in and he opened a dispensary. The medical work was self-supporting from the start. Next came a small church. Macdonald had been preaching in the streets of Wuzhou and gathered a little congregation. Within a few years the mission compound housed not only the fifty-bed hospital but boarding schools for both girls and boys and he bought an island in the river where he created a settlement for leprosy sufferers.

In July 1906 Roderick Macdonald went to the District Synod in Guangzhou. It was the first summer for nine years that he had been away from Wuzhou. The river boat on which he was travelling back was attacked by pirates. Macdonald went to the aid of the wounded captain and while tending him was himself shot. He died instantly.

****

In Britain and Ireland, the families and friends of the dead received the news – whether of murder, shipwreck or fatal illness – long after the event. Many would have called to mind Charles Wesley's words:

---

[22]   M. Macdonald, pp. 32–4.

And let our bodies part,
To different climes repair;
Inseparably joined in heart
The friends of Jesus are.

The vineyard of their Lord
Before his labourers lies;
And lo! We see the vast reward
Which waits us in the skies

Where all our toils are o'er,
Our suffering and our pain;
Who meet on that eternal shore
Shall never part again.[23]

---

[23]   C. Wesley, *Hymns and Sacred Poems*, (Bristol, Felix Farley, 1749).

Conclusion
A New Century

What tasks, spite of all hindrances and weaknesses, the past century has seen accomplished! Fiji, from an outpost of hell, become a home of Christian light; the Britains [sic] overseas, in their swift incalculable spread, leavened by the Methodist witness, chaplained by the Methodist preacher, so that the British Empire today is as definitely Christian in its outlying provinces as at its centre; our tutelage of West Indian negrodom, from an ancestry of fetishism and a childhood of slavery up to the full-grown man in Christ Jesus; our array of missionary graves, and of vigorous native Churches, in West Africa; the contribution of our Missions to the Christianization of the thought and conscience of India; our contingent to the army of Christ in China, planted in its commanding centres, furnished with the most modern appliances of the Gospel warfare: such are the 'labours into which we are entered'; they are our heritage, our vantage-ground, – and our challenge![1]

This purple passage was written for the WMMS centenary in 1913, its object to stimulate enthusiasm for the missionary cause and the task ahead. Its positive slant is selective; the achievements, however gratifying, were not the whole story; the task was not merely unfinished, it was scarcely begun. The sacrifices, faithful perseverance and heroism of nineteenth century missionaries had indeed reaped a remarkable harvest in Tonga and Fiji, but only moderate growth in Africa and scant reward elsewhere, even in the Caribbean, where membership peaked in the 1840s and then went into decline. Kenneth Latourette, the eminent American historian of Christian mission, described the 'long nineteenth century' which ended in 1914 as 'The Great Century'.[2] The achievements of Protestant Missionary Societies on both sides of the Atlantic were undoubtedly great in terms of geographical expansion, but the results in terms of conversions were small, by comparison with the rapid numerical growth of the church almost everywhere except Europe over the next hundred years.

It was nonetheless in a mood of hopefulness that all five branches of Methodism entered the new century. There was no sign of the remarkable movements which would soon produce tens of thousands of new Christians in south-west China and the Ivory Coast. They would take Methodism by surprise; no carefully laid plan

---

[1]   Findlay and Findlay, p. 219.
[2]   K.S. Latourette, *A History of the Expansion of Christianity*, (7 vols, New York & London, Harper, 1937–47).

evoked them. The most ambitious plans for the future were related to bricks and mortar: better school and hospital premises and church buildings not just adequate in size but sturdy in structure and worthy of the Lord they honoured. The other critical focus was training an indigenous ministry. With standards of education in general gradually improving, the pace of ministerial training could accelerate; theological educators were a pressing need.

These plans were implemented and interrupted, in the context of world wars, decolonization, the accelerating pace of travel and telecommunications, the reunion of divided Methodism, wider schemes of church union which included striking successes and dismal failures and constant theological debate between 'progressive/liberal' and 'conservative/fundamentalist' Christians. A collection of essays on such themes is to be found in the companion volume, *Methodists and their Missionary Societies 1900–1996.*

Bibliography

Methodist Periodicals and Reports

Wesleyan:

The Arminian Magazine, 1778–1797
The Methodist Magazine, 1798–1821
The Wesleyan–Methodist Magazine, 1822–1897
Missionary Notices, 1816–1904
Work and Workers in the Mission Field, 1892–1904
Wesleyan Methodist Missionary Society Annual Reports, 1789–1932
Ladies' Committee Occasional Papers, 1859–1898
Ladies'/Women's Auxiliary Annual Reports, 1881–1918
Minutes of the Conference, 1744–1932

Primitive Methodist:

The Primitive Methodist Magazine, 1834–1898
Primitive Methodist Missionary Notices, 1851–1869
Records of Missionary Work, 1870–1892
The Record of the Primitive Methodist Missionary Society, 1893–1904
Primitive Methodist Missionary Society Annual Reports, 1843–1931
Minutes of the Conference, 1820–1932

Methodist New Connexion:

Minutes of the Conference, 1796–1907

United Methodist Free Churches:

The Missionary Echo, 1894–1907
The United Methodist Free Churches Magazine, 1858–1892
Annual Reports, 1868–1907
Minutes of the Proceedings of the Annual Assembly, 1856–1907

Bible Christian:

Minutes of the Annual Conference, 1818–1907

Irish Methodist:

The Irish Evangelist, 1859–1883
Irish Christian Advocate, first published 1883
Minutes of the Methodist Conferences in Ireland

Non-specific:

Proceedings of the Wesley Historical Society, first published 1897
Epworth Review, 1974–2011
Methodist History (USA), first published 1962

Printed Sources

Arthur, W., *A Mission to the Mysore* (London, Partridge & Oakey, 1847)
——— *Italy in Transition (*London, Hamilton, Adams & Co., 1860)
——— *Women's Work in India* (London, T. Woolmer, 1882)
Asbury, F., *Journal* (New York, N. Bangs & T. Mason, 1821)
Baldwin, A., *A Missionary Outpost in Central Africa* (London, PM Young People's Missionary Department, 1914)
Balia, D., 'Charles Pamla and the 1866 Revival' in P. Denis (ed.), *The Making of an Indigenous Clergy in Southern Africa* (Pietermaritzburg, Cluster Publications, 1995)
Barber, B.A., *A Methodist Pageant* (London, Holborn, 1932)
Barber, W.T.A., *David Hill, Apostle to the Chinese* (London, Wesleyan Book Room, 1906)
Bartels, F.L., *The Roots of Ghana Methodism* (Cambridge, Cambridge University Press, 1965)
Barton, J.L., *The Missionary and his Critics* (New York, Fleming H. Revell Co., 1906)
Beckerlegge, O.A., *The United Methodist Free Churches* (London, Epworth Press, 1957)
Bickford, J., *An Autobiography of Christian Labour, 1838–1888* (London, Charles H. Kelly, 1890)
Birtwhistle, N.A., *Thomas Birch Freeman* (London, Cargate Press, 1950)
——— *In his Armour: The Life of John Hunt* (London, Cargate Press, 1954)
——— *William Threlfall: A Study in Missionary Vocation* (London, Cargate Press, 1966)
——— *Methodist Missions* in Davies, George and Rupp (eds), *History*, vol. 3 (London, Epworth Press, 1983)
Bleby, H., *Death Struggles of Slavery* (London, Hamilton, Adams, & Co., 1853)

Bohr, P.R., 'Liang Fa's Quest for Moral Power' in S.W. Barnett and J.K. Fairbank (eds), *Christianity in China: Early Protestant Missionary Writings* (Cambridge, Mass, Harvard University Press, 1985)

Bonk, J.J., *Missions and Money* (New York, Orbis Books, 1991)

Boocock, N., *Our Fernandian Missions* (London, W.A. Hammond, 1912)

Bourne, F.W., *The Bible Christians: Their Origin and History* (London, BC Book Room, 1905)

Boyce, W.B., *Notes on South African Affairs* (London, John Mason, 1839)

Brailsford, E.J., *Richard Watson, theologian and missionary advocate* (London, Charles H. Kelly, 1906)

Brewin, R., *Memoirs of Mrs Rebecca Wakefield* (London, Andrew Crombie, 1888)
———— *The Martyrs of Golbanti* (London, Andrew Crombie, 1888?)

Broadbent, S., *A narrative of the first introduction of Christianity amongst the Barolong tribe of Bechuanas, South Africa* (London, Wesleyan Mission House, 1865)

Brown, G., *George Brown, pioneer missionary and explorer: an autobiography* (London, Hodder & Stoughton, 1908)

Burns, A.C., *History of Nigeria* (London, Allen & Unwin, 1929)

Byrne, L., *The Hidden Journey* (London, SPCK, 1993)

Calvert, J., *Fiji and the Fijians* (London, Alexander Heylin, 1858)

Candlin, G.T., *John Innocent: A Story of Mission Work in North China* (London, United Methodist Publishing House, 1909)

Carey, W., *An Enquiry into the Obligations of Christians to Use Means for the Conversion of the Heathens* (Leicester, Ann Ireland, 1792; Kindle edition, 2004)

Cheeseman, T., *The story of William Threlfall, missionary martyr of Namaqualand, with some account of Jacob Links and Johannes Jager* (Cape Town, Methodist Publishing Office, 1910)

Church History Association of India (various authors), *History of Christianity in India* (Bangalore, 1982 and ongoing vols)

Clapham, J., 'Bengal Methodism: First Hundred Years' in N.B. Mitra (ed.), *Methodist in Bengal* (Kolkata, Diamond Art Press, 2007)

Clayton, G.A., *Methodism in Central China* (London, Charles H. Kelly, 1906)

Coke, T., *A History of the West Indies* (3 vols, Liverpool, Nuttall, Fisher, & Dixon, 1808, 1810, 1811)

Coke, T. and Moore, H., *The Life of John Wesley* (London, Paramore, 1792)

Comaroff, J.L. and J., *Of Revelation and Revolution: Christianity, Colonialism and Consciousness in South Africa* (2 vols, Chicago, University of Chicago Press, 1991, 1997)

Cox, J., *Imperial fault lines: Christianity and colonial power in India, 1818–1940* (Stanford, California, Stanford University Press, 2002)

Cracknell, K.R., *Justice, Courtesy and Love* (London, Epworth Press, 1995)

Crafford, D., *Trail-blazers of the Gospel: Black Pioneers in the Missionary History of Southern Africa* (Pretoria, ISWEN, 1991)

Cragg, D., *A Spark of Grace: The Wesleyan Methodist Mission in South Africa 1816–1883* (Cape Town, Methodist Publishing House, 2011)

Crothers, T.D., Longbottom, W., Townsend, W.J., Rider, T., Packer, G. (eds), *The centenary of the Methodist New Connexion 1797–1897* (London, Geo. Burroughs, 1897)

Cumbers, F.H., *Richmond College 1843–1943* (London, Epworth Press, 1944)

Curnock, N. (ed.), *The Journal of the Revd John Wesley* (8 vols, London, Epworth Press, 1911)

da Costa, E.V., *Crowns of glory, tears of blood: the Demerara Slave Rebellion of 1823* (Oxford, Oxford University Press, 1994)

Darch, J., *Missionary Imperialists?* (Milton Keynes, Paternoster, 2009)

Davey, C.J., *The March of Methodism* (London, Epworth Press, 1951)

Davey, C.J. and Thomas, H.E., *Together Travel On* (London, Cargate, 1984)

Davidson, A.K. and Lineham, P.J. (eds), *Transplanted Christianity* (Palmerston North, NZ, Dunmore Press, 1989)

Davies, R.E., George, A.R., Rupp, G. (eds), *A History of the Methodist Church in Great Britain* (4 vols, London, Epworth Press, 1965, 1978, 1983, 1988)

Dickson, M., *The Inseparable Grief: Margaret Cargill of Fiji* (London, Epworth Press, 1976)

Eayrs, G., Townsend, W.J., Workman, H.B. (eds), *A New History of Methodism* (2 vols, London, Hodder & Stoughton, 1909)

Etherington, N. (ed.), *Missions and Empire* (Oxford, Oxford University Press, 2005)

Everett, J., *Wesleyan Takings* (London, Hamilton Adams, 1841)

Farndale, W.E., *The Secret of Mow Cop* (London, Epworth Press, 1950)

Farquhar, D.U., *Caribbean Adventures. Extracts from Missionary Journals* (Boston, Mass, Mt Prospect Press, 1999)

Findlay, G.G. and Findlay, M.G., *Wesley's World Parish* (London, Hodder & Stoughton, 1912)

Findlay, G.G. and Holdsworth, W.W., *The History of the Wesleyan Methodist Missionary Society* (5 vols, London, Epworth Press, 1921–24)

Frederiks, M.T., *We Have Toiled All Night: Christianity in the Gambia 1465–2000* (Zoetemeer, Uitgeverij Boekencentrum, 2003)

Freeman, T.B., *Journal of Various Visits to the Kingdoms of Ashanti, Aku, and Dahomi* (London, John Mason, 1844; 3rd edn, London, Frank Cass, 1968)

Graaff, B., *Modumedi Moleli* (Harare, Mambo Press, 1988)

Gray, S.D., *Frontiers of the Kingdom* (London, Cargate Press, 1930)

Griffiths, L.J., *History of Methodism in Haiti* (Port-au-Prince, Imprimerie Méthodiste, 1991)

Grist, W.A., *Samuel Pollard, Pioneer Missionary in China* (London, United Methodist Publishing House, 1920)

Groves, C.P., *The Planting of Christianity in Africa* (4 vols, London, Lutterworth Press, 1948–58)

Gunnar, P.M., *Here am I, Lord, Send Me: the life of missionary leader William Binnington Boyce* (Sydney, The Federation Press, 2003)

Hall, C.M., *Calvert of Cannibal Fiji* (London, WMMS, 1918)

Harris, E.J., 'Wesleyan Witness in an Interreligious Context' in P.R. Meadows (ed.), *Windows on Wesley* (Oxford, Applied Theology Press, 1997)

Hastings, A., *African Christianity* (London, Geoffrey Chapman, 1976)

—————— *The Church in Africa 1450–1950* (Oxford, Clarendon Press, 1994)

Hedley, J., *Our Mission in North China* (London, Geo. Burrows, 1907)

Hempton, D., *Methodism: Empire of the Spirit* (New Haven, Yale University Press, 2005)

Hewson, L.A., *An Introduction to South African Methodists* (Cape Town, Standard Press, 1950)

Hopkins, A.J., *Trail Blazers and Road Makers* (London, United Methodist Publishing House, 1928)

Hughes, H.P., *Social Christianity* (London, Hodder & Stoughton, 1889)

Jackson, S.I., *In the Shadow of a Mighty Rock* (Oxford, Wesley Historical Society, 2009)

Jackson, T. (ed.), *The Lives of Early Methodist Preachers* (6 vols, London, Wesleyan Book Room, 1865)

John, G., *A Voice from China* (London, James Clarke & Co, 1907)

Kelly, T., *Hymns on Various Passages of Scripture* (Dublin, Marcus Moses, 1820)

Kendall, H.B., *The origin and history of the Primitive Methodist Church* (2 vols, PM Publishing House, 1906)

Kendall, R.E., *Charles New and the East Africa Mission* (Nairobi, Kenya Literature Bureau, 1978)

Kirsop, J., *Life of Thomas H. Carthew, Missionary to East Africa* (London, Andrew Crombie, 1897)

—————— *Life of Robert Moss Ormerod, Missionary to East Africa* (London, Andrew Crombie, 1901)

Krapf, J.L., *Travels, Researches, and Missionary Labours During an Eighteen Years' Residence in Eastern Africa* (London, Trübner & Co., 1860)

Lamb, F., *The Gospel and the Mala* (Mysore, Wesleyan Mission Press, 1913)

Langford, T.A., *Methodist Theology* (London, Epworth Press, 1998)

Lenton, J.H., *John Wesley's Preachers* (Milton Keynes, Paternoster, 2009)

Lewis, A., 'Bicentenary of Rev James Evans' in *WHS Proceedings*, 53, May 2001

Lewis, J., *William Goudie* (London, WMMS, 1923)

Luckcock, J.L., *Thomas of Tonga, 1797–1881: The Unlikely Pioneer* (Peterborough, Methodist Publishing House, 1992)

Macdonald, M., *Roderick Macdonald MD, a servant of Jesus Christ* (London, Robert Culley, 1908)

Maclean, J., *James Evans, inventor of the syllabic system of the Cree language* (Toronto, Methodist Mission Rooms, 1890)

Mears, W.G., *Methodist Torchbearers* (Rondebosch, Methodist Missionary Department, 1955)

———— *Sergeant John Kendrick* (Cape Town, Methodist Publishing House, 1963)

Milburn, G., *Primitive Methodism* (London, Epworth Press, 2002)

Millard, J.A., *Malihambe: Let the Word Spread* (Pretoria, Unisa Press, 1999)

Mitra, N.B. (ed.), *Methodist in Bengal* (Kolkata, Diamond Art Press, 2007)

Moister, W., *Conversations on the Rise, Progress and Present State of Wesleyan Missions in Various Parts of the World* (London, Hamilton Adams & Co, 1869)

Neill, S., *A History of Christian Missions* (London, Penguin Books, 1964)

New, C., *Life, Wanderings and Labours in Eastern Africa* (London, Hodder & Stoughton, 1873)

Nthamburi, Z.J., *A History of the Methodist Church in Kenya* (Nairobi, Uzima, 1982)

Oddie, G.A., *Social Protest in India: British Protestant Missionaries and Social Reforms 1850–1900* (New Delhi, Manohar, 1979)

Piggott, T.C. and Durley, T., *Life and Letters of Henry James Piggott* (London, Epworth Press, 1921)

Pitman, E.R., *Lady Missionaries in Foreign Lands* (London, S.W. Partridge, n.d.)

Porter, A., *Religion versus empire?* (Manchester, Manchester University Press, 2004)

Prickett, B.B., *Island Base* (Banjul, Methodist Church Gambia, 1969)

Pritchard, E.C., *Under the Southern Cross* (London, W.A. Hammond, 1914)

Pritchard, J.R., 'The Untidy Beginnings of Methodist World Mission' in *Epworth Review*, October 1999

———— *Women's Work, Mary Batchelor to Muriel Stennett* in N Virgoe (ed.), *Angels and Impudent Women* (Wesley Historical Society, 2008)

———— *Methodists and their Missionary Societies 1900–1996* (Aldershot, Ashgate Publishing, 2014)

Race, S., *The Two Worlds of Joseph Race* (London, Souvenir Press, 1988)

Rack, H.D., *Reasonable Enthusiast* (London, Epworth Press, 1989)

Rigg, J.H., *Jabez Bunting, a great Methodist leader* (London, Charles H. Kelly, 1905)

Rose, J.R., *A Church Born to Suffer* (London, Cargate Press, 1951)

Rutherford, N., *Shirley Baker and the King of Tonga* (Melbourne, Oxford University Press, 1971)

Ryle, J., *My God, My Land: Interwoven Paths of Christianity and Tradition in Fiji* (Aldershot, Ashgate Publishing, 2010)

Sadler, C., *Never a Young Man: Extracts from the Letters and Journals of the Rev William Shaw* (Cape Town, HAUM, 1967)

Samuel, P., *The Wesleyan Methodist Missions in Jamaica and Honduras Delineated* (London, Partridge & Oakey, 1850)

Senior, G.R., *The China Experience* (Peterborough, Methodist Publishing House, 1994)

———— *Samuel Pollard* (Emsworth, World Methodist Historical Society, 1999)

———— *David Hill, Missionary in Central China* (Oxford, Wesley Historical Society, 2008)

Shaw, B., *Memorials of Southern Africa* (London, John Mason, 1841; reprinted by C. Struik, Cape Town, 1970)

Shaw, W., *A Defence of the Wesleyan Missionaries in southern Africa* (London, John Mason, 1839)

Sheaff, M., *From Tortoise Hill* (Leominster, Orphans Press, 2007)

Small, W.J.T. (ed.), *A History of the Methodist Church in Ceylon* (Colombo, Wesley Press, 1964)

Snowden, R.F., *The Ladies of Wesleydale* (London, Epworth Press, 1957)

Stanley, B., *The Bible and the Flag* (Leicester, Apollos, 1990)

Stevens, A., *A Compendious History of American Methodism* (New York, Phillips & Hunt, 1868)

Susu, E., *The history of Methodist Theological education in Fiji until 1973* (Suva, Fiji, Pacific Theological College, 2009)

Symons, J.C., *Life of the Rev. Daniel James Draper* (Melbourne, Wesleyan Book Depot, 1870)

Taggart, N.W., *The Irish in World Methodism 1760–1960* (London, Epworth Press, 1986)

———— 'Methodist Foreign Missions, The First Half Century' in *WHS Proceedings*, 45, October 1986

———— *William Arthur, First among Methodists* (London, Epworth Press, 1993)

Telford, J., *Makers of our Missions* (London, Charles H. Kelly, 1895)

———— *Women in the Mission Field* (London, Charles H. Kelly, 1895)

———— *A Short History of Wesleyan Methodist Foreign Missions* (London, Charles H. Kelly, 1905)

———— (ed.), *The Letters of John Wesley* (8 vols, London, Epworth Press, 1931)

Thomas, H., *The Slave Trade* (New York, Simon & Schuster, 1997)

Thompson, E.W., *The Methodist Mission House: its history and its treasures* (London, WMMS, 1933?)

Thompson, H.P., *Into All Lands* (London, SPCK, 1951)

Thornley, A., 'The Legacy of Siloam: Tahitian Missionaries in Fiji' in D. Munro and A. Thornley (eds), *The Covenant Makers: Islander Missionaries in the Pacific* (Suva, Institute of Pacific Studies, 1996)

Thorpe, C., *Limpopo to Zambesi* (London, Cargate Press, 1951)

Turner, J.G., *The Pioneer Missionary: Life of the Rev Nathaniel Turner* (Melbourne, George Robertson, 1872)

Vickers, J.A., *Thomas Coke, Apostle of Methodism* (London, Epworth Press, 1969)

———— 'One-man Band: Thomas Coke and the origins of Methodist Missions' in *Methodist History* vol. 34/3, April 1996

———— *Myths of Methodism* (Oxford, Wesley Historical Society, 2008)

Vivian, W., *A Captive Missionary in Mendiland* (London, Andrew Crombie, 1899)

Wakefield, E.S., *Thomas Wakefield: missionary and geographical pioneer in east equatorial Africa* (London, Religious Tract Society, 1904)

Walker, F.D., *William Carey: Missionary Pioneer and Statesman* (London, Cargate Press, 1926)

Warren, M.A.C., *Social History and Christian Mission* (London, SCM Press, 1967)

Webb, P.M., *Women of our Company* (London, Cargate Press, 1958)

Webster, T., *History of the Methodist Episcopal Church in Canada* (Hamilton, Canada Christian Advocate Office, 1870)

Wesley, C., *Hymns and Sacred Poems* (Bristol, Felix Farley, 1742, 1749)

Wesley, J., *An earnest appeal to men of reason and religion* (Bristol, Felix Farley, 1743)

—— *Sermons on several Occasions* (Bristol, J. Grabham & W. Pine, 1760; 4th edn, London, Epworth Press, 1944)

—— *A calm address to our American colonies* (London, R. Hawes, 1775)

—— *Thoughts upon Slavery* (London, R. Hawes, 1784)

Whiteside, J., *History of the Wesleyan Methodist Church of South Africa* (London, Elliot Stock, 1906)

Wigger, J., *American Saint, Francis Asbury and the Methodists* (New York, Oxford University Press, 2009)

Williams, J., *A Narrative of Missionary Enterprises in the South Sea Islands* (London, J. Snow, 1837)

WMMS (corporately compiled), *The missionary controversy: discussion, evidence and report* (London, WMMS, 1890)

Wolstenholme, B., *Not Dear to Themselves* (Loughborough, Teamprint, revised edn, 1998)

Wood, A.H., *Overseas Missions of the Australian Methodist Church* (4 vols, Melbourne, Aldersgate Press, 1975–80)

Wood, A.M., *Woman's Call to Woman* (London, WMMS Ladies' Auxiliary, n.d.)

World Mission Conference, *The History and Records of the Conference, together with Addresses Delivered at the Evening Meetings* (Edinburgh & London, Oliphant, Anderson & Ferrier, 1910)

Young, R., *The Southern World: Journal of a Deputation from the Wesleyan Conference to Australia and Tasmania* (London, John Mason, 1858)

Young, W.J., *The Quiet Wise Spirit* (London, Epworth Press, 2002)

Other Books Quoted

Arthur, W., *The Tongue of Fire* (London, E. Stevenson & F.A. Owen, 1856)

Boyce, W.B., *The Higher Criticism and the Bible* (London, Wesleyan Conference Office, 1881)

Clemmow, F., *Days of Sorrow, Times of Joy* (Kibworth, Matador, 2012)

Darwin, C., *On the Origin of Species* (London, John Murray, 1859)

David, S., *The Indian Mutiny* (London, Penguin Books, 2002)

Davidson, B., *The Story of Africa* (London, Mitchell Beazley, 1984)

Derrick, R.A., *A History of Fiji* (Suva, Government Press, 1946)

Encyclopedia Britannica (Edinburgh, 1797)

Fitzpatrick, D., *Irish Emigration 1801–1921* (Dublin, Dundalgan Press, 1984)

Foote, A.H., *Africa and the American Flag* (New York, D. Appleton & Co., 1862)

Gogerly, D.J., *Ceylon Buddhism* (Colombo, Wesleyan Methodist Book Room, 1908)

Holmes, R., *The Age of Wonder: How the Romantic Generation Discovered the Beauty and Terror of Science* (London, Harper Press, 2008)

Hunt, J., *Letters on Entire Sanctification* (ed. J. Calvert) (London, Wesleyan Conference Office, 1853)

Hurwitz, E.F., *Politics and the Public Conscience: Slave Emancipation and the Abolitionist Movement in Britain* (London, Allen & Unwin, 1973)

Kaye, Sir J.W., *Christianity in India: An Historical Narrative* (London, Smith, Elder & Co., 1859)

Latourette, K.S., *A History of the Expansion of Christianity* (7 vols, New York & London, Harper, 1937–47).

Long, U., (ed.), *The Journals of Elizabeth Lees Price, written in Bechuanaland, 1854–1883* (London, Edward Arnold, 1956)

Lyell, C., *Principles of Geology* (3 vols, London, John Murray, 1830–33)

Macdonald, J., *Memoirs of Joseph Benson* (London, T. Blanshard, 1822)

Mayhew, C., *Men Seeking God* (London, Allen & Unwin, 1955)

Midgley, C., *Women Against Slavery: The British Campaigns 1780–1870* (London, Routledge, 1992)

Nasson, B., *The South African War 1899–1902* (London, Arnold, 1999)

Parks, F., *Wanderings of a pilgrim in search of the picturesque* (2 vols, London, Pelham Richardson, 1850; reprinted Karachi, Oxford University Press, 1975)

Royle, E., 'Writing the Local History of Methodism' in P.S. Forsaith and M. Wellings (eds), *Methodism and History* (Oxford, Applied Theology Press, 2010)

Selby, T.G., *Chinamen at Home* (London, Hodder & Stoughton, 1900)

——— *As the Chinese See Us* (London, T. Fisher Unwin, 1901)

——— *The Chinaman in his own Stories* (London, Charles H. Kelly, 1905)

Sims, G.R. (ed.), *Living London* (London, Cassell & Co, 1902)

Slater, T.E., *The Philosophy of Missions: A Present-Day Plea* (London, James Clarke, 1882)

Spence, J.D., *God's Chinese Son: The Taiping Heavenly Kingdom of Hong Xiuquan* (New York, W.W. Norton, 1996)

Strauss, D.F., *Das Leben Jesu kritisch bearbeitet* (Tübingen, 1835–36)

Thompson, E.P., *The Making of the English Working Class* (London, Gollancz, 1963; reprinted Penguin, 1980)

Thomson, D., *England in the Nineteenth Century* (London, Penguin Books, 1960)

Trüper, U., *The Invisible Woman* (Basel, Basler Afrika Bibliographien, 2006)

Watson, R., *Theological Institutes* (London, John Mason, 1823, 1829)

Wilberforce, W., *Appeal to the Religion, Justice and Humanity of the Inhabitants of the British Empire* (London, J. Hatchard Son, 1823)

Unpublished Material

Anderson, S., 'Masters, Slaves and Missionaries on the Gold Coast, 1838–1851', MMS History Conference paper, 2005
Bishop, E.A., 'Leaving Burma for Good', 2006, privately circulated
Harrison, R., 'Incidents Illustrative of Two Terms in Hunan, 1930–43', privately circulated
Howard, P., 'A case of returned empties – former missionaries in 'home' circuits in the early years', MMS History Conference paper, 2005
Potter, J.M., 'Methodist Missionaries and State Formation in Nineteenth Century Southern Africa', MMS History Conference paper, 2007
James, D.W., 'The hand that guided, the heart that planned', privately circulated
Taggart, N.W., 'The Irish Factor in World Methodism in the Eighteenth and Nineteenth Centuries' (PhD thesis, Queen's University, Belfast, 1981)
Welch, I., 'The Wesleyan Methodist Church and the Evangelization of the Chinese on the Victorian Goldfields in the 19th Century', MMS History Conference paper, 2003

Online Resources [accessed 31 October 2012]

Australian Dictionary of Biography, http://adb.anu.edu.au/biography
Biographical Dictionary of Chinese Christianity, http://www.bdcconline.net/en/stories
Dictionary of African Christian Biography, http://www.dacb.org
Dictionary of Methodism in Britain and Ireland, http://dmbi.wesleyhistoricalsociety.org.uk
Telford, J., *A Short History of Wesleyan Methodist Foreign Missions* (London, 1905): e-version at http://archive.org/details/shorthistorymiss00telfuoft

Index